REA's Test Prep Books Are The Best!

(a sample of the <u>hundreds of letters</u> REA receives each year)

" I did well because of your wonderful prep books... I just wanted to thank you for helping me prepare for these tests. "

Student, San Diego, CA

" My students report your chapters of review as the most valuable single resource they used for review and preparation. "

Teacher, American Fork, UT

" Your book was such a better value and was so much more complete than anything your competition has produced — and I have them all! "

Teacher, Virginia Beach, VA

" Compared to the other books that my fellow students had, your book was the most useful in helping me get a great score. "

Student, North Hollywood, CA

" Your book was responsible for my success on the exam, which helped me get into the college of my choice... I will look for REA the next time I need help. "

Student, Chesterfield, MO

" Just a short note to say thanks for the great support your book gave me in helping me pass the test... I'm on my way to a B.S. degree because of you! "

Student, Orlando, FL

(more on next page)

(continued from front page)

" I just wanted to thank you for helping me get a great score
on the AP U.S. History exam... Thank you for making great test preps! "
Student, Los Angeles, CA

" Your *Fundamentals of Engineering Exam* book was the absolute best
preparation I could have had for the exam, and it is one of the major
reasons I did so well and passed the FE on my first try. "
Student, Sweetwater, TN

" I used your book to prepare for the test and found that the advice and the
sample tests were highly relevant... Without using any other material, I earned
very high scores and will be going to the graduate school of my choice. "
Student, New Orleans, LA

" What I found in your book was a wealth of information sufficient to shore up
my basic skills in math and verbal... The section on analytical ability was
excellent. The practice tests were challenging and the answer explanations most
helpful. It certainly is the *Best Test Prep for the GRE*! "
Student, Pullman, WA

" I really appreciate the help from your excellent book. Please keep up
the great work. "
Student, Albuquerque, NM

" I am writing to thank you for your test preparation... your book helped me
immeasurably and I have nothing but praise for your *GRE* preparation."
Student, Benton Harbor, MI

(more on back page)

The Best Test Preparation for the

CLAST

COLLEGE-LEVEL ACADEMIC SKILLS TEST

With REA's TESTware® on CD-ROM

Written by Florida Educators and CLAST Experts:

Warren Almand, M.A.
Instructor of English
Chipola College
Marianna, Florida

Mamie Webb Hixon, M.A.
Director of the Writing Center
University of West Florida
Pensacola, Florida

Judy Downs, Ph.D.
Assistant Professor of English
University of Tampa
Tampa, Florida

Paul Linnehan, Ph.D.
Assistant Professor of English
University of Tampa
Tampa, Florida

Julienne Empric, Ph.D.
Professor of Literature
Eckerd College
St. Petersburg, Florida

Brenda Shryock, M.S.
Former Mathematics Instructor
Lynn University
Boca Raton, Florida

Ina Steinberg, Ph.D.
Chair, Department of English
Barry University
Miami, Florida

Research & Education Association
Visit our website at
www.rea.com

Research & Education Association
61 Ethel Road West
Piscataway, New Jersey 08854
E-mail: info@rea.com

The Best Test Preparation for the
CLAST (College-Level Academic Skills Test)
With TEST*ware®* on CD-ROM

Published 2008

Printed in the United States of America

Library of Congress Control Number 2006927969

ISBN-13: 978-0-7386-0274-5
ISBN-10: 0-7386-0274-4

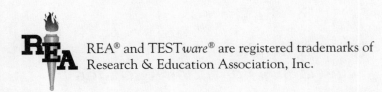

C08-0101

Contents

About Research & Education Association

Founded in 1959, Research & Education Association (REA) is dedicated to publishing the finest and most effective educational materials—including software, study guides, and test preps—for students in middle school, high school, college, graduate school, and beyond.

REA's Test Preparation series includes books and software for all academic levels in almost all disciplines. Research & Education Association publishes test preps for students who have not yet entered high school, as well as high school students preparing to enter college. Students from countries around the world seeking to attend college in the United States will find the assistance they need in REA's publications. For college students seeking advanced degrees, REA publishes test preps for many major graduate school admission examinations in a wide variety of disciplines, including engineering, law, and medicine. Students at every level, in every field, with every ambition can find what they are looking for among REA's publications.

REA presents tests that accurately depict the official exams in both degree of difficulty and types of questions. REA's practice tests are always based upon the most recently administered exams, and include every type of question that can be expected on the actual exams.

REA's publications and educational materials are highly regarded and continually receive an unprecedented amount of praise from professionals, instructors, librarians, parents, and students. Our authors are as diverse as the fields represented in the books we publish. They are well known in their respective disciplines and serve on the faculties of prestigious high schools, colleges, and universities throughout the United States and Canada.

We invite you to visit us at *www.rea.com* to find out how "REA is making the world smarter."

Acknowledgments

In addition to our authors, we would like to thank Larry B. Kling, Vice President, Editorial, for his overall direction; Pam Weston, Vice President, Publishing, for setting the quality standards for production integrity and managing the publication to completion; John Cording, Vice President, Technology, for coordinating the design and development of REA's TEST*ware*® software; Heena Patel, Michelle Boykins, and Amy Jamison, Technology Project Managers, for their software design contributions and software testing efforts; Anne Winthrop Esposito, Senior Editor, for coordinating revisions; Christine Saul, Senior Graphic Designer, for cover design; and Caragraphics for coordinating pre-press electronic file mapping.

STUDY SCHEDULE

The following study schedule will help you to become thoroughly prepared for the CLAST. Although the schedule is designed for a 12-week study program, you may see it as a series of steps that you can tailor to fit your available study time. Be sure to set aside some time each day to study; make your study time as routine as possible. This will not only help you to focus on the material, it will also allow you to reinforce and master the concepts needed for the exam. Try to study for at least one hour a day, if not three. Keep in mind that the more you study for the CLAST, the more prepared and confident you will be on the day of the exam.

Week 1	Read the English Language Skills Review. Make flash cards for any concepts that are new to you, such as misused words or grammar constructs. Carry these cards with you during the week and flip through them periodically. Do all of the drill exercises within the chapter, and check your answers. If you do not understand a given question, go back to the review and study that section once more.
Week 2	Take the English Language Skills Diagnostic Test. Check your answers and refer to the Diagnostic Chart to guide you to review sections that will help you the most. Re-read the sections explaining the skills you missed on the diagnostic test.
Week 3	Read the Essay Writing Review. Do all the drill exercises within the chapter. Compare your responses to the drill sections with the answers given. Show your work to a friend and ask for constructive criticism. Work with the concepts in this chapter until they are reflected in your writing and become second nature.
Week 4	Take the Essay Writing Skills Diagnostic Test. Compare your responses to the answers given. Use the diagnostic chart to refer you to sections of the reviews that will help you strengthen any skills that may still need work.
Week 5	Read the Reading Skills Review. Take all the drills, and read the explanations for any questions you missed. Try to apply the concepts in the review to any reading you do before test time.
Week 6	Take the Reading Skills Diagnostic Test. Check your answers, and use the diagnostic chart to guide you to sections of the review that need more of your attention.
Week 7	Begin working on the Mathematics Review. Concentrate on only one section at a time so as not to overwhelm yourself. Make flash cards of any concepts and formulae that are new to you. Do all of the drill problems, and make sure you understand the explanations of any questions you missed.

Week 8	Take the Mathematics Diagnostic Test. Read the explanations for any questions you got wrong. Use the diagnostic chart to guide you to sections of the review that explain concepts in the questions that you missed. After you have reviewed those concepts, re-do the questions you got wrong, without the help of the review or the explanations, if you can.
Week 9	Take Practice Test 1 on CD-ROM. Work in a quiet, comfortable space that is free of distraction.
Week 10	Read the explanations for any questions you missed on the practice test. Re-read the corresponding section of the review. After studying the concepts again, re-try the questions you missed.
Week 11	Take Practice Test 2 on CD-ROM. Work in a quiet, comfortable space that is free of distraction.
Week 12	Read the explanations for any questions you missed on the practice test. Re-read the corresponding sections of the reviews. After studying the concepts again, take Practice Tests 1 and 2 in this book, for extra practice.

Good luck!

INSTALLING REA's TEST*ware*®

SYSTEM REQUIREMENTS

Pentium 75 MHz (300 MHz recommended), or a higher or compatible processor; Microsoft Windows, 98, NT 4 (SP6), ME, 2000, or XP; 64 MB Available RAM; Internet Explorer 5.5 or higher (Internet Explorer 5.5 is included on the CD); minimum 60 MB available hard-disk space; VGA or higher-resolution monitor, 800x600 resolution setting; Microsoft Mouse, Microsoft Intellimouse, or compatible pointing device.

INSTALLATION

1.   Insert the CLAST TEST*ware*® CD-ROM into the CD-ROM drive.
2.   If the installation doesn't begin automatically, from the Start Menu, choose the RUN command. When the RUN dialog box appears, type d:\setup (where D is the letter of your CD-ROM drive) at the prompt and click OK.
3.   The installation process will begin. A dialog box proposing the directory "Program Files\REA\CLAST" will appear. If the name and location are suitable, click OK. If you wish to specify a different name or location, type it in and click OK.
4.   Start the CLAST TEST*ware*® application by double-clicking on the icon.

REA's CLAST TEST*ware*® is **EASY** to **LEARN AND USE**. To achieve maximum benefits, we recommend that you take a few minutes to go through the on-screen tutorial on your computer.

TECHNICAL SUPPORT

REA's TEST*ware*® is backed by customer and technical support. For questions about **installation or operation of your software**, contact us at:

Research & Education Association
Phone: (732) 819-8880 (9 a.m. to 5 p.m. ET, Monday–Friday)
Fax: (732) 819-8808
Website: http://www.rea.com
E-mail: info@rea.com

Note to Windows XP Users: In order for the TEST*ware*® to function properly, please install and run the application under the same computer-administrator level user account. Installing the TEST*ware*® as one user and running it as another could cause file access path conflicts.

CLAST
COLLEGE LEVEL ACADEMIC SKILLS TEST

Chapter 1

How to Pass
the CLAST

Chapter 1

HOW TO PASS THE CLAST

ABOUT THIS BOOK AND TEST*ware*®

This book provides you with an accurate and complete representation of Florida's College-Level Academic Skills Test (CLAST). Inside you will find brisk subject reviews designed to provide you with the information and strategies needed to pass the exam,* and two full-length practice tests based on the current format of the CLAST.

REA's tests were developed by experts in the Florida higher-education community to adhere to the same timed conditions and content coverage as the actual test. In fact, our practice tests contain every type of question that you can expect to encounter on the CLAST. Following each test, you will find an answer key with detailed explanations designed to help you master the test material.

Practice Tests 1 and 2 are also included on the enclosed TEST*ware*® CD. The software provides timed conditions and instantaneous, accurate scoring, which makes it all the easier to pinpoint your strengths and weaknesses.

ABOUT THE TEST

WHO TAKES THE TEST AND WHAT IS IT USED FOR?

The College-Level Academic Skills Test is administered by the Florida State Department of Education to measure academic skills at the undergraduate level. Tens of thousands of students take the test each year, usually after completing 60 credits on the undergraduate level. The CLAST is the leading means by which Florida's undergraduates demonstrate attainment of basic college-level communication and computational skills. Such proficiency is required of three specific groups of people:

1) Students enrolled in a public community college pursuing an Associate of Arts (A.A.) degree must pass the test before graduating.

* **This book will prepare you effectively for either the paper-based CLAST or the computer-adaptive CLAST, which is better known as the CAT-CLAST.**

2) Students enrolled in a baccalaureate program in many public four-year colleges must pass the CLAST by the time they reach the 60-credit mark.

3) Students enrolled in private institutions must take the CLAST if they are receiving state-funded financial aid. If they fail any section and wish to continue receiving aid, they must enroll in a course that will give them the skills needed to pass.

Students enrolled in public institutions who have failed each section of the CLAST may be required to pass at least three sections before being permitted to earn above 60 college credits. They may also be required to pass all four sections before earning more than 96 credits.

Under provisions of a Florida statute adopted on January 1, 1996, your institution may offer an exemption to the CLAST or to parts of it; for the latest information on how the law is being carried out, you should contact the person or office responsible for administering the CLAST at your college or university.

WHO ADMINISTERS THE TEST?

The CLAST is developed and administered by the Florida Department of Education. The Technical Support Contractor (TSC) works in conjunction with the Commissioner of Education to ensure the security of each test center and to maintain test conditions for each test administration.

WHEN SHOULD THE CLAST BE TAKEN?

Most students take the CLAST by the time they complete 60 undergraduate credits. Students in baccalaureate programs usually take the test by the end of their sophomore year, and students in Associate of Arts programs take the test before graduation.

WHEN AND WHERE IS THE TEST GIVEN?

The CLAST is administered at Florida colleges and universities that are designated as test centers by the Florida Department of Education. The test is usually given on the first Saturday in October and June, and the third Saturday in February. Alternate test dates fall on the Tuesday after the regular administration for students who miss the regular administration for medical or religious reasons.

HOW DO I REGISTER FOR THE CLAST?

All students who are required to take the CLAST are notified by mail. Registration and test date information will be provided at that time. If you believe you are required to take the test, but have not received notification, contact your college registrar.

Should you need further information, or if you wish to request a registration application, contact:

Florida Department of Education
325 West Gaines St., Turlington Building
Tallahassee, FL 32399-0400
Phone: (850) 245-0513
Website: *www.fldoe.org/asp*

IS THERE A REGISTRATION FEE?

To take the CLAST, you will be required to pay a registration fee. You will be notified of the fee when you receive your registration material. If you feel you are eligible for a fee waiver, contact your institution's financial aid office.

HOW TO USE THIS BOOK AND TEST*ware*®

WHAT DO I STUDY FIRST?

Take the diagnostic tests located in the reviews to determine which sections of the CLAST will give you the most difficulty. Carefully reviewing the detailed explanations of the answers will help you to understand what you are doing wrong, while cross-referencing charts will help you to determine which parts of the reviews require most of your time and concentration. These reviews include the information you need to know when taking the exam.

Complete the drills in each section to practice what you have learned. The drills will be very useful in helping you brush up on your skills. If you perform poorly on any drill, study that section of the review again.

After you have studied each review thoroughly, take the first practice test on CD-ROM. Try to simulate actual testing conditions as closely as possible. This sample test will help you to gauge your possible performance on the actual exam. As you check your answers, note which areas still need more work. Review those areas again before taking the second practice test.

To get the most out of your studying time, we recommend that you follow the Study Schedule appearing before this introduction. It suggests a plan to help budget your study time to your best advantage.

WHEN SHOULD I START STUDYING?

It is never too early to start studying for the CLAST. The earlier you begin, the more time you have to sharpen your skills. Do not procrastinate! Last-minute cramming is not helpful for this test. By studying a little bit each day, you can familiarize yourself with the test format and time limits, which will allow you to be confident and calm so that you can pass the CLAST.

FORMAT OF THE CLAST

Section	Time Limit	Number of Questions
Essay	60 minutes	1 free-response
English Language Skills and Reading Skills	80 minutes	40 multiple-choice 41 multiple-choice
Mathematics	90 minutes	55 multiple-choice

Total Testing Time: 3 hours and 50 minutes (for first-time test-takers)

All of the questions on the CLAST, with the exception of the Essay section, will be in multiple-choice format. The number of answer choices varies from section to section. First-time testtakers will be required to adhere to the schedule above; students who are retaking any sections of the test will be granted twice as much time for the section they are retaking. Although the actual time allotted for the test is just under four hours, the whole test—including breaks and paperwork—usually takes approximately five hours.

SECTIONS OF THE CLAST

ESSAY SECTION

The first part of the CLAST consists of a free-response essay question. You will be presented with two topics and be asked to choose one. This section is intended to draw on your writing skills: your ability to develop a thesis relevant to the topic, to support or refute that thesis with sophisticated ideas, and to organize those ideas in a logical fashion. You will also be responsible for using standard written English; readers will look for proper punctuation, diction, sentence flow, and use of the active voice.

ENGLISH LANGUAGE SKILLS AND READING SKILLS SECTION

These two sections are administered during the same time period. The English Language section measures your familiarity with the mechanics of the English language by testing punctuation, grammar, spelling, and word choice. Questions on sentence structure test your ability to construct well-written, grammatically correct sentences.

The Reading section involves critical reading skills. You are required to identify the main idea of given passages, as well as recognize the author's tone, writing method, and approach. Moreover, you are required to understand how the mechanics of writing in the passage function to convey the idea, thesis, or imagery, and how to evaluate their validity.

MATHEMATICS SECTION

The Mathematics section tests a basic understanding of the most fundamental mathematical disciplines. In this subtest, you will find questions covering Arithmetic, Algebra, Geometry, Statistics, and Logic. Multiple-choice questions will involve skills such as solving word problems, interpreting data, and applying mathematical formulas and properties. The Logic section will require you to recognize the relationship between statements in an argument and to change the statements while maintaining their meaning.

ABOUT THE REVIEW SECTIONS

FORMAT OF THE REVIEWS

Our reviews are written to help you understand the concepts behind CLAST test questions. The four reviews in this book correspond to the four subtests of the actual CLAST. Each review chapter is complete with drills to help reinforce the concepts as you learn them. Diagnostic tests help you to pinpoint any weak areas that may need extra attention. By using the reviews in conjunction with the practice tests, you will be able to sharpen your skills and pass the CLAST.

ESSAY WRITING SKILLS REVIEW

Included in this review are tips to keep in mind while developing a well-written essay. Structural suggestions and transitional clues will help you to learn the components of good writing. This review also includes a diagnostic test which gives you practice recognizing the elements of a well-structured passage, and asks you to write or rewrite sections of preexisting writings. This review will help you to focus and polish your skills so that you may pass this section of the CLAST.

ENGLISH LANGUAGE SKILLS REVIEW

The rules of grammar, spelling, and punctuation are outlined in this review. Also covered are diction and sentence structure skills, common grammatical mistakes and how to correct them. As with other reviews, this material is reinforced by drills.

READING SKILLS REVIEW

This review covers the format of the reading questions as well as critical reading skills. By reviewing the concepts and the question stems simultaneously, you can develop the ability to answer the Reading section questions quickly and accurately. Studying this information and completing the drills will improve your performance on the Reading section, and will help you to reinforce your progress with the Essay Writing section as well.

MATHEMATICS SKILLS REVIEW

Covered in this review are the basics of mathematics as they are addressed on the exam. You will find each topic explained in detail in simple and direct language. Sample problems and detailed solutions will help to illustrate the concepts and guide you through the best methods to determine the answer, so that you may learn how to approach similar questions on the actual test.

SCORING THE CLAST

HOW DO I SCORE MY PRACTICE TESTS?

Use this scoring worksheet to track your score improvements from Practice Test 1 to Practice Test 2. The worksheet below is meant to serve as a diagnostic tool to measure your performance; it is not meant to predict your performance on the actual CLAST. Since each multiple-choice section has 5 "developmental" questions that will not be scored, before computing your score with the chart below, subtract 5 from each of your multiple-choice raw scores.

SCORING WORKSHEET

	Test 1		Test 2	
	Number correct (raw score)	**Scaled score**	**Number correct (raw score)**	**Scaled score**
Reading	_____	_____	_____	_____
English Language	_____	_____	_____	_____
Mathematics	_____	_____	_____	_____
Writing:				
1st Reader:	_____		_____	
2nd Reader:	_____		_____	_____

SCORING THE READING, ENGLISH LANGUAGE, AND MATHEMATICS SECTIONS

After you take the Practice Tests, record your scores in the appropriate columns on the scoring worksheet.

Next, refer to the conversion chart on the next page. Match your raw score (Number Correct) with the corresponding scaled score. Write your scaled score in the appropriate column.

After taking both tests, compare your scores and analyze your performance. Did you improve? If your performance was not better on the second test, concentrate more on the areas that gave you trouble.

RAW SCORE CONVERSION CHART

READING, ENGLISH LANGUAGE, AND MATHEMATICS SECTIONS

Number Correct	English Score	Reading Score	Math Score
0	125	105	118
1	153	134	146
2	175	156	168
3	189	170	181
4	198	180	190
5	206	188	198
6	213	195	204
7	219	202	210
8	225	207	214
9	230	213	219
10	235	218	223
11	240	223	227
12	244	228	231
13	248	232	234
14	252	237	237
15	256	240	241
16	260	245	244
17	264	250	247
18	268	254	250
19	272	259	253
20	276	263	256
21	280	267	258
22	284	272	261
23	288	277	264
24	292	281	266
25	296	287	269
26	301	292	272
27	306	298	275
28	311	304	277

Number Correct	English Score	Reading Score	Math Score
29	317	311	280
30	323	318	283
31	330	327	286
32	338	338	289
33	348	352	292
34	361	374	295
35	382	404	298
36		411	301
37			305
38			309
39			312
40			316
41			321
42			326
43			331
44			337
45			343
46			351
47			361
48			374
49			395
50			423

SCORING THE ESSAY WRITING SECTION

The Essay Writing section of the CLAST is scored using a different method, due to the format of this test section. Two readers will rate your essay on a scale of 1-6. To measure your performance on the Essay portion of the practice test, have two people (preferably teachers) read your essays and assign a score between 1 and 6, the lowest score being 1. These two scores will be added together to give you an essay score between 2 and 12.

Should you decide to score your own essay, be objective! Reward yourself if a job is well done, but also determine if there is room for improvement. You can also evaluate your essay in terms of the skills you reviewed in the Essay Writing chapter.

WHAT SCORES DO I NEED TO PASS THE ACTUAL CLAST?

The actual CLAST is scored using statistical formulas and statistical analysis. Each test administration has a different conversion scale and different standards for passing. Usually, the score range is from approximately 100 to 400, although even the range varies to accommodate each test.

As you work through your practice tests, you should try to obtain scores similar to the following:

Reading:	295
English Language:	295
Mathematics:	295
Essay Writing:	6

These scores are provided to give you a general idea of your possible performance on the CLAST. They are not intended to predict or determine your future scores.

WHEN WILL I RECEIVE MY SCORE REPORT AND WHAT WILL IT LOOK LIKE?

Your score report for the CLAST will arrive approximately five weeks after you take the test. The report will list your scaled score for each section, in addition to the breakdown of your performance within the sections. Only the scaled score will be recorded on your transcript; the breakdown of your performance within each section will not appear on your transcript. The passing score for each test will appear on the bottom of your score report.

STUDYING FOR THE CLAST

It is very important for you to choose a time and place for studying that works best for you. Some students set aside a certain number of hours every morning to study, while others may choose to study at night before going to sleep. Other students may study during the day, while waiting on line, or even during lunch. Only you can determine when and where your study time would be most effective. Be consistent and use your time wisely. Work out a study routine and stick to it!

When you take the practice tests on CD-ROM, try to make your testing conditions as much like the actual test as possible. Turn your television and radio off, and sit at a quiet table free of distraction.

Try not to review too much at one time; concentrate on one problem area at a time. One good technique is to reread the question, and then the explanation. Then study the corresponding section in the review chapter until you are confident that you understand the material.

Keep track of your scores and mark them on the scoring worksheet. By doing so, you will be able to gauge your progress and discover your weaknesses. You should carefully study the reviews that cover your areas of difficulty, as this will build your skill in those areas.

TEST-TAKING TIPS...

Whether you're taking the paper-and-pencil or computerized version (CAT) of the CLAST, it's critical that you become comfortable with the format and presentation of the test. Apart from the CAT-CLAST not having the Essay subtest, the two versions are essentially identical. Even so, there still some distinctions you'll want to put to use in your approach to each.

...FOR THE PAPER-BASED CLAST

Work on the easier questions first. If you find yourself working too long on any one question, flag it in your test booklet and move on. After answering all the questions that you can, return to the ones you skipped.

Be sure to mark your answer in the circle that corresponds to the number of the question. Since the multiple-choice sections are graded by machine, marking one answer incorrectly will distort your score. Be especially careful not to let your flagged questions disturb the sequence of your answer marks; you run the risk of throwing off your whole answer grid with one skipped answer. Double-check that your question and answer numbers stay in sync.

...FOR THE CAT-CLAST

Budget your time wisely. This is a timed test, so check in with the clock, but by no means obsess over it. The key is not to spend too much time on any single question. If you don't know the answer, make an educated guess and confidently move on.

Use your keyboard effectively. Use the UP and DOWN arrows on your keyboard to scroll through the reading passages.

Take special care in committing to an answer. Compared with the paper-based test, marking your answer on the computer can seem like a breeze. Don't get lulled into making this too automatic a motion.

The English Language Skills, Reading, and Mathematics subtests are offered as part of the CAT-CLAST for both first-time test takers and retakes. In the event you need to retake the exam, you will be granted a great deal more time. For both the English Language Skills and Reading subtests, regardless of whether you take just one or the pair, you will have 2 hours and 40 minutes; for the Mathematics subtest by itself, you'll get 3 hours.

Finally, it's important to understand that despite its name, the CAT-CLAST is <u>not adaptive</u> but rather linear—just like the paper-based CLAST.

...FOR EITHER VERSION OF THE CLAST

If you're unsure of the answer, guess! There's no penalty for guessing.

THE DAY OF THE TEST

BEFORE THE TEST

Try to be as well-rested and comfortable as possible for the day of the test. Get a good night's sleep and wear comfortable clothes so you are not distracted by the temperature. Wearing layers will allow you to adjust to the temperature.

Make sure to wake up early enough to allow yourself plenty of time to get to the test center. This will not only eliminate the anxiety associated with being late, it will also provide you with enough time to eat a good breakfast.

Try to get to the test center a little early. Any stress added by rushing or getting lost won't help your cause. The doors to the test center should open at 7:45 A.M. and close at about 8:15 A.M. Since the test must be secured, no latecomers or stand-bys will be admitted. The test normally begins at 8:30 A.M.

Be sure to bring your examination admission ticket and two forms of identification. Each form of I.D. should bear your signature, and at least one should have your photo (i.e., driver's license, student I.D., etc.). You will not be admitted into the test center without proper I.D. You should also bring several sharpened No. 2 pencils and a few ballpoint pens, either black or blue.

You will not be permitted to bring calculators, calculator watches, books, papers, slide rules, beepers, compasses, rulers, or dictionaries into the test center.

DURING THE TEST

When you arrive at the test center, try to find a seat where you will be comfortable. You will have the opportunity to walk around and use the rest room during the breaks between sections.

Before the test begins, the Institutional Test Administrator (ITA) will ask the people who are retaking the test to go to another designated room. Retakers are given different time limits than first-time test-takers.

You can write in your test booklet but scrap paper is prohibited, even for the Mathematics section. Mark your responses in the appropriate spaces on the answer sheet. Fill in the oval that corresponds to your answer choice as neatly as possible, and make sure it is dark. You can change your answer, but only if you completely erase your old one. Bear in mind that your test will be scored by an unforgiving machine.

Time limits will be clearly denoted for you. Two breaks will be given: one after the Essay Writing section, and one after the Reading and English Language Skills section. The Mathematics section is usually given last.

AFTER THE TEST

Although the actual time needed for the test is just under four hours (except for repeat takers), you will most likely be in the test center for close to five hours.

When you have finished the test, you will be dismissed from the testing center. Then, go home and relax! Your full score report will arrive in about five weeks.

COLLEGE LEVEL ACADEMIC SKILLS TEST

Chapter 2
English Language
Skills Review

Chapter 2

ENGLISH LANGUAGE SKILLS REVIEW

The requirements for informal spoken English are much more relaxed than the rigid rules for "standard written English"; while slang, colloquialisms, and other informal expressions are acceptable and sometimes very appropriate in casual speech, they are inappropriate in academic and business writing. More often than not, writers, especially student writers, do not make a distinction between the two: they use the same words, grammar, and sentence structure from their everyday speech in their college papers, albeit unsuccessfully.

The English Language Skills (ELS) section of the CLAST is designed to measure your knowledge of these skills: standard written English usage, the kind of English used in most college textbooks, in published documents, and in reputable magazines and newspapers; it is the kind of English you are required to use in your college papers. Standard English is also the kind of English you will be expected to use as a professional.

This test does not necessarily require you to know the grammatical terms, such as *gerund, subject complement,* or *dependent clause,* although general familiarity with such terms may be helpful to you in determining whether a sentence or part of a sentence is correct or incorrect. You should watch for errors in grammar, spelling, punctuation, capitalization, sentence structure, and word choice. Remember: this is a test of *written* language skills; therefore, your responses should be based on what you know to be correct for written work, not what you know to be appropriate for a casual conversation. For instance, in informal speech, you might say *"Who are you going to choose?"* But in formal academic writing, you would write *"Whom are you going to choose?"* Your choices, then, should be dictated by requirements for "written English" rather than "conversational English."

THE DIRECTIONS

The English Language Skills test is taken together with the Reading Skills test. You are given 80 minutes to complete both sections. Since the Reading Skills section is the longer of the two, it is recommended that you take the English Language Skills section first. You should allot 30-40 minutes for this section.

Since there are seven different question formats on the English Language Skills section, there are seven different sets of directions. All questions, however, have only one correct answer. Keep in mind, also, that since your score is based on the number of correct answers, there is no penalty for guessing. Therefore, it is to your advantage to answer every question.

TIPS

- As you work through the drills in this review, read the directions very carefully. If you memorize the directions now, you will save valuable time during the actual test.

- Read the test items with a critical eye, as if you were editing one of your own papers or the paper of a friend.

- Remember: not every item contains a mistake.

- Remember to examine the sentences only for those errors mentioned in the directions.

- For multiple-choice items, do not guess. Read each choice closely and carefully. Choose from the multiple-choice items the response that has no error.

- Look for errors, not for wording that, in your judgment, should be changed. That is, do not decide that an underlined word, for instance, is incorrect simply because you prefer a different word. Determine whether any of the underlined parts of any of the choices contain an error in standard grammar, usage, syntax, or mechanics. For example:

The Secretary of State, as well as the other members of the cabinet <u>were summoned</u> suddenly to the bedside of the <u>ailing</u> President.

The error is *were summoned*. The problem is one of agreement, not one of word choice or word placement. Although *ailing* could be changed to *ill, sick,* or *infirm, ailing* is not incorrect in connotation, denotation, grammar, or spelling. Also, the adverb *suddenly* could precede the verb, but its present position is not incorrect. The verb phrase *were summoned*, however, is grammatically incorrect; the subject of the sentence, *Secretary of State*, is singular; therefore, the verb should also be singular— *was summoned*.

ENGLISH LANGUAGE SKILLS DIAGNOSTIC TEST

The following is a sample CLAST English Language Skills section. It contains 40 items covering word choice, sentence structure skills, grammar, and mechanics—the same categories that are tested by the actual CLAST subtest on English Language Skills. This section does not require you to write an essay; you are required to write an essay for the Essay Subtest. This is a 40-question, 35-minute test. Taking this test should give you a realistic indication not only of your strengths and weaknesses in English language skills, but also of the speed and accuracy of your responses. Therefore, you should time yourself for better, more realistic results.

Answers to each question are presented with a cross-reference to which sections of the English Language Skills review you should study if you answer a question incorrectly.

ENGLISH LANGUAGE SKILLS DIAGNOSTIC TEST

> **DIRECTIONS:** From the given choices, select the word or phrase that best fits the context of the sentence.

1.   The noise distracted me and _____ my concentration.

   (A)   effected

   (B)   affected

   (C)   effects

2.   _____ airlines are feeling the effects of the pilots' strike.

   (A)   Fewer

   (B)   Less

   (C)   A large amount of

3. The statue looks very different _____ the way it used to look.

    (A) then

    (B) than

    (C) from

DIRECTIONS: Select the sentence that clearly and effectively states the idea and has no structural errors.

---

4.   (A) The title of an educational institution does not affect the quality of it's education.

    (B) The title of an educational institution does not affect the quality of its' education.

    (C) The title of an educational institution does not affect the quality of its education.

5.   (A) My father is no more an atheist than me.

    (B) My father is no more an atheist than you or I.

    (C) My father is no more an atheist than you or me.

6.   (A) I was real fortunate to be chose to pitch in an exhibition game.

    (B) I was real fortunate to have been chosen to pitch in an exhibition game.

    (C) I was very fortunate to have been chosen to pitch in an exhibition game.

7.   (A) The director asked me and my roommate to usher at the opening performance of the play.

    (B) The director asked my roommate and I to usher at the opening performance of the play.

    (C) The director asked he and my roommate to usher at the opening performance of the play.

8. (A) A hawk's outstanding eyesight aids them with their vision.

    (B) A hawk's outstanding eyesight aids them with its vision.

    (C) A hawk's outstanding eyesight aids the hawk with its vision.

9. (A) In Wisconsin they produce a lot of cheese.

    (B) They produce a lot of cheese in Wisconsin.

    (C) Wisconsin produces a lot of cheese.

10. (A) Lying on the table is a picture of my husband and me on our wedding day.

    (B) Laying on the table is a picture of my husband and I on our wedding day.

    (C) Lying on the table is a picture of my husband and I on our wedding day.

11. (A) Our dog frightened the electrician even though he was trying to be friendly.

    (B) Even though our dog was trying to be friendly, he frightened the electrician.

    (C) Our dog frightened the electrician which was trying to be friendly.

12. (A) All students including we freshman have to study.

    (B) All students including us freshman have to study.

    (C) Us freshman students have to study.

13. (A) Give the trophy to whomever wins the tennis match.

    (B) Whom do you think will win the tennis match?

    (C) Who do you think will win the tennis match?

14. (A)   A U.S. President was often judged by the number of jobs he creates.

(B)   A U.S. President is often judged by the number of jobs he creates.

(C)   A U.S. President was often judge by the number of jobs he creates.

15. (A)   By the end of this semester, all the students will have went through the program.

(B)   By the end of this semester, all the students went through the program.

(C)   By the end of this semester, all of the students will have gone through the program.

DIRECTIONS: Choose the option that does not contain an error in grammar.

---

16. Two pieces of identification are required for customers <u>which</u> are withdrawing or depositing cash.

(A)   who   (C)   that

(B)   whom   (D)   No change is necessary.

17. It is necessary that your signatures <u>are witnessed</u> by a notary.

(A)   be witnessed   (C)   is to be witnessed

(B)   are witness   (D)   No change is necessary.

18. <u>There's</u> two different things that are selling products today—quality and fashion.

(A)   There is   (C)   There be

(B)   There are   (D)   No change is necessary.

19. The play will be held over for another <u>month, it</u> is the most popular play the theater has ever produced.

(A)   month; it   (C)   month and it

(B)   month it   (D)   No change is necessary.

DIRECTIONS: From the given choices, select the underlined portion which is not needed in the passage and mark its corresponding letter on your answer sheet.

---

20. Recreation, in the form of games and sports, <u>are</u> such a <u>principal</u> part of our
                                                   A   **B**

lives that we can hardly do without <u>it</u>.   <u>No Errors</u>
                                   C   **D**

21. Getting good grades <u>has</u> always been <u>very important</u> to <u>she and her sisters</u>.
                               A   **B**   **C**

<u>No Errors</u>
  D

22. The IRS sent <u>me and my wife</u> our refunds, but most of my friends <u>have</u> not
                       A   **B**

received <u>theirs</u> yet.   <u>No Errors</u>
         C   **D**

23. Each of the participants <u>was asked</u> <u>to complete</u> the questionnaire <u>as quick as</u>
                                 A   **B**   **C**

possible.   <u>No Errors</u>
              D

24. A <u>real popular</u> leisure-time activity <u>among</u> college students <u>is</u> dating.
    A   **B**   **C**

<u>No Errors</u>
  D

DIRECTIONS: Select the sentence that clearly and effectively states the idea and has no structural errors.

---

25. (A) Until neither of us has been outside the United States, we have no idea where the Taj Mahal is.

    (B) Since neither of us has been outside the United States, we have no idea where the Taj Mahal is.

    (C) Neither of us has been outside the United States, but we have no idea where the Taj Mahal is.

26. (A) The Chesapeake Bay provides more seafood to the United States than any other body of water except the Atlantic and Pacific Oceans.

(B)   The Chesapeake Bay provides more seafood to the United States than any body of water except the Atlantic and Pacific Oceans.

(C)   The Chesapeake Bay provides more seafood to the United States than all the bodies of water except the Atlantic and Pacific Oceans.

27.   (A)   A company cannot say a product is endorsed by any group or agency if it is untrue.

      (B)   A company cannot say a product is endorsed by any group or agency if this is untrue.

      (C)   A company cannot say a product is endorsed by any group or agency if this information is untrue.

28.   (A)   Having a job has taught me responsibility, patience, and how to handle money.

      (B)   Having a job has taught me responsibility, patience, and how to budget my money.

      (C)   Having a job has taught me responsibility, patience, and the importance of a budget.

29.   (A)   Plagiarism is when the writer presents the thoughts of another writer or author as her own.

      (B)   Plagiarism occurs when the writer presents the thoughts of another writer or author as her own.

      (C)   Plagiarism is the writer presents the thoughts of another writer or author as her own.

30.   (A)   Poorly typed and hastily proofread, my essay contained several glaring errors.

      (B)   Poorly typed and hastily proofread, several glaring errors appeared in my essay.

      (C)   Poorly typed and hastily proofread, I had several glaring errors in my essay.

31. (A) Daily exercise, a strict sleeping schedule, and eating nutritious foods are all necessary to sound health.

    (B) Daily exercise, a strict sleeping schedule, and eating foods which are nutritious are all necessary to sound health.

    (C) Daily exercise, a strict sleeping schedule, and good nutrition are all necessary to sound health.

32. (A) Neither those in favor of the bill or those opposed to it are happy about the decision.

    (B) Neither those in favor of the bill nor those opposed to it are happy about the decision.

    (C) Either those in favor of the bill nor those opposed to it are happy about the decision.

33. (A) Disney World is as large as, if not larger than, any amusement park in the country.

    (B) Disney World is as large, if not larger than, any other amusement park in the country.

    (C) Disney World is as large as, if not larger than, any other amusement park in the country.

34. (A) The employees are negotiating to get a raise higher than last year.

    (B) The employees are negotiating to get a raise higher than last year's.

    (C) The employees are negotiating to get a raise higher then last years.

35. (A) The performer, while making his way through the crowd, stopping only to sign autographs.

    (B) The performer, while making his way through the crowd and stopping only to sign autographs.

    (C) The performer, while making his way through the crowd, stopped only to sign autographs.

36. (A) The Declaration of Independence was adopted on July 4, 1776; a date that is now a national holiday, the Fourth of July, or Independence Day.

    (B) The Declaration of Independence was adopted on July 4, 1776, a date that is now a national holiday, the Fourth of July, or Independence Day.

    (C) The Declaration of Independence was adopted on July 4, 1776, a date that is now a national holiday, the Fourth of July or Independence Day.

37. (A) Brass instruments are wind instruments that include: the trumpet, French horn, and trombone.

    (B) Brass instruments are wind instruments such as: the trumpet, French horn, and trombone.

    (C) Brass instruments are wind instruments that include the trumpet, French horn, and trombone.

38. (A) "The Invisible Man", winner of the national book award, charts the journey of a black man from the South to Harlem.

    (B) *The Invisible Man,* winner of the national book award, charts the journey of a black man from the South to Harlem.

    (C) "The Invisible Man," winner of the national book award, charts the journey of a black man from the South to Harlem.

39. (A) The article *Namecalling* in *News II* magazine discusses women's odd names such as Lois Price and Carol Christmas.

    (B) The article *Namecalling* in "News II" magazine discusses women's odd names such as "Lois Price" and "Carol Christmas."

    (C) The article "Namecalling" in *News II* magazine discusses women's odd names such as Lois Price and Carol Christmas.

40. (A) Modern technology makes it possible for people who cannot speak to communicate through a "live talker."

    (B) Modern technology makes it possible for people who cannot speak to communicate through a "live talker".

    (C) Modern technology makes it possible for people who cannot speak, to communicate through a "live talker."

ENGLISH LANGUAGE SKILLS REVIEW DIAGNOSTIC TEST ANSWER KEY

Use the chart below to check your answers. If you responded incorrectly, refer to the column on the right to direct you to the review section that will help you.

Question	Answer	*If you answered this question incorrectly, see the section titled:*
1	B	Word Choice Skills: p. 35
2	A	Word Choice Skills: p. 35
3	B	Word Choice Skills: p. 35
4	C	Pronoun-Antecedent Agreement: p. 62
5	B	Pronoun Case: p. 60
6	C	Adjective and Adverb Usage: p. 68
7	A	Pronoun Case: p. 60
8	C	Pronoun-Antecedent Agreement: p. 62
9	C	Pronoun Reference: p. 64
10	A	Verb Forms: p. 52
11	B	Pronoun Reference: p. 64
12	B	Pronoun Case: p. 60
13	C	Pronoun Case: p. 60
14	B	Verb Tense: p. 53
15	C	Verb Forms and Verb Tenses: p. 52 and 53
16	A	Pronoun Case and Pronoun Reference: p. 60
17	A	Verb Forms: p. 52
18	B	Subject-Verb Agreement: p. 54
19	A	Fragments, Run-on/Fused Sentences, and Comma Splices: p. 47
20	A	Subject-Verb Agreement: p. 54
21	C	Pronoun Case: p. 60
22	D	Subject-Verb Agreement and Pronoun Case: p. 54 and p. 60
23	C	Adjective Usage: p. 68
24	A	Adjective Usage: p. 68

Question	Answer	If you answered this question incorrectly, see the section titled:
25	B	Subordination, Coordination, and Predication: p. 48
26	A	Faulty Comparisons: p. 69
27	C	Pronoun Reference: p. 64
28	C	Parallelism: p. 44
29	B	Subordination, Coordination, and Predication: p. 48
30	A	Dangling Modifiers: p. 45
31	C	Parallelism: p. 44
32	B	Parallelism: p. 44
33	C	Faulty Comparisons: p. 69
34	B	Faulty Comparisons: p. 69
35	C	Fragments, Run-on/Fused Sentences, and Comma Splices: p. 47
36	C	Commas: p. 72
37	C	Colons: p. 80
38	B	Quotation Marks and Italics: p. 81
39	C	Quotation Marks, Italics, and Apostrophes: p. 81 and p. 83
40	A	Commas and Quotation Marks: p. 72 and p. 81

DETAILED EXPLANATIONS OF ANSWERS

1. **(B)** The correct answer is (B) since "affected" is used correctly to mean "influenced." (A) and (C) are incorrect since "effected" and "effects", used here as verbs, mean "to have brought about" and "to bring about."

2. **(A)** The correct answer is (A) since "fewer" is used to signal countable nouns. (B) is incorrect because "less" is used only for mass nouns or general amounts, not groups of things (such as airlines) that can be separated into individual, countable components. (C) is incorrect because, like "less", "a large amount of" specifies a mass noun, not a countable noun.

3. **(B)** The correct answer is (B) since "different than" is used when followed by a clause. (A) is incorrect because "then" is an adverb of time, not a conjunction used in comparisons. (C) is also incorrect since "different than" should be used instead of "different from" when a clause follows the expression.

4. **(C)** The correct answer is (C) since "its" is the possessive of "it," which here refers to "educational institution." (A) is incorrect because "it's" is the contraction for "it is"; since this situation calls for a possessive, "it is" is not appropriate. (B) is incorrect because "its'" is a meaningless word that is never used.

5. **(B)** The correct answer is (B) since only the nominative case "I" would allow for the correct continuation of the elliptical clause: "My father is no more an atheist than you or I am." (A) is incorrect because "me" belongs to the objective case and cannot support the completion of the elliptical clause ("me am" is obviously wrong). (C) is incorrect for the same reasons as (A); the addition of "you" changes nothing since only the second pronoun ("me" or "I" in "you and me" or "you and I") matters when completing the elliptical clause.

6. **(C)** The correct answer is (C) since "fortunate" is an adjective correctly modified by an adverb, "very." (A) is incorrect because "real" is an adjective (not an adverb) and therefore cannot modify the adjective "fortunate"; furthermore, "to be chose" is incorrect because "chose" in this instance must act as an adjective and therefore must be "chosen." (B) is incorrect because, like in (A), "real" is an adjective, not an adverb.

7. **(A)** The correct answer is (A) since the objective case pronoun ("me") is required as the direct object of the verb "asked." (B) is incorrect because "I" belongs to the nominative case and cannot act as the object of the verb "asked"; eliminate "my roommate" and the reason becomes easier to understand: "The director asked I" is incorrect. (C) is incorrect because "he" (like "I") belongs to the nominative case, not the objective case which is required here; "him" (rather than "he") would have been an acceptable possibility.

8. **(C)** The correct answer is (C) since the verb "aids" agrees in number with the nouns and pronouns ("hawk's," "hawk," and "its") to which it refers. (A) is incorrect since "A hawk's" calls for a singular object for the verb "aids"; "them," being plural, is thus incorrect. "Their" agrees in number with "them," but since "them" is already incorrect, the agreement is of no consequence. (B) is incorrect because it repeats the same mistake involving "them" which we saw in (A); "its" agrees with the singular "A hawk's" and "aids" but not with the plural "them."

9. **(C)** The correct answer is (C) because the pronoun "they" has no antecedent in choices (A) and (B). If sentence (A) or (B) had appeared in a paragraph in which the pronoun "they" was understood, for example, to refer to a specific company with many factories nationwide, then, the lack of an antecedent in sentence (A) or (B) itself would pose no problem. Since you cannot infer such specifics, though, (C) is the only correct answer.

10. **(A)** The correct answer is (A) because "lying" is the present tense and agrees with the present tense "is"; (A) is also correct because the phrase "picture of" calls for the objective pronoun "me" as the object of the preposition "of." (B) is incorrect because "laying" (past tense) does not agree with "is" (present tense), and because "I" belongs to the nominative case and thus cannot act as the object of "of." (C) is incorrect because "I" belongs to the nominative case and thus cannot act as the object of "of."

11. **(B)** The correct answer is (B) because it is clear in this sentence that "he" refers to the dog, not the electrician. (A) is incorrect since the referent for "he" is ambiguous; the fact that "he" appears directly after "electrician," rather than "dog," gives the impression that it was the electrician who was trying to be friendly. Obviously, the sentence makes more sense if we understand the dog to be the one attempting to be friendly. (C) is incorrect since "who" (not "which") is used when referring to a person (the electrician, in this instance).

12. **(B)** The correct answer is (B) because the objective case pronoun ("us") is used after a preposition ("including"). (A) is incorrect since "we" belongs to the nominative case and cannot act as the object of a preposition. (C) is incorrect because in this instance there is no preposition and therefore the nominative pronoun "we" (not "us") is required.

13. **(C)** The correct answer is (C) since the sentence calls for the nominative case. If you rewrite the sentence and substitute "she" or "her" for "who," the answer becomes clearer: "Do you think she will win the tennis match?" It's sometimes easier to hear that "she"—which is nominative, like "who"—is correct. (A) is incorrect since "whomever" should be "whoever"; in this instance, despite the preposition "to," "whoever" is correct since the object of "to" is not "whoever" but the entire noun phrase "whoever wins the tennis match," in which "whoever" is the subject of the verb "wins." (B) is incorrect since the nominative case (who), not the objective case (whom), is required; as above, when we rewrite the sentence, she/who (not her/whom) is correct.

14. **(B)**   The correct answer is (B) since the tense of the verbs ("is," "creates") remains consistent. (A) is incorrect since the verb phrase "was often judged" in the past tense demands that other actions occurring in the past also be described in the past tense ("created," not "creates"). (C) is incorrect since the first verb phrase "was often judge" requires the past participle "judged" and since, like in (A), "creates" should be "created" in order to correspond with "was."

15. **(C)**   The correct answer is (C) since the sentence is set in the present ("this semester") and correctly uses the future perfect tense ("will have gone through") to look forward to an action that will be completed in the future. (A) is incorrect because the future perfect form of the verb "to go" is "will have gone," not "will have went." (B) is incorrect: "went" signals a completed action, but "this" implies that the semester is not over. The students can only be said to have completed the program when the semester is over, thus the simple past tense of "went" cannot be used.

16. **(A)**   The correct answer is (A) since "who" functions as the subject of the clause, and "which" should not be used to refer to people. (B) is incorrect because the clause can only accept a nominative pronoun ("who") as its subject; for example, you can substitute the nominative "they" in the clause "who/they are withdrawing," but you could not similarly substitute the objective case pronoun "whom" or "them." (C) is incorrect since "that" should not be used to refer to people.

17. **(A)**   The correct answer is (A) since the sentence is in the subjunctive mood (indicated by the phrase "It is necessary that"). (B) is incorrect since "be," not "are," is used to indicate a condition not yet in existence or contrary to fact; in addition, "witness" should be the past participle "witnessed." (C) is incorrect since the present tense, not the future tense, must be used for the subjunctive mood.

18. **(B)**   The correct answer is (B) since the verb must agree in number with its plural subject, which is really "two different things," not the expletive "there." (A) is incorrect because "is" is singular and fails to agree with the plural subject "two different things." Likewise, (C) is incorrect because the subject and verb fail to agree.

19. **(A)**   The correct answer is (A) since the sentence is really two sentences joined by a comma (this is called a comma splice). (B) is incorrect since the removal of the comma fails to separate the two sentences sufficiently. (C) is incorrect since it creates a run-on, rather than correcting the sentence by using a period, a semicolon, a coordinating conjunction, or a subordinating conjunction.

20. **(A)**   The correct answer is (A) since the subject and verb do not agree ("Recreation" is singular, but "are" is plural). Nothing is wrong with (B) since "principal" is used correctly to mean major or foremost. Nothing is wrong with (C); "it" is singular, the antecedent being "Recreation," not the plural "games and sports." (D) is not appropriate because, as shown above, the subject and verb must be made to agree.

21. **(C)** The correct answer is (C) since the preposition "to" takes the objective case pronoun "her," not "she." Nothing is wrong with (A) since "Getting good grades" is a verbal noun using a gerund and thus requires a singular verb, "has" not "have." Nothing is wrong with (B) since the adverb "very" correctly modifies the adjective "important." (D) is not appropriate because the nominative "she" must be changed to the objective "her," as explained above.

22. **(D)** The correct answer is (D) since the sentence need not be changed. Nothing is wrong with (A): "me" belongs to the objective case and correctly serves as an indirect object of the implied construction, "The IRS sent our refunds to me and my wife" ("our refunds" is the direct object of the verb "sent"). Nothing is wrong with (B), the plural verb form "have," since the indefinite pronoun "most" is plural in this instance (implying more than one friend). Nothing is wrong with (C) because "theirs" is the possessive pronoun appropriate for "friends"; "their" would not be appropriate since it is a possessive, but not a possessive pronoun.

23. **(C)** The correct answer is (C) because the adjective "quick" should be the adverb "quickly" (modifying the verb "to complete"). Nothing is wrong with (A) since the singular verb form "was asked" takes the singular subject "Each," not the plural "participants." Nothing is wrong with (B) since the infinitive "to complete" correctly follows the main verb "was asked." (D) is not appropriate since "quick" should be "quickly," as explained above.

24. **(A)** The correct answer is (A) because one adjective ("real") cannot modify another ("popular"); "really popular" is the appropriate usage since "really" is an adverb. Nothing is wrong with (B) since "among" is correctly used for a relationship involving more than two people. Nothing is wrong with (C) since the singular subject "activity" agrees with the singular verb form "is." (D) is not appropriate since "real" must be changed to "really."

25. **(B)** The correct answer is (B) because the sentence's two clauses work logically together. (A) is incorrect because "until" indicates an event that has not yet happened, but the past tense verb form "has been" indicates that the event (not going outside the United States) has in fact happened or is happening. (C) is incorrect because the sentence logically implies the "we" must have travelled outside the United States to know the location of the Taj Mahal, which is in India, not the United States; "but" impedes the logic of the sentence since "but" implies something contrary to the expectations set up in the first clause—the expectations, however, are not disrupted (as suspected, the "we" does not know the location of the Taj Mahal).

26. **(A)** The correct answer is (A) because that comparison is logical and complete. (B) is incorrect because it omits "other" after "any" when comparing one body of water with other bodies of water. (C) is incorrect because it wrongly substitutes "the" for "other" after "any."

27. **(C)**   The correct answer is (C) because it makes clear that "this information" refers to the product endorsement, not to the company, product, group, or agency. (A) is incorrect because "it" is an ambiguous pronoun that could be thought to refer to the company, product, group, or agency, instead of the endorsement. (B) is incorrect because, like "it," "this" fails to refer to the endorsement.

28. **(C)**   The correct answer is (C) because the noun "importance" remains parallel to (continues) the list of nouns preceding it. (A) is incorrect since the phrase "how to" disrupts the parallel construction begun by the list of nouns. (B) is incorrect because, like in (A), "how to" disrupts the parallel construction. There is no meaningful difference between "handle" and "budget" in (A) and (B).

29. **(B)**   The correct answer is (B) because this sentence bears no faulty predication. (A) is incorrect since the construction "is when" is faulty predication ("when" indicates a time and should not be used to define a word or concept). (C) is incorrect because it wrongly implies that "Plagiarism" is a person ("the writer"), rather than a thing or event.

30. **(A)**   The correct answer is (A) because it contains no dangling modifiers. (B) is incorrect because the phrase "Poorly typed and hastily proofread" is a dangling modifier (the phrase wrongly modifies "several glaring errors," rather than "my essay"). (C) is incorrect because it, too, makes the phrase "Poorly typed and hastily proofread" into a dangling modifier by placing "I" (rather than "my essay") directly after it.

31. **(C)**   The correct answer is (C) because it contains parallel items in a series. (A) is incorrect since the item "eating nutritious foods" begins with a gerund ("eating"), thus failing to maintain parallel construction. (B) is incorrect since, like in (A), the parallel series of nouns modified by adjectives ("Daily exercise, a strict sleeping schedule") is disrupted by a gerund ("eating").

32. **(B)**   The correct answer is (B) since it correctly uses the correlative pair "neither...nor." (A) is incorrect because it wrongly follows "neither" with "or" instead of "nor." (C) is incorrect because it wrongly pairs "Either" with "nor."

33. **(C)**   The correct answer is (C) since it correctly uses the phrases "as large as" and "any other." (A) is incorrect since it omits the "other" which should follow "any." (B) is incorrect because it omits the second "as" in "as large as."

34. **(B)**   The correct answer is (B) because it does not contain a faulty comparison. (A) is incorrect because it uses "year" instead of "year's"; the possessive "year's" is necessary since the raise is higher than last *year's* raise, not last *year* raise. (C) is incorrect because "years" omits the apostrophe necessary to make it possessive; it should be "year's," not "year."

35. **(C)** The correct answer is (C) since it is a complete sentence. (A) is incorrect since it contains only dependent clauses and no independent clause. (B) is incorrect since, like (A), it contains only dependent clauses. Neither the comma in (A) nor the "and" in (B) makes the final clause independent since the gerund "stopping" does not change to "stopped."

36. **(C)** The correct answer is (C) since the commas are used correctly to set off the date and the appositive. (A) is incorrect because it sets off the appositive "a date that is now a national holiday" with a semicolon and a comma, instead of two commas. (B) is incorrect because it uses a comma and "or" together when only "or" is necessary.

37. **(C)** The correct answer is (C) since it is not necessary to use a colon following "include." (A) is incorrect because it is never necessary to place a colon after a preposition, such as "include," even when a list follows. (B) is incorrect since "such as," like "include," does not need a colon to introduce a list.

38. **(B)** The correct answer is (B) because it applies the standard rules of capitalization and quotation marks. (A) is incorrect since it uses quotation marks instead of italics to mark a book title, and because it places a comma outside the closing quotation marks. (C) is incorrect because it wrongly uses quotation marks instead of italics to mark a book title.

39. **(C)** The correct answer is (C) since it correctly uses quotation marks and italics. (A) is incorrect since article titles, such as "Namecalling," should be set off with quotation marks, not italics or underlining. (B) is incorrect because it uses italics instead of quotations marks to set off "Namecalling"; uses quotation marks instead of italics to set off the magazine title *News II*; and unnecessarily uses quotation marks to set off the names Lois Price and Carol Christmas.

40. **(A)** The correct answer is (A) since it does not use any unnecessary commas and since it places the period inside the closing quotation marks. (B) is incorrect since the period should never be placed outside of the quotation marks if the quotation marks come at the very end of the sentence. (C) is incorrect because it unnecessarily inserts a comma before the infinitive "to communicate."

WORD CHOICE SKILLS

USAGE

Consider the following sentence:

The high school *principal* resigned for two *principal* reasons.

If you think that the second *principal* is the wrong word (that it should be *principle*), look again. This usage is correct. This kind of problem would be covered in a test on Word Choice Skills, which covers words commonly confused and misused, as well as the use of words based on their grammatical appropriateness in a sentence, such as the grammatical distinction between *principal* and *principle*, *fewer* and *less*, and *a* and *an*. Word choice problems are different from spelling problems, which are tested in the Spelling section. The Word Choice Skills section also includes questions that test your knowledge of connotative versus denotative meanings and wordiness versus conciseness. Study carefully the following list of commonly misused words.

COMMONLY MISUSED WORDS

A
: Used before words with an initial consonant sound
EX: *a* director, *a* historical event

AN
: Used before words with an initial vowel sound
EX: *an* actress, *an* honorable man

(Remember, it is the initial *sound* that determines whether you use **a** or **an**. If the initial sound is a vowel sound, use **an**, even if the word starts with a consonant: *an* FBI agent, *an* MBA degree. If the initial is a consonant, use **a**, even if the initial letter is a vowel: *a* university, *a* union.)

A LOT
: Often misspelled as one word

ACCEPT
: Verb: to take
EX: I graciously *accept* your invitation.

EXCEPT
: Verb: to omit; preposition: but
EX: Teachers are *excepted* from jury duty.
Everyone was excused *except* Joe and me.

ADVICE
: Noun (ending pronounced "ice")
EX: Most good *advice* falls on deaf ears.

ADVISE
: Verb (rhymes with "devise")
EX: The protestors were advised to submit a list of their grievances.

AFFECT
: Verb: to influence
EX: The noise *affects* my concentration.

EFFECT

Noun: result; verb: to bring about
EX: His speech had a positive *effect* on me.
    The President has *effected* a new tax law.

If you are unsure about which word to use in a given sentence, try substituting the verb "influence" and the noun "result." If the sentence makes sense when you use "influence," then the correct word to use is "affect." If the sentence makes sense when you substitute "result," then the correct word to use is "effect."

ALL RIGHT

Often misspelled as one word

ALMOST

Adverb
EX: We sold *almost* all the tickets.

MOST

Adjective or pronoun
EX: We sold *most* of the tickets.
    Most ticketed events sell out early.

AMONG

Used for relationships involving MORE THAN TWO people or things
EX: There is a closeness *among* family members.

BETWEEN

Used for relationships involving ONLY TWO people or things
EX: Lois and Hattie had only fifty cents *between* them.

AMOUNT

Used with singular (mass) nouns
EX: *amount* of work, *amount* of credit

NUMBER

Used with plural (countable) nouns
EX: *number* of classes, *number* of mistakes

AS, AS IF, AS THOUGH

Used before clauses (see LIKE)
EX: It looks *as if* (not LIKE) it is going to rain.
    He acts *as though* (not LIKE) he has Alzheimer's disease.

BE SURE TO

Used before verbs
EX: *Be sure to* close the windows before it rains.

TRY TO

Used before verbs
EX: *Try to* be on time for class.

CAPITAL

Noun: uppercase letter, money to invest, or seat of government; adjective: serious
EX: "B" is *capital* letter b.
    How much *capital* do you have?
    Santa Fe is the *capital* of New Mexico.
    Capital crimes such as murder often result in *capital* punishment.

CAPITOL	Noun: a building in which the seat of government is located. EX: The *capitol* building in our nation's *capital* is a spectacular sight.
COULD HAVE	Used before a verb EX: I *could have* eaten before I left.
SHOULD HAVE	Used before a verb EX: You *should have* eaten before you left.
MIGHT HAVE	Used before a verb EX: He *might have* taken the keys with him.
WOULD HAVE	Used before a verb EX: He *would have* told me to lock the door.
DIFFERENT THAN	Used only before a clause EX: The old plantation is *different than* it used to be.
DIFFERENT FROM	Always used EXCEPT before a clause EX: Her hairdo is *different from* yours.
DUE TO	Used to introduce ADJECTIVE phrases EX: His mistakes were *due to* carelessness.
BECAUSE OF	Used to introduce ADVERB phrases EX: He was dismissed *because of* his dishonesty.
FEWER	Used with countable nouns or specific numbers EX: *fewer* cigarettes, *fewer* people
LESS	Used with mass nouns or general amounts EX: *less* time, *less* money, *less* than one percent
HOPEFULLY	Used as an adverb meaning "in a HOPEFUL manner," not as a sentence modifier
CORRECT:	The children waited *hopefully* for the package to arrive.
INCORRECT:	*Hopefully*, the team will win.
KIND OF/SORT OF	Correctly used preceding nouns, not adjectives; often misused for rather
CORRECT:	I enjoy reading this *kind of* magazine.
INCORRECT:	The movie was *kind of* boring.
CORRECT:	The movie was *rather* boring.

LEAD
Verb (pronounced "leed"): to go first. Its forms are lead, leads, leading, led, and have led
EX: Priests *lead* celibate lives.
The man *led* a life of celibacy before he became a priest.
noun (rhymes with "red"): a type of metal
EX: Coffins are often lined with *lead*.

LEND
Verb: to allow the use of (lending, lent, have lent)
EX: The credit union only *lends* money to members.
I *lent* my book to Betty.
Thank you for *lending* me your car.

LOAN
Noun: something lent for temporary use
EX: I applied for a bank *loan* to buy a car.
He is *loaning* his boat to John for the weekend.

LIE
Verb: to rest (lie, lying, lay, have lain)
EX: I *lie* on the couch every afternoon.
I *lay* on the couch for hours yesterday.
The sweater is still *lying* on the couch.

LAY
Verb: to put (lay, laying, laid, have laid)
EX: Where did I *lay* my book?
I must *have laid* it down somewhere.
I saw you *laying* it down in your room.

LIKE
Preposition used to introduce a PHRASE, not a clause (see **AS, AS IF,** and **AS THOUGH**)
EX: His features are unique *like* a fingerprint.
It looks *like* rain.

PRINCIPAL
Noun: chief official
adjective: major, foremost
EX: She is the school *principal*.
The *principal* reason for waiting is the expense.

PRINCIPLE
Noun: rule, axiom, ethics
EX: Lying to his parents would violate his *principles*.

RISE
Verb: to go up (rise, rising, rose, have risen)
EX: She must *rise* early in the morning to get to work on time.

RAISE
Verb: to push up (raise, raising, raised, have raised)
EX: The landlord must *raise* the rent to cover an increase in taxes.

SET
Verb: to place (set, setting, set, have set)
EX: Please *set* the groceries on the counter.

SIT
Verb: to be seated (sit, sitting, sat, have sat)
EX: Good students usually *sit* in the front row.

THAN	Conjunction EX: Amy is a better tennis play *than* I.
THEN	Adverb of time (often misused for *than*)
CORRECT:	The cashier rang up the sale, *then* gave us our change.
INCORRECT:	He is smarter *then* Bobby.
THAT	Defining or restrictive pronoun, refers to a specific noun EX: The lawn mower *that* is broken is in the garage.
WHICH	Nondefining, nonrestrictive pronoun, does not define the noun being referred to, but adds a fact about it. EX: The lawn mower, *which* is broken, is in the garage.

WORDS THAT SHOULD NOT BE USED IN FORMAL WRITING

DUE TO THE FACT THAT

Misused for BECAUSE

EX: Jim could not run well *because* (NOT due to the fact that) his foot hurt.

ENTHUSE/ENTHUSED

Colloquialism for ENTHUSIASTIC

EX: After hearing about the new project, Dan was *enthusiastic* (NOT enthused).

IRREGARDLESS Misused for REGARDLESS

EX: *Regardless* (NOT irregardless) of her position, Joan was the most powerful member of the team.

IS WHEN/IS WHERE

Should NOT be used to introduce an explanation or a definition

EX: Plagiarism *occurs when* (NOT is when) a writer presents the ideas of another author as his own.

REASON IS BECAUSE/REASON WAS BECAUSE

EX: The *reason* he succeeded is *that* (NOT because) he worked hard.

SUPPOSE TO/USE TO

Incorrect spelling for SUPPOSED TO/USED TO

CORRECT: I *used* to study economics.

He is *supposed to* be home by 10:00.

INCORRECT: I *use to* swim every day.

She is *suppose to* go to New York tomorrow.

CONNOTATIVE AND DENOTATIVE MEANINGS

The denotative meaning of a word is its *literal*, dictionary definition: what the word denotes or "means." The connotative meaning of a word is what the word connotes or "suggests"; it is a meaning apart from what the word literally means. A writer should choose a word based on the tone and context of the sentence; this ensures that a word bears the appropriate connotation while still conveying some exactness in denotation. For example, a gift might be described as "cheap," but the directness of this word has a negative connotation—something cheap is something of little or no value. The word "inexpensive" has a more positive connotation, though "cheap" is a synonym for "inexpensive." Questions of this type require you to make a decision regarding the appropriateness of words and phrases for the context of a sentence.

WORDINESS AND CONCISENESS

Wordiness questions test your ability to detect redundancies (unnecessary repetitions), circumlocution (failure to get to the point), and padding with loose synonyms. Wordiness questions require you to choose sentences that use as few words as possible to convey a message clearly, economically, and effectively.

Effective writing is concise. Wordiness, on the other hand, decreases the clarity of expression by cluttering sentences with unnecessary words. Of course, all short sentences are not better than long ones simply because they are brief. As long as a word serves a function, it should remain in the sentence. However, repetition of words, sounds, and phrases should be used only for emphasis or other stylistic reasons. Editing your writing will reduce its bulk. Notice the difference in impact between the first and second sentences in the following pairs:

INCORRECT: The medical exam that he gave me was entirely complete.

CORRECT: The medical exam he gave me was complete.

INCORRECT: Larry asked his friend John, who was a good, old friend, if he would join him and go along with him to see the foreign film made in Japan.

CORRECT: Larry asked his good, old friend John if he would join him in seeing the Japanese film.

INCORRECT: I was absolutely, totally happy with the present that my parents gave to me at 7 A.M. on the morning of my birthday.

CORRECT: I was happy with the present my parents gave me on the morning of my birthday.

INCORRECT: It seems perfectly clear to me that although he went and got permission from the professor, he still should not have played that awful, terrible joke on the Dean.

CORRECT: It seems clear that although he got permission from the professor, he still should not have played that terrible joke on the Dean.

INCORRECT: He went to England by means of a long boat.

CORRECT: He went to England by boat.

DRILL: WORD CHOICE SKILLS

> **DIRECTIONS:** Choose the correct option.

1. His <u>principal</u> reasons for resigning were his <u>principles</u> of right and wrong.

    (A) principal…principals

    (B) principle…principals

    (C) principle…principles

    (D) No change is necessary.

2. The book tells about Alzheimer's disease—how it <u>affects</u> the patient and what <u>effect</u> it has on the patient's family.

    (A) effects…affect

    (B) affects…affect

    (C) effects…effects

    (D) No change is necessary.

3. The <u>amount</u> of homeless children we can help depends on the <u>number</u> of available shelters.

    (A) number…number

    (B) amount…amount

    (C) number…amount

    (D) No change is necessary.

4. All students are <u>suppose to</u> pass the CLAST before <u>achieving</u> upper-division status.

    (A) suppose to…acheiving

    (B) suppose to…being achieved

    (C) supposed to…achieving

    (D) No change is necessary

5. The reason he <u>succeeded</u> is <u>because</u> he worked hard.

    (A) succeeded…that

    (B) seceded…that

    (C) succede…because of

    (D) No change is necessary.

> **DIRECTIONS:** From the given choices, select the word or phrase that best fits the context of the sentence.

6. The professor explained the _____ of labor unions and how they affected national commerce.

(A)   derivation

(B)   origin

(C)   ancestry

7.   That teakwood chest we saw at the antique store was quite _____.

(A)   charming

(B)   winsome

(C)   delightful

8.   To save money, we decided to give mother a(n) _____ gift for her birthday.

(A)   cheap

(B)   inexpensive

(C)   modest

9.   Everyone likes Jody because she has such a(n) _____ personality.

(A)   flippant

(B)   vivacious

(C)   industrious

10.   Mike is a nice fellow, but he can be really _____.

(A)   talkative

(B)   verbose

(C)   grandiloquent

DIRECTIONS: Select the sentence that clearly and effectively states the idea and has no structural errors.

---

11.   (A)   South of Richmond, the two roads converge together to form a single highway.

(B)   South of Richmond, the two roads converge together to form an interstate highway.

(C)   South of Richmond, the two roads converge to form an interstate highway.

(D)   South of Richmond, the two roads converge to form a single interstate highway.

12.   (A)   The student depended on his parents for financial support.

(B)   The student lacked the ways and means to pay for his room and board, so he depended on his parents for this kind of money and support.

(C)   The student lacked the ways and means or the wherewithal to support himself, so his parents provided him with the financial support he needed.

(D)   The student lacked the means to pay for his room and board, so he depended on his parents for financial support.

13.   (A)   Vincent van Gogh and Paul Gauguin were close personal friends and companions who enjoyed each other's company and frequently worked together on their artwork.

(B)   Vincent van Gogh and Paul Gauguin were friends who frequently painted together.

(C)   Vincent van Gogh was a close personal friend of Paul Gauguin's, and the two of them often worked together on their artwork because they enjoyed each other's company.

(D)   Vincent van Gogh, a close personal friend of Paul Gauguin's, often worked with him on their artwork.

14.   (A)   A college education often involves putting away childish thoughts, which are characteristic of youngsters, and concentrating on the future, which lies ahead.

(B)   A college education involves putting away childish thoughts, which are characteristic of youngsters, and concentrating on the future.

(C)   A college education involves putting away childish thoughts and concentrating on the future.

(D)   A college education involves putting away childish thoughts and concentrating on the future which lies ahead.

15. (A) I had the occasion to visit an oriental pagoda while I was a tourist on vacation and visiting in Kyoto, Japan.

    (B) I visited a Japanese pagoda in Kyoto.

    (C) I had occasion to visit a pagoda when I was vacationing in Kyoto, Japan.

    (D) On my vacation, I visited a Japanese pagoda in Kyoto.

SENTENCE STRUCTURE SKILLS

PARALLELISM

This section tests your recognition of sentence balance, or sentences which use the same kind of grammatical construction for all items in a series—those usually joined by a coordinating conjunction (*and, but, or,* and *nor*). *No smoking, eating, or drinking* is parallel; *No smoking, eating, or food* is not. This skill also requires knowledge of parallel correlative pairs, that is, using the appropriate pairs together, such as *neither...nor, either...or, both* with *and, whether* with *or,* and *not only* with *but also.*

Parallel structure is used to express matching ideas. It refers to the grammatical balance of a series of any of the following:

Phrases
The squirrel ran *along the fence, up the tree,* and *into his burrow* with a mouthful of acorns.

Adjectives
The job market is flooded with *very talented, highly motivated,* and *well educated* young people.

Nouns
You will need a *notebook, pencil,* and *dictionary* for the test.

Clauses
The children were told to decide *which toy they would keep* and *which toy they would give away.*

Verbs
The farmer *plowed, planted,* and *harvested* his corn in record time.

Verbals
Reading, writing, and *calculating* are fundamental skills that all of us should possess.

Correlative Conjunctions

both…and either…or
neither…nor not only…but also
whether…or

Either you will do your homework *or* you will fail.

Note: Correlative conjunctions must be used as pairs and not mixed with other conjunctions, such as *either* with *nor* or *not only* with *also*.

Repetition of Structural Signals
(such as articles, auxiliaries, prepositions, and conjunctions)

INCORRECT: I *have quit* my job, *enrolled* in school, and *am looking* for a reliable babysitter.

CORRECT: I *have quit* my job, *have enrolled* in school, and *am looking* for a reliable babysitter.

Note: Repetition of prepositions is considered formal and is not necessary. You can travel *by car, by plane, or by train*; it's all up to you.

OR

You can travel *by car, plane, or train*; it's all up to you.

"And who" and "and which" constructions are too wordy

INCORRECT: Lesley is a career-oriented young lady *and who* can cook, too.

CORRECT: Lesley is a career-oriented young lady *who* can cook, too.

When a sentence contains items in a series, check for both punctuation and sentence balance. When you check for punctuation, you should make sure the commas are used correctly. When you check for parallelism, you should make sure that the conjunctions connect similar grammatical constructions, such as all adjectives or all clauses.

MISPLACED AND DANGLING MODIFIERS

Modification questions test your ability to recognize sentences containing misplaced word groups. As its name suggests, a misplaced modifier is one that is in the wrong place in the sentence. Misplaced modifiers come in all form—words, phrases, and clauses. Sentences containing misplaced modifiers are often very comical: *Mom made me eat the spinach instead of my brother.* Misplaced modifiers, like the one in this sentence, are usually too far away from the word or words they modify. This sentence should read *Mom made me, instead of my brother, eat the spinach.*

Modifiers like *only, nearly,* and *almost* should be placed next to the word they modify and not in front of some other word, especially a verb, that they are not intended to modify.

A modifier is misplaced if it appears to modify the wrong part of the sentence or if we cannot be certain what part of the sentence the writer intended it to modify. To correct a misplaced modifier, move the modifier next to the word it describes.

INCORRECT: She served hamburgers to the men on paper plates.

CORRECT: She served hamburgers on paper plates to the men.

Split infinitives also result in misplaced modifiers. Infinitives consist of the marker *to* plus the plain form of the verb. The two parts of the infinitive make up a grammatical unit that should not be split. Splitting an infinitive is placing an adverb between the *to* and the verb.

INCORRECT: The weather service expects temperatures to not rise.

CORRECT: The weather service expects temperatures not to rise.

Sometimes a split infinitive may be natural and preferable, though it may still bother some readers.

EX: Several U.S. industries expect *to* more than *triple* their use of robots within the next decade.

A squinting modifier is one that may refer to either a preceding or a following word, leaving the reader uncertain about what it is intended to modify. Correct a squinting modifier by moving it next to the word it is intended to modify.

INCORRECT: Snipers who fired on the soldiers often escaped capture.

CORRECT: Snipers who often fired on the soldiers escaped capture.

OR

Snipers who fired on the soldiers escaped capture often.

A dangling modifier is a modifier or verb in search of a subject: the modifying phrase (usually an *-ing* word group, an *-ed* or *-en* word group, or a *to + a verb* word group—participle phrase or infinitive phrase respectively) either appears to modify the wrong word or has nothing to modify. It is literally dangling at the beginning or the end of a sentence. The sentences often look and sound correct: *To be a student government officer, your grades must be above average.* (However, the verbal modifier has nothing to describe. Who is *to be a student government officer?* Your grades?) Questions of this type require you to determine whether a modifier has a headword or whether it is dangling at the beginning or the end of the sentence.

To correct a dangling modifier, reword the sentence by either: 1) changing the modifying phrase to a clause with a subject, or 2) changing the subject of the sentence to the word that should be modified. The following are examples of a dangling gerund, a dangling infinitive, and a dangling participle:

INCORRECT: Shortly after leaving home, the accident occurred.

Who is <u>leaving home</u>, the accident?

CORRECT: Shortly after we left home, the accident occurred.

INCORRECT:	To get up on time, a great effort was needed.
	<u>To get up</u> needs a subject.
CORRECT:	To get up on time, I made a great effort.

FRAGMENTS

A fragment is an incomplete construction which may or may not have a subject and a verb. A complete construction, such as a sentence or an independent clause, expresses a complete thought. Specifically, a fragment is a group of words pretending to be a sentence. Not all fragments appear as separate sentences, however. Often, fragments are separated by semicolons, by writers who cannot distinguish between independent and dependent clauses.

INCORRECT:	Traffic was stalled for ten miles on the freeway. Because repairs were being made on potholes.
CORRECT:	Traffic was stalled for ten miles on the freeway because repairs were being made on potholes.
INCORRECT:	It was a funny story; one that I had never heard before.
CORRECT:	It was a funny story, one that I had never heard before.

RUN-ON/FUSED SENTENCES

A run-on/fused sentence is not necessarily a long sentence or a sentence that the reader considers too long; in fact, a run-on may be two short sentences: *Dry ice does not melt it evaporates.* A run-on results when the writer fuses or runs together two separate sentences without any correct mark of punctuation separating them. Questions of this type test your ability to recognize both fused sentences and comma splices as incorrect.

A run-on or fused sentence is two independent clauses which are not separated by any punctuation.

INCORRECT:	Knowing how to use a dictionary is no problem each dictionary has a section in the front of the book telling how to use it.
CORRECT:	Knowing how to use a dictionary is no problem. Each dictionary has a section in the front of the book telling how to use it.

Even if one or both of the fused sentences contains internal punctuation, the sentence is still a run-on.

INCORRECT:	Bob bought dress shoes, a suit, and a nice shirt he needed them for his sister's wedding.
CORRECT:	Bob bought dress shoes, a suit, and a nice shirt. He needed them for his sister's wedding.

COMMA SPLICES

A comma splice is the unjustifiable use of only a comma to combine what really is two separate sentences.

INCORRECT: One common error in writing is incorrect spelling, the other is the occasional use of faulty diction.

CORRECT: One common error in writing is incorrect spelling; the other is the occasional use of faulty diction.

Both run-on sentences and comma splices may be corrected in one of the following ways:

RUN-ON: Neal won the award he had the highest score.

COMMA SPLICE: Neal won the award, he had the highest score.

Separate the sentences with a period
Neal won the award. He had the highest score.

Separate the sentences with a comma and a coordinating conjunction (*and,***
but, or, nor, for, yet, so)**
Neal won the award, for he had the highest score.

Separate the sentences with a semicolon
Neal won the award; he had the highest score.

Separate the sentences with a subordinating conjunction such as *although,*
because, since, if
Neal won the award because he had the highest score.

SUBORDINATION, COORDINATION, AND PREDICATION

Suppose, for the sake of clarity, you wanted to combine the information in these two sentences to create one statement:

I studied a foreign language. I found English quite easy.

How you decide to combine this information should be determined by the relationship you'd like to show between the two facts. *I studied a foreign language, and I found English quite easy* seems rather illogical. The **coordination** of the two ideas (connecting them with the coordinating conjunction *and* is ineffective. Using **subordination** instead (connecting the sentences with a subordinating conjunction) clearly shows the degree of relative importance between the expressed ideas:

After I studied a foreign language, I found English quite easy.

When using a conjunction, be sure that the sentence parts you are joining are in agreement.

INCORRECT: She loved him dearly but not his dog.

CORRECT: She loved him dearly but she did not love his dog.

A common mistake that is made is to forget that each member of the pair must be followed by the same kind of construction.

INCORRECT: They complimented them both for their bravery and they thanked them for their kindness.

CORRECT:	They both complimented them for their bravery and thanked them for their kindness.

While refers to time and should not be used as a substitute for *although, and,* or *but.*

INCORRECT:	While I'm usually interested in Fellini movies, I'd rather not go tonight.
CORRECT:	Although I'm usually interested in Fellini movies, I'd rather not go tonight.

Where refers to time and should not be used as a substitute for *that.*

INCORRECT:	We read in the paper where they are making great strides in DNA research.
CORRECT:	We read in the paper that they are making great strides in DNA research.

After words like *reason* and *explanation,* use *that,* not *because.*

INCORRECT:	His explanation for his tardiness was because his alarm did not go off.
CORRECT:	His explanation for his tardiness was that his alarm did not go off.

DRILL: SENTENCE STRUCTURE SKILLS

DIRECTIONS: Select the sentence that clearly and effectively states the idea and has no structural errors.

1. (A) Many gases are invisible, odorless, and they have no taste.

   (B) Many gases are invisible, odorless, and have no taste.

   (C) Many gases are invisible, odorless, and tasteless.

2. (A) Everyone agreed that she had neither the voice or the skill to be a speaker.

   (B) Everyone agreed that she had neither the voice nor the skill to be a speaker.

(C)   Everyone agreed that she had either the voice nor the skill to be a speaker.

3.   (A)   The mayor will be remembered because he kept his campaign promises and because of his refusal to accept political favors.

      (B)   The mayor will be remembered because he kept his campaign promises and because he refused to accept political favors.

      (C)   The mayor will be remembered because of his refusal to accept political favors and he kept his campaign promises.

4.   (A)   While taking a shower, the doorbell rang.

      (B)   While I was taking a shower, the doorbell rang.

      (C)   While taking a shower, someone rang the doorbell.

5.   (A)   He swung the bat, while the runner stole second base.

      (B)   The runner stole second base while he swung the bat.

      (C)   While he was swinging the bat, the runner stole second base.

6.   (A)   After a defense attorney represents the accused, a prosecuting attorney represents the state.

      (B)   Because a defense attorney represents the accused, a prosecuting attorney represents the state.

      (C)   A defense attorney represents the accused, and a prosecuting attorney represents the state.

7.   (A)   Many people went to the interstate fair located on the outskirts of town.

      (B)   Located on the outskirts of town, many people went to the interstate fair.

      (C)   Many people, located on the outskirts of town, went to the interstate fair.

8.   (A)   I only need ten more credit hours to graduate.

(B)   I need only ten more credit hours to graduate.

(C)   I need ten more credit hours only to graduate.

DIRECTIONS: Choose the correct option.

---

9.   Nothing grows as well in Mississippi as <u>cotton. Cotton</u> being the state's principal crop.

   (A)   cotton, cotton   (C)   cotton cotton

   (B)   cotton; cotton   (D)   No change is necessary.

10.   It was a heartwrenching <u>movie; one</u> that I had never seen before.

   (A)   movie and   (C)   movie. One

   (B)   movie, one   (D)   No change is necessary.

11.   Traffic was stalled for three miles on the <u>bridge. Because</u> repairs were being made.

   (A)   bridge because   (C)   bridge, because

   (B)   bridge; because   (D)   No change is necessary.

12.   The ability to write complete sentences comes with <u>practice writing</u> run-on sentences seems to occur naturally.

   (A)   practice, writing   (C)   practice and

   (B)   practice. Writing   (D)   No change is necessary.

13.   Even though she had taken French classes, she could not understand native French <u>speakers they</u> all spoke too fast.

   (A)   speakers, they   (C)   speaking

   (B)   speakers. They   (D)   No change is necessary.

14.   Brad had participated in the school chorus for <u>years and</u> now he was looking forward to joining the new show choir.

   (A)   years, and   (C)   years; and

   (B)   years. And   (D)   No change is necessary.

15. Sam completed his <u>studies, then</u> he went on to become an engineer.

   (A)   studies; then

   (B)   studies and

   (C)   studies then

   (D)   No change is necessary.

16. The thinning ozone layer poses a serious threat to <u>tanners; however</u>, research-ers are developing various forms of safe, sunless tans.

   (A)   tanners, however

   (B)   tanners however

   (C)   tanners. However

   (D)   No change is necessary.

17. In 1982, eight people were killed by cyanide-laced Tylenol <u>capsules, conse-quently,</u> regulations were passed which require tamper-resistant packaging for all over-the-counter medications.

   (A)   capsules. Consequently

   (B)   capsules consequently

   (C)   capsules and consequently,

   (D)   No change is necessary.

18. Alaska became the forty-ninth state <u>in 1959, and</u> Hawaii became the fiftieth state later that year.

   (A)   in 1959, but

   (B)   in 1959, since

   (C)   in 1959: and

   (D)   No change is necessary.

19. Each state has two <u>senators because</u> the number of representatives per state depends on the population of the state.

   (A)   senators but

   (B)   senators since

   (C)   senators; and

   (D)   No change is necessary.

20. The reason the mayoral candidate will not run for office again <u>is because</u> his defeat in yesterday's election was overwhelming.

   (A)   is because of

   (B)   is that

   (C)   is since

   (D)   No change is necessary.

VERBS

VERB FORMS

This section covers the principal parts of some irregular verbs including trouble-some verbs like *lie* and *lay*. The use of regular verbs like *look* and *receive* poses no real problem to most writers since the past and past participle forms end in *-ed*; it is the irregular forms which pose the most serious problems—for example, *seen, written,* and *begun.*

VERB TENSES

The questions in this section address special and conventional uses of the present tense and other main tenses.

Tense sequence indicates a logical time sequence.

Use **present tense:**

> In statements of universal truth:
>> I learned that the sun *is* ninety-million miles from the earth.

> In statements about the contents of literature and other published work:
>> In this book, Sandy *becomes* a nun and *writes* a book on psychology.

Use **past tense:**

> In statements concerning writing or publication of a book:
>> He *wrote* his first book in 1949, and it *was published* in 1952.

Use **present perfect tense:**

> For an action that began in the past but continues into the future:
>> I *have lived* here all my life.

Use **past perfect tense:**

> For an earlier action that is mentioned in a later action:
>> Cindy ate the apple that she *had picked.*

> (First she picked it, then she ate it.)

Use **future perfect tense:**

> For an action that will have been completed at a specific future time:
>> By May, I *shall have graduated.*

Use a **present participle:**

> For action that occurs at the same time as the verb:
>> *Speeding* down the interstate, I saw a cop's flashing lights.

Use a **perfect participle:**

> For action that occurred before the main verb:
>> *Having read* the directions, I started the test.

Use the **subjunctive mood:**

> To express a wish or state a condition contrary to fact:
>> *If it were not raining,* we could have a picnic.

> in that clauses after verbs like **request, recommend, suggest, ask, require,** and **insist;** and after such expressions as **it is important** and **it is necessary:**
>> It is necessary that all papers *be* submitted on time.

SUBJECT-VERB AGREEMENT

Agreement is the grammatical correspondence between the subject and the verb of a sentence: *I do, we do, they do; he, she, it does.* This test section requires you to choose sentences whose subjects and verbs agree in number—both are singular or both are plural. Since the principal source of confusion for many students is which verb form is singular and which is plural, this sections focuses first on making that distinction and second, on identifying the real subject of a sentence. Finally, this section identifies subjects that are commonly construed as singular and those that are constructed as plural.

Every English verb has five forms, two of which are the bare form (plural) and the -s form (singular). Simply put, singular verb forms end in -s; plural forms do not.

Study these rules governing subject-verb agreement:

A verb must agree with its subject, not with any additive phrase in the sentence such as a prepositional or verbal phrase. Ignore such phrases.

Your *copy* of the rules *is* on the desk.

The latest U2 tape will not be available until the *dispute* over the distribution rights *is* settled.

Ms. Craig's *record* of community service and outstanding teaching *qualifies* her for promotion.

In an inverted sentence beginning with a prepositional phrase, the verb still agrees with its subject.

At the end of the summer *come* the best *sales.*

Under the house *are* some old Mason *jars.*

Prepositional phrases beginning with compound prepositions such as **along with**, **together with**, **in addition to**, and **as well as** should be ignored, for they do not affect subject-verb agreement.

Gladys Knight, as well as the Pips, *is* riding the midnight train to Georgia.

A verb must agree with its subject, not its subject complement.

Taxes are a problem.

A *problem is* taxes.

His main *source* of pleasure *is* food and women.

Food and women are his main source of pleasure.

When a sentence begins with an expletive such as **there, here**, or **it**, the verb agrees with the subject, not the expletive.

> Surely, there *are* several *alumni* who would be interested in forming a group.
>
> There *are* 50 *students* in my English class.
>
> There *is* a horrifying *study* on child abuse in *Psychology Today*.

Indefinite pronouns such as **each, either, one, everyone, everybody**, and **everything** are singular.

> *Somebody* in Detroit *loves* me.
>
> *Does either* [one] of you have a pencil?
>
> *Neither* of my brothers *has* a car.

Indefinite pronouns such as **several, few, both**, and **many** are plural.

> *Both* of my sorority sisters *have* decided to live off campus.
>
> *Few seek* the enlightenment of transcendental meditation.

Indefinite pronouns such as **all, some, most**, and **none** may be singular or plural depending on their referents.

> *Some* of the food *is* cold.
>
> *Some* of the vegetables *are* cold.
>
> I can think of some retorts, but *none seem* appropriate.
>
> *None* of the children *is* as sweet as Sally.

Fractions such as **one-half** and **one-third** may be singular or plural depending on the referent.

> *Half* of the mail *has* been delivered.
>
> *Half* of the letters *have* been read.

Subjects joined by **and** take a plural verb unless the subjects are considered one item or unit. Also, use of an **ampersand** instead of **and** tends to call for consideration of the subject as a single unit.

> *Jim* and *Tammy were* televangelists.
>
> *Simon and Garfunkel was* one of the top folk-pop groups of the sixties.
>
> *Earth, Wind & Fire is* part of the classic-rock pantheon.

In cases when the subjects are joined by **or, nor, either...or,** or **neither...nor,** the verb must agree with the subject closer to it.

Either the teacher or the *students are* responsible.

Neither the students nor the *teacher is* responsible.

Relative pronouns, such as **who, which,** or **that,** which refer to plural antecedents require plural verbs. However, when the relative pronoun refers to a singular subject, the pronoun takes a singular verb.

She is one of the girls *who cheer* on Friday nights.

She is the only cheerleader *who has* a broken leg.

Subjects preceded by **every, each,** and **many a** are singular.

Every man, woman, and child *was* given a life preserver.

Each undergraduate *is* required to pass a proficiency exam.

Many a tear *has* to fall before one matures.

A collective noun, such as **audience, faculty, jury,** etc., requires a singular verb when the group is regarded as a whole, and a plural verb when the members of the group are regarded as individuals.

The *jury has* made its decision.

The *faculty are* preparing their grade rosters.

Subjects preceded by **the number of** or **the percentage of** are singular, while subjects preceded by **a number of** or **a percentage of** are plural.

The number of vacationers in Florida *increases* every year.

A number of vacationers *are* young couples.

Titles of books, companies, name brands, and groups are singular or plural depending on their meaning.

Trix are for kids.

Snickers satisfies you.

Great Expectations is my favorite novel.

The *Rolling Stones are* performing in the Super Dome.

Certain nouns of Latin and Greek origin have unusual singular and plural forms.

Singular	**Plural**
criterion	criteria
alumnus	alumni
datum	data
medium	media

The *data are* available for inspection.

The only *criterion* for membership *is* a high GPA.

Some nouns such as *deer, shrimp,* and *sheep* have the same spellings for both their singular and plural forms. In these cases, the meaning of the sentence will determine whether they are singular or plural.

Deer are beautiful animals.

The spotted *deer is* licking the sugar cube.

Some nouns like *scissors, jeans,* and *wages* have plural forms but no singular counterparts. These nouns almost always take plural verbs.

The *scissors are* on the table.

My new *jeans fit* me like a glove.

Words used as examples, not as grammatical parts of the sentence, require singular verbs.

Can't is the contraction for "cannot."

Cats is the plural form of "cat."

Mathematical expressions of subtraction and division require singular verbs, while expressions of addition and multiplication take either singular or plural verbs.

Ten *divided* by two *equals* five.

Five *times* two *equals* ten. OR Five *times* two *equal* ten.

Nouns expressing time, distance, weight, and measurement are singular when they refer to a unit and plural when they refer to separate items.

Fifty yards is a short distance.

Ten years have passed since I finished college.

Expressions of quantity are usually plural.

Nine out of ten dentists *recommend* that their patients floss.

Some nouns ending in **-ics**, such as *economics* and *ethics*, take singular verbs when they refer to principles or a field of study; however, when they refer to individual practices, they usually take plural verbs.

Ethics is being taught in the spring.

His unusual business *ethics àre* what got him into trouble.

Some nouns like *measles*, *news*, and *calculus* appear to be plural but are actually singular in number. These nouns require singular verbs.

Measles is a very contagious disease.

Calculus requires great skill in algebra.

A verbal noun (infinitive or gerund) serving as a subject is treated as singular, even if the object of the verbal phrase is plural.

Hiding your mistakes *does* not make them go away.

To run five miles *is* my goal.

A noun phrase or clause acting as the subject of a sentence requires a singular verb.

What I need is to be loved.

Whether there is any connection between them is unknown.

Clauses beginning with **what** may be singular or plural depending on the meaning, that is, whether *what* means "the thing" or "the things."

What I want for Christmas is a new motorcycle.

What matters are Clinton's ideas.

A plural subject followed by a singular appositive requires a plural verb; similarly, a singular subject followed by a plural appositive requires a singular verb.

When the girls throw a party, *they* each bring a *gift*. The *board*, all ten members, *is* meeting today.

DRILL: VERBS

DIRECTIONS: Choose the option that does not contain an error in grammar.

---

1. If you <u>had been concerned</u> about Marilyn, you <u>would have went</u> to greater lengths to ensure her safety.

    (A)   had been concern…would have gone

    (B)   was concerned…would have gone

    (C)   had been concerned…would have gone

    (D)   No change is necessary.

2. Susan <u>laid</u> in bed too long and missed her class.

    (A)   lays   (C)   lied

    (B)   lay   (D)   No change is necessary.

3. The Great Wall of China <u>is</u> fifteen hundred miles long; it <u>was built</u> in the third century B.C.

    (A)   was…was built   (C)   has been…was built

    (B)   is…is built   (D)   No change is necessary.

4. Joe stated that the class <u>began</u> at 10:30 a.m.

    (A)   begins   (C)   was beginning

    (B)   had begun   (D)   No change is necessary.

5. The ceiling of the Sistine Chapel <u>was</u> painted by Michelangelo; it <u>depicted</u> scenes from the Creation in the Old Testament.

    (A)   was…depicts   (C)   has been…depicting

    (B)   is…depicts   (D)   No change is necessary.

6. After Christmas <u>comes</u> the best sales.

    (A)   has come   (C)   is coming

    (B)   come   (D)   No change is necessary.

7. The bakery's specialty <u>are</u> wedding cakes.

   (A) is   (C) be

   (B) were   (D) No change is necessary.

8. Every man, woman, and child <u>were given</u> a life preserver.

   (A) have been given   (C) was given

   (B) had gave   (D) No change is necessary.

9. Hiding your mistakes <u>don't</u> make them go away.

   (A) doesn't   (C) have not

   (B) do not   (D) No change is necessary.

10. The Board of Regents <u>has recommended</u> a tuition increase.

   (A) have recommended   (C) had recommended

   (B) has recommend   (D) No change is necessary.

PRONOUNS

PRONOUN CASE

Pronoun case questions test your knowledge of the use of nominative and objective case pronouns:

Nominative Case	Objective Case
I	me
he	him
she	her
we	us
they	them
who	whom

This review section answers the most frequently asked grammar questions: when to use *I* and when to use *me*; when to use *who* and when to use *whom*. Some writers avoid *whom* altogether, and instead of distinguishing between *I* and *me*, many writers incorrectly use *myself*. This section not only answers the I-me, who-whom questions, but it also proves how a change in the function of a pronoun determines its form.

Use the **nominative case** (subject pronouns):

For the subject of a sentence:
We students studied until early morning for the final.
Alan and *I* "burned the midnight oil," too.

For pronouns in apposition to the subject:
Only two students, Alex and *I*, were asked to report on the meeting.

For the predicate nominative/subject complement:
The actors nominated for the award were *she* and *I*.

For the subject of an elliptical clause:
Molly is more experienced than *he*.

For the subject of a subordinate clause:
Robert is the driver *who* reported the accident.

For the complement of an infinitive with no expressed subject:
I would not want to be *he*.

When a conjunction connects two pronouns or a pronoun and a noun, remove the "and" and the other pronoun or noun to determine what the correct pronoun form should be:

Mom gave ~~Tom and~~ myself a piece of cake.

Mom gave ~~Tom and~~ I a piece of cake

Mom gave ~~Tom and~~ me a piece of cake.

Removal of these words reveals what the correct pronoun should be:

Mom gave *me* a piece of cake.

The only pronouns that are acceptable after **between** and other prepositions are: **me, her, him, them,** and **whom**. When deciding between **who** and **whom**, try substituting *he* for **who** and *him* for **whom**; then follow these easy transformation steps:

1. Isolate the **who** clause or the **whom** clause:

   who we can trust

2. Invert the word order, if necessary. Place the words in the clause in the natural order of an English sentence, subject followed by the verb:

   we can trust who

3. Read the final form with the *he* or *him* inserted:

   We can trust ~~whom~~ him.

When a pronoun follows a comparative conjunction like *than* or *as*, complete the elliptical construction to help you determine which pronoun is correct.

> EX: She has more credit hours than me [do].
> She has more credit hours than I [do].

Use the **objective case** (object pronouns):

For the direct object of a sentence:
> Mary invited *us* to her party.

For the object of a preposition:
> The books that were torn belonged to *her*.
> Just between you and *me*, I'm bored.

For the indirect object of a sentence:
> Walter gave a dozen red roses to *her*.

For the appositive of a direct object:
> The committee elected two delegates, Barbara and *me*.

For the object of an infinitive:
> The young boy wanted to help *us* paint the fence.

For the object of a gerund:
> Enlisting *him* was surprisingly easy.

For the object of a past participle:
> Having called the other students and *us*, the secretary went home for the day.

For a pronoun that precedes an infinitive (the subject of an infinitive):
> The supervisor told *him* to work late.

For the complement of an infinitive with an expressed subject:
> The fans thought the best player to be *him*.

For the object of an elliptical clause:
> Bill tackled Joe harder than *me*.

For the object of a verb in apposition:
> Charles invited two extra people, Carmen and *me*, to the party.

PRONOUN-ANTECEDENT AGREEMENT

These kinds of questions test your knowledge of using an appropriate pronoun to agree with its antecedent in number (singular or plural form) and gender (masculine, feminine, or neuter). An antecedent is a noun or pronoun to which another noun or pronoun refers.

Here are the two basic rules for pronoun reference-antecedent agreement:

1. Every pronoun must have a conspicuous antecedent.

2. Every pronoun must agree with its antecedent in number, gender, and person.

When an antecedent is one of dual gender like *student, singer, artist, person, citizen*, etc., use **his** or **her**. Some careful writers change the antecedent to a plural noun to avoid using the sexist, singular masculine pronoun his:

INCORRECT: Everyone hopes that he will win the lottery.

CORRECT: Most people hope that they will win the lottery.

Ordinarily, the relative pronoun **who** is used to refer to people, **which** to refer to things and places, **where** to refer to places, and **that** to refer to places or things. The distinction between **that** and **which** is a grammatical distinction (see the section on Word Choice Skills).

Many writers prefer to use **that** to refer to collective nouns.

EX: A family *that* traces its lineage is usually proud of its roots.

Many writers, especially students, are not sure when to use the reflexive case pronoun and when to use the possessive case pronoun. The rules governing the usage of the reflexive case and the possessive case are quite simple.

Use the **possessive case:**

Before a noun in a sentence:
Our friend moved during the semester break.

My dog has fleas, but *her* dog doesn't.

Before a gerund in a sentence:
Her running helps to relieve stress.

His driving terrified her.

As a noun in a sentence:
Mine was the last test graded that day.

To indicate possession:
Karen never allows anyone else to drive *her* car.

Brad thought the book was *his,* but it was someone else's.

Use the **reflexive case:**

As a direct object to rename the subject:
I kicked *myself.*

As an indirect object to rename the subject:
Henry bought *himself* a tie.

As an object of a prepositional phrase:
Tom and Lillie baked the pie for *themselves.*

As a predicate pronoun:
She hasn't been *herself* lately.

Do not use the reflexive in place of the nominative pronoun:
INCORRECT: Both Randy and *myself* plan to go.
CORRECT: Both Randy and *I* plan to go.

INCORRECT: *Yourself* will take on the challenges of college.
CORRECT: *You* will take on the challenges of college.

INCORRECT: Either James or *yourself* will paint the mural.
CORRECT: Either James or *you* will paint the mural.

Watch out for careless use of the pronoun form:
INCORRECT: George *hisself* told me it was true.
CORRECT: George *himself* told me it was true.

INCORRECT: They washed the car *theirselves.*
CORRECT: They washed the car *themselves.*

Notice that reflexive pronouns are not set off by commas:
INCORRECT: Mary, *herself,* gave him the diploma.
CORRECT: Mary *herself* gave him the diploma.

INCORRECT: I will do it, *myself.*
CORRECT: I will do it *myself.*

PRONOUN REFERENCE

Pronoun reference questions require you to determine whether the antecedent is conspicuously written in the sentence or whether it is remote, implied, ambiguous, or vague, none of which results in clear writing. Make sure that every italicized pronoun has a conspicuous antecedent and that one pronoun substitutes only for another noun or pronoun, not for an idea or a sentence.

Pronoun reference problems occur in the following instances:

When a pronoun refers to either of two antecedents.
INCORRECT: Joanna told Tim that *she* was getting fat.
CORRECT: Joanna told Tim, "I'm getting fat."

When a pronoun refers to a remote antecedent.

INCORRECT: A strange car followed us closely, and *he* kept blinking his lights at us.

CORRECT: A strange car followed us closely, and its driver kept blinking his lights at us.

When **this**, **that**, and **which** refer to the general idea of the preceding clause or sentence rather than the preceding word.

INCORRECT: The students could not understand the pronoun reference handout, which annoyed them very much.

CORRECT: The students could not understand the pronoun reference handout, a fact which annoyed them very much.

OR

The students were annoyed because they could not understand the pronoun reference handout.

When a pronoun refers to an unexpressed but implied noun.

INCORRECT: My husband wants me to knit a blanket, but I'm not interested in it.

CORRECT: My husband wants me to knit a blanket, but I'm not interested in knitting.

When **it** is used as something other than an expletive to postpone a subject.

INCORRECT: It says in today's paper that the newest shipment of cars from Detroit, Michigan, seems to include outright imitations of European models.

CORRECT: Today's paper says that the newest shipment of cars from Detroit, Michigan, seems to include outright imitations of European models.

INCORRECT: The football game was canceled because it was bad weather.

CORRECT: The football game was canceled because the weather was bad.

When **they** or **it** is used to refer to something or someone indefinitely, and there is no definite antecedent.

INCORRECT: At the job placement office, they told me to stop wearing ripped jeans to my interviews.

CORRECT: At the job placement office, I was told to stop wearing ripped jeans to my interviews.

When the pronoun does not agree with its antecedent in number, gender, or person.

INCORRECT: Any graduate student, if they are interested, may attend the lecture.

CORRECT: Any graduate student, if he or she is interested, may attend the lecture.

OR

All graduate students, if they are interested, may attend the lecture.

INCORRECT: Many Americans are concerned that the overuse of slang and colloquialisms is corrupting the language.

CORRECT: Many Americans are concerned that the overuse of slang and colloquialisms is corrupting their language.

INCORRECT: The Board of Regents will not make a decision about tuition increase until their March meeting.

CORRECT: The Board of Regents will not make a decision about tuition increase until its March meeting.

When a noun or pronoun has no expressed antecedent.

INCORRECT: In the President's address to the union, he promised no more taxes.

CORRECT: In his address to the union, the President promised no more taxes.

DRILL: PRONOUNS

DIRECTIONS: Choose the option that does not contain an error in grammar.

---

1. My friend and <u>myself</u> bought tickets for *Cats*.

   (A) I

   (B) me

   (C) us

   (D) No change is necessary.

2. Alcohol and tobacco are harmful to <u>whomever</u> consumes them.

   (A) whom

   (B) who

   (C) whoever

   (D) No change is necessary.

3. Everyone is wondering <u>whom</u> her successor will be.

   (A) who   (C) who'll

   (B) whose   (D) No change is necessary.

4. Rosa Lee's parents discovered that it was <u>her who</u> wrecked the family car.

   (A) she who   (C) her whom

   (B) she whom   (D) No change is necessary.

5. A student <u>who</u> wishes to protest <u>his or her</u> grades must file a formal grievance in the Dean's office.

   (A) that…their   (C) whom…their

   (B) which…his   (D) No change is necessary.

6. One of the best things about working for this company is that <u>they pay</u> big bonuses.

   (A) it pays   (C) they paid

   (B) they always pay   (D) No change is necessary.

7. Every car owner should be sure that <u>their</u> automobile insurance is adequate.

   (A) your   (C) its

   (B) his or her   (D) No change is necessary.

8. My mother wants me to become a teacher, but I'm not interested in <u>it</u>.

   (A) this   (C) that

   (B) teaching   (D) No change is necessary.

9. Since I had not paid my electric bill, <u>they</u> sent me a delinquent notice.

   (A) the power company   (C) it

   (B) he   (D) No change is necessary.

10. Margaret seldom wrote to her sister when <u>she</u> was away at college.

    (A) who   (C) her sister

    (B) her   (D) No change is necessary.

ADJECTIVES AND ADVERBS

CORRECT USAGE

Be careful and *Drive carefully* are sentences that illustrate the differences that this section tests: the proper use of an adjective or an adverb as a single-word modifier, including distinctions between *bad* and *badly* and *good* and *well.*

Adjectives are words that modify nouns or pronouns by defining, describing, limiting, or qualifying those nouns or pronouns.

Adverbs are words that modify verbs, adjectives, or other adverbs and that express such ideas as time, place, manner, cause, and degree. Use adjectives as subject complements with linking verbs; use adverbs with action verbs.

EX:	The oldman's speech was *eloquent.*	ADJECTIVE
	Mr. Brown speaks *eloquently.*	ADVERB
	Please be *careful.*	ADJECTIVE
	Please drive *carefully.*	ADVERB

GOOD AND WELL

Good is an adjective; its use as an adverb is colloquial and nonstandard.

INCORRECT:	He plays *good.*
CORRECT:	He looks *good* to be an octogenarian.
	The quiche tastes very *good.*

Well may be either an adverb or an adjective. As an adjective, **well** means "in good health."

CORRECT:	He plays *well.*	ADVERB
	My mother is not *well.*	ADJECTIVE

BAD OR BADLY

Bad is an adjective used after sense verbs such as *look, smell, taste, feel,* or *sound,* or after linking verbs (is, am, are, was, were).

INCORRECT:	I feel *badly* about the delay.
CORRECT:	I feel *bad* about the delay.

Badly is an adverb used after all other verbs.

INCORRECT:	It doesn't hurt very *bad*
CORRECT:	It doesn't hurt very *badly.*

REAL OR REALLY

Real is an adjective; its use as an adverb is colloquial and nonstandard. It means "genuine."

INCORRECT:	He writes *real* well.	
CORRECT:	This is *real* leather.	

Really is an adverb meaning "very."

INCORRECT:	This is *really* diamond.	
CORRECT:	Have a *really* nice day.	
EX:	This is *real* amethyst.	ADJECTIVE
	This is *really* difficult.	ADVERB
	This is a *real* crisis	ADJECTIVE
	This is *really* important.	ADVERB

SORT OF AND KIND OF

Sort of and **kind of** are often misused in written English by writers who actually mean *rather* or *somewhat*.

INCORRECT:	Jan was *kind of* saddened by the results of the test.
CORRECT:	Jan was *somewhat* saddened by the results of the test.

FAULTY COMPARISONS

These questions include comparisons that use adjectives and adverbs with certain conjunctions, such as *than* and *as*, to indicate a greater or lesser degree of what is specified in the main part of the sentence. Errors occur when the comparison being made is illogical, redundant, or incomplete. Watch for **-er** and **-est** forms of words *more* and *most*, and correlative pairs like *as…as*. Other clues are *than* and *other*. Usually, sentences containing a faulty comparison sound correct because their problem is not one of grammar but of logic. Read these sentences closely to make sure that like things are being compared, that the comparisons are complete, and that the comparisons are logical.

When comparing two persons or things, use the comparative, not the superlative form, of an adjective or an adverb. Use the superlative form for comparison of more than two persons or things. Use *any*, *other*, or *else* when comparing one thing or person with a group of which it/he or she is a part.

Most one- and two-syllable words form their comparative and superlative degrees with -er and -est suffixes. Adjectives and adverbs of more than two syllables form their comparative and superlative degrees with the addition of *more* and *most*.

Positive	Comparative	Superlative
good	better	best
old	older	oldest
friendly	friendlier	friendliest
lonely	lonelier	loneliest
talented	more talented	most talented
beautiful	more beautiful	most beautiful

When in doubt, consult a dictionary. Look up the positive form; the dictionary will usually give the comparative and superlative forms.

A double comparison occurs when the degree of the modifier is changed incorrectly by adding both **-er** and *more* or **-est** and *most* to the adjective or adverb.

INCORRECT: He is the *most nicest* brother.

CORRECT: He is the *nicest* brother.

INCORRECT: She is the *more meaner* of the sisters.

CORRECT: She is the *meaner* sister.

Illogical comparisons occur when there is an implied comparison between two things that are not actually being compared or that cannot be logically compared.

INCORRECT: The interest at a loan company is higher *than* a bank.

CORRECT: The interest at a loan company is higher *than* that *at* a bank.

OR

The interest at a loan company is higher *than at* a bank.

Ambiguous comparisons occur when elliptical words (those omitted) create for the reader more than one interpretation of the sentence.

INCORRECT: I like Mary better than you. (than you *what?*)

CORRECT: I like Mary better than I like you.

OR

I like Mary better than you do.

Incomplete comparisons occur when the basis of the comparison (the two categories being compared) is not explicitly stated.

INCORRECT: Skywriting is *more* spectacular.

CORRECT: Skywriting is *more* spectacular *than* billboard advertising.

Do not omit the words **other**, **any**, or **else** when comparing one thing or person with a group of which it/he or she is a part.

INCORRECT: Joan writes better *than any* student in her class.

CORRECT: Joan writes better *than any other* student in her class.

Do not omit the second **as** of **as...as** when making a point of equal or superior comparison.

INCORRECT: The University of West Florida is *as large* or larger than the University of North Florida.

> CORRECT: The University of West Florida is *as large as* or larger than the University of Northern Florida.

Do not omit the first category of the comparison, even if the two categories are the same.

INCORRECT: This is one of the best, if not the best, college in the country.

CORRECT: This is one of the best colleges in the country, if not the best.

The problem with the incorrect sentence is that *one of the best* requires the plural word *colleges*, not *college*.

DRILL: ADJECTIVES AND ADVERBS

DIRECTIONS: Choose the option that does not contain an error in grammar.

---

1.   Although the band performed <u>badly</u>, I feel <u>real bad</u> about missing the concert.

   (A)   badly…real badly   (C)   badly…very bad

   (B)   bad…badly   (D)   No change is necessary.

2.   These reports are <u>relative simple</u> to prepare.

   (A)   relatively simple   (C)   relatively simply

   (B)   relative simply   (D)   No change is necessary.

3.   He did <u>very well</u> on the test although his writing skills are not <u>good</u>.

   (A)   real well…good   (C)   good…great

   (B)   very good…good   (D)   No change is necessary.

4.   Shake the medicine bottle <u>good</u> before you open it.

   (A)   very good   (C)   well

   (B)   real good   (D)   No change is necessary.

5.   Though she speaks <u>fluently</u>, she writes <u>poorly</u> because she doesn't observe <u>closely</u> or think <u>clear</u>.

   (A)   fluently, poorly, closely, clearly

(B)   fluent, poor, close, clear

(C)   fluently, poor, closely, clear

(D)   No change is necessary.

DIRECTIONS: Select the sentence that clearly and effectively states the idea and has no structural errors.

---

6.   (A)   Los Angeles is larger than any city in California.

    (B)   Los Angeles is larger than all the cities in California.

    (C)   Los Angeles is larger than any other city in California.

7.   (A)   Art history is as interesting as, if not more interesting than, music appreciation.

    (B)   Art history is as interesting, if not more interesting than, music appreciation.

    (C)   Art history is as interesting as, if not more interesting, music appreciation.

8.   (A)   The baseball team here is as good as any other university.

    (B)   The baseball team here is as good as all the other universities.

    (C)   The baseball team here is as good as any other university's.

9.   (A)   I like him better than you.

    (B)   I like him better than I like you.

    (C)   I like him better.

PUNCTUATION

COMMAS

The notion that a writer should place commas according to pauses is incorrect. Commas should be placed according to standard rules of punctuation for purpose, clarity, and effect. CLAST questions of this type test your knowledge of such rules. The proper use of commas is explained in the following rules and examples:

In a **series**:

> When more than one adjective describes a noun, use a comma to separate and emphasize each adjective. The comma takes the place of the word **and** in the series.
>
> the long, dark passageway
>
> another confusing, sleepless night
>
> an elaborate, complex, brilliant plan
>
> the old, grey, crumpled hat

Some adjective-noun combinations are thought of as one word. In these cases, the adjective in front of the adjective-noun combination needs no comma. If you inserted **and** between the adjective-noun combination, it would not make sense.

> a stately oak tree
>
> an exceptional wine glass
>
> my worst report card
>
> a china dinner plate

The comma is also used to separate words, phrases, and whole ideas (clauses); it still takes the place of **and** when used this way.

> an apple, a pear, a fig, and a banana
>
> a lovely lady, an elegant dress, and many admirers
>
> She lowered the shade, closed the curtain, turned off the light, and went to bed.

The only question that exists about the use of commas in a series is whether or not one should be used before the final item. It is standard usage to do so, although many newspapers and magazines have stopped using the final comma. Occasionally, the omission of the comma can be confusing.

INCORRECT: Would you like to shop at Sak's, Lord and Taylor's and Gimbels?

He got on his horse, tracked a rabbit and a deer and rode on to Canton.

We planned the trip with Mary and Harold, Susan, Dick and Joan, Gregory and Jean and Charles.

With a **long introductory phrase:**

Usually if a phrase of more than five or six words or a dependent clause precedes the subject at the beginning of a sentence, a comma is used to set it off.

After last night's fiasco at the disco, she couldn't bear the thought of looking at him again.

Whenever I try to talk about politics, my wife leaves the room.

Provided you have said nothing, they will never guess who you are.

It is not necessary to use a comma with a short sentence.

In January she will go to Switzerland.

After I rest I'll feel better.

During the day no one is home.

If an introductory phrase includes a verb form that is being used as another part of speech (a **verbal**), it must be followed by a comma.

INCORRECT: When eating Mary never looked up from her plate.

CORRECT: When eating, Mary never looked up from her plate.

INCORRECT: Because of her desire to follow her faith in James wavered.

CORRECT: Because of her desire to follow, her faith in James wavered.

INCORRECT: Having decided to leave Mary James wrote her a letter.

CORRECT: Having decided to leave Mary, James wrote her a letter.

To separate sentences with **two main ideas:**

To understand this use of the comma, you need to be able to recognize compound sentences. When a sentence contains more than two subjects and verbs (clauses), and the two clauses are joined by a conjunction (**and, but, or, nor, for, yet**), use a comma before the conjunction to show that another clause is coming.

I thought I knew the poem by heart, but he showed me three lines I had forgotten.

Are we really interested in helping the children, or are we more concerned with protecting our good names?

He is supposed to leave tomorrow, but he is not ready to go.

Jim knows you are disappointed, and he has known it for a long time.

If the two parts of the sentence are short and closely related, it is not necessary to use a comma.

He threw the ball and the dog ran after it.

Jane played the piano and Michael danced.

I am going to take English 101 or Creative Writing.

Be careful not to confuse a sentence that has a compound verb and a single subject with a compound sentence. If the subject is the same for both verbs, there is no need for a comma.

INCORRECT: Charles sent some flowers, and wrote a long letter explaining why he had not been able to attend.

CORRECT: Charles sent some flowers and wrote a long letter explaining why he had not been able to attend.

INCORRECT: Last Thursday we went to the concert with Julia, and afterwards dined at an old Italian restaurant.

CORRECT: Last Thursday we went to the concert with Julia and afterwards dined at an old Italian restaurant.

INCORRECT: For the third time, the teacher explained that the literacy level for high school students was much lower than it had been in previous years, and, this time, wrote the statistics on the board for everyone to see.

CORRECT: For the third time, the teacher explained that the literacy level for high school students was much lower than it had been in previous years and this time wrote the statistics on the board for everyone to see.

In general, words and phrases that stop the flow of the sentence or are unnecessary for the main idea are set off by commas.

Abbreviations after names
Did you invite John Paul, Jr., and his sister?
Martha Harris, Ph.D., will be the speaker tonight.

Interjections (An exclamation without added grammatical connection)
Oh, I'm so glad to see you.
I tried so hard, alas, to do it.
Hey, let me out of here.

Direct address
Roy, won't you open the door for the dog?
I can't understand, Mother, what you are trying to say.
May I ask, Mr. President, why you called us together?
Hey, lady, watch out for that car!

Tag questions
I'm really hungry, aren't you?
Jerry looks like his father, doesn't he?

Geographical names and addresses
The concert will be held in Chicago, Illinois, on August 12.
The letter was addressed to Mrs. Marion Heartwell, 1881 Pine Lane, Palo Alto, California 95824.

Note: No comma is needed before the zip code because it is already clearly set off from the state name.

Transitional words and phrases

On the other hand, I hope he gets better.

In addition, the phone rang constantly this afternoon.

I'm, nevertheless, going to the beach on Sunday.

You'll find, therefore, that no one is more loyal than I am.

Parenthetical words and phrases

You will become, I believe, a great statesman.

We know, of course, that this is the only thing to do.

In fact, I planted corn last summer.

The Mannes affair was, to put it mildly, a surprise.

Unusual word order

The dress, new and crisp, hung in the closet.

Intently, she stared out the window.

With **nonrestrictive elements**:

Parts of a sentence that modify other parts are sometimes essential to the meaning of the sentence and sometimes not. When a modifying word or group of words is not vital to the meaning of the sentence, it is set off by commas. Since it does not restrict the meaning of the words it modifies, it is called "nonrestrictive." Modifiers that are essential to the meaning of the sentence are called "restrictive" and are not set off by commas.

ESSENTIAL: The girl *who wrote the story* is my sister.

NONESSENTIAL: My sister, *the girl who wrote the story*, has always loved to write.

ESSENTIAL: John Milton's famous poem *Paradise Lost* tells a remarkable story.

NONESSENTIAL: Dante's greatest work, *The Divine Comedy,* marked the beginning of the Renaissance.

ESSENTIAL: The cup *that is on the piano* is the one I want.

NONESSENTIAL: The cup, *which my brother gave me last year*, is on the piano.

ESSENTIAL: The people *who arrived late* were not seated.

NONESSENTIAL: George, *who arrived late*, was not seated.

To set off **direct quotations**:

Most direct quotes or quoted materials are set off from the rest of the sentence by commas.

"Please read your part more loudly," the director insisted.

"I won't know what to do," said Michael, "if you leave me."

The teacher said sternly, "I will not dismiss this class until I have silence."

Who was it who said "Do not ask for whom the bell tolls; it tolls for thee"?

Note: Commas always go inside the closing quotation mark, even if the comma is not part of the material being quoted.

Be careful not to set off indirect quotes or quotes that are used as subjects or complements.

"To be or not to be" is the famous beginning of a soliloquy in Shakespeare's *Hamlet.* (subject)

She said she would never come back. (indirect quote)

Back then my favorite poem was "Evangeline." (complement)

To set off contrasting elements:

Her intelligence, not her beauty, got her the job.

Your plan will take you a little further from, rather than closer to, your destination.

It was a reasonable, though not appealing, idea.

He wanted glory, but found happiness instead.

In dates:

Both forms of the date are acceptable.

She will arrive on April 6, 1998.

He left on 5 December 1980.

In January 1967, he handed in his resignation.

On October 22, 1992, Frank and Julie were married.

Usually, when a subordinate clause is at the end of a sentence, no comma is necessary preceding the clause. However, when a subordinate clause introduces a sentence, a comma should be used after the clause. Some common subordinating conjunctions are:

after	since
although	so that
as	though
as if	till
because	unless
before	until
even though	when
if	whenever
inasmuch as	while

SEMICOLONS

Questions testing semicolon usage require you to be able to distinguish between the semicolon and the comma, and the semicolon and the colon. This review section covers the basic uses of the semicolon: to separate independent clauses not joined by a coordinating conjunction, to separate independent clauses separated by a conjunctive adverb, and to separate items in a series with internal commas. It is important to be consistent; if you use a semicolon between *any* of the items in the series, you must use semicolons to separate *all* of the items in the series.

Usually, a comma follows the conjunctive adverb. Note also that a period can be used to separate two sentences joined by a conjunctive adverb. Some common conjunctive adverbs are:

accordingly	nevertheless
besides	next
consequently	nonetheless
finally	now
furthermore	on the other hand
however	otherwise
indeed	perhaps
in fact	still
moreover	therefore

Then is also used as a conjunctive adverb, but it is not usually followed by a comma.

Use the **semicolon**:

To separate independent clauses which are not joined by a coordinating conjunction:

I understand how to use commas; the semicolon I have not yet mastered.

To separate two independent clauses connected by a conjunctive adverb:

He took great care with his work; therefore, he was very successful.

To combine two independent clauses connected by a coordinating conjunction if either or both of the clauses contain other internal punctuation:

Success in college, some maintain, requires intelligence, industry, and perseverance; *but* others, fewer in number, assert that only personality is important.

To separate items in a series when each item has internal punctuation:

I bought an old, dilapidated chair; an antique table which was in beautiful condition; and a new, ugly, blue and white rug.

Call our customer service line for assistance: Arizona, 1-800-555-6020; New Mexico, 1-800-555-5050; California, 1-800-555-3140; or Nevada, 1-800-555-3214.

Do not use the semicolon:

To separate a dependent and an independent clause:

INCORRECT: You should not make such statements; even though they are correct.

CORRECT: You should not make such statements even though they are correct.

To separate an appositive phrase or clause from a sentence:

INCORRECT: His immediate aim in life is centered around two things; becoming an engineer and learning to fly an airplane.

CORRECT: His immediate aim in life is centered around two things: becoming an engineer and learning to fly an airplane.

To precede an explanation or summary of the first clause:

Note: Although the sentence below is punctuated correctly, the use of the semicolon provides a miscue, suggesting that the second clause is merely an extension, not an explanation, of the first clause. The colon provides a better clue.

WEAK: The first week of camping was wonderful; we lived in cabins instead of tents.

BETTER: The first week of camping was wonderful: we lived in cabins instead of tents.

To substitute for a comma:

INCORRECT: My roommate also likes sports; particularly football, basketball, and baseball.

CORRECT: My roommate also likes sports, particularly football, basketball, and baseball.

To set off other types of phrases or clauses from a sentence:

INCORRECT: Being of a cynical mind; I should ask for a recount of the ballots.

CORRECT: Being of a cynical mind, I should ask for a recount of the ballots.

INCORRECT: The next meeting of the club has been postponed two weeks; inasmuch as both the president and vice-president are out of town.

CORRECT: The next meeting of the club has been postponed two weeks, inasmuch as both the president and vice-president are out of town.

Note: The semicolon is not a terminal mark of punctuation; therefore, it should not be followed by a capital letter unless the first word in the second clause ordinarily requires capitalization.

COLONS

While it is true that a colon is used to precede a list, one must also make sure that a complete sentence precedes the colon. The colon signals the reader that a list, explanation, or restatement of the preceding will follow. It is like an arrow, indicating that something is to follow. The difference between the colon and the semicolon and between the colon and the period is that the colon is an introductory mark, not a terminal mark. Look at the following examples:

The Constitution provides for a separation of powers among the three branches of government.

government.	The period signals a new sentence.
government;	The semicolon signals an interrelated sentence.
government,	The comma signals a coordinating conjunction followed by another independent clause.
government:	The colon signals a list.

The Constitution provides for a separation of powers among the three branches of *government:* executive, legislative, and judicial.

Ensuring that a complete sentence precedes a **colon** means following these rules:

Use the colon to introduce a list (one item may constitute a list):

I hate this one course: English.

Three plays by William Shakespeare will be presented in repertory this summer at the University of West Florida: *Hamlet, Macbeth,* and *Othello.*

To introduce a list preceded by **as follows** or **the following**:

The reasons he cited for his success are as follows: integrity, honesty, industry, and a pleasant disposition.

To separate two independent clauses, when the second clause is a restatement or explanation of the first:

All of my high school teachers said one thing in particular: college is going to be difficult.

To introduce a word or word group which is a restatement, explanation, or summary of the first sentence:

These two things he loved: an honest man and a beautiful woman.

To introduce a formal appositive:

I am positive there is one appeal which you can't overlook: money.

To separate the introductory words from a quotation which follows, if the quotation is formal, long, or paragraphed separately:

The actor then stated: "I would rather be able to adequately play the part of Hamlet than to perform a miraculous operation, deliver a great lecture, or build a magnificent skyscraper."

The colon should only be used after statements that are grammatically complete.

Do *not* use a colon after a verb.

INCORRECT: My favorite holidays are: Christmas, New Year's Eve, and Halloween.

CORRECT: My favorite holidays are Christmas, New Year's Eve, and Halloween.

Do *not* use a colon after a preposition.

INCORRECT: I enjoy different ethnic foods such as: Greek, Chinese, and Italian.

CORRECT: I enjoy different ethnic foods such as Greek, Chinese, and Italian.

Do *not* use a colon interchangeably with the dash.

INCORRECT: Mathematics, German, English: These gave me the greatest difficulty of all my studies.

CORRECT: Mathematics, German, English—these gave me the greatest difficulty of all my studies.

Information preceding the colon should be a complete sentence regardless of the explanatory information following the clause.

Do *not* use the colon before the words **for example**, **namely**, **that is**, or **for instance** even though these words may be introducing a list.

INCORRECT: We agreed to it: namely, to give him a surprise party.

CORRECT: There are a number of well-known American women writers: for example, Nikki Giovanni, Phillis Wheatley, Emily Dickinson, and Maya Angelou.

Colon usage questions test your knowledge of the colon preceding a list, restatement, or explanation. These questions also require you to be able to distinguish between the colon and the period, the colon and the comma, and the colon and the semicolon.

APOSTROPHES

Apostrophe questions require you to know when an apostrophe has been used appropriately to make a noun possessive, not plural. Remember the following rules when considering how to show possession:

Add 's to singular nouns and indefinite pronouns:

Tiffany's flowers

a dog's bark

everybody's computer

at the owner's expense

today's paper

Add 's to singular nouns ending in s, unless this distorts the pronunciation:
>Deloris's paper
>
>the boss's pen
>
>Dr. Yots' class
>
>for righteousness' sake
>
>Dr. Evans's office OR Dr. Evans' office

Add **an apostrophe** to plural nouns ending in s or *es*:
>two cents' worth
>
>ladies' night
>
>thirteen years' experience
>
>two weeks' pay

Add 's to plural nouns not ending in s:
>men's room
>
>children's toys

Add 's to the last word in compound words or groups:
>brother-in-law's car
>
>someone else's paper

Add 's to the last name when indicating joint ownership:
>Joe and Edna's home
>
>Julie and Kathy's party
>
>women and children's clinic

Add 's to both names if you intend to show ownership by each person:
>Joe's and Edna's trucks
>
>Julie's and Kathy's pies
>
>Ted's and Jane's marriage vows

Possessive pronouns change their forms *without* the addition of an apostrophe:
>her, his, hers
>
>your, yours
>
>their, theirs
>
>it, its

Use the possessive form of a noun preceding a gerund:
>His driving annoys me.
>
>My bowling a strike irritated him.
>
>Do you mind our stopping by?
>
>We appreciate your coming.

Add 's to words and initials to show that they are plural:
>No if's, and's, or but's
>
>the do's and don't's of dating

three A's

IRA's are available at the bank.

Add **s** to numbers, symbols, and letters to show that they are plural:

TVs

VCRs

the 1800s

the returning POWs

QUOTATION MARKS AND ITALICS

These kinds of questions test your knowledge of the proper use of quotation marks with other marks of punctuation, with titles, and with dialogue. These kinds of questions also test your knowledge of the correct use of italics and underlining with titles and words used as sample words (for example, *the word is is a common verb*).

The most common use of double quotation marks (") is to set off quoted words, phrases, and sentences.

"If everybody minded their own business," said the Duchess in a hoarse growl, "the world would go round a great deal faster than it does."

"Then you would say what you mean," the March Hare went on.

"I do," Alice hastily replied: "at least—at least I mean what I say—that's the same thing, you know."

—from Lewis Carroll's *Alice in Wonderland*

Single quotation marks are used to set off quoted material within a quote.

"Shall I bring 'Rhyme of the Ancient Mariner' along with us?" she asked her brother.

Mrs. Green said, "The doctor told me, 'Go immediately to bed when you get home!'"

"If she said that to me," Katherine insisted, "I would tell her, 'I never intend to speak to you again! Goodbye, Susan!'"

When writing dialogue, begin a new paragraph each time the speaker changes.

"Do you know what time it is?" asked Jane.

"Can't you see I'm busy?" snapped Mary.

"It's easy to see that you're in a bad mood today!" replied Jane.

Use quotation marks to enclose words used as words (sometimes italics are used for this purpose).

"Judgment" has always been a difficult word for me to spell.

Do you know what "abstruse" means?

"Horse and buggy" and "bread and butter" can be used either as adjectives or as nouns.

If slang is used within more formal writing, the slang words or phrases should be set off with quotation marks.

Harrison's decision to leave the conference and to "stick his neck out" by flying to Jamaica was applauded by the rest of the conference attendees.

When words are meant to have an unusual or specific significance to the reader, for instance irony or humor, they are sometimes placed in quotation marks.

For years, women were not allowed to buy real estate in order to "protect" them from unscrupulous dealers.

The "conversation" resulted in one black eye and a broken nose.

To set off titles of TV shows, poems, stories, and book chapters, use quotation marks. (Book, motion picture, newspaper, and magazine titles are underlined when handwritten and italicized when printed.)

The article "Moving South in the Southern Rain," by Jergen Smith in the *Southern News*, attracted the attention of our editor.

The assignment is "Childhood Development," Chapter 18 of *Human Behavior*.

My favorite essay by Montaigne is "On Silence."

"Happy Days" led the TV ratings for years, didn't it?

You will find Keats' "Ode on a Grecian Urn" in Chapter 3, "The Romantic Era," in Lastly's *Selections from Great English Poets*.

Errors to avoid:

Be sure to remember that quotation marks always come in pairs. Do not make the mistake of using only one set.

INCORRECT: "You'll never convince me to move to the city, said Thurman. I consider it an insane asylum."

CORRECT: "You'll never convince me to move to the city," said Thurman. "I consider it an insane asylum."

INCORRECT: "Idleness and pride tax with a heavier hand than kings and parliaments," Benjamin Franklin is supposed to have said. If we can get rid of the former, we may easily bear the latter."

CORRECT: "Idleness and pride tax with a heavier hand than kings and parliaments," Benjamin Franklin is supposed to have said. "If we can get rid of the former, we may easily bear the latter."

When a quote consists of several sentences, do not put the quotation marks at the beginning and end of each sentence; put them at the beginning and end of the entire quotation.

INCORRECT: "It was during his student days in Bonn that Beethoven fastened upon Schiller's poem." "The heady sense of liberation in the verses must have appealed to him." "They appealed to every German." —John Burke

CORRECT: "It was during his student days in Bonn that Beethoven fastened upon Schiller's poem. The heady sense of liberation in the verses must have appealed to him. They appealed to every German." —John Burke

---

Instead of setting off a long quote with quotation marks, if it is longer than five or six lines you may want to indent and single space it. If you do indent, do not use quotation marks.

In his *First Inaugural Address,* Abraham Lincoln appeals to the war-torn American people:

> We are not enemies, but friends. We must not be enemies. Though passion may have strained, it must not break, our bonds of affection. The mystic chords of memory, stretching from every battlefield and patriot grave to every living heart and hearthstone all over this broad land, will yet swell the chorus of the Union when again touched, as surely they will be, by the better angels of our nature.

Be careful not to use quotation marks with indirect quotations.

INCORRECT: Mary wondered "if she would get over it."

CORRECT: Mary wondered if she would get over it.

INCORRECT: The nurse asked "how long it had been since we had visited the doctor's office."

CORRECT: The nurse asked how long it had been since we had visited the doctor's office.

When you quote several paragraphs, it is not sufficient to place quotation marks at the beginning and end of the entire quote. Place quotation marks at the *beginning of each paragraph,* but only at the *end of the last paragraph.* Here is an abbreviated quotation for an example:

"Here begins an odyssey through the world of classical mythology, starting with the creation of the world...

"It is true that themes similar to the classical may be found in any corpus of mythology...Even technology is not immune to the influence of Greece and Rome...

"We need hardly mention the extent to which painters and sculptors...have used and adapted classical mythology to illustrate the past, to reveal the human body, to express romantic or antiromantic ideals, or to symbolize any particular point of view."

Remember that commas and periods are *always* placed inside the quotation marks even if they are not actually part of the quote.

INCORRECT: "Life always gets colder near the summit", Nietzsche is purported to have said, "—the cold increases, responsibility grows".

CORRECT: "Life always gets colder near the summit," Nietzsche is purported to have said, "—the cold increases, responsibility grows."

INCORRECT: "Get down here right away", John cried. "You'll miss the sunset if you don't."

CORRECT: "Get down here right away," John cried. "You'll miss the sunset if you don't."

INCORRECT: "If my dog could talk", Mary mused, "I'll bet he would say, 'Take me for a walk right this minute'".

CORRECT: "If my dog could talk," Mary mused, "I'll bet he would say, 'Take me for a walk right this minute'."

Other marks of punctuation, such as question marks, exclamation points, colons, and semicolons, go inside the quotation marks if they are part of the quoted material. If they are not part of the quotation, however, they go outside the quotation marks. Be careful to distinguish between the guidelines for the comma and period, which always go inside the quotation marks, and those for other marks of punctuation.

INCORRECT: "I'll always love you"! he exclaimed happily.

CORRECT: "I'll always love you!" he exclaimed happily.

INCORRECT: Did you hear her say, "He'll be there early?"

CORRECT: Did you hear her say, "He'll be there early"?

INCORRECT:	She called down the stairs, "When are you going"?
CORRECT:	She called down the stairs, "When are you going?"
INCORRECT:	"Let me out"! he cried. "Don't you have any pity"?
CORRECT:	"Let me out!" he cried. "Don't you have any pity?"

Remember to use only one mark of punctuation at the end of a sentence ending with a quotation mark:

INCORRECT:	She thought out loud, "Will I ever finish this paper in time for that class?".
CORRECT:	She thought out loud, "Will I ever finish this paper in time for that class?"
INCORRECT:	"Not the same thing a bit!", said the Hatter. "Why, you might just as well say that 'I see what I eat' is the same thing as 'I eat what I see'!".
CORRECT:	"Not the same thing a bit!" said the Hatter. "Why, you might just as well say that 'I see what I eat' is the same thing as 'I eat what I see'!"

DRILL: PUNCTUATION

DIRECTIONS: Choose the option that does not contain an error in grammar.

1. Indianola, <u>Mississippi, where B.B. King and my father grew up,</u> has a population of less than 50,000 people.

    (A) Mississippi, where B.B. King and my father grew up,

    (B) Mississippi where B.B. King and my father grew up,

    (C) Mississippi; where B.B. King and my father grew up,

    (D) No change is necessary.

2. John Steinbeck's best known novel *The Grapes of Wrath* is the story of the <u>Joads and Oklahoma family</u> who were driven from their dustbowl farm and forced to become migrant workers in California.

    (A) Joads, an Oklahoma family

    (B) Joads, an Oklahoma family,

    (C) Joads; an Oklahoma family

    (D) No change is necessary.

3. All students who are interested in student teaching next <u>semester, must submit an application to the Teacher Education Office</u>.

    (A) semester must submit an application to the Teacher Education Office.

    (B) semester, must submit an application, to the Teacher Education Office.

    (C) semester: must submit an application to the Teacher Education Office.

    (D) No change is necessary.

4. Whenever you travel by <u>car, or plane, you</u> must wear a seatbelt.

    (A) car or plane you

    (B) car, or plane you

    (C) car or plane, you

    (D) No change is necessary.

5. Wearing a seatbelt is not just a good <u>idea, it's</u> the law.

    (A) idea; it's

    (B) idea it's

    (C) idea. It's

    (D) No change is necessary.

6. Senators and representatives can be reelected <u>indefinitely; a</u> president can only serve two terms.

    (A) indefinitely but a

    (B) indefinitely, a

    (C) indefinitely a

    (D) No change is necessary.

7. Students must pay a penalty for overdue library <u>books, however, there</u> is a grace period.

    (A) books; however, there

    (B) books however, there

    (C) books: however, there

    (D) No change is necessary.

8. Among the states that seceded from the Union to join the Confederacy in 1860-1861 <u>were</u>: Mississippi, Florida, and Alabama.

    (A) were

    (B) were;

    (C) were.

    (D) No change is necessary.

9. The art exhibit displayed works by many famous <u>artists such as</u>: Dali, Picasso, and Michelangelo.

    (A) artists such as;

    (B) artists such as

    (C) artists. Such as

    (D) No change is necessary.

10. The National Shakespeare Company will perform <u>the following plays:</u> *Othello, Macbeth, Hamlet,* and *As You Like It.*

   (A) the following plays,   (C) the following plays

   (B) the following plays;   (D) No change is necessary.

11. There are three things that contributed to <u>his success: his</u> achievements, his personal demeanor, and his industriousness.

   (A) his success; his   (C) his success, his

   (B) his success. His   (D) No change is necessary.

12. <u>Your's</u> is the only one of the <u>children's</u> stories to be chosen for publication.

   (A) yours…childrens'   (C) your's…childrens'

   (B) yours…children's   (D) No change is necessary.

13. The westward movement of vast numbers of <u>Americans'</u> was a great milestone in our <u>history's</u> growth.

   (A) Americans'…historys'   (C) American's…histories

   (B) Americans…history's   (D) No change is necessary.

14. Joan <u>Rivers'</u> gossip and George <u>Burns'</u> jokes make my <u>boss's</u> workdays exciting.

   (A) River's…Burn's…bosses   (C) Rivers's…Burns's…boss's

   (B) Rivers'…Burns'…boss'   (D) No change is necessary.

15. <u>The Joneses'</u> have gone on vacation two <u>July's</u> in a row.

   (A) The Joneses…Julys   (C) The Jones'…Julys

   (B) The Jones's…Julys   (D) The Jones's…July's

DIRECTIONS: Select the sentence that clearly and effectively states the idea and has no structural errors.

---

16. (A) It was John Donne who wrote "No man is an island, entire of itself".

   (B) It was John Donne who wrote "No man is an island, entire of itself."

   (C) It was John Donne who wrote: "no man is an island entire of itself."

17. (A) In one of his speeches, Dr. Martin Luther King, Jr., said, "Whatever your life's work is, do it well."

    (B) In one of his speeches, Dr. Martin Luther King, Jr., said, Whatever your life's work is, do it well.

    (C) In one of his speeches, Dr. Martin Luther King, Jr., said, "Whatever your life's work is, do it well".

18. (A) "You can stop going to school, Aunt Maggie said, "but you never stop learning."

    (B) "You can stop going to school, Aunt Maggie said, but you never stop learning."

    (C) "You can stop going to school," Aunt Maggie said, "but you never stop learning."

CAPITALIZATION

Capitalization questions test your ability to recognize correct use and application of capitalization rules for course titles, seasons, compass directions, proper names, book and other titles of printed and visual works, job titles, holidays, places, etc.

When a word is capitalized, it calls attention to itself. This attention should be for a good reason. There are standard uses for capital letters. In general, capitalize 1) all proper nouns, 2) the first word of a sentence, and 3) a direct quotation.

You should also capitalize

Names of ships, aircraft, spacecraft, and trains:

Apollo 13	Mariner IV
DC-10	S.S. United States
Sputnik 11	Boeing 707

Names of deities:

God	Jupiter
Allah	Holy Ghost
Buddha	Venus
Jehovah	Shiva

Geological periods:

Neolithic age	Cenozoic era
late Pleistocene times	Ice Age

Names of astronomical bodies:

Mercury	Big Dipper
the Milky Way	Halley's comet
Ursa Major	North Star

Note: Sun, moon, and earth are not capitalized unless they are used with other astronomical terms that are capitalized.

Mars, Venus, and Earth are three of the planets in our solar system.

Personifications:

Reliable **Nature** brought her promised **Spring**.

Bring on **Melancholy** in his sad might.

She believed that **Love** was the answer to all her problems.

Historical periods:

the Middle Ages	World War I
Reign of Terror	Great Depression
Christian Era	Roaring Twenties
Age of Louis XIV	Renaissance

Organizations, associations, and institutions:

Girl Scouts	North Atlantic Treaty Organization
Kiwanis Club	League of Women Voters
New York Yankees	Unitarian Church
Smithsonian Institution	Common Market
Library of Congress	Franklin Glen High School
New York Philharmonic	Harvard University

Government and judicial groups:

United States Court of Appeals	Senate
Committee on Foreign Affairs	Parliament
New Jersey City Council	Peace Corps
Arkansas Supreme Court	Census Bureau
House of Representatives	Department of State

A general term that accompanies a specific name is capitalized only if it follows the specific name. If it stands alone or comes before the specific name, it is put in lowercase:

Washington State	the state of Washington
Senator Dixon	the senator from Illinois
Central Park	the park
Golden Gate Bridge	the bridge
President Ford	the president of the United States
Pope John XXIII	the pope
Queen Elizabeth I	the queen of England
Tropic of Capricorn	the tropics
Monroe Doctrine	the doctrine of expansion
the Mississippi River	the river
Easter Day	the day
Treaty of Versailles	the treaty
Webster's Dictionary	the dictionary
Equatorial Current	the equator

Use a capital to start a sentence:
> Our car would not start.
>
> When will you leave? I need to know right away.
>
> Never!
>
> Let me in! Please!

When a sentence appears within a sentence, start it with a capital letter:
> We had only one concern: When would we eat?
>
> My sister said, "I'll find the Monopoly game."
>
> He answered, "We can only stay a few minutes."

It is the usual practice to capitalize the first word in each line of a poem, even if the word is in the middle of a sentence:
> When I consider everything that grows
> Holds in perfection but a little moment,
> That this huge stage produceth naught but shows,
> Whereon the stars in secret influence comment.
> > —William Shakespeare

> She dwells with Beauty—Beauty that must die;
> And Joy, whose hand is ever at his lips
> Bidding Adieu.
> > —John Keats

The most important words of titles are capitalized. Those words not capitalized are conjunctions (*and, or, but*) and short prepositions (*of, on, by, for*). The first and last word of a title must always be capitalized:

A Man for All Seasons	*Crime and Punishment*
Of Mice and Men	*Rise of the West*
Strange Life of Ivan Osokin	"Sonata in G Minor"
"Let Me In"	"Ode to Billy Joe"
"Rubaiyat of Omar Khayyam"	
"All in the Family"	

Capitalize newspaper and magazine titles:

> *U.S. News & World Report*
> *National Geographic*
> the *New York Times*
> the *Washington Post*

Capitalize radio and TV station call letters:

ABC	NBC
WNEW	WBOP
CNN	HBO

Do not capitalize compass directions or seasons:

west	north
east	south
spring	winter
autumn	summer

Capitalize regions:

the South	the Northeast
the West	Eastern Europe

BUT: the south of France
            the east part of town

Capitalize specific military units:

the U.S. Army
the 7th Fleet
the German Navy
the 1st Infantry Division

Capitalize political groups and philosophies:

Democrat	Communist
Marxist	Nazism
Whig	Federalist
Existentialism	Transcendentalism

BUT: do not capitalize systems of government or individual adherents to a philosophy:

democracy	communism
fascist	agnostic

DRILL: CAPITALIZATION

DIRECTIONS: Choose the correct option.

---

1. Mexico is the southernmost country in <u>North America</u>. It borders the United States on the north; it is bordered on the <u>south</u> by Belize and Guatemala.

    (A)   north America…South   (C)   North america…south

    (B)   North America…South   (D)   No change is necessary.

2. (A)   Until 1989, Tom Landry was the only Coach the Dallas cowboys ever had.

(B)   Until 1989, Tom Landry was the only coach the Dallas Cowboys ever had.

(C)   Until 1989, Tom Landry was the only Coach the Dallas Cowboys ever had.

3.   The <u>Northern Hemisphere</u> is the half of the <u>earth</u> that lies north of the <u>Equator.</u>

(A)   Northern hemisphere…earth…equator

(B)   Northern hemisphere…Earth…Equator

(C)   Northern Hemisphere…earth…equator

(D)   No change is necessary.

4.   (A)   My favorite works by Ernest Hemingway are "The Snows of Kilimanjaro," *The Sun Also Rises,* and *For Whom the Bell Tolls.*

(B)   My favorite works by Ernest Hemingway are "The Snows Of Kilimanjaro," *The Sun Also Rises,* and *For Whom The Bell Tolls.*

(C)   My favorite works by Ernest Hemingway are "The Snows of Kilimanjaro," *The Sun also Rises,* and *For whom the Bell Tolls.*

5.   Aphrodite (<u>Venus in Roman Mythology</u>) was the <u>Greek</u> goddess of love.

(A)   Venus in Roman mythology…greek

(B)   venus in roman mythology…Greek

(C)   Venus in Roman mythology…Greek

(D)   No change is necessary.

6.   The <u>Koran</u> is considered by <u>Muslims</u> to be the holy word.

(A)   koran…muslims   (C)   Koran…muslims

(B)   koran…Muslims   (D)   No change is necessary.

7.   (A)   The freshman curriculum at the community college includes english, a foreign language, Algebra I, and history.

(B)   The freshman curriculum at the community college includes English, a foreign language, Algebra I, and history.

(C)   The Freshman curriculum at the Community College includes English, a foreign language, Algebra I, and History.

8.   At the <u>spring</u> graduation ceremonies, the university awarded over 2,000 <u>bachelor's</u> degrees.

(A)   Spring…Bachelor's   (C)   Spring…bachelor's

(B)   spring…Bachelor's   (D)   No change is necessary.

SPELLING

Spelling questions test your ability to recognize misspelled words. This section reviews spelling tips and rules to help you spot inventive and creative spellings. Problems such as the distinction between *to* and *too* and *lead* and *led* are covered under the Word Choice Skills section of this review.

* Remember, **i** before **e** except after **c**, or when sounded as "a" as in neighbor and weigh.

* There are only three words in the English language that end in -**ceed**: proceed, succeed, exceed

* There are several words that end in -**cede**: secede, recede, concede, precede

* There is only one word in the English language that ends in -sede: supersede

Many people learn to read English phonetically; that is, by sounding out the letters of the words. However, many English words are not pronounced the way they are spelled, and those who try to spell English words phonetically often make spelling *errors*. It is better to memorize the correct spelling of English words rather than relying on phonetics to spell correctly.

DRILL: SPELLING

<u>DIRECTIONS:</u> Choose the correct option.

1.   <u>Preceding</u> the <u>business</u> session, lunch will be served in a <u>separate</u> room.

(A)   preceeding…business…seperate

(B)   proceeding…bussiness…seperate

(C)   proceeding…business…seperite

(D)   No change is necessary.

2. Monte <u>inadvertently</u> left <u>several</u> of his <u>libary</u> books in the cafeteria.

    (A) inadverdently…serveral…libery

    (B) inadvertently…several…library

    (C) inadvertentely…several…librery

    (D) No change is necessary.

3. Sam wished he had more <u>liesure</u> time so he could <u>persue</u> his favorite hobbies.

    (A) leisure…pursue   (C) leisure…persue

    (B) liesure…pursue   (D) No change is necessary.

4. One of my <u>favrite charecters</u> in <u>litrature</u> is Bilbo from *The Hobbit.*

    (A) favrite…characters…literature

    (B) favorite…characters…literature

    (C) favourite…characters…literature

    (D) No change is necessary.

5. Even <u>tho</u> Joe was badly hurt in the <u>accidant</u>, the company said they were not <u>lible</u> for damages.

    (A) though…accidant…libel   (C) though…acident…liable

    (B) though…accident…liable   (D) No change is necessary.

ENGLISH LANGUAGE SKILLS

ANSWER KEY

DRILL: WORD CHOICE SKILLS

1.	**(D)**	5.	**(A)**	9.	**(B)**	13.	**(B)**
2.	**(D)**	6.	**(B)**	10.	**(A)**	14.	**(C)**
3.	**(A)**	7.	**(A)**	11.	**(C)**	15.	**(B)**
4.	**(C)**	8.	**(B)**	12.	**(A)**		

DRILL: SENTENCE STRUCTURE SKILLS

1.	**(C)**	6.	**(C)**	11.	**(C)**	16.	**(D)**
2.	**(B)**	7.	**(A)**	12.	**(B)**	17.	**(A)**
3.	**(B)**	8.	**(B)**	13.	**(B)**	18.	**(D)**
4.	**(B)**	9.	**(A)**	14.	**(D)**	19.	**(D)**
5.	**(A)**	10.	**(B)**	15.	**(A)**	20.	**(B)**

DRILL: VERBS

1.	**(C)**	4.	**(A)**	7.	**(A)**	10.	**(D)**
2.	**(B)**	5.	**(A)**	8.	**(C)**		
3.	**(D)**	6.	**(B)**	9.	**(A)**		

DRILL: PRONOUNS

1.	**(A)**	4.	**(A)**	7.	**(B)**	10.	**(C)**
2.	**(C)**	5.	**(D)**	8.	**(B)**		
3.	**(A)**	6.	**(A)**	9.	**(A)**		

DRILL: ADJECTIVES AND ADVERBS

1.	**(C)**	4.	**(C)**	6.	**(C)**	8.	**(C)**
2.	**(A)**	5.	**(A)**	7.	**(A)**	9.	**(B)**
3.	**(D)**						

DRILL: PUNCTUATION

1.	**(D)**	6.	**(D)**	11.	**(D)**	16.	**(B)**
2.	**(A)**	7.	**(A)**	12.	**(B)**	17.	**(A)**
3.	**(A)**	8.	**(A)**	13.	**(D)**	18.	**(C)**
4.	**(C)**	9.	**(B)**	14.	**(D)**		
5.	**(A)**	10.	**(D)**	15.	**(A)**		

DRILL: CAPITALIZATION

1.	**(D)**	3.	**(C)**	5.	**(C)**	7.	**(B)**
2.	**(B)**	4.	**(A)**	6.	**(D)**	8.	**(D)**

DRILL: SPELLING

1.	**(D)**	3.	**(A)**	5.	**(B)**
2.	**(B)**	4.	**(B)**		

ENGLISH LANGUAGE SKILLS

DETAILED EXPLANATIONS OF ANSWERS

DRILL: WORD CHOICE SKILLS

1.   **(D)**   Choice (D) is correct. No change is necessary. *Principal*, functioning as an adjective in this instance, means "first in rank" or "chief." *Principle* is a noun meaning "axiom" or "rule of conduct."

2.   **(D)**   Choice (D) is correct. No change is necessary. *Affect* is a verb meaning "to influence" or "to change." *Effect* is a noun meaning "result."

3.   **(A)**   Choice (A) is correct. Use *amount* with noncountable, mass nouns (*amount* of food, help, money); use *number* with countable, plural nouns (*number* of children, classes, bills).

4.   **(C)**   Choice (C) is correct. *Supposed to* and *used to* should be spelled with a final *d*. *Achieving* follows the standard spelling rule—*i* before *e*.

5.   **(A)**   Choice (A) is correct. Use *that*, not *because*, to introduce clauses after the word *reason*.

6.   **(B)**   Choice (B) is correct. Although each word choice given is a synonym for *origin*, the sense of the sentence requires a word with the literal meaning of "beginning." *Ancestry* refers to lineage, usually of a family, and *derivation* refers to the source, usually of a word.

7.   **(A)**   Choice (A) is correct. *Charming* is an appropriate adjective to apply to a piece of antique furniture. While both *winsome* and *delightful* have very similar meanings, *winsome* is more appropriately applied to people, and *delightful* usually refers to people or events, rather than furniture.

8.   **(B)**   Choice (B) is correct. *Cheap* bears a negative connotation, implying that the gift would be worthless. *Inexpensive*, while a synonym for *cheap*, has a less harsh connotation; it implies that the gift would not be expensive. *Modest* would be an illogical choice for this sentence.

9. **(B)** Choice (B) is correct. *Vivacious*, which implies that a person is outgoing and fun to be around, is the best choice for this sentence. *Flippant* implies that a person is smug and talks back, while *industrious* suggests that a person is hard-working.

10. **(A)** Choice (A) is correct. *Talkative* suggests that one talks quite a lot. While *verbose* and *grandiloquent* are synonyms of *talkative*, both carry different connotations. *Verbose* is usually associated with wordiness, particularly in speeches. *Grandiloquent* suggests pomposity.

11. **(C)** Choice (C) is correct. *Converge together* is redundant, and *single* is not needed to convey the meaning of *a highway*.

12. **(A)** Choice (A) is correct. It is economical and concise. The other choices contain unnecessary repetition.

13. **(B)** Choice (B) is correct. Choices (A) and (C) pad the sentences with loose synonyms that are redundant. Choice (D), although a short sentence, does not convey the meaning as clearly as choice (B).

14. **(C)** Choice (C) is correct. The other choices all contain unnecessary repetition.

15. **(B)** Choice (B) is correct. Choices (A) and (C) contain circumlocution; they fail to get to the point. Choice (D) does not express the meaning of the sentence as concisely as choice (B).

DRILL: SENTENCE STRUCTURE SKILLS

1. **(C)** Choice (C) is correct. Each response contains items in a series. In choices (A) and (B), the word group after the conjunction is not an adjective like the first words in the series. Choice (C) contains three adjectives.

2. **(B)** Choice (B) is correct. Choices (A), (C), and (D) combine conjunctions incorrectly.

3. **(B)** Choice (B) is correct. Choices (A) and (C) appear to be parallel because the conjunction *and* connects two word groups that both begin with *because*, but the structure on both sides of the conjunction are very different. *Because he kept his campaign promises* is a clause; *because of his refusal to accept political favors* is a prepositional phrase. Choice (B) connects two dependent clauses.

4. **(B)** Choice (B) is correct. Choices (A) and (C) contain the elliptical clause *While...taking a shower.* It appears that the missing subject in the elliptical clause is the same as that in the independent clause—the *doorbell* in choice (A) and *someone* in choice

(C), neither of which is a logical subject for the verbal *taking a shower*. Choice (B) removes the elliptical clause and provides the logical subject.

5. **(A)** Choice (A) is correct. Who swung the bat? Choices (B) and (C) both imply that it is the runner who swung the bat. Only choice (A) makes it clear that as *he* swung the bat, someone else (the *runner*) stole second base.

6. **(C)** Choice (C) is correct. It simply states information without a qualifying word *before* or *after* that would require additional information.

7. **(A)** Choice (A) is correct. *Located on the outskirts of town* has been placed to modify *people* in choices (B) and (C); the obvious intent is for this phrase to describe *the interstate fair.*

8. **(B)** Choice (B) is correct. *Only* should be used to modify what is intended, in this case *only ten more credit hours.*

9. **(A)** Choice (A) is correct. The punctuation in the original sentence and in choice (B) creates a fragment. *Cotton being the state's principal crop* is not an independent thought because it lacks a complete verb—*being* is not a complete verb.

10. **(B)** Choice (B) is correct. The punctuation in the original sentence and in choice (A) creates a fragment. Both the semicolon and the period should be used to separate two independent clauses. The word group *one that I have never seen before* does not express a complete thought and therefore is not an independent clause.

11. **(C)** Choice (C) is correct. The dependent clause *because repairs were being made* in choices (B) and (C) is punctuated as if it were a sentence. The result is a fragment.

12. **(B)** Choice (B) is correct. Choices (A) and (C) do not separate the complete thoughts in the independent clauses with the correct punctuation.

13. **(B)** Choice (B) is correct. Choices (A) and (C) do not separate the independent clauses with the correct punctuation.

14. **(D)** Choice (D) is correct. The clause *and now he was looking forward to joining the show choir* is not a complete thought; therefore, it is not an independent clause and the sentence is not a run-on sentence. Choices (A) and (B) are incorrect because they punctuate the sentence as if the clause were independent.

15. **(A)** Choice (A) is correct. The original sentence contains a comma splice; choice (B) contains a run-on; choice (C) separates the sentences with a coordinating conjunction but omits the comma.

16. **(D)** Choice (D) is correct. Choice (A) contains a comma splice, and choice (B) is a run-on sentence.

17. **(A)**   Choice (A) is correct. Choice (B) is a run-on, and the original sentence contains a comma splice.

18. **(D)**   Choice (D) is correct. Choice (A) suggests a chronological relationship between the two ideas, and choice (B) suggests a cause-and-effect relationship.

19. **(D)**   Choice (D) is correct. The ideas are of equal importance, so they need to be coordinated. Choice (A) coordinated them, but with a conjunction of contrast. Choice (B) subordinated the second idea, suggesting that it is of lesser importance than the first.

20. **(B)**   Choice (B) is correct. Choices (A) and (C) contain faulty predication; that is, the complement of each sentence is not structurally correct. Choice (A) uses a compound preposition to introduce a clause, and the original sentence uses an adverb clause instead of a noun clause as the subject complement.

DRILL: VERBS

1.   **(C)**   Choice (C) is correct. The past participle form of each verb is required because of the auxiliaries (helping verbs) *had been* (concerned) and *would have* (gone).

2.   **(B)**   Choice (B) is correct. The forms of the irregular verb meaning *to rest* are *lie (rest), lies (rests), lay (rested),* and *has lain (has rested).* The forms of the verb meaning *to put* are *lay (put), lays (puts), laying (putting), laid (put),* and *have laid (have put).*

3.   **(D)**   Choice (D) is correct. The present tense is used for universal truths and the past tense is used for historical truths.

4.   **(A)**   Choice (A) is correct. The present tense is used for customary happenings. Choice (B), *had begun,* is not a standard verb form. Choice (C), *was beginning,* indicates that 10:30 a.m. is not the regular class time.

5.   **(A)**   Choice (A) is correct. The past tense is used for historical statements, and the present tense is used for statements about works of art.

6.   **(B)**   Choice (B) is correct. The subject of the sentence is the plural noun *sales,* not the singular noun *Christmas,* which is the object of the prepositional phrase.

7.   **(A)**   Choice (A) is correct. The subject *specialty* is singular.

8.   **(C)**   Choice (C) is correct. Subjects preceded by *every* are considered singular and therefore require a singular verb form.

9.   **(A)**   Choice (A) is correct. The subject of the sentence is the gerund *hiding*, not the object of the gerund phrase *mistakes*. *Hiding* is singular; therefore, the singular verb form *does* should be used.

10.   **(D)**   Choice (D) is correct. Though the form of the subject *Board of Regents* is plural, it is singular in meaning.

DRILL: PRONOUNS

1.   **(A)**   Choice (A) is correct. Do not use the reflexive pronoun *myself* as a substitute for I.

2.   **(C)**   Choice (C) is correct. In the clause *whoever consumes them*, *whoever* is the subject. *Whomever* is the objective case pronoun, and should be used only as the object of a sentence, never as the subject.

3.   **(A)**   Choice (A) is correct. Use the nominative case pronoun *who* as the subject complement after the verb *is*.

4.   **(A)**   Choice (A) is correct. In this sentence use the nominative case/subject pronouns *she who* as the subject complement after the *be* verb *was*.

5.   **(D)**   Choice (D) is correct. *Student* is an indefinite, genderless noun that requires a singular personal pronoun. While *his* is a singular personal pronoun, a genderless noun includes both the masculine and feminine forms and requires *his or her* as the singular personal pronoun.

6.   **(A)**   Choice (A) is correct. The antecedent *company* is singular, requiring the singular pronoun *it*, not the plural *they*.

7.   **(B)**   Choice (B) is correct. Choice (A) contains a person shift: *Your* is a second person pronoun, and *his* and *her* are third person pronouns. The original sentence uses the third person plural pronoun *their* to refer to the singular antecedent *every car owner*. Choice (B) correctly provides the masculine and feminine forms *his or her* required by the indefinite, genderless *every car owner*.

8.   **(B)**   Choice (B) is correct. The implied antecedent is *teaching*. Choices (A) and (C) each contain a pronoun with no antecedent. Neither *it* nor *this* are suitable substitutions for *teacher*.

9.   **(A)**   Choice (A) is correct. The pronoun *they* in the original sentence has no conspicuous antecedent. Since the doer of the action is obviously unknown (and therefore genderless), choice (B), *he*, is not the correct choice.

10. **(C)** Choice (C) is correct. The original sentence is ambiguous: the pronoun *she* has two possible antecedents; we don't know whether it is Margaret or her sister who is away at college.

DRILL: ADJECTIVES AND ADVERBS

1. **(C)** Choice (C) is correct. *Bad* is an adjective; *badly* is an adverb. *Real* is an adjective meaning *genuine* (*a real problem, real leather*). To qualify an adverb of degree to express how bad, how excited, how boring, etc., choose *very*.

2. **(A)** Choice (A) is correct. Use an adverb as a qualifier for an adjective. *How simple? Relatively simple.*

3. **(D)** Choice (D) is correct. *Good* is an adjective; *well* is both an adjective and an adverb. As an adjective, *well* refers to health; it means "not ill."

4. **(C)** Choice (C) is correct. All the other choices use *good* incorrectly as an adverb. *Shake* is an action verb that requires an adverb, not an adjective.

5. **(A)** Choice (A) is correct. The action verbs *speaks, writes, observes,* and *think* each require adverbs as modifiers.

6. **(C)** Choice (C) is correct. The comparisons in choices (A) and (B) are illogical: these sentences suggest that Los Angeles is not in California because it *is larger than any city in California.*

7. **(A)** Choice (A) is correct. Do not omit the second *as* of the correlative pair *as…as* when making a point of equal or superior comparison, as in choice (B). Choice (C) omits *than* from "if not more interesting [than]".

8. **(C)** Choice (C) is correct. Choice (A) illogically compares *baseball team* to a *university,* and choice (B) illogically compares *baseball team* to *all the other universities.* Choice (C) logically compares the baseball team here to the one at any other university, as implied by the possessive ending on university—*university's.*

9. **(B)** Choice (B) is correct. Choices (A) and (C) are ambiguous; because these sentences are too elliptical, the reader does not know where to place the missing information.

DRILL: PUNCTUATION

1.   **(D)**   Choice (D) is correct. Nonrestrictive clauses, like other nonrestrictive elements, should be set off from the rest of the sentence with commas.

2.   **(A)**   Choice (A) is correct. Use a comma to separate a nonrestrictive appositive from the word it modifies. "An Oklahoma family" is a nonrestrictive appositive.

3.   **(A)**   Choice (A) is correct. Do not use unnecessary commas to separate a subject and verb from their complement. Both choices (B) and (C) use superfluous punctuation.

4.   **(C)**   Choice (C) is correct. Do not separate two items in a compound part with commas. The original sentence incorrectly separates "car or plane." Choice (A) omits the comma after the introductory clause.

5.   **(A)**   Choice (A) is correct. Use a semicolon to separate two independent clauses/ sentences that are not joined by a coordinating conjunction, especially when the ideas in the sentences are interrelated.

6.   **(D)**   Choice (D) is correct. Use a semicolon to separate two sentences not joined by a coordinating conjunction.

7.   **(A)**   Choice (A) is correct. Use a semicolon to separate two sentences joined by a conjunctive adverb.

8.   **(A)**   Choice (A) is correct. Do not use a colon after a verb or a preposition. Remember that a complete sentence must precede a colon.

9.   **(B)**   Choice (B) is correct. Do not use a colon after a preposition, and do not use a colon to separate a preposition from its objects.

10.   **(D)**   Choice (D) is correct. Use a colon preceding a list that is introduced by words such as *the following* and *as follows*.

11.   **(D)**   Choice (D) is correct. Use a colon preceding a list. Do not use a period or a semicolon to indicate the end of this sentence since there is a list following the completed thought.

12.   **(B)**   Choice (B) is correct. Possessive pronouns (*yours, ours, hers, his, its*) are spelled without an apostrophe.

13.   **(D)**   Choice (D) is correct. Add only an apostrophe to an already plural noun ending in -s to make it possessive (Americans'). To make a singular noun like history possessive, use the 's possessive marker at the end of the word.

14. **(D)** Choice (D) is correct. Use an apostrophe and -s to form the possessive of a singular noun ending in -s unless the addition of the 's produces a distorted or false pronunciation. *Rivers'*, not Rivers's, *Burns'*, not Burns's. If, however, the apostrophe and -s combination are needed to produce the extra syllable, add both the apostrophe and the -s: *witnesses', waitresses'*. Some singular nouns ending in -s need the apostrophe and the -s to create the extra syllable: *boss's, Tess's*.

15. **(A)** Choice (A) is correct. Do not use an apostrophe to form the plural of a noun. *Julys* is the plural of *July*. *The Joneses* is the plural of *Jones*.

16. **(B)** Choice (B) is correct. Place directly quoted phrases and expressions in quotation marks, even if they are commonly known and used.

17. **(A)** Choice (A) is correct. Place dialogue and quoted material in quotation marks, and place periods inside the closing quotation mark.

18. **(C)** Choice (C) is correct. Place both parts of a divided quotation in quotation marks.

DRILL: CAPITALIZATION

1. **(D)** Choice (D) is correct. *North America*, like other proper names, is capitalized. No*rth, south, east,* and *west* are only capitalized when they refer to geographic regions (*the Southwest, Eastern Europe);* as compass directions, they are not capitalized.

2. **(B)** Choice (B) is correct. Although persons' names are capitalized, a person's title is not (*coach*, not *Coach*). Capitalize the complete name of a team, school, river, etc. (Dallas Cowboys).

3. **(C)** Choice (C) is correct. Capitalize all geographic units, and capitalize *earth* only when it is mentioned with other planets. *Equator* is not capitalized.

4. **(A)** Choice (A) is correct. Capitalize the first word in a title and all other words in a title except articles, prepositions with fewer than five letters, and conjunctions.

5. **(C)** Choice (C) is correct. Capitalize proper adjectives (proper nouns used as adjectives): *Greek* goddess, *Roman* mythology.

6. **(D)** Choice (D) is correct. Capitalize all religious groups, books, and names referring to religious deities.

7. **(B)** Choice (B) is correct. Do not capitalize courses unless they are languages (English) or course titles followed by a number (Algebra I).

8. **(D)** Choice (D) is correct. Do not capitalize seasons unless they accompany the name of an event such as *Spring Break*. Do not capitalize types of degrees (*bachelor's degrees*); capitalize only the name of the degree (*Bachelor of Arts degree*).

DRILL: SPELLING

1. **(D)** Choice (D) is the best response. *Business* has only three -s's. Separate has an -e at the beginning and the end, not in the middle.

2. **(B)** Choice (B) is the best response. *Library* has two r's.

3. **(A)** Choice (A) is the best response. *Leisure* is one of the few English words that does not follow the *i* before *e* except after *c* rule. *Pursue* has two **u**'s and only one **e**.

4. **(B)** Choice (B) is the best response. "Favorite," "characters," and "literature" are commonly mispronounced, and when someone who mispronounces them tries to spell them phonetically, he or she often misspells them.

5. **(B)** Choice (B) is the best response. Advertisements often misspell words to catch the consumer's eye (*lite* for light, *tho* for though, etc.), and these misspellings are becoming more common in student writing. "Accident" and "liable" are examples of words that are not pronounced the way they are spelled.

CLAST
COLLEGE LEVEL ACADEMIC SKILLS TEST

Chapter 3

Essay Writing
Skills Review

Chapter 3

ESSAY WRITING SKILLS REVIEW

People write essays for many reasons, and not just to complete tests. Some of our best thinkers have written essays which we continue to read from generation to generation. Essays offer the reader a logical, coherent, and imaginative written composition showing the nature or consequences of a single controlling idea considered from the writer's unique point of view. Writers use essays to communicate their opinion or position on a topic to readers who are not present at that time. Writers use essays to help their readers understand or learn about something that readers should or might want to know or do. Essays always express more or less directly the author's opinion, belief, position, or knowledge (backed by evidence) about the idea or object in question.

This chapter will help you refresh your writing skills and determine your current knowledge of essay-writing skills. In writing your essay, you'll be asked to defend your point of view with facts, examples, and logical reasons. Step-by-step, this review will take you through the essay-writing process, from brainstorming to beginnings, middles, and ends, and to self-editing, including time constraints and other challenges.

Even good writers should familiarize themselves with the material in the review and get a feel for what to expect in writing the essay on the actual exam. By taking the diagnostic test and reading through the review, you will improve your chances of doing well on this section of the test.

Remember, you are not writing the Great American Novel. You want to write a clear, coherent, organized essay with effective support and interesting ideas; this goal is completely achievable. Writing is somewhat like learning to play the piano: the more you study and practice, the better you'll be. This review can help you to review, build, and polish your skills.

THE DIRECTIONS

The first of the CLAST is the Essay Writing section. In this section, two essay topics are given, and you are asked to choose one. You are then given 60 minutes to develop a well-written, well-structured essay.

TIPS

WHAT GOOD WRITERS KNOW ABOUT WRITING

Seasoned writers:

- Value process over product and are willing to do lots of planning and revising.

- Realize that an effective essay stimulates people to think with its strong thesis, supporting details, and logical argument.

- Are willing to take risks, say something that is unpopular or unusual, and share their work with others to get outside opinions and critiques.

- Frequently write from personal experience as a springboard for issues, characters, and events.

- Are avid readers, using other writers as models, inspiration, and sources of information.

- Use standard practice for spelling, punctuation, and capitalization.

- Observe the conventions of standard American English grammar usage.

ESSAY WRITING SKILLS DIAGNOSTIC TEST

To prepare you for the requirements of CLAST, do the exercises in this section. The CLAST requires that you be able to focus and organize your essays, and that you be able to write in effective Standard American English. Accordingly, this diagnostic offers exercises to test your skills in paragraphing and basic issues in grammar and sentence style. For the answers to the issues raised in the exercises, refer to the Answer Key on page 117. As you discover the gaps in your knowledge about paragraphing and grammar, make a point to use the sections of this book that are relevant to study and resolve your problems effectively in preparation for the test. Mark your answers on the answer sheet on the next page.

ESSAY WRITING SKILLS TEST

PARAGRAPH DIAGNOSTIC

> **DIRECTIONS:** Answer the following questions based on the paragraphs below.

After reading the paragraph below, answer the questions that follow.

[1]So many athletic shoes are on the market now; so many are so expensive! [2]Buying a pair for yourself or your kids can make even those of us who are blessed with a fair amount of discretionary income feel like paupers. [3]For example, those running shoes I used to buy for $20 a few years ago, now cost—on average—over $150. [4]With the advance of miracle materials and space age technology, my old leather hiking boots have gone from about $20 a pair to upwards of $180! [5]Tennis shoes that I could buy for that good old $20 bill, now cost the average income earner the wages of half a good day's work—or more, depending upon how vain you are. [6]No, it takes a rich man, now, to have fun in only amateur recreation. [7]And forget allowance; your kid needs a trust fund.

1.   What is the number of the topic sentence?

2.   Which of the sentences in the paragraph offer evidence for the writer's topic sentence?

3.   Which of the sentences in the paragraph offer rhetorical support for the topic sentence?

4.   Below is a sentence that could be used as the focus, or topic sentence, of a paragraph. On a separate piece of paper, write a paragraph which uses this sentence as its focus.

Word processing programs on the market today have made writing a less cumbersome task.

5.   Choose which one of the sample paragraphs below would make the best conclusion for a complete essay.

The days of paper books, then, are numbered. Environmental considerations, such as the destruction of oxygen-producing trees discussed above, limit the quality of paper itself that a publisher can use to offer a lasting product. Electronic writing and desktop publishing will more and more obviate the need to buy expensive editions in stores. In the not too distant future, libraries will be full of disks, not dusty volumes, and for the busy traveller, books listened to on tape on the road will replace curling up in a big old cushy chair. We will not turn pages for much longer; we will turn switches on and off instead.   [1]

Small electric cars, though limited in range, are fun, and could be used for short business and workaday commuting. The less expensive cars are always small. People will understand that polluting the air with fossil fuel exhausts is unnecessary. American car manufacturers continue to make gas monsters. Soon however, many electric cars will be affordable for the average American. Everyone is different, so it is up to the individual to choose what the future will hold.   [2]

6.   Read the sample paragraph. Select the sentence from the three choices below which offers the best transition for the reader, and offers the best ending for the paragraph.

To reduce weight and improve one's cardiovascular system, the advantages of walking far outweigh those of jogging. Walking gets the heart rate up with less stress on the joints. For those of us who balk at sweat and strain, walking is an activity that is hard for even the most desultory to claim as "too difficult." Walking burns calories at a slightly lower rate than jogging, but all you really need to do is increase your time. If you are a senior, you risk less with walking than you do with jogging. Unlike jogging, walking does not entail any highly specialized or expensive equipment. All you need is sneakers and an interest in breathing fresh air.

(A)   The advantages of walking are many and jogging will just cause you pain and run you down.

(B)   Thus, walking and jogging are not equal, and walking's advantages far outweigh those of jogging.

(C)   So, the next time you think about what would be the better exercise for you, think twice before you decide to jog.

GRAMMAR DIAGNOSTIC

DIRECTIONS: All of the sentences that follow have some grammatical or stylistic error. Some have more than one. Write corrections for each of the sentences. Once having attempted to correct the sentences on your own, you may wish to refer to the English Language Skills Review section for more information on grammatical errors and how to correct them.

1.   Using only the tool available in the truck, the bathroom could not be completed on time.

2.   The radical newspaper was lying on the table, however, the president ignored it.

3.   Since the carbonation in the product was excessive. Removed it from the market.

4.   Each of the players were notified of the cancellation but they all thought it was unnecessary.

5.   Just between you and I, John's car is a real lemon!

6.   Who's idea this is we are not sure, but for it's convenience, the ladies salon is on the first floor.

7. We go to the stores on Tuesday, and we bought items on sale.

8. Our department recently purchased a new PC, a new desk, and new software, which was cumbersome to use.

9. The files are in the office of the President with the metal detectors in the cabinet by the window.

10. We will be going to England, visiting London, and to tour Dover.

11. I go to the store with who I please.

12. The compact car is more cheaper than the luxury model.

13. Of the two jobs available, I like that of Chief Engineer best.

14. John works greedy for his paltry company paycheck.

15. Harold works in the city with Lance, and he can't make the commute on time.

16. Peter asked father if he still loved the west or if he intended to move south.

17. It was decided by the committee that George should be included by Mary in the project.

ESSAY WRITING SKILLS REVIEW DIAGNOSTIC TEST ANSWER KEY

Use the chart below to check your answers. If you had trouble with a question, refer to the column on the right to direct you to the review section that will help you.

PARAGRAPH DIAGNOSTIC

Question	If you had trouble with this question, see the section titled:
1	The Topic Sentence: Writing Skills, p. 127
2	Supporting Paragraphs: Writing Skills, p. 127
3	Refuting Your Ideas: Writing Skills, p. 129
4	Supporting Paragraphs: Writing Skills, p. 127
5	The Mission of the Conclusion: Writing Skills, p. 131
6	Why the Reader Needs Transitions: Writing Skills, p. 129

GRAMMAR DIAGNOSTIC

Question	If you had trouble with this question, see the section titled:
1	Misplaced and Dangling Modifiers: English Skills, p. 45
2	Run-On/Fused Sentences: English Skills, p. 47
3	Fragments: Essay Writing Skills, p. 133; English Skills, p. 47; Pronoun Reference: English Skills, p. 64
4	Subject-Verb Agreement: Writing Skills, p. 133; English Skills, p. 54
5	Subordination, Coordination, and Predication: English Skills, p. 54
6	Pronoun Case: English Skills, p. 60
7	Apostrophes: English Skills, p. 83
8	Verb Tense: Writing Skills, p. 133
9	Misplaced and Dangling Modifiers: English Skills, p. 45
10	Parallelism: English Skills, p. 44
11	Pronoun Case: English Skills, p. 60
12	Faulty Comparison: English Skills, p. 69
13	Faulty Comparison: English Skills, p. 69
14	Correct Usage: English Skills, p. 68
15	Pronoun Reference: English Skills, p. 35
16	Capitalization: English Skills, p. 90
17	Avoiding the Passive: Writing Skills, p. 135

DETAILED EXPLANATIONS OF ANSWERS

PARAGRAPH DIAGNOSTIC

1.   Sentence 2 is correct. Sentence 1 is incorrect. Though it introduces the topic of expense, sentence 1 offers no real thesis, or point of view on the part of the writer. No reasonable person would argue that athletic shoes are not expensive. However, they could claim, unlike the writer, that athletic shoes—on the contrary—make buyers feel rich because they *can* afford them. The topic sentence of a paragraph, when it is explicit, always states some opinion, judgement, or observation that the writer is obliged to support with evidence or examples. Sentence 6 is incorrect because the focus of the paragraph is not how rich the buyer is, but how it makes him or her feel poor. This sentence is a form of hyperbole—pointing to how one very well might have to be rich to buy these shoes. Sentence 7 is incorrect because the focus of the paragraph is not children's allowances or forming trust funds for them, but again, through hyperbole and sarcasm, how the buyer must be rich to support buying shoes for children. The writer, therefore, implies its opposite: that not being able to afford these shoes makes the buyer feel like a pauper if s/he cannot meet the needs of his or her children.

2.   Sentences 3, 4, and 5 are correct. All of these sentences offer the reader anecdotal evidence and facts to support the topic sentence that the shoes are expensive and that, by implication, they make the buyer feel like a pauper. The writer implies that buying them will take quite a bit of money out of one's "discretionary income" even though one is lucky enough to have a "good" income. Sentences 1, 2, 6, and 7 are incorrect because they function differently in the paragraph. These sentences present or modify ideas; they do not offer measurable supporting evidence. See also the answer to part A for further explanation.

3.   Sentences 6 and 7 are correct. These two sentences offer hyperbolic and sardonic support for the writer's thesis. See also the answer to part A above.

4.   To write a successful paragraph to support this topic sentence, you may organize your response in one of several ways. But no matter how you decide to write your paragraph, a paragraph that opens with the topic sentence cited above *must* have a combination of ingredients to be effective: unity, coherence, and evidence. All the sentences must support a single unifying idea. The evidence may be of several types: facts, statistics, anecdotal, life experience, the testimony of authority, or a working hypothetical illustration.

   "Transitions provide coherence which help move forward the writer's narrative or logic. Paragraphs are a sort of "show and tell." The writer "tells" you an opinion, judgement, or observation, and then "shows" you that "thesis," or main idea expressed in a topic sentence, has merit by offering backup evidence to lend credence to the opinion, judgement, or observation expressed.

5.   Sentence 1 is the better conclusion. This paragraph offers a useful transition ("then") in the first sentence to indicate a rhetorical move toward a summing up. The rest of the sentences then do sum up what the writer discussed earlier in the essay ("discussed above"), keeping the reader's attention on what the essay covered. Finally, the writer offers a "clincher" sentence and ends on a slightly sardonic note, implying that the changes under discussion will be a change in lifestyle and will be fundamental as well: "We will not turn pages for much longer; we will turn switches on an off instead."

Paragraph 2 is not the best choice. Each sentence in the paragraph seems to be its own thesis, thus no unity is supplied. No transitions are used to show summation or the trends of the writer's thought. No idea is subordinated to another in time, place, or logic. Finally, the writer, instead of taking a real stand and holding to a position, cops out at the end by using the old getaway line about leaving it all up to the individual. A good conclusion takes a strong stand and supports it forcefully with summary evidence and effective coherence.

6.   **(C)**   (C) is the best choice. This sentence offers a fine unobtrusive transition ("So…") to lead the reader to a sense of summing up, and it offers a "clincher" with which to end the discussion in the form of an action that the reader may or ought to take: "think twice." (A) is not the best choice because it offers no actual verbal link to the ideas that preceded it, and it makes a different point than the paragraph supports, losing both unity and coherence. (B) is not the best choice because while it does offer a logical transitional word that points toward summing up ("Thus…"), it sounds artificial in tone—the diction of a formal professor, not the writer's friendly, direct voice—and the sentence just reiterates the point made earlier in a mechanical way, not offering a development of thought toward something new as in (C).

GRAMMAR DIAGNOSTIC

Note: The sentences in this exercise may be corrected in many ways. The corrections offered here illustrate the resolution of specific problems. To understand other ways to correct these errors, work with someone whose knowledge you trust and try out variations. The best way to control these errors is to learn to spot them and then to make corrections on your own.

1.   Correction: Using the only tool available in the truck, the plumber could not complete the bathroom on time.

The original sample sentence is incorrect because it leads with a **dangling modifier** ("Using"), so called because it is not clear what subject it modifies. The way it is written, "the bathroom" appears to be the one "using" the tool in question. This doesn't make sense. To correct this error, make it clear who or what is doing the "using."

2.   Correction: The radical newspaper was lying on the table; however, the president ignored it.

The original sample sentence is incorrectly punctuated with commas, making it into a kind of **run-on sentence**. It is really two sentences: the first one ends with "table"; the second begins with "however." Commas link words, phrases, and clauses, not sentences. You may use only two forms of punctuation to end sentences, a period or its equivalent [.] [?] [!] or a semicolon [;].

3. Correction: Since the carbonation in the product was excessive, the company removed the product from the market.

These two word groups in the original samples are both **sentence fragments**. You cannot begin a sentence with a subordinating conjunction leading the first clause ("Since...") and end it with a period [.] without linking to an independent clause. The second word group is a fragment because there is no subject in it for the verb "removed." To correct them, the first clause must be linked to the second phrase which, in turn, must have a subject added to become an independent clause, so that the sentence can stand on its own as a complete thought.

The second word group also has a problem with a **vague pronoun reference**, "it." What, exactly, is "it"? The "product" or the "carbonation"? Since the reader may misunderstand, the writer should identify exactly what "it" is so as to avoid any confusion.

4. Correction: Each of the players was notified of the cancellation, but they all thought the notification was unnecessary.

The original sample sentence has incorrect **subject-verb agreement**. In English, "Each" always refers to the understood subjective pronoun "one." The prepositional phrase "of the players" only modifies "Each" [one]; "players" is not the subject. Thus, the verb "to be" used here should agree in number with "one," not the plural "players"; so, "were" should be changed to "was."

The second major fault is that there was no comma before the "but" at the beginning of the second clause of the sentence. This makes the sentence a type of run-on sentence. Commas must be placed before the **coordinating conjunction** [, and] that leads into a second complete clause that could be a complete sentence by itself without the coordinating conjunction.

5. Correction: Just between you and me, John's car is a real lemon!

The original sample sentence is incorrect because the case of the subjective pronoun "I" cannot be the object of a preposition ("between"). Instead, the writer must use the form of the pronoun known as the **objective case**. In this instance, the correct form would be "me." The other case for personal pronouns in English is called the **possessive case** (my, mine). Learn the difference in use among these personal pronouns.

6.   Correction: Whose idea this is we are not sure, but for its convenience, the ladies' salon is on the first floor.

The original sample sentence is incorrect because it uses **apostrophes** incorrectly. In addition, the writer does not employ the possessive case for pronouns when necessary, but mistakenly uses contractions instead. "Who's" means "who is," and does not indicate possession. "Whose" is the correct form. Similarly, "it's" means "it is" and cannot be the possessive form of the pronoun "it." "Its" is the correct form. Finally, "ladies" does not show possession in the original version of this sentence. When a noun is used to show possession before another noun, then the writer must use an apostrophe to demonstrate that. Thus, since the "salon" belongs to, or is to be used only by the "ladies," and since it is a plural noun, the apostrophe must be used with it and placed after the "s" to show plurality.

7.   Correction: We go to the stores on Tuesday, and we buy items on sale.

The original sample sentence is incorrect because the verbs shift tense unnecessarily and illogically. Both the "going" and the "buying" take place at the same time, and since the sentence begins in the present tense it should stay in the same time.

8.   Correction: Our department recently purchased a new PC that was cumbersome to use, a new desk and new software.

The original sample sentence uses the relative pronoun "which" ambiguously to start a subordinate clause that modifies a noun. The problem is that because of its placement at the end of the sentence, the reader cannot tell clearly to which single noun "which" refers. Modifiers should always be placed as close to the noun modified as possible. In addition, "which" should never be used to indicate a quality essential to the identity of a noun. In this case, it is the PC that is "cumbersome to use," so the writer should use "that" to introduce the clause and place it as close to the noun modified as possible. Of course, the writer may have meant that the desk was "cumbersome to use." But if that is what was meant, then the sentence should read as follows:

Our department recently purchased a new PC, a new desk that was cumbersome to use, and new software.

9.   Correction: The files are in the President's office with the metal detectors in the cabinet by the window.

The original sample sentence is incorrect because it **misplaces modifying phrases** and rambles from prepositional phrase to prepositional phrase to prepositional phrase without logic. The way the original is written suggests that the "President" has "metal detectors." Often, this error can be corrected by eliminating the offending phrase altogether, or by turning that phrase into an adjective (Thus "of the President" becomes "President's.")

10.   Correction: We will be going to England, visiting London, and touring Dover.

The original sample sentence is incorrect because it has **faulty parallelism**. If you use words, phrases, or clauses in a sequence, you should keep the form of the sequence the same. In this case, the writer uses the present participle "-ing" form and then switches to the infinitive phrase "to tour" at the end. The form should be consistent, or parallel, with the others. So, changing it to "touring" solves the problem.

11.   Correction: I go to the store with whom I please.

The original sample sentence is incorrect because it uses the wrong case of the pronoun, "who." Since "who" is the object of the preposition "with," the form the pronoun should take is "whom," or the **objective case**. See also explanations 5 and 6 above.

12.   Correction: The compact car is cheaper than the luxury model.

The original sample sentence is incorrect because the writer uses the wrong comparative form for the adjective "cheap." Words of one or two syllables—not counting exceptions such as "worse"—are modified for comparison by the model.

one	two	among three or more
pretty	prettier	prettiest

Words of three syllables (say "beautiful") or more are modified on the model

one	two	among three or more
beautiful	more beautiful than	most beautiful

13.   Correction: Of the two jobs available, I like that of Chief Engineer better.

The original sample sentence is incorrect because it uses the wrong comparative form for "good." "Good" is a comparative adjective that is an exception to the pattern and actually changes its whole spelling, not just its form. If you got this one wrong learn the comparative forms and the exceptions.

one	two	among three or more
good	better	best

14.   Correction: John works greedily for his paltry company paycheck.

The original sample sentence is incorrect because it uses an incorrect adjective/adverb form. Sometimes writers do the reverse, of course. In this case, the base noun "greed" modifies the verb "works," describing how John works, not some other noun, or John. So, it must be "greedily." If the word "greed," were a complement to "is" in the sentence, then "greedy," would be correct since it modifies "John," not the verb "is":

John is greedy about his company paycheck.

15. Correction: Harold works in the city with Lance, and Harold can't make the commute on time.

    Another common error. The original sample sentence is incorrect because the subjective pronoun "he" in the second clause is an **ambiguous pronoun**. Since both of the antecedents to "he" are one man, the "he" could refer to either one of them. So, who has trouble with the commute is moot. Clarify by naming the subject of the verb in the second clause. See also explanations 3, 5, and 6 above.

16. Correction: Peter asked Father if he still loved the West or if he intended to move south.

    The original sample sentence lacks correct capitalization. "Father" should be capitalized when it is used not as a common noun but as the name of the writer's father. "West" should be capitalized because it is referred to as a geographical region, not a direction in which to move. The key to this is that the regional term is usually accompanied with the definite article "the." When the word for direction is used as such, no capitalization is necessary—as in the case of "south" in this sentence.

17. Correction: The committee decided that Mary should include George in the project.

    The original sample sentence is not grammatically wrong. However, its **passive voice** structure is one that good writers stay away from. Notice how long the original is. Notice how it has the pattern "was…-ed by…" and "be…-ed by…." This structure is called passive voice. Some form of the verb "to be" is coupled with a past participle [-ed, -n, -t; is review**ed**, will be show**n**, are deal**t**] to form the passive voice.

    The correction, you will notice, removes both the form of the verb "to be" and the "by…" phrase, making the sentence shorter and more direct. This correction is called active voice because the action is done directly by the subject of the verb.

    Active voice style is to be preferred, though passive voice is not wrong. With passive voice, however, the subject of the verb is acted upon; in active voice, the subject does the action. Thus:

Passive voice: The car **was purchased by** John.

Active voice: **John purchased** the car.

USING THE WRITING PROCESS

Most people mistakenly think that writers just sit down and churn out wonderful essays or poems in one sitting, in a flash of genius and inspiration. This is not true! Writers use the writing process from start to finish to help them develop a well-composed document. If you do not reflect on your composition in stages and make changes as you develop it, you will not see all the problems or errors in it. Don't try to write an essay all at one time and then leave the room. Stay and look through it. Reflect upon it using the writing process in the following way.

HANDLING TIME CONSTRAINTS: THE CASE OF THE TICKING CLOCK

Writing under pressure can be frustrating, but if you study this review, practice and polish your essay skills before the exam, and have a realistic sense of what to expect, you can turn problems into possibilities.

A good way to organize your time during the essay exam is as follows:

1. First five minutes: carefully read the directions and topic, then brainstorm on paper (when you use written brainstorming, you're already writing!).

2. Next 20 minutes: write a rough, working draft of your essay, focusing more on content than correctness.

3. Next 20 minutes: reread your essay for organization, interesting ideas, quality of examples and support, logical flow, and completeness, and revise where necessary.

4. Next 10 minutes: rewrite and edit your revised draft for grammar, punctuation, and spelling, paying particular attention to run-ons and fragments.

5. Final 5 minutes: proofread with attention to detail.

Adjust the schedule to your personal writing style and needs, and practice before the exam with a clock to see where you need to expand or limit certain time periods.

The best hint here: during the first working draft, let the ideas flow without editing and censoring yourself. Your ideas will be more authentic, fresh, and true to what you really believe and want to say. Creative expression cannot be forced.

PRE-WRITING

Read the essay question and decide on your purpose: Do you want to persuade your reader? Or, do you want to explain something?

Sample: "Television is bad for people." Do you agree or disagree with this statement?

Decide. Take a stand. Don't be wishy-washy. Write the statement of your position.

Sample: I agree that television is bad for people.

Or: Television is an excellent learning tool and is good for most people.

One of these is your thesis, depending on your point of view.

CONSIDER YOUR AUDIENCE

The writer's responsibility is to write clearly, honestly, and cleanly for the reader's sake. Essays would be pointless without an audience. Why write an essay if no one wants or needs to read it? Why add evidence, organize your ideas, or correct bad grammar? The reason to do any of these things is because someone out there needs to understand what you mean or say. What would the audience need to know in order to believe you or to come over to your position? Imagine someone you know (visualize her—name him) listening to you declare your position or opinion and then saying, "Oh, yeah? Prove it!" Don't you know someone like that? Sure you do. It's the wiseguy, your history teacher. These are the people—write to them. When you write your essay, make sure to answer the following questions so that you will not be confronted with a person who says, "Prove it!"

What evidence do you need to prove your idea to this skeptic?

What would s/he disagree with you about?

What does s/he share with you as common knowledge? What does s/he need to be told by you?

CONTROL YOUR POINT OF VIEW

People may write essays from one of three points of view, depending upon whom the audience is for the essay. The points of view below are discussed from Informal → Formal.

1. Subjective/Personal Point of View:

    "I think
    "I believe $\Big\}$ cars are more trouble than they are worth."
    "I feel

2. Second Person Point of View (We…You; I…You): "If **you** own a car, **you** will soon find out that it is more trouble than it is worth."

3. Third Person Point of View: (focuses on the idea, not what "I" think of it): "**Cars** are more trouble than **they** are worth."

Stick with one, or another; don't switch your "point of view" in the middle of the essay. Any one is OK.

CONSIDER YOUR EVIDENCE

During the pre-writing stage, jot down a few phrases that show ideas and examples which support your point of view. Do this quickly on a separate piece of paper spending no more than **five minutes** on the task. Don't try to outline, just **list things** you think may be important to discuss. After you have listed several ideas, pick at least three to five things you want or need to discuss and number them in the order of importance to prove your point.

THE FOUNDATIONS OF A GREAT ESSAY

Sample topic: By the time a student finishes twelfth grade, he or she will have watched 18,000 hours of television, but spent only 11,000 hours in the classroom. Sociologists, psychologists, and educational groups generally tend to give television low marks in educating and nurturing young minds. Does television have a primarily positive or negative effect on young people? Should television-watching be restricted, even forbidden, for children? Take a stand, and give specific examples to defend your response.

GETTING STARTED

While using the sample topic from above on the effects of television on children, let's talk about how you can immediately get started on this topic or any other, and never be stuck again.

There are many ways to start an essay: with a question, a quote, a line from a poem or song, a definition, a statistic or fact, or an illustration or anecdote. The primary job of the introduction is to **give a sense of the scope of the essay** (how much will the writer discuss?) and **hook the reader's attention** (as a writer, you never get a second chance at a first impression).

One method for introductions is to **start with a story**. For example, here's a story opening for the television and children topic above:

> Bobby Romano, eight years old, comes home from school, kisses his mother, grabs a banana, and plops down on the sofa to watch Batman. When Bobby's mother asks him how school was, he says in annoyance, "Fine," and goes back to watching the show. Bobby's mother suggests that he go out to play or finish homework, but Bobby remains glued to his seat, his eyes a glassy stare. He has three pages of math homework and a book report to finish, but at this moment his mind is deep in the Bat Cave. Like millions of American schoolchildren, Bobby Romano is the victim of a mindless activity that robs him of his creative energies: television.

Story openings, or human interest stories, capture the reader at a powerful, emotional level and are almost always effective. Once you start with a story, the supporting paragraphs must break away from the narrative (story-telling) and get on with the defense of the major point (thesis). Your essay should not be one long story, but a series of well-supported reasons and ideas.

Readers also like the use of facts and statistics (evidence of knowledge and research) because such evidence appeals to reason and logic. The statistics given in the sample topic above are a good example of such evidence made to prove the point that schoolchildren spend more time watching television than working in school.

Starting with a question and suggesting an answer can also be effective; for example, "Does television have a positive or negative effect on young children?" would be a good way to start an essay on the subject.

Remember, like the opening scenes of a movie, the introduction stimulates the reader's interest and sets the tone for all that follows, so the reader's sense of expectation must be high and positive. Readers enjoy stories such as the one above about Bobby Romano because most of them can relate to the experience, and the story builds a common ground between writer and reader.

THE TOPIC SENTENCE

The topic sentence usually appears at the end of the introductory paragraph. This sentence allows your reader to understand the point and direction of your essay. While the introductory paragraph provides background information and prepares your reader for your discussion; the topic sentence or thesis sentence will clearly state the issue you will argue during the essay, along with your stance on that issue.

The thesis is the heart of the essay. Without it, readers won't know what your major message or central idea is in the essay.

The **thesis must be something that can be argued or needs to be proven**, not just an accepted fact. For example, "Animals are used every day in cosmetic and medical testing," is a fact in the public domain that needs no proof. But if the writer says, "Using animals for cosmetic and medical testing is cruel and should be stopped," we have something about which to argue and debate a point that must be supported and defended by the writer.

A good thesis takes a stand and challenges the writer to provide credible evidence, while stimulating the reader to think.

The thesis can be placed in any paragraph of the essay, but in an essay of 300–600 words, especially one written for evaluative exam purposes, the thesis is best-placed in the last sentence of the opening paragraph. See the "Bobby Romano" example above for placement of thesis at the end of the opening paragraph, which argues that television has a negative effect ("mindless activity") on children.

STAYING ON TOPIC AND HAMMERING IT HOME

Have you ever known anyone who started a story, then drifted off of the topic or digressed for 20 minutes, leaving you totally confused and unsure (and irritated) about the point being made? Your readers expect you to choose a topic, take a stand, and not introduce points that have not been explained and defended.

SUPPORTING PARAGRAPHS

Let's continue the Bobby Romano-television and children essay example, then **analyze the supporting paragraphs** in terms of show vs. tell writing, use of transitions, building ideas in order of ascendancy for momentum and drama, and writing in readable sound bites (effective paragraph and sentence length).

Television is not a totally bad medium. Educational shows on PBS, documentaries such as the one on the Civil War, and certain programs, movies, and specials teach viewers more about the world. Television, which has been called "the 19-inch neighborhood," lets us travel to places we've never been and experience people and cultures who are different from us. But children such as Bobby Romano do not always use television to its productive advantage. Television becomes an electronic babysitter, a passive activity that requires nothing from the viewer. When parents fail to supervise viewing or do not talk to their children about the barrage of conflicting images on the screen, children do not develop the critical skills they need to judge what they see and hear.

Although many American schools are trying to integrate television viewing into their educational programs, they have lagged behind in addressing the power and influence television has, especially on young viewers such as Bobby Romano. Children often lack the skills to discern and discriminate, to choose between fantasy and reality, to separate the abstract from the concrete. Violent images such as blood being splattered everywhere, people shooting each other for petty reasons, inappropriate references to sex, and music television with a host of sexist messages should all be filtered for young viewers. Schools need to recognize that television, good and bad, is here to stay and can be used as an effective teaching device, but Bobby and his friends need help knowing how to be selective in their viewing.

An additional use of television and the primary one—advertising—is perhaps television's greatest influence on children. Children's programming in particular has been criticized by the National Coalition on Children's Television for running shows that are actually 30-minute advertisements for toys, action figures, or games. One study of six-year-olds indicated they did not know where the show stopped and the commercials began. Also, the message to children, like Bobby, about most products is that they must have this doll, this kind of running shoe, or this pair of jeans to belong and be cool. American television advertising does not encourage children to be secure in their own beings and heavily promotes active toys for boys (how to do something) and passive toys for girls (dressing pretty dolls).

We now have 492 words on the subject of children's television viewing. Let's analyze the content and organization to see how the essay is supported and developed, then write and discuss the conclusion.

YOUR WRITING AS A WINDOW: SHOW VS. TELL

If you go on a vacation and later show a friend the pictures, she will have a much clearer view of what you saw and did, and of your observations and experiences, than if you only tell him about the trip. Good writing operates in much the same way. Think of your writing as a window: **it is your job as a writer to show the reader what you see** (feel, taste, touch, and hear) out that window. You must help the reader to participate in your writing through the use of specific examples and mental images.

How does the Bobby Romano essay example use "show" writing? The introduction and supporting paragraphs use specific images and examples throughout to support the thesis that television viewing in general is not good for children. Here are a few examples of "show" writing from the essay (remember, we still have to write and discuss the conclusion)—"eight years old...kisses his mother, grabs a banana, and plops down on the sofa to watch Batman...three pages of math homework and a book report to finish... his mind is deep in the Bat Cave...'the 19-inch neighborhood'...electronic babysitter...blood being splattered everywhere...one study of six-year olds...running shoe."

One after the other, **specific examples and images help the reader** to relate to, understand, and **believe the writer's main point**, even if the reader disagrees with the stand being taken.

REFUTING YOUR IDEAS

A good writer will anticipate any counter-arguments a reader may have, and use them to further prove his or her own argument. By explaining the inaccuracy of any objections to your thesis, you can make your own ideas seem stronger.

When refuting your ideas, provide evidence that will convince your reader of the problems inherent in the counter-argument. In the "Bobby Romano" passage, the writer refutes his or her argument:

Television is not a totally bad medium... But children such as Bobby Romano do not always use television to its productive advantage.

In this case, the writer has anticipated the objections of television advocates. To this objection, the writer responds: theoretically television is not all that bad, but realistically, few children benefit from educational programming. By explaining the flaw in the counter-argument, the writer has strengthened his or her own thesis.

WHY THE READER NEEDS TRANSITIONS

Transitions are like the links of a bracelet, holding the beads or major points together. They help the reader follow the smooth flow of your ideas and show a connection between major and minor ideas.

Simple transitions are words such as "first, second, next, in addition, also, therefore, in contrast, on the other hand, but, for example, as a result" and the like. Like signposts or signals, simple transitions help the reader move from one idea to the next, and provide linkages among both key and minor points.

Complex transitions mean repeating or echoing key phrases or ideas from above. Notice in the children's television essay example that the words "Bobby Romano," "children," "young viewers," and "television" run like a red thread throughout the essay. These transitions serve to keep the reader on track, to unify the essay, and to give a sense of smoothness and flow to the essay.

Without transitions, you will jar the reader and distract him from your own good ideas.

Here are some typical transitional words and phrases.

Linking similar ideas

again	for example	likewise
also	for instance	moreover
and	further	nor
another	furthermore	of course
besides	in addition	similarly
equally important	in like manner	too

Linking dissimilar/contradictory ideas

although	however	otherwise
and yet	in spite of	provided that
as if	instead	still
but	nevertheless	yet
conversely	on the contrary	
even if	on the other hand	

Indicating cause, purpose, result

as	for	so
as a result	for this reason	then
because	hence	therefore
consequently	since	thus

Indicating time or position

above	before	meanwhile
across	beyond	next
afterwards	eventually	presently
around	finally	second
at once	first	thereafter
at the present time	here	thereupon

Indicating an example or summary

as a result	in any event	in short
as I have said	in brief	on the whole
for example	in conclusion	to sum up
for instance	in fact	
in any case	in other words	

ORDER OF IDEAS

One of the "tricks" that good writers know is that you don't give your strongest ideas away at the beginning. Effective writers lead their readers in increments of tolerance, often saving their best or most effective reasons for the middle or last supporting paragraphs.

In the Bobby Romano essay example, the strongest criticism of television (its use of advertising) appears as the last supporting paragraph. Ideas about sex and violence on television appear not at the beginning (before the reader is disposed to them) but in the second paragraph, by which time the reader is comfortable with the writer's style and message.

PARAGRAPH AND SENTENCE LENGTH

No hard and fast rules exist for paragraph and sentence length; however, some helpful rules of thumb apply, especially when writing a short essay.

A paragraph length of five to seven sentences enhances readability and keeps the writer from going on and on, making the reader's eyes glaze over in boredom.

The average, written English sentence is 15-20 words (again, no hard and fast rules apply for sentence length, either). If you want to know if your writing is choppy (sentences too short, marching through your paper without flow), give your practice essay the choppiness test: count the total number of words in the first ten sentences and divide by ten to get an average sentence length. If the answer is fewer than ten words per sentence, you may have a tendency to be choppy in your writing; if greater than 15 words, your essay may be wordy. A happy medium will improve readability and impress the reader with your concise, succinct style.

THE MISSION OF THE CONCLUSION

Let's look at the conclusion for the Bobby Romano–children's television essay, and then **discuss what effective conclusions do**, including: how signal words work; giving a sense of closure; offering solutions, recommendations, or future prospects for the topic; an important rule for conclusions—no new topics; and writing a clincher that sizzles:

> Overall, television is both friend and foe to children. When children like Bobby Romano use television as a substitute for play, interaction, and thought, they fall prey to T.V.'s negative influences. When they bug their parents for a pair of name-brand shoes or jeans, they become victims of the fallacy that, "Everybody's doing it, and I'm no one until I do it, too." In contrast, when children watch shows like "Reading Rainbow," they partake of the best that television has to offer. Schools, parents, broadcasters, and advertisers must all work together to turn the glassy stare of a Bobby Romano into the alert, excited gaze of a child involved in that most precious pursuit—learning.

With the conclusion, we now have a 600-word essay, developed, supported, coherent, and properly summarized.

HOW SIGNAL WORDS MAY HELP

Notice the use of the word "Overall" at the beginning of the conclusion to signal the reader that the writer is about to summarize and end the paper. Similar signal words such as "In conclusion, Therefore, In summary, To sum up..." announce to the reader your intention to wrap up your ideas. By restating the thesis and major points from the essay (but not in the same words), the writer helps to remind the reader of the essay's message and leaves the reader with a sense of wholeness and completeness, knowing that the business of the written essay is properly finished.

In the Bobby Romano example, both the negative and positive effects of television are restated, but the essay continues to deliver its message that the overall effects of television on children are negative. No doubt is left in the reader's mind about the writer's stance, but the writer does take care to acknowledge opposing viewpoints.

OFFERING SOLUTIONS, RECOMMENDATIONS, OR FUTURE PROSPECTS FOR YOUR TOPIC

In the Bobby Romano essay example, the essay ends by recommending that all interested parties work together to address and solve the problems caused by undiscerning children watching television. Other recommendations, such as more study and research, more time spent in schools discussing television's influence, or limiting the number of hours children watch television, could also be given.

Remember, don't raise more questions than you answer. If you raise an issue, suggest an answer or a resource for finding an answer in order to strengthen your credibility with the reader.

AN IMPORTANT RULE FOR CONCLUSIONS: NO NEW TOPICS

If you were watching a movie that suddenly shifted plot and characters at the end, you would be disappointed or even angry. Similarly, **conclusions must not drift away from the major focus** and message of the paper. Make sure your conclusion is clearly on the topic and represents your perspective without any confusion about what you really mean and believe. The reader will respect you for staying true to your intentions.

WRITING A CLINCHER THAT SIZZLES

One of the reasons soap operas are so successful is that each day ends with a cliffhanger, and Friday's episode ends with a major cliffhanger. While your essay might not end with a cliffhanger, you should create the same sense of drama in the last sentence, like the dramatic end of a movie. The sizzler is your last chance to grab and impress the reader.

Notice how the last sentence of the Bobby Romano essay uses emotional phrases such as "must all work together," "glassy stare," "alert, excited gaze of a child," and "that most precious pursuit—learning," to give a dramatic, even noble finish to the essay. You can even use humor, if appropriate, but a dramatic close will remind the reader you are serious, even passionate, about what you believe.

REVISING, EDITING, AND PROOFREADING

Once you've written the essay, it's time to edit it for grammar, punctuation, and spelling. Reviewing important areas of concern before the exam will strengthen your skills as you write the rough, working draft.

REVISING AND ORGANIZING THE PARAGRAPHS

The unit of work for revising is "the paragraph." After you have written what you want to say based on your pre-writing list, spend about **ten minutes** revising your draft, looking to see if you need to indent for paragraphs anywhere. If you do, make a little proofreader's mark (¶) to indicate that you think a paragraph should begin at that point. Check to see if you want to add anything that would make your point of view more convincing. Be sure to supply useful transitions to keep up the flow of your ideas. If you don't have room on the paper, or if your new paragraph shows up out of order, add that paragraph and indicate with a number or some other mark where you want it to go. Check to make sure that you provide examples and illustrate your statements.

POLISHING AND EDITING THE ESSAY SENTENCES

If the unit of work for revising is the paragraph, the unit of work for editing is the sentence. In **the last five to ten minutes**, check your paper for mistakes by editing.

POLISHING CHECKLIST

- Are all your sentences really sentences, or have you written some fragments or run-on sentences?

- Are you using your vocabulary correctly?

- Have you used some inappropriate words that you would never use with your history teacher?

- Did you leave out punctuation anywhere? Did you capitalize correctly? Did you check for commas, periods, and quotation marks?

Be sure to **read every word** during this time and make corrections as you go.

COMMON WRITING ERRORS

The four writing errors most often made by beginning writers are run-ons (also known as fused sentences), fragments, lack of subject-verb agreement, and incorrect use of object:

1. **Run-ons:** "She swept the floor it was dirty" is a run-on, because the pronoun "it" stands as a noun subject and starts a new sentence. A period or semicolon is needed after "floor."

2. **Fragments:** "Before Jimmy learned how to play baseball" is a fragment, even though it has a subject and verb (Jimmy learned). The word

"before" fragmentizes the clause, and the reader needs to know what happened before Jimmy learned how to play baseball.

3. **Problems with subject-verb agreement**: "Either Maria or Robert are going to the game," is incorrect because either Maria is going or Robert is going, but not both. The sentence should say, "Either Maria or Robert is going to the game."

4. **Incorrect object**: Probably the most common offender in this area is saying "between you and I," which sounds nice but is incorrect. "Between" is a preposition which takes the objective case, "me." So you always say "between you and me."

CLAST graders also cite lack of thought, misspellings, incorrect pronoun or use of antecedent, and lack of development as frequently occurring problems. Keep in mind: clear, coherent handwriting always works to your advantage. Readers will appreciate an essay they can read with ease.

Refer to the English Language Skills Review section for more information on common grammatical errors and how to correct them.

FIVE WORDS WEAK WRITERS OVERUSE

Weak and beginning writers overuse the vague pronouns "you, we, they, this, and it," often without telling exactly who or what is represented by the pronoun.

Beginning writers often **shift to second person "you,"** when the writer means, "a person." This shift confuses readers and weakens the flow of the essay. Although "you" is commonly accepted in creative writing, journalism, and other arenas, for the purpose of a short, formal essay, it's best to avoid "you" altogether.

"We" is another pronoun that should be avoided. If by "we," the writer means "Americans" or "society" or some other group, then say so.

"They" is misused in essay writing, because it is so overused in conversation: "I went to the doctor, and they told me to take some medicine." Tell who "they" are.

"This" is usually used incorrectly without a referent: "She told me she received a present. This sounded good to me." This what? This idea? This news? This present? Be clear, and don't make your readers guess about what you mean. The word "this" should be followed by a noun or referent.

"It" is a common problem among weak writers. To what does "it" refer? Your readers want to know and won't appreciate vagueness, so take the time to be clear and complete in your expression of ideas.

VERB TENSE: STAY IN THE SAME TIME ZONE

Make sure to remain in the same verb tense in which you began your essay. If you start in the past, make sure all verbs are past tense. Staying in the same verb tense improves the continuity and flow of ideas. Avoid phrases such as "now was," a confusing blend of present and past. Consistency of time is essential to the reader's understanding.

USING YOUR OWN VOCABULARY

Is it a good idea on the CLAST essay or any other essay to use big words that sound good in the dictionary or thesaurus, but that you don't really use or understand? No. So **whose vocabulary should you use? Your own.** You will be most comfortable with your own language style, your own voice, your own way of saying things.

This "comfort zone" doesn't give the writer license to be informal in a formal setting or to be ungrammatical, but if you try to write in a style that is not yours, your writing will be awkward and lack a true voice.

You should certainly improve and build your vocabulary at every opportunity (reading for pleasure helps), but remember: you should not attempt to change your vocabulary level at this point.

AVOIDING THE PASSIVE VOICE

In writing, the active voice is preferable because it is emphatic and direct. A weak passive verb leaves the doer unknown or seemingly unimportant. However, the passive voice is essential when the action of the verb is more important than the doer, when the doer is unknown, or when the writer wishes to place the emphasis on the receiver of the action rather than on the doer.

THE K.I.S.S. RULE FOR GRAMMAR, SPELLING, AND PUNCTUATION

Most writers have a grammatical level they can handle, one with which they are fairly sure they are writing correctly. The K.I.S.S rule means "Keep it Simple, Sweetie." In other words, do not try to construct sentences, spell words, and use punctuation you really do not know how to use correctly.

A common example is misuse of the semicolon. Student writers use the semicolon because it looks good on paper, but few know how to use it correctly.

So, unless and until you are sure as a writer that you can use advanced techniques, K.I.S.S.! Meanwhile, practice using your own straightforward style to the best of your abilities. Brush up on grammar, punctuation, and spelling, and use a variety of sentence types, but stay true to what you know you can accomplish.

PROOFREADING WITH CARE

In the last two or three minutes, read your paper, word for word, forward and then backward from the end to the beginning. Read it out loud if possible, but read it! By doing so, you will notice a certain number of errors that you may have missed by having read forward only. For example, read the sentence before this one backward, starting with "only," and see if you spot any more errors than you read the first time. **Effective proofreading means both attention to big ideas and attention to detail.** Do not let small errors distract from your good ideas, and make sure your good ideas are served by the grammatical structures you choose.

ESSAY STRATEGIES

Before the test, you should:

- Study the review to be clear about all the in's and out's of essay writing.

- Take the diagnostic test and use the cross-referencing to clear up points of confusion.

- Be familiar with the directions that explain how to write the essay part of the exam, because the actual directions will be similar.

During the test, you should:

- Take a stand on the issue presented and don't back down. You should acknowledge opposing viewpoints, but make sure yours is clearly and strongly stated.

- Use a little time to brainstorm and organize your thoughts with lists, pictures, outlines, and whatever helps you make sense of your ideas.

- Write a quick, working draft of the essay on scratch paper. Don't edit along the way, but circle problem areas, or jot notes to yourself about changes you want to make in the final draft.

After writing your essay, you should:

- Do a quick reading for soundness and organization of ideas. Make sure your essay clearly and strongly states your point of view, along with logical support and defense of your ideas.

- Proofread your essay for grammar, spelling, and punctuation, and make revisions.

- Copy the final version of your essay onto the lined pages of the Writing Sample answer sheet.

- If time allows, do a final reading to make sure you are satisfied with the outcome.

DRILL: ESSAY WRITING

<u>DIRECTIONS:</u> Write a 300 to 600 word essay on the topic given.

TOPIC:

In the last 20 years, the deterioration of the environment has become a growing concern among both scientists and ordinary citizens. Choose one pressing environmental problem, explain its negative impact, and discuss possible solutions.

ESSAY WRITING SKILLS

ANSWER KEY

DRILL: ESSAY WRITING

This "Answer Key" provides sample essays which represent possible responses to the essay topic. Compare your own response to those given on the next few pages. Allow the strengths and weaknesses of the sample essays help you to critique your own essay and to improve your writing skills.

POOR ESSAY

The most pressing environmental problem today is that lots of people and companies don't care about the environment, and they do lots of things that hurt the environment.

People throw littur out car windows and don't use trash cans, even if their all over a park, soda cans and fast food wrappers are all over the place. Cigarette butts are the worst cause the filters never rot. Newspapers and junk mail get left to blow all over the neighborhood, and beer bottles to.

Companies pollute the air and the water. Sometimes the ground around a company has lots of tocsins in it. Now companies can buy credits from other companies that let them pollute the air even more. They dump all kinds of chemacals into lakes and rivers that kills off the fish and causes acid rain and kills off more fish and some trees and small animuls and insects and then noone can go swimming or fishing in the lake.

Too many people drive instead of taking the bus and they don't tune the cars and so they could avoid pollution if they would just take car of the car but they don't and so the car's emissions are too high and makes smog and effects the ozone layer.

People need to respect the environment because we only have one planet, and if we keep polluting it pretty soon nothing will grow and then even the people will die.

WHY THIS ESSAY IS POOR

The writer of this essay does not define his or her thesis for this essay. Because of this lack of a clear thesis, the reader is left to infer the topic from the body of the essay. It is possible to perceive the writer's intended thesis; however, the support for this thesis is very superficial. The writer presents a list of common complaints about polluters, without any critical discussion of the problems and possible solutions. Many sentences are run-on sentences and the writer has made several spelling errors. While the author manages to communicate his or her position on the issue, he or she does so on such a superficial level and with so many errors in usage and mechanics that the writer fails to demonstrate an ability to effectively communicate.

AVERAGE ESSAY

A pressing environmental problem today is the way we are cutting down too many trees and not planting any replacements for them. Trees are beneficial in many ways, and without them, many environmental problems would be much worse.

One of the ways trees are beneficial is that, like all plants, they take in carbon dioxide and produce oxygen. They can actually help clean the air this way. When too many trees are cut down in a small area, the air in that area is not as good and can be unhealthy to breath.

Another way trees are beneficial is that they provide homes for many types of birds, insects, and animals. When all the trees in an area are cut down, these animals lose their homes and sometimes they can die out and become extinct that way. Like the spotted owls in Oregon, that the loggers wanted to cut down the trees they lived in. If the loggers did cut down all the old timber stands that the spotted owls lived in, the owls would have become extinct.

But the loggers say that if they can't cut the trees down then they will be out of work, and that peoples' jobs are more important than birds. But this is the attitude that has led to so many species getting extinct. People need to realize that destroying even one specie can throw the whole food chain out of balance and then other species die off too.

The loggers can do two things—they can either get training so they can do other jobs, or they can do what they should have done all along, and start replanting trees. For every mature tree they cut down, they should have to plant at least one tree seedling. If logging companies would do that, then pretty soon, we would have all of our forests again, and there would never be a shortage of lumber. Many species that have almost died out might grow stronger again, too. This would help the economy too because the loggers would have more work, and the price of lumber would go down, which would make the cost of new housing go down too.

Another problem with cutting down too many trees can be seen in the tropical rain forests, where so many trees are being cut down that it is said that dozens of species of plants and animals are becoming extinct every day! The real tragedy is that a lot of these plants might have medicinal value—some of them might even have given us the cure for cancer, but we'll never know.

The people who live near the rain forests want the land for their crops or for grazing their animals. They think the land is really rich because this really lush forest is there, but really, it is the forest itself that keeps the land from being desolate. The roots of the big trees hold the soil so that the other plants can grow. When the big trees are cut down, there is nothing left to hold the soil and so it all erodes away in the monsoon season. The land doesn't have all the minerals needed for a lot of crops, either, so in the end there will just be big deserts where the rain forests were.

People need to teach the people who are cutting down the rain forests how to make the land they already have be more productive. If they knew how to do things like rotate crops and irrigate, they could get by with less land for farming.

Cutting down the trees that we need for life, and that lots of other species depend on, is a big environmental problem that has a lot of long term consaquences. Trees are too important for all of us to cut them down without thinking about the future.

WHY THIS ESSAY IS AVERAGE

This essay has a clear thesis, which the author does support with good examples. But the writer shifts between the chosen topic, which is that indiscriminate tree-cutting is a pressing environmental problem, and a list of the ways in which trees are beneficial and a discussion about the logging profession. Also, while there are few mistakes in usage and mechanics, the writer does have some problems with sentence structure. The writing is pedestrian and the writer does not elaborate on the topic as much as he or she could have. The writer failed to provide the kind of critical analysis that the topic required.

EXCELLENT ESSAY

There are many pressing environmental problems facing both this country and the world today. Pollution, the misuse and squandering of resources, and the cavalier attitude many people express all contribute to the problem. But one of the most pressing problems this country faces is the apathetic attitude many Americans have towards recycling.

Studies have shown that if Americans would just recycle the Sunday newspaper, we could save over 500,000 trees a year! There have been other studies that clearly show that the benefits of recycling plastic, glass, aluminum, and other solid household waste would have similar results. Unfortunately, less than half of us recycle regularly, and even those who do recycle do not recycle everything.

Some municipalities have begun to take matters into their own hands and have passed laws that legally require residents to recycle. New York City, for example, recently passed laws requiring all apartment and condominium complexes to recycle. Many communities in other parts of the East also have mandatory recycling programs. But these programs frequently limit compulsory recycling to glass, aluminum cans, and newspaper, while tons of plastic, aluminum foil, magazines, and junk mail still go into landfills. And these obligatory recycling laws are still very uncommon in other parts of the country that are not faced with the problem of lack of landfill space.

Why is mandatory recycling so imperative? There are several reasons. First, recycling previously used materials conserves precious national resources. Many people never stop to think that reserves of metal ores are not unlimited. There is only so much gold, silver, tin, and other metals in the ground. Once it has all been mined, there will never be any more unless we recycle what has already been used.

Second, the United States daily generates more solid waste than any other country on earth. Our disposable consumer culture consumes fast food meals in paper or styrofoam containers, uses disposable diapers with plastic liners that do not biodegrade, receives pounds, if not tons, of unsolicited junk mail every year, and relies more and more on prepackaged rather than fresh food. All of these factors, and more, mean that we are burying ourselves in garbage. Cities on the East Coast, where land is already scarce, have either shipped their garbage out of state to an area that has plenty of open land left, or have shipped it out to sea and dumped it off shore. But these solutions are, by their very nature, temporary. Recently, more stringent regulations have been passed forbidding off shore dumping and interstate transportation of garbage. There have been newspaper stories detailing the fruitless, months-long trips of garbage barges hunting for a port that will let them off load tons of rotting, stinking garbage.

Landfills are becoming so full that their garbage heaps tower ten, twenty, or even thirty feet in the air, posing serious health problems for surrounding neighborhoods. But there is nowhere else to put all the trash. The sensible solution, then, is to reduce the amount of trash that has to go into the landfills. Recycling accomplishes that goal.

Another important benefit of recycling is the advantages for the environment in the form of reduced pollution. Recycling aluminum for cans reducing the emissions by 95%. Recycling plastic also produces less toxic gasses and less waste. Paper recycling also requires less processing than producing new paper, which also reduces the water and air pollution associated with paper mills.

Many people claim that they are willing to recycle, but that it is too complicated to separate all the different types of waste. This is a feeble excuse. All that is necessary are three or four bins and a regular trashcan. One bin can be used for aluminum, one for glass, one for plastic, and the last for newspaper, while food scraps and other non-recyclable garbage can go in the trashcan. Many communities offer curbside pickup of recyclable materials, even in areas where recycling is not mandatory. Some communities even pickup discarded appliances and used automotive oil.

Other countries have already taken steps to require mandatory recycling. Australia, for example, has encouraged cities to establish recycling programs and provided government grants to set up these programs. Americans pride themselves on being world leaders, but we have been criminally slow to deal with the problem of garbage.

Perhaps the solution is to take another approach and appeal to the country's patriotic spirit to encourage recycling. During and after World War II, this country conducted paper and scrap metal drives to support the war effort. The materials collected this way were recycled to produce the necessary wartime commodities faster and for a lower cost. Scrap metal, for example, was melted down to be recast as shell casings for bullets and artillery ammunition. If Americans could be inspired to unite and collect recyclable materials in a similar way, maybe recycling programs would be more successful. There have been some successful attempts to teach school age children to recycle at school and at home. Many adults who recycle say that they do so because their children insist on it!

Another aspect of the problem that needs to be addressed is the cost of recycling. Many communities that have mandated recycling complain that they are losing money with their recycling programs. Companies that pick up and haul recycled goods claim that higher fees are necessary because they have to separate the materials. But if the consumer separates materials at home and then the hauling company collects each type of material separately, the costs should not be so high. Some companies are already using collection trucks with separate compartments for glass, plastic, and aluminum. Another solution that is being used in some areas are conveyor belts that use magnets to separate non-aluminum metals, and then use workers who sort plastic, aluminum, and glass into different bins. But the most important step is to encourage companies that produce recyclable products to reuse these materials. If a company that made glassware received a tax break for using recycled glass, and the size of that benefit increased with the amount of recycled material the company used, it would provide a real incentive for manufacturers. Perhaps a combination of all of these possibilities is the answer.

Regardless of what the final answer is, the problem is clear. We have to stop covering our land with garbage, and the best ways to do this are to reduce our dependence on prepackaged goods and to minimize the amount of solid waste disposed of in landfills. The best way to reduce solid waste is to recycle it. Americans need to band together to recycle, to preserve our irreplaceable natural resources, reduce pollution, and preserve our precious environment.

WHY THIS ESSAY IS EXCELLENT

This essay presents a clearly defined thesis and the writer elaborates on this thesis in a thoughtful and sophisticated manner. Various aspects of the problem under consideration are presented and explored, along with possible solutions. The support provided for the writer's argument is convincing and logical. There are few usage or mechanical errors to interfere with the writer's ability to communicate effectively. This writer demonstrates a comprehensive understanding of the rules of written English.

Chapter 4

Reading Skills Review

Chapter 4

READING SKILLS REVIEW

Adequate reading skills are crucial for success in the academic and business worlds. Close and accurate reading skills involve more than simple reading and retention; university students must be able to recognize patterns and relationships within and between the form and content of written works. Students must also be able to understand, identify, and analyze the author's argument, while recognizing how language is used in the text to communicate that argument.

The CLAST Reading Skills section measures your critical reading ability: the ability to analyze and respond to written text. This is a skill you are expected to use throughout college and beyond.

All the information you will need to answer these questions can be found directly in the passage. This means you must pay very close attention to the ideas presented in the passage, and the manner of presentation. As you read, do not be afraid to analyze the text critically. Be aware of bias and opinion thinly disguised as fact. Consider the Reading Test a game of detection: you are the detective searching for the right answers to the questions. You will find the clues to the correct answers in the passages themselves. Just as in a mystery story, some of the clues will be less obvious than others—but they will be there!

THE DIRECTIONS

The Reading Test on the CLAST is taken together with the English Language Skills test during the same 80-minute period. Since the Reading Test is more time-consuming than the English Test, you should probably take the English Test first and try to leave 50 or 60 minutes for the Reading Test.

The Reading Skills section consists of a series of approximately two passages of various lengths and subject matter. Each passage is followed by multiple-choice questions. You will be asked a total of 41 questions based on these passages.

TIPS

- **Mind your watch** so that you will have time to answer all of the questions. Remember, you will have approximately one hour to answer 41 questions. Therefore, you should answer about 11 questions every 15 minutes.

- **Read the question stems first.** It's easier to find something if you know what you are looking for. Read the questions but not the answer choices, before you read the passage itself.

- **Skim the passage before reading it.** Skimming a passage is like surveying the scene of a crime: your eye roams quickly down the page, looking for clues as to what the passage is all about, what the main point is, and how that point is developed.

- **Use your pencil.** As you read the passage, mark in the margin the location of the sentence which you think best expresses the author's main point. Circle words or phrases that answer or relate to the questions you have read beforehand. And finally, use your pencil as a pacesetter. As you read, move the tip of the pencil steadily from left to right below each line of print without touching the page. This will help you to keep reading at a steady pace.

- **Read all the answer choices before answering a question.** At times you will be tempted to select one of the answers before you have read all the other choices. Don't be fooled! You may find that another answer choice is preferable.

- **Guess the answer if you are stumped.** If you can eliminate one or more wrong choices, you are in good shape. There is no penalty for guessing on this test; your score is determined only by the total number of correct answers. But once again, use your pencil: put a question mark beside that question so that you can return to it if you have time.

READING SKILLS DIAGNOSTIC TEST

The following diagnostic test is designed to help you find your strengths and weaknesses in the reading comprehension skills tested on the CLAST. The test consists of 41 questions, and the suggested time is 55 minutes. If you get questions wrong on a particular section of the Reading Skills Review, the chart following the test will direct you to the appropriate section to study.

READING SKILLS DIAGNOSTIC TEST

DIRECTIONS: Read the passage and answer the questions that follow.

Passage A (from Fyodor Dostoyevsky, "Something about Lying," 1873)

Why is everybody here lying—every single man? I am convinced that I will be immediately stopped and that people will start shouting: "Oh, what nonsense, by no means everybody! You have no topic, and so you are inventing things in order to begin in a more imposing fashion." I have already been
5 upbraided for the lack of themes. But the point is that now I am earnestly convinced of the universality of our lying. One lives 50 years with an idea, one perceives and feels it, and all of a sudden it appears in such an aspect as to make it seem that one had hitherto not known it at all.

Lately, I was suddenly struck by the thought that in Russia, among our
10 educated classes, there cannot be even one man who wouldn't be addicted to lying. This is precisely because among us even quite honest people may be lying. I am certain that in other nations, in the overwhelming majority of them, only scoundrels are lying; they are lying for the sake of material gain, that is, with directly criminal intent.

15 Well, in our case, even the most esteemed people may be lying for no reason at all, and with most honorable aims. We are lying almost invariably for the sake of hospitality. One wishes to create in the listener an aesthetical impression, to give him pleasure, and so one lies even, so to speak, sacrificing oneself to the listener.

1. The central idea of this passage is that

    (A) people all over the world lie for the sake of material gain.

    (B) only scoundrels lie; respectable people do not.

    (C) everybody in Russia is lying, almost always for the sake of the listener.

    (D) there can be nothing wrong with lying since everybody is doing it.

2. In developing the passage, the organizational pattern used by the author could be described as

    (A) definition.

    (B) statement and clarification.

    (C) cause and effect.

    (D) classification.

3. In this passage, what is the meaning of the word "upbraided" (line 5)?

    (A) Reprimanded   (C) Distinguished

    (B) Complimented   (D) Noticed

4. What is the relationship between the sentence beginning in line 11 ("This is precisely…") and the sentence beginning in line 9 ("Lately, I was…")?

    (A) Statement and clarification

    (B) Generalization and example

    (C) Comparison and contrast

    (D) Cause and effect

Passage B (from Thomas Hardy, "The Profitable Reading of Fiction," 1888)

If we speak of deriving good from a story, we usually mean something more than the gain of pleasure during the hours of its perusal. Nevertheless, to get pleasure out of a book is a beneficial and profitable thing, if the pleasure be of a kind which, while doing no moral injury, affords relaxation and relief when
5 the mind is overstrained or sick of itself. The prime remedy in such cases is change of scene, by which change of the material scene is not necessarily implied. A sudden shifting of the mental perspective into a fictitious world, combined with rest, is well known to be often as efficacious for renovation as a corporeal journey afar.

10 In such a case the shifting of scene should manifestly be as complete as if the reader had taken the hind seat on a witch's broomstick. The town man finds what he seeks in novels of the country, the countryman in novels of society, the indoor class generally in outdoor novels, the villager in novels of the mansion, the aristocrat in novels of the cottage.

15 The narrative must be of a somewhat absorbing kind, if not absolutely fascinating. To discover a book or books which shall possess, in addition to the special scenery, the special action required, may be a matter of some difficulty, though not always of such difficulty as to be insuperable; and it may be asserted that after every variety of spiritual fatigue there is to be found refresh-

20 ment, if not restoration, in some antithetic realm of ideas which lies waiting in the pages of romance.

5. The first sentence of this passage indicates that the author's purpose is to

   (A)   suggest that people read only for pleasure.

   (B)   analyze the benefits of reading stories.

   (C)   defend the view that reading is a waste of time.

   (D)   entertain the reader by telling a story.

6. In this passage the author shows bias in favor of

   (A)   reading nonfiction.   (C)   reading for relaxation.

   (B)   reading thrillers.   (D)   city life over country life.

7. The image of the reader taking a ride on a witch's broomstick (line 11) is used to illustrate

   (A)   the frivolousness of reading merely for pleasure.

   (B)   the complete change of scenery which reading can provide.

   (C)   the wickedness of trying to escape reality.

   (D)   the dangerous power of storytellers.

8. From this passage you could infer that the author

   (A)   is a novelist trying to promote the reading of novels.

   (B)   disapproves of pleasure reading.

   (C)   believes there are other benefits to reading stories.

   (D)   leads an unhappy life.

Passage C (from Heinrich Heine, "London and the English," 1828)

    The stranger who wanders through the great streets of London, and does not chance right into the regular quarters of the multitude, sees little or nothing of the fearful misery existing there. Only here and there at the mouth of some dark alley stands a ragged woman with a suckling babe at her weak
5 breast, and begs with her eyes. Perhaps if those eyes are still beautiful, we glance into them, and are shocked at the world of wretchedness visible within. The common beggars are old people, generally blacks, who stand at the corners of the streets cleaning pathways—a very necessary thing in muddy London— and ask for "coppers" in reward. It is in the dusky twilight that Poverty with
10 her mates Vice and Crime glide forth from their lairs. They shun daylight the more anxiously since their wretchedness there contrasts more cruelly with the pride of wealth which glitters everywhere; only Hunger sometimes drives them at noonday from their dens, and then they stand with silent, speaking eyes, staring beseechingly at the rich merchant who hurries along, busy and jingling
15 gold, or at the lazy lord who, like a surfeited god, rides by on his high horse, casting now and then an aristocratically indifferent glance at the mob below, as though they were swarming ants, or rather a mass of baser beings, whose joys and sorrows have nothing in common with his feelings.

9.   The author of this passage has created a tone that could be described as

    (A)   apathetic.   (C)   bitter.

    (B)   arrogant.   (D)   sympathetic.

10.   What is the relationship between the sentence beginning on line 3 ("Only here and there...") and the first sentence ("The stranger who...")?

    (A)   Contrast

    (B)   Statement and clarification

    (C)   Addition

    (D)   Generalization and example

11.   Which statement below most accurately describes the main idea of this passage?

    (A)   London is a marvelous city to visit if you avoid the shabby sections.

    (B)   The wretchedness of London's poor is not obvious to the casual visitor.

(C)   In London the rich and the poor live side by side in harmony.

(D)   London should do something to hide the poor from the public eye.

Passage D

The Democrats obviously know how to handle the economy better than the Republicans. Right after Bill Clinton, a Democrat, was elected President, the economy began to improve.

12.   Is the argument in the above sentences valid or invalid?

(A)   Valid

(B)   Invalid

Passage E (from Edgar Allan Poe, "Philosophy of Furniture," 1840)

The rage for glitter—because its idea has become, as we before observed, confounded with that of magnificence in the abstract—has led us, also, to the exaggerated employment of mirrors. We line our dwellings with great British plates, and then imagine we have done a fine thing. Now, the slightest thought
5   will be sufficient to convince any one, who has an eye at all, of the ill effect of numerous looking-glasses, and especially of large ones. Regarded apart from its reflection, the mirror presents a continuous, flat, colorless, unrelieved surface—a thing always and obviously unpleasant. Considered as a reflector, it is potent in producing a monstrous and odious uniformity; and the evil is here
10   aggravated, not in merely direct proportion with the augmentation of its sources, but in a ratio constantly increasing. In fact, a room with four or five mirrors arranged at random is, for all purposes of artistic show, a room of no shape at all. If we add to this evil the attendant glitter upon glitter, we have a perfect farrago of discordant and displeasing effects. The veriest bumpkin, on entering
15   an apartment so bedizened, would be instantly aware of something wrong, although he might be altogether unable to assign a cause for his dissatisfaction. But let the same person be led into a room tastefully furnished, and he would be startled into an exclamation of pleasure and surprise.

13.   The first sentence of this paragraph indicates that the author's purpose is to

(A)   define the abstract term "magnificence."

(B)   criticize the overuse of mirrors in decoration.

(C)　show how the use of mirrors has led to the popularity of "glitter."

(D)　compare the usefulness of mirrors with the usefulness of windows.

14.　The author's statement beginning in line 4 ("Now the slightest thought...") is a statement of

(A)　fact.

(B)　opinion.

15.　In this context, the word "augmentatation" (line 10) means

(A)　quality.　　　　　　　(C)　variety.

(B)　decline.　　　　　　　(D)　increase.

16.　The author of this passage has created a tone that could be described as

(A)　critical.　　　　　　　(C)　optimistic.

(B)　amused.　　　　　　　(D)　nostalgic.

17.　In developing the passage, the organizational pattern used by the author could be described as

(A)　statement and clarification.

(B)　classification.

(C)　addition.

(D)　time order.

Passage F (from Leo Tolstoy, "On Art," c. 1895-1897)

　　　The process of "creation"—one common to all men and therefore known to each of us by inner experience—occurs as follows: a man surmises or dimly feels something that is perfectly new to him, which he has never heard of from anybody. This something new impresses him, and in ordinary conversation he
5　points out to others what he perceives, and to his surprise finds that what is apparent to him is quite unseen by them. They do not see or do not feel what he tells them of. This isolation, discord, disunion from others, at first disturbs him, and verifying his own perception the man tries in different ways to communicate to others what he has seen, felt, or understood; but these others
10　still do not understand what he communicates to them, or do not understand it as he understands or feels it. And the man begins to be troubled by a doubt

as to whether he imagines and dimly feels something that does not really exist, or whether others do not see and do not feel something that does exist. And to solve this doubt he directs his whole strength to the task of making his discov-
15 ery so clear that there cannot be the smallest doubt, either for himself or for other people, as to the existence of what he has seen, understood, or felt, others at once see, understand, and feel as he does, and it is this effort to make clear and indubitable to himself and to others what both to others and to him had been dim and obscure, that is the source from which flows the production of
20 man's spiritual activity in general, or what we call works of art—which widen man's horizon and oblige him to see what had not been perceived before.

18. The main idea expressed in this passage is that

  (A) works of art arise from an individual's attempt to clarify a new percep-
       tion or discovery.

  (B) society little appreciates the artists in its midst and is undeserving of
       their artistic creations.

  (C) society forces the creative individual into conformity to its common-
       place perceptions of the world.

  (D) the artistic individual never doubts his own superior perceptions.

19. What is the relationship between the sentence beginning on line 11 ("And the
     man begins...") and the previous sentence beginning on line 7 ("This isola-
     tion, discord...")?

  (A) Statement and clarification

  (B) Cause and effect

  (C) Addition

  (D) Generalization and example

20. The fact that the man tries first to communicate his discovery to others in
     ordinary conversation (line 5) is used to show

  (A) how the impetus for creation arises from a need to communicate.

  (B) how little attention ordinary people pay to the artists in society.

  (C) that creative people are ordinary in every way.

  (D) the difficulty of being an artist these days.

21.   The statement in lines 17-21 ("it is this effort...perceived before") is a statement of

(A)   fact.

(B)   opinion.

Passage G (from Miguel de Unamuno, "Large and Small Towns," 1917)

Great cities are levelling; they lift up the low and depress the high; they exalt mediocrity and abase superlativeness—the result of the action of the mass, as powerful in social life as in chemistry.

Soon after I came to this ancient city of Salamanca which has now become
5   so dear to me, a city of some thirty thousand souls, I wrote to a friend and told him that if after two year's residence here he should be informed that I spent my time playing cards, taking siestas and strolling round the square for a couple of hours every day, he might give me up for lost; but if at the end of that time I should still be studying, meditating, writing, battling for culture in
10   the public arena, he might take it that I was better off here than in Madrid. And so it has proved to be.

I remember that Guglielmo Ferrero's conclusion, based upon a review of ancient Greece, of the Italy of the Renaissance and of the Germany of a century ago, is that for the life of the spirit, small cities of a population like
15   that of Salamanca are the best—better than very small towns or large ones of over a hundred thousand inhabitants.

This depends, of course, upon the quality of the spirit in question. I am convinced that the monastic cloister, which so often atrophies the soul and reduces the average intelligence to a lamentable slavery to routine, has in
20   certain exceptional cases exalted the spirit by its arduous discipline.

Great cities are essentially democratic, and I must confess that I feel an invincible platonic mistrust of democracies. In great cities culture is diffused but vulgarized. People abandon the quiet reading of books to go to the theatre, that school of vulgarity; they feel the need of being together; the gregarious
25   instinct enslaves them; they must be seeing one another.

22.   What does the sentence beginning in line 17 ("This depends...") do in relation to the sentence beginning in line 12 ("I remember that...")?

(A)   It draws a conclusion based on the statement beginning in line 12.

(B)   It offers a qualification of the statement beginning in line 12.

(C) It gives a specific example of what is stated in the sentence beginning in line 12.

(D) It flatly contradicts the statement beginning in line 12.

23. From this passage, you could infer that

(A) the author believes that great cities are essentially democratic.

(B) given a choice, the author would prefer to live in a small city.

(C) the author has never lived in a small town or out in the country.

(D) the author believes that democracy is the best form of government.

24. Identify the statement below which gives the most accurate statement of the central idea of this passage.

(A) Great cities tend to reduce everyone to the same level and are therefore not conducive to the life of the spirit.

(B) The cloistered life of monks and nuns is perhaps the best way of life for the person interested in spiritual growth.

(C) Smaller cities are not conducive to spiritual and intellectual growth because they are too sleepy and inactive.

(D) As far as the spiritual life is concerned, great cities are superior both to small cities and to life in the country.

25. In developing the passage, the organizational pattern used by the author could be described

(A) simple listing.

(B) time order.

(C) classification.

(D) statement and clarification.

Passage H

Those senators in Washington are all millionaires. They don't know anything about the problems of the average working person, and even if they did know, they wouldn't care because they have no financial worries themselves.

26. The argument in the above sentences is

(A) valid.

(B) invalid.

Passage I (from Oscar Wilde, "Impressions of America," 1882)

The first thing that struck me on landing in America was that if the Americans are not the most well-dressed people in the world, they are the most comfortably dressed. Men are seen there with the dreadful chimney-pot hat, but there are very few hatless men; men wear the shocking swallow-tail coat,
5 but few are to be seen with no coat at all. There is an air of comfort in the appearance of the people which is a marked contrast to that seen in this country, where, too often, people are seen in close contact with rags.

The next thing particularly noticeable is that everybody seems in a hurry to catch a train. This is a state of things which is not favourable to poetry or
10 romance. Had Romeo or Juliet been in a constant state of anxiety about trains, or had their minds been agitated by the question of return-tickets, Shakespeare could not have given us those lovely balcony scenes which are so full of poetry and pathos.

America is the noisiest country that ever existed. One is waked up in the
15 morning not by the singing of the nightingale, but by the steam whistle. It is surprising that the sound practical sense of the Americans does not reduce this intolerable noise. All Art depends upon exquisite and delicate sensibility, and such continual turmoil must ultimately be destructive of the musical faculty.

27. The example of Romeo and Juliet in line 10 is introduced in order to

   (A) criticize Americans for their ignorance of Shakespeare.

   (B) suggest humorously that their poetic and romantic world would be impossible in America.

   (C) underscore the need for silence if Art is to thrive.

   (D) contrast the drabness of American dress with Romeo and Juliet's exquisite dress.

28. The word "faculty," as used in line 18 means

   (A) professors.   (C) instrument.

   (B) a power of the mind. (D) ease.

29. The first sentence of this passage ("The first thing…comfortably dressed.") indicates that the author's purpose is to

   (A) give a comprehensive, objective analysis of American society.

   (B) compare the ways Americans dress with the ways Europeans dress.

(C)   offer some personal observations on America from a foreigner's perspective.

(D)   ridicule Americans for the way they dress, eat, and live.

30.   The author's statement, beginning in line 17, that "All Art depends upon exquisite and delicate sensibility" is a statement of

(A)   fact.

(B)   opinion.

Passage J

The tiny island, shaped like a three-quarter moon, was situated about two hundred yards offshore. At first glance, it seemed to be composed of nothing but rock and shell. _____(1)_____ when we disembarked from our little rowboat, we could see clumps of light brown grass or weed flourishing here and there. Other than those meager signs of life, _____(2)_____, the island was quite barren. We walked carefully around its perimeter, searching for signs of previous visitors—a beer can or soda can, perhaps, an old shoe, a discarded matchbox. We were strangely disappointed to see no litter at all. _____(3)_____, just as we were heading back to the boat, we spotted the gold coin half buried in the sand.

31.   The most appropriate word for blank (1) would be

(A)   And.   (C)   But.

(B)   Therefore.   (D)   Moreover.

32.   The most appropriate word(s) for blank (2) would be

(A)   however.   (C)   whereupon.

(B)   of course.   (D)   hereafter.

33.   The most appropriate word for blank (3) would be

(A)   Since.   (C)   Because.

(B)   Then.   (D)   After.

Passage K (from Alexis de Tocqueville, *Democracy in America*, 1840)

In democratic armies the desire of advancement is almost universal: it is ardent, tenacious, perpetual; it is strengthened by all other desires and extinguished only with life itself. But it is easy to see that, of all armies in the world, those in which advancement must be slowest in time of peace are the armies of
5 democratic countries. As the number of commissions is naturally limited while the number of competitors is almost unlimited, and as the strict law of equality is over all alike, none can make rapid progress; many can make no progress at all. Thus the desire of advancement is greater and the opportunities of advancement fewer than elsewhere. All the ambitious spirits of a democratic army
10 are consequently ardently desirous of war, because war makes vacancies and warrants the violation of that law of seniority which is the sole privilege natural to democracy.

We thus arrive at this singular consequence, that, of all armies, those most ardently desirous of war are democratic armies, and of all nations, those most
15 fond of peace are democratic nations; and what makes these facts still more extraordinary is that these contrary effects are produced at the same time by the principle of equality.

34. The central idea of this passage is that

   (A) democratic armies desire war, whereas democratic nations desire peace.

   (B) no one can be promoted in a democratic army because all are equal.

   (C) war is the only means by which an army can justify its existence.

   (D) in a democracy, war is justified by the common will of the people.

35. The author of this passage has created a tone that could be described as

   (A) objective.   (C) malicious.

   (B) impassioned.   (D) depressed.

36. The author implies that

   (A) democracy is an inferior form of government.

   (B) the principle of equality has both good and bad effects.

   (C) armies everywhere should be abolished because they become corrupted.

   (D) democracy is the best form of government ever devised.

Passage L (from Thomas B. Macaulay, "History," 1828)

The effect of historical reading is analogous, in many respects, to that produced by foreign travel. The student, like the tourist, is transported into a new state of society. He sees new fashions. He hears new modes of expression. His mind is enlarged by contemplating the wide diversities of laws, of morals,

5 and of manners. But men may travel far, and return with minds as contracted as if they had never stirred from their own market-town. In the same manner, men may know the dates of many battles and the genealogies of many royal houses, and yet be no wiser. Most people look at past times as princes look at foreign countries. More than one illustrious stranger has landed on our island

10 amidst the shouts of a mob, has dined with the King, has hunted with the master of the stag-hounds, has seen the guards reviewed, and a knight of the garter installed, has cantered along Regent Street, has visited Saint Paul's, and noted down its dimensions; and has then departed, thinking that he has seen England. He has, in fact, seen a few public buildings, public men, and public

15 ceremonies. But of the vast and complex system of society, of the fine shades of national character, of the practical operation of government and laws, he knows nothing. He who would understand these things rightly must not confine his observations to palaces and solemn days. He must see ordinary men as they appear in their ordinary business and in their ordinary pleasures. He must

20 mingle in the crowds of the exchange and the coffee-house. He must obtain admittance to the convivial table and the domestic hearth. He must bear with vulgar expression. He must not shrink from exploring even the retreats of misery. He who wishes to understand the condition of mankind in former ages must proceed on the same principle. If he attends only to public transactions,

25 to wars, congresses, and debates, his studies will be as unprofitable as the travels of those imperial, royal, and serene sovereigns who form their judgment of our island from having gone in state to a few fine sights, and from having held formal conferences with a few great officers.

37. In developing the paragraph, the organizational pattern used by the author could be described as

   (A) comparison.   (C) cause and effect.

   (C) time order.   (D) classification.

38. The sentence (line 5) "But men may travel far, and return with minds as contracted as if they had never stirred from their own market-town" is a statement of

    (A) fact.

    (B) opinion.

39. This paragraph indicates that the author's purpose is to

    (A) describe what the typical visitor to England sees.

    (B) point out the differences between traveling and reading history.

    (C) show how the study of history is similar to foreign travel.

    (D) mock those who think they know England but do not.

Passage M

Jonathan is an outstanding baseball player and has done great work with the kids at the YMCA, so I am sure he will have great success as a computer sales representative.

40. Is the argument in the above sentences valid or invalid?

    (A) Valid

    (B) Invalid

READING SKILLS REVIEW DIAGNOSTIC TEST ANSWER KEY

Use the chart below to check your answers. If you responded incorrectly, refer to the column on the right to direct you to the review section that will help you.

Question	Answer	If you answered this question incorrectly, see the section titled:
1	C	Recognizing the Central Idea: p. 170
2	B	Identifying Organizational Pattern: p. 176
3	A	Determining Contextual Meaning p. 172
4	D	Identifying Relationships Between Sentences: p. 184
5	B	Recognizing the Author's Purpose: p. 175
6	C	Detecting Bias: p. 179
7	B	Identifying Supporting Details: p. 171
8	C	Drawing Logical Inferences and Conclusions: p. 187
9	D	Recognizing Tone: p. 181
10	A	Relationships Between Sentences: p. 184
11	B	Recognizing the Central Idea: p. 170
12	B	Recognizing Valid and Invalid Arguments: p. 185
13	B	Recognizing the Author's Purpose: p. 175
14	B	Distinguishing Between Fact and Opinion: p. 178
15	D	Determining Contextual Meaning p. 172
16	A	Recognizing Tone: p. 181
17	A	Identifying Organizational Pattern: p. 176
18	A	Recognizing the Central Idea: p. 170
19	C	Identifying Relationships Between Sentences: p. 184
20	A	Identifying Supporting Details: p. 171
21	B	Distinguishing Between Fact and Opinion: p. 178
22	B	Identifying Relationships Between Sentences: p. 184
23	B	Drawing Logical Inferences and Conclusions: p. 187
24	A	Recognizing the Central Idea: p. 170
25	D	Identifying Organizational Pattern: p. 176
26	B	Recognizing Valid and Invalid Arguments: p. 185

Question	Answer	If you answered this question incorrectly, see the section titled:
27	B	Identifying Supporting Details: p. 171
28	B	Determining Contextual Meaning: p. 172
29	C	Recognizing the Author's Purpose: p. 175
30	B	Distinguishing Between Fact and Opinion: p. 178
31	C	Identifying Relationships Within Sentences: p. 182
32	A	Identifying Relationships Within Sentences: p. 182
33	B	Identifying Relationships Within Sentences: p. 182
34	A	Recognizing the Central Idea: p. 170
35	A	Recognizing Tone: p. 181
36	B	Drawing Logical Inferences and Conclusions: p. 187
37	A	Identifying Organizational Pattern: p. 176
38	B	Distinguishing Between Fact and Opinion: p. 178
39	C	Recognizing the Author's Purpose: p. 175
40	B	Recognizing Valid and Invalid Arguments: p. 185

DETAILED EXPLANATIONS OF ANSWERS

1.   **(C)**   (C) is correct because the passage is specifically about lying in Russia. (A) contradicts reasons for lying given in the third paragraph; (B) contradicts material in the second paragraph; (D) is not implied by the passage.

2.   **(B)**   (B) is correct because the passage explains more fully the author's statement that everybody is lying. The passage does not work to show what conditions led to universal lying (C), does not divide the subject into categories (D), or seek to define any particular word or term (A).

3.   **(A)**   (A) is correct because lines 1-4 suggest that the author expected a negative response to his topic and (A) has a negative connotation. (B) has a positive meaning; (C) and (D) are more neutral.

4.   **(D)**   (D) is correct because the sentence beginning in line 12 provides a cause for the condition described in the first sentence, rather than providing a specific example of that condition (B), seeking to explain it more carefully (A), or show differences or similarities to it (C).

5.   **(B)**   (B) is correct because the author refers to gaining pleasure from reading stories without himself telling a story (D). Because the author clearly indicates that he does not believe reading is a waste of time, (C) is incorrect; he also suggests the possibility of benefits beyond reading only for pleasure, so (A) is incorrect.

6.   **(C)**   (C) is correct because the author describes reading as a pleasant means of relieving spiritual fatigue. (B) is more specific than the author is. (A) is incorrect because the author specifically refers to reading stories, a form of fiction. (D) refers to one particular example used to illustrate the relaxing effect reading can have.

7.   **(B)**   (B) is correct because the following sentence clearly describes examples of scenery changes. (A) contradicts the main point of the passage; (C) and (D) have more negative meanings than the author intended.

8.   **(C)**   (C) is correct because although the author treats the relaxing effects of reading, he refers to the possibility of "something more than the gain of pleasure…" (B) contradicts the main point of the passage. There is no evidence that the author is himself a novelist or that he leads an unhappy life, so (A) and (D) are incorrect.

9.   **(D)**   (D) is correct because the author describes poor people with sympathy; (C) is incorrect because while the author treats the rich people who ignore the poor with some bitterness, the general mood of the passage is sympathetic. The author shows no arrogance (B) towards anyone he describes, and his use of emotional language suggests that he is not at all apathetic (A).

10. **(A)** (A) is correct because the second sentence contrasts the reality of the ragged woman with the great streets which the stranger in the first sentence sees; the forcefulness of this contrast makes (D) incorrect because (D) suggests a weaker connection between the sentences. (B) is incorrect because the second sentence does not explain the first sentence more fully; (C) is incorrect because the second sentence doesn't provide a specific example of what the stranger does see.

11. **(B)** (B) is correct because the passage treats both the wretchedness of the poor and the visitor who doesn't see this wretchedness. While the author may imply (A), it is not the point he wants to make in this passage; (C) is incorrect because the author does not describe harmony between the rich and the poor; (D) contradicts the sympathetic tone of the passage.

12. **(B)** (B) is correct, because the statement relies on a post hoc argument, assuming that because the economy improved after Clinton's election, Clinton must have done something to improve it.

13. **(B)** (B) is correct because it refers to the overuse of mirrors implied by "exaggerated employment." (A) is incorrect because the author refers to "magnificence" only in passing; (C) is incorrect because it switches the causal order the author suggests— the author suggests that the popularity of glitter led to the use of mirrors, not the other way around. (D) is incorrect because the author never mentions windows.

14. **(B)** The correct response is (B). It is impossible to check the accuracy of this statement.

15. **(D)** (D) is correct because the sentence contains the word "increasing" and appears to be about something getting larger; also, the author is referring to large mirrors. (B) is incorrect because "decline" suggests something getting smaller. (A) and (C) are incorrect because they do not refer to size changes.

16. **(A)** (A) is correct because the tone of the passage is clearly negative; (B) and (C) both suggest a positive tone, and (D) suggests bittersweetness.

17. **(A)** (A) is correct because the author clarifies his initial statement with a series of sentences explaining it more fully; because the sentences clarify this point, the author does more than list point after point (C). (B) is incorrect because he never describes different categories of mirrors; (D) is incorrect because there are no references to time or chronology in the passage.

18. **(A)** (A) is correct because the passage describes the process an artist goes through as he works to communicate his new perceptions. The passage refers to the difficulties artists experience only as they are unable to communicate their ideas, making (D) incorrect; because the artist suggests that in overcoming those difficulties, the artist creates a work of art, (B) and (C) are incorrect.

19. **(C)** (C) is correct because neither sentence clearly results from the other. (B) is incorrect because the first sentence does not describe conditions leading to anything in the second sentence and vice versa. (A) is incorrect because the second sentence shows a development, not an explanation; (D) is incorrect because the second sentence provides no specific example of any general statement made in the first sentence.

20. **(A)** (A) is correct because the passage describes the ways in which the need to communicate ideas leads to the creation of art. (B) and (C) are incorrect because the author is not seeking to describe ordinariness or the responses of ordinary people, but to show what leads to actual creation of art. Because the author never refers directly to the difficulties of being an artist, now or at any other time, (D) is incorrect.

21. **(B)** (B) is the correct response. It is impossible to prove factually how works of art allow us to perceive things.

22. **(B)** (B) is correct because the second sentence develops the point made in the first sentence; since it develops rather than contradicts the point, (D) is incorrect. (C) is incorrect because the second sentence does not provide a specific example of a general statement in the first sentence. (A) is incorrect because the second statement is not conclusive.

23. **(B)** (B) is correct because the author in lines 14-16 praises small cities, and throughout the passage is critical of great cities. (A) is incorrect because the author directly states this point. (D) is incorrect because the author clearly indicates that he mistrusts democracies. There is no evidence in the passage indicating (C).

24. **(A)** (A) summarizes points the author makes in the first and last paragraphs. Because the author refers to cloisters but doesn't consider them *best* for spiritual growth, (B) is incorrect. (C) contradicts the point he makes in lines 8-11; (D) contradicts the main point of the passage.

25. **(D)** (D) is correct; the sentences in the passage explain more fully the main point of the author's argument. (A) is incorrect because rather than simply listing points, the author arranges his points to explain his main point more fully. (C) is incorrect because while he does classify cities by size, the author does this to clarify the point he wants to make about great cities. Because there is no evidence of time or chronology, (B) is incorrect.

26. **(B)** (B) is correct, because the argument is an ad hominem argument, attacking the senators for being millionaires rather than criticizing their arguments, ideas, or policies.

27. **(B)** (B) is correct. Because the author is pointing out that Romeo and Juliet did not worry about hurrying for trains, (A) and (D) are incorrect; (C) is incorrect because the paragraph containing line 10 about hurry, not noise.

28. **(B)** (B) is correct; the third paragraph describes noise and hearing and uses the word "sensibility," all of which are abstract ideas related to the way people's minds perceive things. (D) is incorrect, because while "ease" is an abstract idea, it does not relate to how people perceive things; (A) and (C) are not abstract ideas.

29. **(C)** (C) is correct. While the author does seem to ridicule Americans, he does not suggest in the first sentence that he intends to, making (D) incorrect. (B) is incorrect because the author never mentions how Europeans dress. (A) is incorrect not only because the author's tone is not objective, but his treatment of American society is not comprehensive, but very focused on specific things such as dress, hurry, and noise.

30. **(B)** This is a statement of opinion. Whether or not continual turmoil will destroy the musical faculty, or whether or not Art depends on this sensibility, is not something that can be factually checked.

31. **(C)** (C) is correct because the information in that sentence contrasts with the information in the previous sentence; (A) and (D) are words indicating addition, and (B) suggests cause and effect.

32. **(A)** (A) is correct; the sentence contrasts with the previous sentence. (C) and (D) indicate chronology and (B) indicates agreement, none of which are indicated in this sentence.

33. **(B)** (B) is correct because the sentence requires a word involving the passing of time; (D) also suggests time passing, but the previous sentence provides no "before" information corresponding to "after." (A) and (C) are incorrect because no cause and effect is suggested.

34. **(A)** (A) is correct, because it contains important points made in each paragraph. While (B) is implied, it is not the central idea of the passage. (C) and (D) are incorrect because the author makes no statements justifying the existence of armies or of war itself.

35. **(A)** (A) is correct because the author's tone is very neutral. (B), (C), and (D) are incorrect because the author shows little evidence of any passion or emotion.

36. **(B)** (B) is correct because the passage describes both good and bad attributes of democracy, a political system based on equality. (A), (C), and (D) all take either an all-good or all-bad position; however, the author is careful to treat both good and bad effects.

37. **(A)** (A) is correct because the author is comparing traveling with reading history. Because there is no causal relationship suggested, (C) is incorrect. (D) is incorrect because the author does not seek to divide up one subject; (B) is incorrect because there is no narration of chronological events.

38. **(B)**   This is a statement of opinion, because it is not possible to check with any accuracy the contraction of minds as the author has described it.

39. **(C)**   The correct response is (C), because throughout the passage the author compares history with foreign travel; (B) contradicts the author's first sentence. (A) and (D) are incorrect because the author uses travel in England as a detail supporting his main point about similarities between travel and reading history.

40. **(B)**   The argument is invalid because it is a non sequitur. Jonathan's success as a computer sales representative is not necessarily guaranteed by his skill at baseball and the quality of his work with children.

LITERAL COMPREHENSION SKILLS

RECOGNIZING THE CENTRAL IDEA

Approximately four questions on the test will ask you to identify the main idea of a passage or paragraph. If you see that one of the questions following a passage asks for the main (or central or controlling) idea, you need to read with this question in mind: "What is the author's point? What is the writer getting at throughout the passage?"

Frequently the author will express the main idea in a single sentence, called the thesis statement or topic sentence.

Example: Find the main idea by reading the following passage and then answer the question.

Passage A (from *National Geographic,* 1917)

The eruption of Mount Katmai in June, 1912, was one of the most tremendous volcanic explosions ever recorded. A mass of ash and pumice whose volume has been estimated at nearly five cubic miles was thrown into the air. In its fall this material buried an area as large as the state of Connecticut to a
5 depth varying from 10 inches to over 10 feet, while small amounts of ash fell as much as 900 miles away.

Great quantities of very fine dust were thrown into the higher regions of the atmosphere and were quickly distributed over the whole world, so as to have a profound effect on the weather, being responsible for the notoriously cold, wet
10 summer of that year.

The comparative magnitude of the eruption can be better realized if one should imagine a similar eruption of Vesuvius. Such an eruption would bury Naples under 15 feet of ash; Rome would be covered nearly a foot deep; the sound would be heard at Paris; dust from the crater would fall in Brussels and
15 Berlin, and the fumes would be noticeable far beyond Christiania, Norway.

Fortunately the volcano is situated in a country so sparsely inhabited that the damage caused by the eruption was insignificant—very much less than in many relatively small eruptions in populous districts, such as that of Vesuvius, which destroyed Pompeii and Herculaneum. Indeed, so remote and little known
20 is the volcano that there were not any witnesses near enough to see the eruption, and it was not until the National Geographic Society's expeditions explored the district that it was settled definitely which of several near-by volcanoes was really the seat of the disturbance.

The most important settlement in the devastated district is Kodiak, which,
25   although a hundred miles from the volcano, was buried nearly a foot deep in
ash. This ashy blanket transformed the "Green Kodiak" of other days into a
gray desert of sand, whose redemption and revegetation seemed utterly hope-
less. When I first visited it, a year later, it presented an appearance barren and
desolate. It seemed to every one there that it must be many years before it
30   could recover its original condition.

Which statement below most accurately describes the main idea of this passage?

(A)   Volcanic explosions are the most destructive events in nature.

(B)   The eruption of Mount Katmai was one of the largest volcanic explosions on record.

(C)   Mount Katmai is so remotely located that no one witnessed its eruption.

(D)   The most important settlement in the area of Mount Katmai is Kodiak.

The passage makes a statement like choice (B) right at the beginning. But is it the main idea? The passage describes the size and extent of the explosion, tries to help us appreciate its magnitude by describing what a similar eruption of Vesuvius would do to the cities of Europe, explains that this tremendous explosion caused little damage because of its remoteness, and describes its effects on a settlement named Kodiak.

Everything in the passage seems related to the idea that the eruption of Mount Katmai was one of the greatest volcanic explosions ever. It may be true that volcanic explosions are the most destructive in nature, but nowhere in the passage does the author make this claim or compare volcanic eruptions with other destructive natural events such as earthquakes and hurricanes. Choice (A), therefore, cannot be right. The passage does state that Mount Katmai is so remote that no one witnessed the eruption. But how can this be the main idea? The first three paragraphs focus not on the remoteness of the volcano but on the great size of the eruption. The point about the volcano's remote location is made only to explain why such a terrific explosion caused such little damage. Choice (C), therefore, cannot be right. The fact that Kodiak is the most important settlement in the area of Mount Katmai is used to illustrate the size and power of Mount Katmai's eruption. Even though the village is 100 miles away from the mountain, it was still covered by a layer of ash 12 inches deep. Again, the author's main point is that the eruption was one of the most tremendous on record. Therefore, choice (D) cannot be right. Choice (B) is the best answer.

IDENTIFYING SUPPORTING DETAILS

In addition to recognizing an author's main idea, it is important to notice how the author supports that idea with facts, examples, illustrations, or related arguments. The second literal comprehension skill tested by CLAST, therefore, is detecting supporting details.

Before you read a passage, read the questions. This way, if any of the questions are about supporting details, you will know *in advance* which details to focus on. When you come to those details in your reading, make a mark in the margin.

Sometimes a question about details asks you to identify the only one of four details that is *not* in the passage. In this case, after you read the passage, check off each detail that you remember being in the passage. If more than one remains, skim the passage again until you can check off all but one. That one will be your answer.

Example: Answer the following question based on the earlier passage about Mount Katmai

The example that Naples would be buried in 15 feet of ash is used to illustrate

    (A)   the enormous size of the eruption of Mount Katmai.

    (B)   the folly of building cities and towns in the vicinity of a volcano.

    (C)   the tremendous power of Mount Vesuvius.

    (D)   the fact that ancient volcanic eruptions are much like modern ones.

The sentence preceding the example about Naples reads, "The comparative magnitude of the eruption can be better realized if one should imagine a similar eruption of Vesuvius." The author is trying to help us appreciate the enormous devastation that Mount Katmai *could have* caused if it were not so remote from population centers. Choice (A), therefore, must be correct.

It may very well be foolish to build near a volcano, but the author's focus here is not on the proximity of Naples to Vesuvius. It is on the spectacular power of Mount Katmai's eruption. Choice (B), therefore, is incorrect.

The author asks us to imagine what would happen if Vesuvius erupted with an explosion the size of Mount Katmai's. The actual power of Vesuvius is beside the point, making (C) incorrect. Choice (D) is incorrect because the passage says nothing about the similarity of ancient and modern eruptions.

DETERMINING CONTEXTUAL MEANINGS

The third and last literal comprehension skill tested is identifying the meaning of words by examining and understanding their context—that is, the sentence and passage in which the word occurs.

Even if you have never before seen a particular word, you can take a pretty good guess at its meaning by paying close attention to the whole sentence and passage. For example, if you do not know the word "obstreperous," try to figure it out by reading this sentence: "The obstreperous youngsters burst through the kitchen door shouting, arguing, and loudly demanding, 'Hey, what's for lunch?'"

If you guessed something like "unruly," "noisy," "boisterous," or "clamorous," you were right!

If you understand the sentence as a whole, you have a good chance of determining the meaning of an unfamiliar word. In the sentence above, the words "burst," "shouting," "arguing," and "loudly" tell us how the youngsters are behaving, so we assume that "obstreperous" must have something to do with wild, noisy behavior.

Even when you already know the meaning of a word, be careful. Words can have more than one meaning; the meaning you are thinking of may not be the one called for by the context. So pay attention to the context clues to determine the meaning of the word in the given sentence.

Example: Read the following sentence and answer the question.

Indeed, so remote and little known is the volcano that there were not any witnesses near enough to see the eruption, and it was not until the National Geographic Society's expeditions explored the district that it was *settled* definitely which of several near-by volcanoes was really the seat of the disturbance.

In this context, the word "settled" means

(A)   inhabited.

(C)   determined.

(B)   subsided.

(D)   quieted down.

All of the above choices are various meanings of "settled," but only choice (C) ("determined") describes what is meant here: that the scientists had to explore the area before they could *determine* which volcano had erupted.

DRILL: LITERAL COMPREHENSION SKILLS

DIRECTIONS: Read the passage and answer the questions that follow.

Passage B (Adapted from: "Religion Without Dogma," by C.S. Lewis)

Professor Hostead, in his article "Modern Agnosticism Justified," argues that a) religion is basically belief in God and immortality, b) most religions consist of "accretions of dogma and mythology" that science has disproven, c) it would be desirable, if it were possible, to keep the basic religious belief
5   without those accumulations of religious notions and legends, but that d) science has rendered even the basic elements of religion almost as incredible as the "accretions." For the doctrine of immortality involves the view that man is a composite creature, a soul in a state of symbiosis with a physical organism.

But science can successfully regard man only monastically, as a single organism
10 whose psychological characteristics all arise from his physical nature; the soul
then becomes indefensible. In conclusion, Professor Hostead asserts that our
only hope rests in empirical, observable evidence for the existence of the soul;
in fact, in the findings of physical research.

My disagreement with Professor Hostead starts at the beginning. I do not
15 consider the essence of religion as simply the belief in God and immortality.
Early Judaism, for example, didn't accept immortality. The human soul in
Sheol (the afterworld) took no account of Jehovah, and God in turn took no
account of the soul. In Sheol all things are forgotten. The religion revolved
around the ritual and ethical demands of God and on the blessings people
20 received from him. During earthly life these blessings were usually material in
nature: happy life, many children, good health, and such. But we do see a
more religious note also. The Jew hungers for the living God; he obeys God's
laws devoutly; he considers himself as impure and sinful in Jehovah's presence.
God is the sole object of worship. Buddhism makes the doctrine of immortal-
25 ity vital, while we find little in the way of that which is religious. The existence
of the gods is not denied, but it has no religious significance. In Stoicism again
both the practice of religion and the belief in immortality are variables, not
absolute traits of religion. Even within Christianity itself we find, as in Stoicism, the subordinate position of immortality.

1.   Which of the following best defines the phrase "accretions of dogma and
mythology" as it is used in the first paragraph?

    (A)   Combinations of fact and fiction

    (B)   Conflicts of sound principles and unsound theories

    (C)   Implications and ideas of religion

    (D)   Religious ideas and fables that have gradually accumulated to form
accepted religious belief

2.   What is the main idea of the entire passage?

    (A)   Belief in God is scientifically valid.

    (B)   Professor Hostead's assumption that the essence of religion is the belief
in God and immortality is incorrect.

(C)   Neither Judaism, Buddhism, Stoicism, nor Christianity fit into Hostead's definition of religion.

(D)   Judaism, Buddhism, Stoicism, and Christianity are all valid ideologies in their regard for immortality and belief in God.

3.   The writer's purpose in this passage is to

(A)   outline basic tenets of Judaism, Buddhism, Stoicism, and Christianity.

(B)   establish scientific credibility of four ideologies so as to undermine Hostead's positions.

(C)   attack Hostead's views by establishing the vulnerability of Hostead's first position.

(D)   define the essence of religion.

4.   The writer uses Judaism, Buddhism, Stoicism, and Christianity to illustrate

(A)   the superiority of Christianity over the other three religions.

(B)   that the essence of religion is not necessarily belief in God and immortality.

(C)   empirical evidence for the soul, the physical research, which Hostead requires as proof for the soul.

(D)   the validity of religious thought over a scientific system devoid of religious, spiritual beliefs.

CRITICAL COMPREHENSION SKILLS

RECOGNIZING THE AUTHOR'S PURPOSE

The first critical comprehension skill that you are asked to demonstrate is the ability to spot the author's purpose or intention. The author's purpose—that is, what the author is trying to accomplish—is closely related to the author's main idea. But purpose and idea are not identical. If a friend rushed into your room and shouted, "Fire!", the main idea would be that the building is on fire. Your friend's *purpose* would be not merely to communicate that idea but to urge you to leave the building. An author's purpose might be to inform, describe, define, explain, analyze, compare, suggest, persuade, amuse, etc.

Determining the author's purpose is a little more difficult than identifying the main idea, because the purpose is usually implied rather than stated directly. But if we correctly interpret what the author is saying, it is usually only a short jump for us to determine why he or she is saying it.

Example: Reread the following paragraph and then answer the question.

The eruption of Mount Katmai in June, 1912, was one of the most tremendous volcanic explosions ever recorded. A mass of ash and pumice whose volume has been estimated at nearly five cubic miles was thrown into the air. In its fall this material buried an area as large as the state of Connecticut to a depth varying from 10 inches to over 10 feet, while small amounts of ash fell as much as 900 miles away.

This paragraph indicates that the author's purpose is to

    (A)   explain how a volcanic eruption comes about.

    (B)   analyze the effects of the eruption on plant and animal life.

    (C)   compare the size of Mount Katmai to the state of Connecticut.

    (D)   describe the magnitude of Mount Katmai's eruption.

Choice (D) is the correct answer, since the whole paragraph describes the size and magnitude of the eruption, which is the author's purpose. Choice (A) is incorrect, since the paragraph is not about volcanoes in general, but about the *effects* of one particular volcano. Although it discusses the effects of the eruption, the paragraph does not mention plant or animal life. Therefore, choice (B) is incorrect. While Connecticut is mentioned, its size is compared to the area covered by ash, *not* to the volcano itself, making choice (C) incorrect.

IDENTIFYING ORGANIZATIONAL PATTERN

Depending on the author's purpose, he or she will organize information and ideas according to a particular pattern or arrangement. If, for example, his or her purpose is to describe the differences between a horse and a donkey, the author would most likely choose the organizational pattern called *contrast*. The second critical reading skill tested on the CLAST is the ability to identify the organizational pattern of a passage.

Fortunately, there are not very many different ways in which authors normally develop their material. Here is a list of types of patterns you may be asked to identify, along with the purposes for which each pattern is used. Study the list to familiarize yourself with the different patterns. Then try to answer the question about a sample passage.

Organizational Pattern	Purpose
(1) time order	to narrate events in chronological order
(2) location order	to describe a scene or object in an orderly way (e.g., top to bottom)
(3) comparison	to call attention to the *similarities* between two things, people, or events
(4) contrast	to call attention to the *differences* between two things, people, or events
(5) summary	to sum up in brief what has already been said at greater length
(6) definition	to clarify the meaning of a word or term by defining it precisely
(7) classification	to divide up a subject into different categories or classes
(8) addition	to develop a subject simply by making one point after another
(9) simple listing	to make a list of items, qualities, characteristics, etc.
(10) cause and effect	to demonstrate how an event came about due to certain conditions or causes
(11) statement and clarification	to explain more fully and clearly what is said at the beginning of the passage
(12) generalization and example	to support a general statement by giving one or more specific examples that illustrate its truth

Read the following passage and answer the question.
(As always, read the question first, then read the passage.)

Passage C (from Henry David Thoreau, *Civil Disobedience*, 1849)

In the morning, our breakfasts were put through the hole in the door, in small oblong-square tin pans, made to fit, and holding a pint of chocolate, with brown bread, and an iron spoon. When they called for the vessels again, I was green enough to return what bread I had left; but my comrade seized it, and said that I should lay that up for lunch or dinner. Soon after he was let out to work at haying in a neighboring field, whither he went every day, and would not be back till noon; so he bade me good-day, saying that he doubted if he should see me again.

In developing the passage, the organizational pattern used by the author could be described as

    (A)   contrast.

    (B)   addition.

    (C)   statement and clarification.

    (D)   time order.

First, consider the purpose of this passage: someone, apparently a prisoner, is describing what happened one morning. Choice (D), time order, is clearly the correct answer because the paragraph is telling what happened in chronological order. There is no contrasting of two things (A). There is an "adding" of one statement to another (B), but these statements are not points or arguments but rather particular events in time. Finally, the paragraph does not proceed by statement and clarification (C) because the second and third sentences do not clarify the first sentence.

DISTINGUISHING BETWEEN FACT AND OPINION

Critical readers do not accept everything they read as true. They realize that many kinds of writing are mixtures of objective facts and the author's opinions, and critical readers are able to tell which is which. A few questions on the CLAST, therefore, will ask you to indicate whether a particular statement is a statement of fact or a statement of opinion.

In answering these questions, keep in mind that a "statement of fact" must be proved or provable by objective means—for example, the means may be checking the date of Washington's birth in an encyclopedia, finding the spelling of "abacus" in a dictionary, or discovering the winner of the 1967 World Series in an almanac. If a statement cannot be verified or disproved by "looking it up," then it must be a statement of opinion.

Even if an author's opinion or view seems to be obviously true, it is still a statement of opinion. You may agree strongly, for example, that "Americans spend too much time watching TV." But that is still an opinion: a personal view that cannot be proved or disproved by "looking it up."

On the other hand, a "statement of fact" may be made in error and still remain a "statement of fact." For example, an author might mistakenly write, "Bill Clinton is our 52nd president." That is a "statement of fact" even though it is not true. (Clinton is our 42nd president.) What makes it a "statement of fact" is that it can be verified or disproved by looking it up, by checking the facts.

Example: Determine whether the following statements are statements of fact or statements of opinion.

1.   The statement that "The United States made a mistake in selling wheat to Russia" is a statement of

    (A)   fact.

    (B)   opinion.

2.   The statement, "The day after the sale of wheat to Russia, the stock market rose 50 points" is a statement of

(A)   fact.

(B)   opinion.

3.   The statement, "The best seasoning to use with Italian dishes is oregano" is a statement of

(A)   fact.

(B)   opinion.

Question 1 gives us a statement of opinion: people might disagree as to whether or not the sale was a mistake. Question 2 is a statement of fact: we could check its accuracy by looking up the date of the sale and the stock market reports for that day and the following day. Question 3 is a statement of opinion: even if 99.99% of all people in the world agree that oregano is "the best" seasoning, it is still a statement of opinion, a matter of taste.

DETECTING BIAS

Closely related to the ability to distinguish between fact and opinion is the ability to detect an author's bias. Bias is a predisposition in favor of or against someone or something: it is a liking for or a dislike of a person or thing. "Prejudice" is close in meaning to "bias," but "prejudice" is a more negative word; it implies a lack of reasonableness, an irrational prejudgment, and it is usually a dislike of a certain group or race.

By contrast, bias is simply a person's feeling for or against something. While it is important to recognize an author's bias, we should not condemn the writer for having a bias. Most readers enjoy learning how an author feels about the subject matter. Bias makes writing more human. Without it, most writing would be too dry.

How do you detect bias in a passage or statement? Watch for these tell-tale signs:

(1)   The author assumes the truth of something that she or he does not try to argue or defend: "It goes without saying that German cars are the best designed in the world."

(2)   The author uses very emotional language in making a point: "They should collect every handgun in the country and dump them all in the ocean."

(3)   The author exaggerates: "Television has ruined this great country!

(4)   The author stereotypes: "French waiters must go to a special school to learn rudeness."

(5)   The author resorts to name-calling: "Those illiterate, foul-mouthed, bare-chested fans ruined the game for me."

On the CLAST you may be asked to identify which subject the author shows bias in favor of or against. You also may be given four statements and be asked which one shows bias.

Example: Read the following passage and see if you can spot the biased statement.

Passage D (from Henry Adams, *History of the United States of America during the Administration of Thomas Jefferson*, 1884-1885)

That Americans should not have been liked was natural; but that they should not have been understood was more significant by far. After the downfall of the French republic they had no right to expect a kind word from Europe, and during the next twenty years they rarely received one. The liberal
5   movement of Europe was cowed, and no one dared express democratic sympathies until the Napoleonic tempest had passed. With this attitude Americans had no right to find fault, for Europe cared less to injure them than to protect herself. Nevertheless, observant readers could not but feel surprised that none of the numerous Europeans who then wrote and spoke about America seemed
10 to study the subject seriously. The ordinary traveler was apt to be little more reflective than a bee or an ant, but some of these critics possessed powers far from ordinary; yet Talleyrand alone showed that had he but seen America a few years later than he did, he might have suggested some sufficient reason for apparent contradictions that perplexed him in the national character.

The author shows bias when he says

(A)   "during the next twenty years they rarely received one." (line 4)

(B)   "Europe cared less to injure them than to protect herself." (lines 7-8)

(C)   "The ordinary traveler was apt to be little more reflective than a bee or an ant." (lines 10-11)

(D)   "he might have suggested some sufficient reason for apparent contradictions that perplexed him in the national character." (lines 13-14)

Choice (C) says that "the ordinary traveler" was no more thoughtful or "reflective" than bees or ants. This definitely shows bias against ordinary travelers as a group by stereotyping them. Choice (A) seems to be based on historical fact; it is therefore not biased. Choice (B) says that Europe was most concerned with protecting herself, which is a reasonable statement. Choice (D) speculates about what Talleyrand might have said if he had visited America a few years later. It is complimentary of Talleyrand's intelligence, but certainly not nearly as biased as choice (C).

RECOGNIZING TONE

In any piece of writing the tone is the underlying attitude or feeling that the writer seems to be expressing. The different tones that a writer may create are as numerous as the different feelings, or shades of feeling, that we experience in daily life. An author's tone may be described as serious or lighthearted, angry or joyful, despairing or hopeful, bitter or buoyant, sarcastic or playful, and so on. Authors communicate a particular tone primarily by their choice of words but also through sentence structure, figures of speech (such as the metaphor "all the world's a stage"), and rhetorical devices (such as the rhetorical question "How can Americans save to buy a home when inflation erodes their savings?").

For most students the difficulty of these questions lies not so much in recognizing the feeling behind a passage as in knowing the meanings of the words used to describe tone. Examine the following list of "feeling" words, and look up in a good dictionary the definitions of the words you don't know.

ambivalent	exasperated	malicious
amiable	exuberant	melancholic
apathetic	farcical	nostalgic
ardent	genial	obsequious
arrogant	haughty	remorseful
benevolent	impassioned	righteous
bewildered	incredulous	satiric
caustic	indignant	subdued
evasive	ironic	vindictive

Example: Read the following passage and answer the question about tone. (As always, look at the question *first!*)

Passage E (from Mark Twain, "Some Rambling Notes of an Idle Excursion," 1877-1878)

There was a good deal of pleasant gossip about old Captain "Hurricane" Jones, of the Pacific Ocean—peace to his ashes! Two or three of us present had known him; I particularly well, for I had made four sea-voyages with him. He was a very remarkable man. He was born in a ship; he picked up what little
5　education he had among his shipmates; he began life in the forecastle, and climbed grade by grade to the captaincy. More than fifty years of his sixty-five were spent at sea. He had sailed all oceans, seen all lands, and borrowed a tint from all climates. When a man has been fifty years at sea he necessarily knows nothing of men, nothing of the world but its surface, nothing of the world's
10　thought, nothing of the world's learning but its A B C: and that much is blurred and distorted by the unfocused lenses of an untrained mind. Such a man is only a gray and bearded child. That is what old Hurricane Jones was— simply an innocent, lovable old infant.

The author of this passage has created a tone that could be described as

    (A)   critical.   (C)   incredulous.

    (B)   melancholic.   (D)   admiring.

"Admiring," (D), is the right choice. The author expresses admiration for Captain "Hurricane" Jones in the phrases "Peace to his ashes!"; "He was a remarkable man"; climbed grade by grade to the captaincy"; "He had sailed all oceans"; and "simply an innocent, lovable infant."

You might be tempted to choose "critical," (A), because the author says the captain "knows nothing of men, nothing of the world but its surface..." But in the context of the passage it is a virtue to know the world so little. The man is innocent and untainted by the world. "Melancholic," (B), meaning sad or mournful, is clearly the wrong choice. The passage describes an interesting, unusual character in an upbeat way. "Incredulous," (C), means disbelieving or skeptical. Nothing indicates that the author is skeptical of anything.

IDENTIFYING RELATIONSHIPS WITHIN SENTENCES

The skill tested here is very similar to the second critical comprehension skill, identifying organizational patterns, since both skills involve seeing logical relationships. The only difference is that earlier you were asked to spot relationships within a whole passage, whereas here you are asked to see relationships within a simple sentence.

The kinds of relationships within a sentence are also similar to the kinds of organizational patterns in a whole passage which we saw earlier. For example, a passage may be organized according to the principle of contrast, such as the author enumerating the differences between a horse and a donkey. And a single sentence in that passage may also contain a relationship of contrast: "The horse makes a high-pitched neigh, *but* the donkey emits a loud, harsh sound called a bray." In this sentence the connecting word "but" tips us off to the kind of relationship between the two parts of the sentence: "but" signals a contrast between the preceding statement and the following one.

What kinds of relationships might you be asked to identify within sentences? Here is a list of the most common ones, along with the connecting words and phrases that signal the relationship.

Kind of Relationship	Connecting Words
addition	and, in addition, moreover, furthermore
contrast	but, however, on the other hand, by contrast, nevertheless, yet, although
comparison	similarly, likewise, just as
cause and effect	thus, so, hence, because, as a result, since, consequently, therefore

The CLAST may ask you to identify relationships between sentences in two different ways. One way is to correct sentences which omit the connecting words. Another way is to examine a sentence and identify, from four choices, the kind of relationship that exists between two parts of a sentence. An example of each type of question follows.

Example: The following passage has some words deleted. For each blank, choose the word or phrase that best completes the passage.

Passage F (from Sarah Orne Jewett, "A White Heron," 1886)

The woods were already filled with shadows one June evening, just before eight o'clock, _____(1)_____ a bright sunset still glimmered faintly among the trunks of the trees. A little girl was driving home her cow, a plodding, dilatory, provoking creature in her behavior, _____(2)_____ a valued companion for all that. They were going away from whatever light there was, and striking deep into the woods, but their feet were familiar with the path, _____(3)_____ it was no matter whether their eyes could see it or not.

1. The most appropriate word for blank (1) would be

    (A) therefore.   (C) similarly.

    (B) though.   (D) so.

2. The most appropriate word for blank (2) would be

    (A) but.   (C) for.

    (B) and.   (D) thus.

3. The most appropriate word for blank (3) would be

    (A) but.   (C) nevertheless.

    (B) since.   (D) and.

4. Read the following sentence and then select the word or phrase that best describes the relationship between the first part of the sentence ("Hard work...rewarded") and the second part ("irresponsibility...dismissal").

    "Hard work and diligence will be rewarded; irresponsibility, on the other hand, will lead to dismissal."

    (A) Addition   (C) Contrast

    (B) Comparison   (D) Cause and effect

Answer:

1.   The correct choice is (B) "though." The first part of the sentence emphasizes the shadows in the woods; the second part mentions "a bright sunset." So the relationship is one of *contrast*, which is best expressed by the word "though."

2.   The correct choice is (A) "but." Before the blank, the cow is called a "plodding, dilatory, provoking creature" (all negative qualities). After the blank, the cow is called a "valued companion." Again, the relationship is one of contrast, expressed by the word "but."

3.   The correct choice is (D) "and." Before the blank, the paragraph states that the travelers' feet are familiar with the path. Following the blank is the statement that it did not matter that they could not see. Since these ideas are similar, the best connecting word is "and."

4.   The correct choice is (C) "contrast." The contrast between "hard work and diligence" in the first part of the sentence and "irresponsibility" in the second part is signaled by the phrase "on the other hand."

IDENTIFYING RELATIONSHIPS BETWEEN SENTENCES

The only difference between this skill and the previous one is that here you will be asked to identify relationships *between* sentences instead of relationships within a single sentence. Some of the relationships are the same as within a sentence: addition, comparison, contrast, and cause and effect. Other possibilities are statement and clarification, generalization and example, and summary.

Example: Read the following passage and then answer the question.

Passage G (from Mark Twain, *Life on the Mississippi*, 1875)

When I was a boy, there was but one permanent ambition among my comrades in our village on the west bank of the Mississippi River. That was, to be a steamboatman. We had transient ambitions of other sorts, but they were only transient. When a circus came and went, it left us all burning to become
5   clowns; the first negro minstrel show that ever came to our section left us all suffering to try that kind of life; now and then we had a hope that, if we lived and were good, God would permit us to be pirates. These ambitions faded out, each in its turn; but the ambition to be a steamboatman always remained.

1. What is the relationship between the second sentence ("That was…") and the first sentence ("When I was a boy…")?

    (A) Statement and clarification   (C) Cause and effect

    (B) Contrast   (D) Addition

2. What is the relationship between the third sentence ("We had transient ambitions…") and the second sentence ("That was…")?

    (A) Statement and clarification   (C) Cause and effect

    (B) Contrast   (D) Addition

Answer:

1. The second sentence tells us specifically that the boys wanted to be steamboatmen. This explains what the author meant in the first sentence by "one permanent ambition." Therefore, the correct answer is (A).

2. The third sentence mentions other "transient" (passing) ambitions, but these are in contrast to the "permanent" ambition to be a steamboatman, making (B) the correct answer.

RECOGNIZING VALID AND INVALID ARGUMENTS

Approximately four questions on the CLAST are designed to test your ability to distinguish valid arguments from invalid arguments and possibly to recognize the names of certain fallacies, or errors in logical reasoning.

Most of these questions will give you a statement and ask you whether the statement is valid or invalid. Since there are only two choices, you have at least a 50/50 chance of getting the question right. When in doubt, choose "invalid" because most of these statements on CLAST tests tend to be invalid.

How are you to know whether a statement is valid or invalid? Your common sense is a good first guide. You can usually tell when a friend gives you an invalid argument: "What's bad about cheating? Everybody does it." Here your common sense or reason tells you that your friend's argument makes no sense. The rightness or wrongness of an action does not depend on how many people are doing it. Besides, even if many are cheating, it is very doubtful that everyone is cheating.

As an aid to common sense, it is good to be aware of certain errors in logical argument called fallacies. In the example above, your friend is guilty of the fallacy called "bandwagon"—that is, appealing to what "everyone" or "most people" do or believe. Below are listed ten other common fallacies that may be used on the CLAST. To the right of each fallacy name is a brief definition and an example of its use.

Fallacy	Definition	Example
circular thinking	Merely repeating in other words the thing you are trying to prove or argue	"The poor need our help because they are so destitute." ("Poor" and "destitute" mean the same thing.)
ad hominem (against the person)	Attacking one's opponent rather than his or her arguments	"What do *you* know about child care reform? You've been divorced twice!"
faulty analogy	Comparing two situations that are quite different in some ways	"Unemployment's up, the stock market is falling—we're in for another Depression."
hasty generalization	Drawing a conclusion based on too few cases	"That's the third cat I've seen. This town is full of cats."
begging the question	*Assuming* that part of your argument is true rather than providing evidence.	"Since the grading system is unfair, we need to change it." (But *is* it unfair? That needs to be argued.)
non sequitur (it doesn't follow)	Drawing a conclusion which is not logically connected to the preceding statements	"She was an Olympic athlete, so I'm sure she'll be a great Secretary of Labor."
either/or (false dilemma)	Reducing an issue to only two alternatives when others exist.	"America—love it or leave it." (It is possible to be critical of one's government without wanting to leave the country.)
post hoc, ergo propter hoc (after this, therefore because of this)	Assuming that because one event followed another, the first must have caused the second.	"You're sneezing! I knew you'd catch a cold at that concert last night."

Fallacy	Definition	Example
red herring	Introducing an irrelevant issue to distract attention from the real issue	"Before we go and elect this woman mayor, I'd like to remind you that our last female mayor resigned in disgrace."
ad populum (to the people)	Playing upon expected emotional responses of readers to certain words, phrases, or concepts	"To keep this great country of ours second to none, we need to vote for higher tariffs on imports."

Example: Find the best answer.

1. "The French are rude. I know three different people who have been to France, and they all talk about how rude the French are."

    Is the argument in the above quotation valid or invalid?

    (A) Valid

    (B) Invalid

2. "Every Swiss citizen has access to health care. If their system works there, it will work in the U.S., too."

    Which of the following fallacies does the above argument use?

    (A) Ad hominem (to the man)   (C) Faulty analogy

    (B) Circular thinking   (D) Bandwagon

    Answer:

1. The argument is invalid, (B). It is a hasty generalization based on too few cases.

2. The statement uses a faulty analogy, (C), assuming that the U.S. is the same as Switzerland, but there are many differences which could make the Swiss system unworkable in the U.S.

DRAWING LOGICAL INFERENCES AND CONCLUSIONS

The last critical reading comprehension skill is the ability to determine what an author implies—that is, what an author does not say directly but what we can reasonably assume the author believes based on what he has said. When we say what an author implies, we are drawing inferences. Closely related to an inference is a conclusion: based on your reading, what might you reasonably conclude about the subject or about the author's attitudes or beliefs?

In answering questions about inferences and conclusions, make sure that an answer choice is a statement that can be inferred or concluded on the basis of the given passage. Some answer choices may sound true by themselves, but that does not mean they are implied in the passage. Also, be sure that the statement you choose is not actually in the passage itself; if it is, then it cannot be an inference or a conclusion since it is directly stated.

Example: Read the following passage and answer the question.

"From that moment on, my life changed. My heart grew cold. Whenever someone happened to look at me, I turned aside. If an acquaintance called to me on the street, I pretended not to notice. When the phone rang, I did not answer."

From this passage, you could infer that

(A)   the author's life changed.

(B)   the author was more sociable before "that moment."

(C)   the author was never a very nice person.

(D)   the author had no friends.

Since the author's life changed, and since the author behaved unsociably after the change, we may infer that the author was more sociable before the change. Choice (B) seems correct, but consider the others. It is true that the author's life changed, (A), but the author states that directly. We cannot infer what is directly stated. We do not have enough evidence to assume that the author was never "nice," (C). In fact, the passage seems to imply that before the change, he or she was more friendly. We cannot conclude that the author had no friends, (D). Someone calls to him on the street, and someone telephones. In any case, there is no way of knowing about the author's friends or lack of friends.

DRILL: CRITICAL COMPREHENSION SKILLS

DIRECTIONS: Select the word or phrase that best suits the blanks below.

Consumers who believe a company is well run and shows promise of doing well in the stock market will invest in that company's stock. If the companys shows a profit, the investor will receive a dividend check. Buying United States Savings Bonds is another well-known way of investing money.

Some companies offer a dividend reinvestment plan: the profits, instead of being sent to the investor in the form of a check, can be reinvested automatically in the company's stock. To encourage this practice, companies offer several incentives. _____(1)_____, if the dividend is too small to buy a whole share, most companies allow the investor to purchase part of a share until enough dividends accumulate for a whole share. _____(2)_____, some companies offer shareholders a discount off the market price of their stock. A five percent discount is the usual rate. _____(3)_____, about 70 percent of companies charge no fee if the stockholder wishes to purchase more shares for cash.

1. (A) Although   (C) In other words
   (B) Eventually   (D) For example

2. (A) Moreover   (C) As a result
   (B) In addition   (D) First

3. (A) Finally   (C) Second
   (B) Later   (D) In contrast

DIRECTIONS: Read the arguments below. If they are fallacious, determine which fallacy applies.

---

4. Girls are bad at math because females are not mathematically inclined.

   (A) Non sequitur   (C) Either/or
   (B) Faulty analogy   (D) Circular logic

5. My opponent is unfit for office because he is a card-carrying liberal.

   (A) Red herring   (C) Bandwagon appeal
   (B) Faulty cause and effect (D) Begging the question

DIRECTIONS: Read the passage, then select the best answer.

In the battle of Atlanta during the American Civil War, Sherman defeated the Confederates by turning the flank of their defenses. The Germans used the same strategy successfully in their initial attack on France in World War II.

6.   Which of the following conclusions can be inferred from the above passage?

(A)   History can produce scientific knowledge.

(B)   History can be an instructive guide to action.

(C)   The lessons of history can be used for good as well as evil purposes.

(D)   History repeats itself.

(E)   The Germans must have studied several types of warfare.

DIRECTIONS: Decide if the argument is fact or opinion.

7.   Capitalism is the best economic system because it works in America and America is great.

(A)   Fact

(B)   Opinion

READING SKILLS

ANSWER KEY

DRILL: LITERAL COMPREHENSION SKILLS

1. **(D)**
2. **(B)**
3. **(C)**
4. **(B)**

DRILL: CRITICAL COMPREHENSION SKILLS

1. **(D)**
2. **(B)**
3. **(A)**
4. **(D)**
5. **(A)**
6. **(B)**
7. **(B)**

READING SKILLS

DETAILED EXPLANATIONS OF ANSWERS

DRILL: LITERAL COMPREHENSION SKILLS

1. **(D)** Choice (D) in the first paragraph refers to this term with a correct definition: "those accumulations of religious notions and legends."

2. **(B)** Hostead's first assumption makes that statement about the essence of religion while the second sentence in paragraph two disputes it.

3. **(C)** The first two sentences of the second paragraph state this purpose exactly.

4. **(B)** The writer states this in the second sentence of the second paragraph, and proceeds to illustrate his point with those four beliefs.

DRILL: CRITICAL COMPREHENSION SKILLS

1. **(D)** Choice (D), "For example," is the only phrase which introduces the first idea without comment or contrast.

2. **(B)** Choice (B), "In addition," introduces the second idea without comment or contrast.

3. **(A)** Choice (A), "Finally," introduces the third main idea, and indicates that this idea concludes the paragraph.

4. **(D)** The fallacy is circular logic because the refutation merely restates the assertion.

5. **(A)** The fallacy is red herring because the argument uses the phrase "card-carrying" to distract the listener instead of discussing the opponent's lack of governing skills.

6. **(B)** Since the passage directly states a reference to history and an effort on behalf of the Germans to use a historical strategy, we can only infer that "history can be used as an instructive to action."

7. **(B)** Arguments containing superlatives, such as "the best" are usually opinions unless supported by empirical data. Since the only refutation is another opinion: "America is great," the refutation is not sufficient to make this assertion factual.

Chapter 5

Mathematics
Skills Review

Chapter 5

MATHEMATICS SKILLS REVIEW

The CLAST Mathematics Subtest consists of 55 multiple-choice items that must be completed in 90 minutes. The test covers five areas: arithmetic, algebra, geometry and measurement, probability, and logical reasoning.

Within each broad area, specific computational skills are tested. This review will take you through each skill, showing you how to approach the problem and find the answer quickly and accurately.

THE DIRECTIONS

As with all other sections of the CLAST, there is only one correct answer for each Mathematics question. Read each item carefully to figure out what the question is asking you to do. Each question will ask you to perform a different type of computation.

Additionally, some questions on the CLAST Mathematics Subtest will refer to information such as diagrams, graphs, or tables. In these instances, the test will clearly state what information pertains to which questions.

TIPS

- Avoid lengthy computations. Use approximations where possible to save valuable time. Once you have enough information to solve a problem, move on. For example:

    $4.7586 + 7.2967 =$

    (A) 11.9   (B) 12.1   (C) 12.0   (D) 11.5

Since the answer is expressed as a number with one decimal place, it is not necessary to add all the places in the original expression. Therefore, it is much quicker to round the numbers to the tenths place before adding. This gives you $4.8 + 7.3 = 12.1$.

- Look at the answer choices before trying to work out the problem. If all the choices are in a specific format, you want to do your work in that format. For example, if the measurements in a problem are given in feet, but the answer choices are given in inches, you must convert feet to inches when working out the problem.

- Remember to work in only one unit and convert if more than one is presented in the problem. For example, if a problem gives numbers in decimals and fractions, convert one in terms of the other and then work out the problem.

- After working out an equation, make sure your result is actually answering the question. Otherwise, you may have to perform extra steps. For example, although you may solve an equation for a specific variable, this may not be the final answer. You may have to use this answer to find another quantity.

MATHEMATICS SKILLS DIAGNOSTIC TEST

The following 20-item diagnostic test will allow you to assess your strengths and weaknesses in the mathematics skills tested on the CLAST. For any question you answer incorrectly, study the review section cross-referenced in the chart following the test.

There is only one correct answer for each item. Do not use any books, calculators, slide rules, or rulers, since they are not allowed during the actual test.

MATHEMATICS SKILLS DIAGNOSTIC TEST

DIRECTIONS: Select the best answer.

---

1. $-2\frac{1}{2} \div 3\frac{1}{3} =$

    (A) $-\frac{3}{4}$ (C) $-1\frac{1}{3}$

    (B) -2 (D) $\frac{1}{4}$

2. If you decrease 40 to 25, what is the percent of decrease?

    (A) 40%   (C) 32.5%

    (B) 30%   (D) 37.5%

3. Identify the place value of the underlined digit: 329.7$\underline{4}$6

    (A) $\frac{1}{10}^{4}$ (C) $\frac{1}{10}$

    (B) $\frac{1}{10}^{2}$ (D) 10^{0}

4. $6.\overline{3}$ ☐ $6.\overline{32}$

(A) <   (C) =

(B) >   (D) ≤

5.   Joe worked from 1:00 to 4:00 in the afternoon. Mary works $\frac{1}{5}$ as long as Joe. How long did Mary work?

(A) 36 minutes   (C) 1.5 hours

(B) 2 hours   (D) 50 minutes

6.   What is the length of the missing side?

(A) 50 cm

(B) 5 cm

(C) 5 m

(D) 50 m

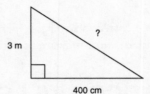

7.   What is the volume of a cone with a radius of 5 cm and a height of 10 cm?

(A) 83π (C) 250π

(B) $(83\frac{1}{3})\pi$ (D) 125π

8.   Lines J and K are parallel. Lines M and N are parallel. What is the measure of $\angle 10$?

(A) 40°

(B) 120°

(C) 60°

(D) 65°

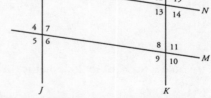

9.   What is the surface area of a cylinder with radius 4 cm and height 16 cm?

(A) 160π (C) 160

(B) 144π (D) 144

10. $5\sqrt{7} + 7\left(\sqrt{35} \times 4\sqrt{5}\right) - 2\sqrt{18} =$

(A) $145\sqrt{2} - 6\sqrt{7}$ (C) $151\sqrt{2}$

(B) $130\sqrt{5} - 4\sqrt{7}$ (D) $145\sqrt{7} - 6\sqrt{2}$

11. $750,000,000 \times 0.0000006 =$

   (A) 3.5×10

   (B) 3.5×10^2

   (C) 4.5×10

   (D) 4.5×10^2

12. Solve for x: $7x - 4 < 2x + 8$

   (A) $x > \frac{12}{5}$

   (B) $x < \frac{12}{5}$

   (C) $x > -\frac{12}{5}$

   (D) $x < -\frac{12}{5}$

13. Solve for x and y in the following set of equations:
    $$x - y = 40$$
    $$3x + 2y = 15$$

   (A) $\{(19, 21)\}$

   (B) $\{(17, -30)\}$

   (C) $\{(19, -21)\}$

   (D)   The empty set

14. It takes two people six hours to move a rock. How long does it take three people to move the same rock?

   (A)   2 hours

   (B)   3 hours

   (C)   4 hours

   (D)   4.5 hours

15. Which of the following mathematically represents the statement:
    "The sum of the squares of two consecutive even integers equals the smaller integer to the 5th power."

   (A) $(2n)^2 + (2n + 2)^2 = (2n)^5$

   (B) $(n)^2 + (n + 2)^2 = (n)^5$

   (C) $(2n)^2 + (2n + 1)^2 = (2n)^5$

   (D) $[(2n) + (2n + 2)]^2 = (2n)^5$

16. What is the mode of the following list?
    $6, 7, 9, 5, 4.5, 8, 9$

   (A)   9

   (B)   8

   (C)   4.5

   (D)   There is no mode.

17. Henry has two sets of shoes, seven pairs of pants, and three sweaters. How many different ways can he dress?

   (A)   42

   (B)   48

   (C)   84

   (D)   21

18. If you roll a six-sided die two times, what is the probability that you will not get two 1's or two 2's in a row?

(A) $\frac{1}{18}$ (C) $\frac{1}{36}$

(B) $\frac{17}{18}$ (D) $\frac{35}{36}$

19. Select the statement that is logically equivalent to:
    If all mice are white, then all lizards are green.

(A) Some mice are white, or all lizards are green.

(B) Some mice are not white, or all lizards are green.

(C) All mice are white, and all lizards are green.

(D) If no mice are white, then no lizards are green.

20. Select the conclusion which makes the following argument valid:
    Jane eats candy bars or she doesn't drink soda.
    Jane drinks soda.

(A) Jane doesn't eat candy bars.

(B) Jane doesn't drink soda.

(C) Jane eats candy bars.

(D) Jane drinks soda and eats candy bars.

MATHEMATICS SKILLS REVIEW DIAGNOSTIC TEST ANSWER KEY

Use the chart below to check your answers. If you responded incorrectly, refer to the column on the right to direct you to the review section that will help you.

Question	Answer	*If you answered this question incorrectly, see the section titled:*
1	A	Rational Numbers, Multiplication and Division: p. 209
2	D	Percent, Percentage of Increase and Decrease: p. 215
3	B	Exponents and Base-Ten Numeration: p. 218
4	B	Order Relation: p. 225
5	A	Word Problems: p. 233
6	C	Triangles: p. 264
7	B	Geometric Formulas: p. 269
8	C	Parallel Lines: p. 261
9	A	Geometric Formulas: p. 269
10	D	Algebra Skills, Real Numbers: p. 286
11	D	Decimals, Multiplication and Division: p. 212
12	B	Linear Inequalities: p. 294
13	C	Systems of Linear Equations: p. 302
14	C	Word Problems: p. 233
15	A	Exponents and Base-Ten Numeration: p. 218; Word Problems: p. 233
16	A	Mean, Median, and Mode: p. 353
17	A	The Fundamental Counting Principle: p 357
18	B	Probability: p. 362
19	B	Determining Equivalence or Non-Equivalence Statements: p. 385
20	C	Reasoning Patterns: p. 397

DETAILED EXPLANATIONS OF ANSWERS

1. **(A)** $-2\frac{1}{2} = -\frac{5}{2}, 3\frac{1}{3} = \frac{10}{3}$

   $-\frac{5}{2} \div \frac{10}{3} = -\frac{5}{2} \times \frac{3}{10} = -\frac{3}{4}$

2. **(D)** $40 - 25 = 15$

   part/total = fraction of decrease: $\frac{15}{40} = 0.375$

   $0.375 \times 100\% = 37.5\%$

3. **(B)**   Write out the digits in the following chart:

10^2	10^1	10^0	.	$1/10^1$	$1/10^2$	$1/10^3$	$1/10^4$
3	2	9	.	7	4	6	

The 4 falls in the $\frac{1}{10}^2$ slot, so this must be its place value.

4. **(B)**   Write out the digits after the decimal point.

$6.\overline{3} = 6.3333\ldots,$ $6.\overline{32} = 6.3232\ldots$
One's place: 6 and 6
Tenths place: 3 and 3
Hundredths place: 3 and 2

In the hundredths place, the first digit is larger than the second. Therefore, choose >.

5. **(A)**   There are three hours between 1:00 and 4:00, so Joe worked three hours.
Mary worked

   $\frac{1}{5} \times 3$ hours $= \frac{3}{5}$ hours.

Since this does not appear as a choice, convert to minutes.

   $\frac{3}{5} \times 60$ minutes/hour $= 36$ minutes

6. **(C)**   Convert all measures to m.

   400 cm $= 4$ m.

Then, use the Pythagorean Theorem: $a^2 + b^2 = c^2$.

   $a = 3, b = 4$
   $c^2 = 3^2 + 4^2 = 9 + 16 = 25$
   $c = 5$

7. **(B)** The formula for the volume of a cone is:

$V = \frac{1}{3} \times \pi \times \text{radius}^2 \times \text{height}$

radius = 5 cm, height = 10 cm

$$V = \frac{1}{3} \times \pi \times 5^2 \times 10 = \frac{1}{3} \times \pi \times 25 \times 10$$
$$V = (\tfrac{250}{3})\pi$$
$$V = (83\tfrac{1}{3})\pi$$

8. **(C)** Angle 3 is supplementary to the 120° angle. Therefore, $m\angle 3 = 180° - 120° = 60°$.

Angle 3 and angle 6 are corresponding angles, so their measures are equal. Therefore, $m\angle 6 = 60°$

Angle 6 and angle 10 are corresponding angles, so their measures are equal. Therefore, $m\angle 10 = 60°$

9. **(A)** A cylinder's surface area is given by:

the area of its top and bottom circles: $2 \times \pi \times \text{radius}^2$
the area around: $2 \times \pi \times \text{radius} \times \text{height}$

radius = 4 cm, height = 16 cm

$$SA = 2 \times \pi \times (4)^2 + 2 \times \pi \times 4 \times 16$$
$$SA = 32\pi + 128\pi$$
$$SA = 160\pi$$

10. **(D)** $5\sqrt{7} + 7\left(\sqrt{35} \times 4\sqrt{5}\right) - 2\sqrt{18}$

$$= 5\sqrt{7} + \left(7 \times 4\right) \left(\sqrt{35} \times \sqrt{5}\right) - 2\sqrt{18}$$

$$= 5\sqrt{7} + 28\left(\sqrt{7} \times \sqrt{5} \times \sqrt{5}\right) - 2\left(\sqrt{9} \times \sqrt{2}\right)$$

$$= 5\sqrt{7} + 28(5)\sqrt{7} - 2(3)\sqrt{2}$$

$$= 145\sqrt{7} - 6\sqrt{2}$$

11. **(D)**

$750{,}000{,}000 = 7.5 \times 10^8$

$0.0000006 = 6 \times 10^{-7}$

$$(7.5 \times 10^8) \times (6 \times 10^{-7}) = (7.5 \times 6) \times (10^8 \times 10^{-7})$$
$$= 45 \times 10^1$$
$$= 4.5 \times 10^2$$

12. **(B)**

$$7x - 4 < 2x + 8$$

$$\underline{-2x \quad\quad -2x} \qquad\qquad \text{Subtract } 2x \text{ from both sides.}$$

$$5x - 4 < \quad 8$$

$$\underline{+4 \quad\quad +4} \qquad\qquad \text{Add 4 to both sides.}$$

$$\frac{5x}{5} \quad < \quad \frac{12}{5} \qquad\qquad \text{Divide by 5 on both sides.}$$

$$x < {}^{12}\!/_5 \qquad\qquad \text{No change of direction in inequality.}$$

13. **(C)** Multiply the first equation by 2: $2(x - y = 40)$

$$2x - 2y = 80$$
$$\underline{3x + 2y = 15} \qquad\qquad \text{Add equations.}$$
$$5x = 95$$
$$x = 19 \qquad\qquad \text{Solve for } x.$$
$$19 - y = \quad 40 \qquad\qquad \text{Substitute into first equation.}$$
$$y = -21 \qquad\qquad \text{Solve for } y.$$

14. **(C)** This problem is an inverse variation since as the number of workers increases, the amount of time required decreases.

Use the formula: # workers × time = # workers × time

$$2 \text{ people} \times 6 \text{ hours} = 3 \text{ people} \times T \text{ hours}$$
$$2 \times 6 = 3 \times T$$
$$12 = 3 \times T$$
$$4 = T$$

15. **(A)**

Two consecutive even integers:	$2n, 2n + 2$
The smaller one:	$2n$
The fifth power of the smaller one:	$(2n)^5$

The statement says: $(2n)^2 + (2n + 2)^2 = (2n)^5$

16. **(A)** The mode is the number which appears most frequently. 9 appears twice in the list. No other number appears more than once. Therefore, 9 is the solution.

17. **(A)** All the clothes are independent events, so use the counting principle: Multiply all possible outcomes.

2 sets of shoes × 7 pairs of pants × 3 sweaters

$$2 \times 7 \times 3 = 42$$

18. **(B)** Each roll of the die is independent, so multiply the probabilities for each roll.

Probability for a 1 to come up: $\frac{1}{6}$
Probability for a 2 to come up: $\frac{1}{6}$

Prob. for a 1 to show 2 times: $\frac{1}{6} \times \frac{1}{6} = \frac{1}{36}$

Prob. for a 2 to show 2 times: $\frac{1}{6} \times \frac{1}{6} = \frac{1}{36}$

Prob. for a 1 to show 2 times or a 2 to show 2 times: $\frac{1}{36} \times \frac{1}{36} = \frac{1}{18}$

Prob. for this not to happen: $P(E') = 1 - P(E)$

$$P(E') = 1 - \frac{1}{18} = \frac{17}{18}$$

19. **(B)** p = all mice are white
        q = all lizards are green

The statement is: (If p, then q)

This is equivalent to: $\sim p$ or q

Negation rule: "all are" ==> "some are not"

Therefore, $\sim p$ = some mice are not white

The transformed statement is:

   Some mice are not white or all lizards are green.

20. **(C)** p = Jane eats candy bars
        q = Jane drinks soda

Statement 1: p or $\sim q$
Statement 2: q
Therefore, p = Jane eats candy bars.

ARITHMETIC SKILLS

RATIONAL NUMBERS

ADDITION AND SUBTRACTION

A rational number is any number that can be expressed as a fraction $\frac{a}{b}$, where both a and b are elements of the set of integers with the exception that b cannot be zero.

Any integer is a rational number, because an integer can be written with a denominator of 1, such as $3 = \frac{3}{1}$.

Some examples of rational numbers are:

$$\frac{1}{4} \qquad -\frac{5}{2} \qquad \frac{20}{3} \qquad \frac{5}{9} \qquad -7$$

To add or subtract two rational numbers, follow these steps:

(1) If it is a subtraction problem, convert the problem to an addition problem by changing the subtraction sign to an addition sign and changing the sign on the term following the subtraction symbol.

(2) Find a common denominator and rewrite the terms with the common denominator.

(3) Regrouping may be necessary before computing.

(4a) Combine the numerators and write the value over the common denominator.

(4b) Combine the integer parts if necessary. Then use the following addition rules to compute:

- If the signs of the numbers are alike, add the absolute values of the numbers and assign to the answer the sign of the original values.

- If the signs are unlike, subtract the lesser absolute value term from the greater absolute value term and assign to the answer the sign of the original value with the greater absolute value.

(5) Regroup to simplify the answer if necessary.

Example: $2\frac{1}{3} + \frac{5}{7} =$

Solution:	$2\frac{7}{21} + \frac{15}{21}$	(2) Find a common denominator.
	$= 2\frac{22}{21}$	(4) Add.
	$= 3\frac{1}{21}$	(5) Regroup to simplify.

Example: $-3 + 1\frac{3}{5} =$

    Solution: $-2\frac{5}{5} + 1\frac{3}{5}$ (3) Regroup with a common denominator.

            $= -1\frac{2}{5}$ (4) Subtract.

Example: $-1\frac{3}{4} - (-2) =$

    Solution: $-1\frac{3}{4} + 2$ (1) Rewrite as an addition problem.

            $= -1\frac{3}{4} + 1\frac{4}{4}$ (3) Regroup with a common denominator.

            $= \frac{1}{4}$ (4) Subtract.

Example: $-\frac{1}{2} - \frac{2}{7} =$

    Solution: $-\frac{1}{2} + (-\frac{2}{7})$ (1) Rewrite as an addition problem.

            $= -\frac{7}{14} + (-\frac{4}{14})$ (2) Find a common denominator.

            $= -\frac{11}{14}$ (4) Add.

MULTIPLICATION AND DIVISION

To multiply or divide two rational numbers, follow these steps:

(1)   Convert any mixed numbers to improper fractions.

(2)   If it is a division problem, convert the problem to a multiplication problem by inverting the second term and replacing the division sign with a multiplication sign.

(3)   Simplify if possible.

(4a) Multiply the numerators.

(4b) Multiply the denominators.

      Use the following rules to determine the sign of the answer.

- If the signs are alike, the answer is positive.

- If the signs are not alike, the answer is negative.

(5)   Rewrite the answer as a mixed number if possible.

Example: $\frac{2}{3} \times 1\frac{3}{5} =$

    Solution: $\frac{2}{3} \times \frac{8}{5}$ (1) Convert to improper fractions.

            $= \frac{16}{15}$ (4) Multiply.

            $= 1\frac{1}{15}$ (5) Rewrite as a mixed number.

Example: $-5 \times 1\frac{4}{5} =$

Solution: $-\frac{5}{1} \times \frac{9}{5}$ (1) Convert to improper fractions.

$= -\frac{1}{1} \times \frac{9}{1}$ (3) Simplify.

$= -9$ (4) Multiply.

Example: $-5\frac{1}{3} \div (-\frac{3}{4}) =$

Solution: $-\frac{16}{3} \div (-\frac{3}{4})$ (1) Convert to improper fractions.

$= -\frac{16}{3} \times (-\frac{4}{3})$ (2) Convert to multiplication.

$= \frac{64}{9}$ (4) Multiply.

$= 7\frac{1}{9}$ (5) Rewrite as a mixed number.

DRILL: RATIONAL NUMBERS

DIRECTIONS: Select the best answer.

1. $\frac{2}{3} + 1\frac{1}{4} =$
   (A) $1\frac{3}{7}$ (C) $3\frac{2}{3}$
   (B) $1\frac{11}{12}$ (D) 1

2. $-3\frac{5}{9} + 7 =$
   (A) $3\frac{4}{9}$ (C) $4\frac{4}{9}$
   (B) $4\frac{5}{9}$ (D) $10\frac{5}{9}$

3. $-8\frac{1}{8} - 2\frac{2}{3} =$
   (A) $-10\frac{19}{24}$ (C) $6\frac{13}{24}$
   (B) $5\frac{13}{24}$ (D) $-10\frac{13}{24}$

4. $-5 - (-2\frac{1}{6}) =$
   (A) $2\frac{5}{6}$ (C) $3\frac{5}{6}$
   (B) $-7\frac{1}{6}$ (D) $-2\frac{5}{6}$

5. $-\frac{2}{3} \times (-\frac{4}{5}) =$

    (A) $-\frac{2}{15}$ (C) $-\frac{8}{15}$

    (B) $\frac{8}{15}$ (D) $-\frac{10}{12}$

6. $5\frac{1}{3} \times \frac{3}{8} =$

    (A) $\frac{4}{11}$ (C) $\frac{8}{5}$

    (B) 2   (D) $5\frac{1}{8}$

7. $-5\frac{1}{4} \div (-\frac{7}{10}) =$

    (A) $-2\frac{4}{7}$ (C) $5\frac{19}{20}$

    (B) $-7\frac{1}{2}$ (D) $7\frac{1}{2}$

8. $-7 \div 2\frac{1}{4} =$

    (A) $3\frac{1}{9}$ (C) $-5\frac{1}{4}$

    (B) $-3\frac{1}{9}$ (D) $4\frac{3}{4}$

DECIMALS

ADDITION AND SUBTRACTION

To add or subtract two rational numbers in decimal form, follow these steps:

(1)   If it is a subtraction problem, convert the problem to an addition problem by changing the subtraction sign to an addition sign and changing the sign on the term following the subtraction symbol.

(2)   If the two terms do not have the same number of decimal places, add zeros to the deficient term until both terms have an equal number of decimal places.

(3a) If the signs of the terms are alike, write the numbers in a column making sure the decimal points are lined up, one beneath the other. Add the numbers as usual, placing the decimal point in the sum so that it is still in line with the others. The sign of the answer is the same sign as the original values.

(3b) If the signs of the terms are not alike, write the greater absolute value term above the lesser absolute value term in a column, making sure the decimal points are lined up, one beneath the other. Subtract the numbers as usual, placing the decimal point in the sum so that it is still in line with the others. The sign of the answer is the sign of the term with the greater absolute value.

Example:　6.3195 + 0.821 =

Solution:　6.3195 + 0.8210　　(2) Add zeros.

$$\begin{array}{r} 6.3195 \\ +\ 0.8210 \\ \hline 7.1405 \end{array}$$

(3) Line up the terms and
add as usual.
Determine sign of the answer.

Example:　5.9313 + (−13.49) =

Solution:　5.9313 + (−13.4900)　　(2) Add zeros.

$$\begin{array}{r} 13.4900 \\ -\ 5.9313 \\ \hline 7.5587 \end{array}$$

(3) Greater absolute value term.
Lesser absolute value term.
Subtract as usual.

− 7.5587　　Determine sign of the answer.

Example:　−3.1 − 8.15 =

Solution:　−3.1 + (−8.15)　　(1) Rewrite as an addition problem.

−3.10 + (−8.15)　　(2) Add zeros.

$$\begin{array}{r} 3.10 \\ +\ 8.15 \\ \hline 11.25 \end{array}$$

(3) Line up the terms and
add as usual.

− 11.25　　Determine sign of the answer.

MULTIPLICATION AND DIVISION

To multiply two rational numbers in decimal form, follow these steps:

(1)　Ignore the decimal place and multiply the numbers as usual.

(2)　Count the number of decimal places in the two given factors and count off that many decimal places in the product. Place the decimal point at that location.

(3)　Use the following rules to determine the sign of the answer:

- If the sign of the two factors are alike, the product is positive.

- If the sign of the two factors are not alike, the product is negative.

Example:　5.18 × (−3.4) =

Solution:

$$\begin{array}{r} 5.18 \quad \text{(2 decimal places)} \\ \times\ \ 3.4 \quad \text{(1 decimal place)} \\ \hline 2072 \\ 1554\ \ \\ \hline 17612 \end{array}$$

(1) Multiply as usual.

17.612　(3 decimal places)　　(2) Locate decimal point.

− 17.612　　(3) Determine sign of the answer.

Example: $-7 \times (-0.005) =$

Solution:

$$
\begin{array}{r}
7.3 \\
\times\ 0.005 \\
\hline
365
\end{array}
$$

(1 decimal place)
(3 decimal places)

(1) Multiply as usual.

0.0365   (4 decimal places)

(2) Locate the decimal point.

0.0365

(3) Determine the sign of the answer.

To divide two rational numbers in decimal form, follow these steps:

(1)   Move the decimal point to the right in the given factor to make the given factor a whole number. Move the decimal point the exact same number of places to the right in the product as in the given factor. If there are not enough places in the product, add zeros until there are enough places. Place a decimal point in the missing factor, directly in line with the decimal point in the product.

(2)   Divide as usual.

(3)   Use the following rules to determine the sign of the answer.

  • If the sign of the given factor and the product are alike, the answer is positive.

  • If the sign of the given factor and the product are not alike, the answer is negative.

Example: $12.93 \div 0.3$

Solution:

$$
0.3\overline{)12.93} \quad \begin{array}{r} 43.1 \end{array}
$$

$$
\begin{array}{r}
43.1 \\
0.3\,)\,\overline{12.93} \\
-\ 12 \\
\hline
9 \\
-\ 9 \\
\hline
3 \\
-\ 3 \\
\hline
0
\end{array}
$$

(1) Locate the decimal point in the missing factor.

(2) Divide.

Answer: 43.1

(3) Determine sign of the answer.

Example: $-0.08 \div 1.6 =$

Solution:

$$
\begin{array}{r}
0.05 \\
1.6\,)\,\overline{0.0\,80} \\
-\ 80 \\
\hline
0
\end{array}
$$

(1) Locate the decimal point in the missing factor.

(2) Divide.

Answer: -0.05

(3) Determine sign of the answer.

DRILL: DECIMALS

DIRECTIONS: Select the best answer.

---

1. $-3.28 + 7.151 =$
   (A) 3.871
   (B) -3.871
   (C) 4.123
   (D) 4.131

2. $-12.9215 + (-0.383) =$
   (A) 12. 9598
   (B) -12.9598
   (C) -13.3045
   (D) 13.3045

3. $4.123 - (-11.9) =$
   (A) 15.023
   (B) -5.323
   (C) 16.023
   (D) -44.1107

4. $1.949 - 4 =$
   (A) -2.051
   (B) 3.051
   (C) 5.949
   (D) -5.949

5. $1.03 \times (-2.6) =$
   (A) -2.18
   (B) -2.678
   (C) 2.78
   (D) -3.38

6. $5.32 \times 0.04 =$
   (A) 0.2128
   (B) 2.128
   (C) 21.28
   (D) 1.33

7. $-25.2 \div 0.3 =$
   (A) $-.84$
   (B) -8.04
   (C) 8.4
   (D) -84

8. $14.95 \div (-6.5) =$
   (A) -2.3
   (B) 20.3
   (C) -23
   (D) -230

PERCENT

PERCENTAGE OF INCREASE AND DECREASE

A percent is a way of expressing the relationship between part and whole, where the whole is defined as 100%. A percent can be defined by a fraction with a denominator of 100. Decimals can also represent a percent. For example, 56% = $\frac{56}{100}$ = 0.56.

To calculate the resultant of increasing or decreasing a given amount by a given percentage:

(1)   Write the multiplication expression with the given amount and the given percentage as an amount out of 100.

(2)   Simplify if possible.

(3)   Multiply.

(4a) For a percent increase, add the original value to the calculated amount.

(4b) For a percent decrease, subtract the original value from the calculated amount.

Example: If you increase 90 by 40%, what is the result?

Solution:	$90 \times \frac{40}{100}$ =	(1) Given amount and given percentage.
	= $\frac{9}{1} \times \frac{4}{1}$	(2) Simplify.
	= 36	(3) Multiply.
	= 90 + 36 = 126	(4) Add to find the result.

Example :   If you decrease 240 by 25%, what is the result?

Solution:	$240 \times \frac{25}{100}$ =	(1) Given amount and given percentage.
	= $\frac{60}{1} \times \frac{1}{1}$	(2) Simplify.
	= 60	(3) Multiply.
	240 − 60 = 180	(4) Subtract to find the result.

To calculate a percent increase or a percent decrease, follow these steps:

(1)   Identify the original amount.

(2)   Subtract the lesser amount from the greater amount.

(3)   Divide this difference by the original amount.

(4)   Set up a proportion with the term from step 3 and the percent increase or decrease.

(5)   Solve the proportion.

Example: If 45 is increased to 54, what is the percent increase?

Solution: 45 (1) Original amount.

$54 - 45 = 9$ (2) Subtract.

$\frac{9}{45}$ (3) Divide difference by original amount.

$\frac{9}{45} = \frac{x}{100}$ (4) Set up proportion.

$\frac{1}{5} = \frac{x}{100}$ Simplify.

$100 = 5x$ (5) Solve the proportion.

$20 = x$

Answer: 20% increase

Example: If 80 is decreased to 20, what is the percent decrease?

Solution: 80 (1) Original amount.

$80 - 20 = 60$ (2) Subtract.

$\frac{60}{80}$ (3) Divide difference by original amount.

$\frac{60}{80} = \frac{x}{100}$ (4) Set up proportion.

$\frac{3}{4} = \frac{x}{100}$ Simplify.

$4x = 300$ (5) Solve the proportion.

$x = 75$

Answer: 75% decrease

PERCENTAGE OF A NUMBER

To find the missing term of "a% of b is c," follow these steps:

(1) Write the equation

$\frac{a}{100} \times b = c$ or $c = \frac{a}{100} \times b$.

(2) Substitute the given values for the appropriate variables.

- The verb "is" represents the equals sign.
- "Of" represents multiplication.
- The "a" term is the percent and is a value out of 100.
- The "b" term is the original number and usually follows the word "of."
- The "c" term is the remaining term and is on the opposite side of the "is" from the given percent.

a% of b is c c is a% of b

or

$\frac{a}{100} \times b = c$ $c = \frac{a}{100} \times b$

(3) Calculate for the missing term.

Example: What is 90% of 400?

Solution: $c = \frac{a}{100} \times b$ (1) Write the equation.

$c = \frac{90}{100} \times 400$ (2) Substitute the givens.

$= \frac{90}{100} \times \frac{400}{1}$ (3) Solve for c.

$= \frac{90}{1} \times \frac{4}{1}$

$= 360$

Example: What percent of 200 is 4?

Solution: $\frac{a}{100} \times b = c$ (1) Write the equation.

$\frac{a}{100} \times 200 = 4$ (2) Substitute the givens.

$\frac{a}{100} \times \frac{200}{1} = 4$ (3) Solve for a.

$\frac{a}{1} \times \frac{2}{1} = 4$

$2a = 4$

$a = 2$

Answer: 2%

Example: 10 is 200% of what number?

Solution: $c = \frac{a}{100} \times b$ (1) Write the equation.

$10 = \frac{200}{100} \times b$ (2) Substitute the givens.

$10 = 2 \times b$ (3) Solve for b.

$5 = b$

DRILL: PERCENT

DIRECTIONS: Select the best answer.

---

1.   If you increase 12 by 150%, what is the result?

(A)   18   (C)   180

(B)   30   (D)   13.8

2.   If you decrease 300 by 5%, what is the result?

(A)   15   (C)   285

(B)   150   (D)   315

3.   What is 3% of 80?

    (A)   0.24   (C)   24

    (B)   2.4   (D)   240

4.   What is 125% of 400?

    (A)   425   (C)   525

    (B)   500   (D)   600

5.   140 is 20% of what number?

    (A)   28   (C)   112

    (B)   70   (D)   700

6.   35 is what percent of 25?

    (A)   110   (C)   40

    (B)   140   (D)   120

EXPONENTS AND BASE-TEN NUMERATION

When a number is multiplied by itself a specific number of times, it is said to be raised to a power. The way this is written is $a^n = b$ where a is a number or base, n is the exponent or power that indicates the number of times the number is to be multiplied by itself, and b is the product of this multiplication.

In the expression 3^2, 3 is the base and 2 is the exponent. This means that 3 is multiplied by itself 2 times and the product is 9.

To assist in recognizing the meaning of exponents, here are a few examples of what to expect on the CLAST.

Example: $(3^4)(7^2) = (3)(3)(3)(3)(7)(7)$

Example: $\dfrac{9^2}{2^5} = \dfrac{(9)(9)}{(2)(2)(2)(2)(2)}$

Example: $4^3 + 6^4 = (4)(4)(4) + (6)(6)(6)(6)$

Example: $5^2 - 8^3 = (5)(5) - (8)(8)(8)$

Example: $(7^3)^2 = (7^3)(7^3)$

Two important facts to remember when working with exponents are:

•   A number raised to the first power is itself. $a^1 = a$

- A nonzero number raised to the zero power is 1. $a^0 = 1$

When working with base-ten numeration, use the following place value chart:

Millions	Thousands	Hundreds	Hundredths	Thousandths	Millionths
units	hundreds · tens · units	hundreds · tens · units	shtnet · hundredths · units	tenths · hundreds · units	units
10^6 10^5	10^4 10^3 10^2	10^1 10^0	$1/10^1$ $1/10^2$ $1/10^3$	$1/10^4$ $1/10^5$	$1/10^6$

When asked to write a numeral in expanded form, use the above place value chart and follow these steps:

(1) Write the given numeral under the appropriate headings lining up the decimal points.

(2) Add together the terms of the number under the heading multiplied by the appropriate heading eliminating any zero terms since zero times a number is zero.

Example: Select the expanded notation for 9,205.07.

Solution:

$$\frac{10^4 \quad 10^3 \quad 10^2 \quad 10^1 \quad 10^0 \; . \; 1/10^1 \quad 1/10^2 \quad 1/10^3}{9 \quad\;\; 2 \quad\;\; 0 \quad\;\; 5 \; . \;\; 0 \quad\quad 7}$$

$(9 \times 10^3) + (2 \times 10^2) + (5 \times 10^0) + (7 \times 1/10^2)$

When asked to identify the place value associated with a particular location within a numeral, use the above place value chart and follow these steps:

(1) Write the given numeral under the appropriate headings lining up the decimal points.

(2) The answer is the heading associated with the location of the underlined digit.

Example: Select the place value associated with the underlined digit.

$$53.89\underline{1}8$$

Solution: $$\frac{10^2 \ 10^1 \ 10^0 \ \times \ 1/10^1 \ 1/10^2 \ 1/10^3 \ 1/10^4 \ 1/10^5 \ 1/10^6}{5 \ 3 \ \times \ 8 \ 9 \ \underline{1} \ 8}$$

Answer: $1/10^3$

When asked to write a numeral from the expanded form, use the above place value chart and follow these steps:

(1)   Write each digit under the corresponding power in the chart lining up the new decimal point with the one in the chart.

(2)   If between the written digits there are headings without a digit, write in a zero.

(3)   Write out the resulting numeral.

Example: Select the numeral for

$$(6 \times 10^2) + (4 \times 10) + (9 \times 1/10) + (1 \times 1/10^4)$$

Solution: $$\frac{10^3 \ 10^2 \ 10^1 \ 10^0 \ \times \ 1/10^1 \ 1/10^2 \ 1/10^3 \ 1/10^4 \ 1/10^5}{6 \ 4 \ \times \ 9 \ 1}$$

$$\frac{10^3 \ 10^2 \ 10^1 \ 10^0 \ \times \ 1/10^1 \ 1/10^2 \ 1/10^3 \ 1/10^4 \ 1/10^5}{6 \ 4 \ 0 \ \times \ 9 \ 0 \ 0 \ 1}$$

Answer: 640.9001

DRILL: EXPONENTS AND BASE-TEN NUMERATION

DIRECTIONS: Select the best answer.

---

1. $(8^2) \ (5^3) =$

(A)   (16) (15)

(B) 40^6

(C)   (8 + 8) (5 + 5 + 5)

(D)   (8) (8) (5) (5) (5)

2. $\dfrac{5^3}{7^2} =$

   (A) $\dfrac{(5)(5)(5)}{(7)(7)}$

   (C) $\dfrac{5+5+5}{7+7}$

   (B) $\dfrac{15}{49}$

   (D) $\dfrac{1}{2}$

3. $2^3 - 6^3 =$

   (A) $(2 + 2 + 2) - (6 + 6 + 6)$

   (C) $(2)(2)(2) - (6)(6)(6)$

   (B) $(2 - 6)^3$

   (D) $(2 - 6)^6$

4. $9^2 + 3^4 =$

   (A) 12^6

   (C) 12^8

   (B) $(9 + 9) + (3 + 3 + 3 + 3)$

   (D) $(9)(9) + (3)(3)(3)(3)$

5. $(4^5)^3 =$

   (A) $(4)(5)(3)$

   (C) $(4 \times 5)^3$

   (B) $(4^5)(4^5)(4^5)$

   (D) 4^8

6. Select the correct expanded notation for 3.0205.

   (A) $(3 \times 10^0) + (2 \times \frac{1}{10}) + (5 \times \frac{1}{10}^4)$

   (B) $(3 \times 10) + (2 \times \frac{1}{10}^1) + (5 \times \frac{1}{10}^3)$

   (C) $(3 \times 10^0) + (2 \times \frac{1}{10}^2) + (5 \times \frac{1}{10}^4)$

   (D) $(3 \times 10) + (2 \times 10^2) + (5 \times 10^4)$

7. Select the place value associated with the underlined digit.
   30$\underline{5}$.251

   (A) 10

   (C) 10^0

   (B) 5

   (D) $\frac{1}{10}^1$

8. Select the numeral for
   $(5 \times 10^4) + (7 \times 10) + (3 \times \frac{1}{10}^2)$.

   (A) $50{,}070.03$

   (C) $5{,}007.003$

   (B) 57.3

   (D) $50{,}007.03$

CONVERTING DECIMALS, PERCENTS, AND FRACTIONS

To convert a fractional number to a decimal:

(1) Whether the fractional number is a simple fraction or a mixed number, divide the numerator by the denominator until termination or a repeating pattern appears.

(2) If the fractional number was a mixed number, combine the whole number part with the fractional part.

Example: Convert $\frac{5}{8}$ to a decimal.

Solution:
$$8\overline{)5.000}$$

$$
\begin{array}{r}
.625 \\
8\overline{)5.000} \\
-\,48 \\
\hline
20 \\
-\,16 \\
\hline
40 \\
-\,40 \\
\hline
0
\end{array}
$$

(1) Divide.

Example: Convert $3\frac{1}{5}$ to a decimal.

Solution:
$$
\begin{array}{r}
.2 \\
5\overline{)1.0} \\
-\,10 \\
\hline
0
\end{array}
$$

(1) Divide.

Answer: 3.2

(2) Combine whole part with decimal part.

To convert a fractional number to a percent:

(1) If the fractional number is a mixed number, convert the mixed number to an improper fraction by multiplying the whole number by the denominator of the fraction and add the numerator. This new term becomes the numerator and the denominator remains the same.

(2) Set up a proportion with the fraction equal to the term $\frac{a}{100}$ since percent means per 100.

(3) Solve the proportion for the missing term a, which is the percent.

Example: Convert $2\frac{3}{4}$ to a percent.

Solution: $2\frac{3}{4} = \frac{11}{4}$

(1) Convert to an improper fraction.

$\frac{11}{4} = \frac{a}{100}$

(2) Set up the proportion.

$$11 \times 100 = 4 \times a \qquad \text{(3) Solve for } a.$$

$$1,100 = 4a$$

$$275 = a$$

Answer: 275%

To convert a percent to a decimal:

(1)   Remember that a percent is per 100, so simply divide by 100.

Example: Convert 115% to a decimal.

Solution: $^{115}/_{100}$

$$^{115}/_{100} = 1.15$$

To convert a percent to a fraction:

(1)   Again remember that a percent is per 100, so write the given percent over 100.

(2)   If there is a decimal part to the numerator, multiply both the numerator and denominator by the power of 10 necessary to form a whole number.

(3)   Reduce the fraction to simplest form.

Example: Convert 15.2% to a fraction.

Solution: $^{15.2}/_{100}$ (1) Meaning of percent.

$^{15.2}/_{100} \times ^{10}/_{10}$ (2) Multiply by $^{10}/_{10}$ since there is one decimal place.

$= ^{152}/_{1,000}$

$= ^{19}/_{125}$ (3) Reduce.

To convert a decimal to a percent:

(1)   Multiply the decimal by 100.

Example: Convert 1.285 to a percent.

Solution: $1.285 \times 100 = 128.5\%$

To convert a decimal to a fraction:

(1)   Write the decimal over 1.

(2)   Multiply both the numerator and denominator by a power of 10 sufficient to convert the numerator into a whole number.

(3)   Reduce the resulting fraction to simplest terms.

Example: Convert 0.738 to a fraction.

Solution: $^{.738}/_1$ (1) Write over 1.

$^{.738}/_1 \times {^{1,000}}/_{1,000}$ (2) Multiply to eliminate decimal.

$= {^{738}}/_{1,000}$ (3) Simplify.

$= {^{369}}/_{500}$

DRILL: CONVERTING DECIMALS, PERCENTS, AND FRACTIONS

DIRECTIONS: Select the best answer.

---

1. $^{13}/_{20} =$
   (A)   .65%   (C)   .13
   (B)   65%   (D)   6.5

2.   84% =
   (A) $^1/_{84}$ (C) $^{17}/_{25}$
   (B)   8.4   (D) $^{21}/_{25}$

3. $4^3/_5 =$
   (A)   4.35   (C)   4.6%
   (B)   4.6   (D)   46%

4.   3.61 =
   (A)   361%   (C) $^{3.61}/_{100}$
   (B)   36.1%   (D)   3.061%

5.   0.003 =
   (A) $^3/_{1,000}$ (C)   3%
   (B) $^3/_{100}$ (D)   .00003%

ORDER RELATION

In this section, you will be asked to compare two pairs of numbers which may be fractions, mixed numbers, decimals, or nonperfect square roots by choosing from the symbols = (equal to), < (less than), or > (greater than).

Before beginning any work, if one of the terms is positive and the other negative, the positive term is obviously greater. Answer the question without any further work and proceed to the next question. If, however, the signs of the two terms are alike, the appropriate steps for the various combinations are as follows.

To compare two fractions or mixed numbers:

(1) Rewrite the fraction or fractional part with a common denominator.

(2) Since the denominators are now equal and provided the whole part of any mixed numbers are equivalent, the fraction with the greater numerator has the greater overall value.

Example: $\frac{2}{7} \; \Box \; \frac{1}{3}$

Solution: $\frac{6}{21} \; \Box \; \frac{7}{21}$

Since 6 < 7,

$\frac{2}{7} < \frac{1}{3}$

Example: $3\frac{3}{4} \; \Box \; 3\frac{7}{10}$

Solution: $3\frac{15}{20} \; \Box \; 3\frac{14}{20}$

Since 15 > 14,

$3\frac{3}{4} > 3\frac{7}{10}$

Example: $-\frac{11}{15} \; \Box \; -\frac{13}{18}$

Solution: $-\frac{66}{90} \; \Box \; -\frac{65}{90}$

Since −66 < −65,

$-\frac{11}{15} < -\frac{13}{18}$

To compare two decimal numbers:

(1) Compare corresponding place value digits of each number beginning at the left most digits. Continue the comparison until one digit is not equal to the other, the number with the greater digit is the decimal with greater value.

(2) It may be necessary to add zeros to terminating decimals or expand repeating decimals to reach a conclusion.

Example: $6.8 \; \Box \; 6.\overline{8}$

Solution: $6.8 = 6.8\underline{0}$

$6.\overline{8} = 6.8\underline{8}888\ldots$

Since 0 < 8 in the thousandths position,
6.80 < 6.88... and

$$6.8 < 6.\overline{8}$$

Example: 98.6$\overline{7}$ ☐ 98.$\overline{67}$

Solution: 98.6$\overline{7}$ = 98.67$\underline{7}$7...

98.$\overline{67}$ = 98.67$\underline{6}$7...

Since 7 > 6 in the thousandths position,
98.6777... > 98.6767... and

$$98.6\overline{7} > 98.\overline{67}$$

To compare a fraction and a decimal:

(1) Convert the fraction to a decimal by dividing the numerator by the denominator.

(2) Proceed as described above for comparing two decimal numbers.

Example: 5.45 ☐ 5⁴/₉

Solution:
$$9\overline{)\,4.0} \quad 0.\overline{4}$$
$$\underline{-\ 3\ 6}$$
$$4$$

5⁴/₉ = 5.$\overline{4}$

Since 5 > 4 in the hundredths position,

5.45 > 5.44... and

5.45 > 5⁴/₉

If one of the terms is a nonperfect square root, one of two procedures is necessary. The first involves less computation and is usually quicker; however, it does not, in some circumstances, provide enough information to arrive at a conclusion.

(1) Determine the perfect squares that are consecutively greater and less than the integer. This will be your range.

(2) Examine the answer choices and eliminate those that don't fall within this range.

If this does not prove fruitful, try the following:

(1) Square both sides. A square root squared is simply the number beneath the radical. The other term squared can sometimes be an estimate.

(2) Compare the squared terms. If the terms were both positive, the greater squared value corresponds to the greater nonsquared term. If the terms

were both negative, the greater squared value corresponds to the lesser nonsquared term.

Note: The square root of a nonperfect square number is an irrational number. That is, as a decimal, it does not terminate or repeat. This means that the square root of a nonperfect square number must be greater than or less than and cannot equal a repeating or terminating decimal.

Example: $\sqrt{65}\ \square\ 7.8$

Solution: $\sqrt{65}$ is between 8 and 9 ($8^2 = 64$, $9^2 = 81$, and $64<65<81$).

Since $\sqrt{65}$ is greater than 8 and 8 is greater than 7.8,

$\sqrt{65} > 7.8$

Example: $2.5\ \square\ \sqrt{7}$

Solution: $\sqrt{7}$ is between 2 and 3 ($2^2 = 4$, $3^2 = 9$, and $4 < 7 < 9$).
This does not provide enough information to decide which symbol to use. Proceed to the second method and square both sides.

$2.5^2 = 6.25$

$(\sqrt{7})^2 = 7$

Since $6.25 < 7$,

$2.5 < \sqrt{7}$

DRILL: ORDER RELATION

DIRECTIONS: Select the best answer.

1. $-\frac{4}{5}\ \square\ \frac{7}{12}$
   (A) =
   (B) <
   (C) >
   (D) ≤

2. $4\frac{5}{7}\ \square\ 4\frac{3}{4}$
   (A) =
   (B) <
   (C) >
   (D) ≥

3. $-\frac{3}{8} \ \square \ -\frac{4}{9}$

    (A) =   (C) >

    (B) <

4. $7.\overline{3} \ \square \ 7.\overline{32}$

    (A) =   (C) >

    (B) <

5. $\frac{13}{52} \ \square \ .25$

    (A) =   (C) >

    (B) <

6. $\sqrt{48} \ \square \ 7.1$

    (A) =   (C) >

    (B) <   (D) $\geq$

7. $\sqrt{120} \ \square \ 10.9$

    (A) =   (C) >

    (B) <   (D) $\geq$

ESTIMATION

To quickly and correctly answer any question from this section, make a rough estimate by rounding the given information in the problem before computing.

For any type of problem in this section, follow these steps:

(1) Round off the given data. Usually a single significant digit is sufficient.

(2) Compute.

   • If a sum is asked for, add the rounded values.

   • If a product is asked for, multiply the rounded values.

   • If an average is asked for, add the rounded values and divide by the total number of values.

Example: For a friend's birthday, I spent $21.97 for the present, $2.95 for the gift wrap, $.85 for a bow, and $2.25 for a card. What is a reasonable estimate of the total amount spent on my friend's birthday?

Solution: $21.97 ==> $22.00   (1) Round each value.

2.95 ==>   3.00

.85 ==>   1.00

2.25 ==> + 2.00

$28.00   (2) Sum the rounded values.

Example: Children in a kindergarten class were asked to bring in bottle caps to use for a class project. Following is a list of the number of caps each child brought in:

Child	Number of Caps
Robert	42
Brandon	14
Wil	29
Douglas	37
Ryan	53
Samantha	11
Vanessa	30
Valery	24
J.P.	7
Kara	35
Katie	16

What is a reasonable estimate of the average number of caps brought in by each child?

Solution: 42 ==>   40   (1) Round each value.

14 ==>   10

29 ==>   30

37 ==>   40

53 ==>   50

11 ==>   10

30 ==>   30

24 ==>   20

7 ==>   10

35 ==>   40

16 ==> + 20

300   (2) Sum the rounded values.

There are 11 students, so round to 10.

$300/_{10} = 30$

About 30 caps per student.

Example: The same kindergarten class of 11 students mentioned above measured the heights of each student at the beginning of the year. The shortest person was 34 inches and the tallest person was 47 inches. What is a reasonable estimate of the average height of a child in the class?

Solution: The average height could be any value ranging from slightly more than 34 inches to slightly less than 47 inches. As this will be a multiple-choice question, choose a value between 34 and 47. There should be only one such value.

DRILL: ESTIMATION

DIRECTIONS: Select the best answer.

1. Joni bought 3.5 gallons of milk at the grocery store. Each gallon costs $3.35. Which of the following is a reasonable estimate of the cost of the milk?

   (A) $3.00   (C) $12.00

   (B) $4.00   (D) $16.00

2. The French club had a car wash last weekend to raise funds for a trip over spring break. They charged $3.00 per car and $5.00 per van. Which of the following would be a reasonable estimate of the average price per vehicle made by the club?

   (A) $2.00   (C) $3.65

   (B) $2.90   (D) $5.00

NUMBER RELATIONSHIPS

To identify a missing term from a list of related number pairs:

(1) Examine the first number pair given. See if the second term is obtainable from the first by

    a. adding or subtracting a constant (1 through 10),

    b. multiplying or dividing by a constant (2, 3, 4, or 5), or

    c. squaring or taking the square root of the first term.

(2) Check your rule(s) out on the second pair.

(3) If your rule holds, continue to check the remaining given pairs. If your rule does not hold, go back to step 1 and examine other alternatives for the rule.

(4)   Once you have a rule which holds consistently for all the given number pairs, apply the rule to the number pair with the missing term.

Example: Look at the relationship between the numbers of each pair. Identify the missing term.

$$(3, 9) \quad (\tfrac{1}{3}, 1) \quad (-5, -15) \quad (\tfrac{4}{3}, 4) \quad (\tfrac{5}{2}, \underline{\quad})$$

Solution: $(3, 9)$	(1) The first pair.
$3 \times \underline{3} = 9$ $3 + \underline{6} = 9$	Ways of obtaining the second term from the first term.
$3^{\underline{2}} = 9$	
$(\tfrac{1}{3}, 1)$	(2) The second pair.
$\tfrac{1}{3} \times 3 = 1$ $\tfrac{1}{3} + 6 \neq 1$ $(\tfrac{1}{3})^2 \neq 1$	Multiply by 3 rule holds. Add 6 rule does not hold. Square rule does not hold.
$-5 \times 3 = -15$ $\tfrac{4}{3} \times 3 = 4$	(3) Remaining pairs.
$\tfrac{5}{2} \times 3 = \tfrac{15}{2}$	(4) Missing term from rule.

Example: Look at the relationship between the numbers of each pair. Identify the missing term.

$$(6, 0) \quad (-1.4, -7.4) \quad (5\tfrac{1}{4}, -\tfrac{3}{4}) \quad (3, -3) \quad (1, \underline{\quad})$$

Solution: $(6, 0)$	(1) The first pair.
$6 \times \underline{0} = 0$ $6 - \underline{6} = 0$	Ways of obtaining the second term from the first term.
$(-1.4, -7.4)$	(2) The second pair.
$-1.4 \times 0 \neq -7.4$ $-1.4 - 6 = -7.4$	Multiply by 0 rule does not hold. Subtract 6 rule holds.
$5\tfrac{1}{4} - 6 = -\tfrac{3}{4}$ $3 - 6 = -3$	(3) Remaining pairs.
$1 - 6 = -5$	(4) Missing term from rule.

To identify a missing term given a progression of numbers:

(1)   Begin with the first two or three terms of the progression.

(2)   Determine if the progression is arithmetic, geometric, or harmonic with the following information:

   a. Arithmetic progressions are formed by adding or subtracting a constant term to each successive term of the progression.

   b. Geometric progressions are formed by multiplying or dividing a constant term to each successive term of the progression.

       c. Harmonic progressions will have a numerator of 1 and a denominator, which if taken alone, is an arithmetic progression.

(3)   If the progression is

       a. arithmetic: Find the term which is being added or subtracted to use to identify the missing term.

       b. geometric: Find the term which is being multiplied or divided to use to identify the missing term.

       c. harmonic: Find the term which is being added to the denominator to use to identify the missing term.

Example: Identify the next term of the following progression.

$$6, 3, 0, -3, -6, -9, \ldots$$

Solution:	$6, 3, 0, \ldots$	(1) The first few terms.
	$6 - 3 = 3$	(2) The progression is arithmetic.
	$3 - 3 = 0$	
	$0 - 3 = -3$	
	etc…	
	$-9 - 3 = -12$	(3) Subtract 3 to find the missing term.

Example: Identify the next term of the following progression.

$$1, -2, 4, -8, 16, -32, \ldots$$

Solution:	$1, -2, 4, \ldots$	(1) The first few terms.
	$1 \times (-2) = -2$	(2) The progression is geometric.
	$-2 \times (-2) = 4$	
	$4 \times (-2) = -8$	
	etc…	
	$-32 \times (-2) = 64$	(3) Multiply by -2 to find the missing term.

Example: Identify the next term of the following progression.

$$\tfrac{1}{3}, \tfrac{1}{9}, \tfrac{1}{15}, \tfrac{1}{21}, \tfrac{1}{27}, \ldots$$

Solution:	$\tfrac{1}{3}, \tfrac{1}{9}, \tfrac{1}{15}, \ldots$	(1) The first few terms.
	The numerators are all 1. The denominators all increase by 6.	(2) The progression is harmonic.
	$27 + 6 = 33$ $\tfrac{1}{33}$	(3) Add 6 to the denominator to find the missing term.

DRILL: NUMBER RELATIONSHIPS

DIRECTIONS: Select the best answer.

1. Look at the relationship between the numbers of each pair. Identify the missing term.

    $(4, 1)$ $(10, 2.5)$ $(-9, -\frac{9}{4})$ $(1.2, 0.3)$ $(\frac{1}{5}, \underline{\quad})$

    (A) $-2\frac{4}{5}$ (C) $3\frac{1}{5}$

    (B) $\frac{1}{25}$ (D) $\frac{1}{20}$

2. Look at the relationship between the numbers of each pair. Identify the missing term.

    $(5, 7)$ $(0.2, 2.2)$ $(-1\frac{1}{3}, 1\frac{1}{3})$ $(10, 12)$ $(-2, \underline{\quad})$

    (A) -22 (C) -4

    (B) 0 (D) 4

3. Look at the relationship between the numbers of each pair. Identify the missing term.

    $(7, 49)$ $(0.2, 0.04)$ $(\frac{1}{3}, \frac{1}{9})$ $(-8, 64)$ $(-2, \underline{\quad})$

    (A) -1 (C) -4

    (B) 1 (D) 4

WORD PROBLEMS

Problems in this skill area can be found in business, social studies, industry, education, economics, environmental studies, the arts, physical science, sports, or consumer relations. Since the area of coverage is so vast and problem types are almost unlimited, the following problem solving tips may help.

(1)   Read the problem carefully to understand what is being asked.

(2)   Identify the relevant information and eliminate that which is irrelevant. Also, check for unit measure consistency.

(3)   Solve the problem.

(4)   Reread the problem to be sure you have answered the question being asked and that your answer is reasonable.

Example: A cellular phone can be rented for a week for $75.00. Local calls cost $0.85. Long distance calls cost $1.20 plus $0.30 per minute. Ms. Bartlow was on a two-week business trip to San Francisco so she rented a phone. She placed 12 local calls and 2 long distance calls, one for 3 minutes and the other for 8 minutes. What was the total cost of the phone and the calls?

Solution:

Cost of phone:	2×75	=	$150.00
Local calls:	12×0.85	=	10.20
Long distance calls:	2×1.20	=	2.40
Number of minutes:	11×0.30	= +	3.30
			$165.90

Example: Gasoline prices are $1.17 for 93 octane and $1.43 for 95 octane. If your car holds 13.5 gallons of gasoline and is virtually empty, what will it cost to fill the tank with 95 octane gasoline?

Solution: Price of gasoline: $1.43
Number of gallons: $\times$ 13.5
$19.31

Example: One hundred twenty children are enrolled in camp this summer. Half of the campers chose swimming as their free activity while $\frac{1}{5}$ chose arts and crafts. How many more children chose swimming over arts and crafts?

Solution: $120 \times \frac{1}{2} = 60$ 60
$120 \times \frac{1}{5} = 24$ −24
36

PERCENTAGE WORD PROBLEMS

Example: A popular bookstore gives a 10% discount to students. What does a student actually pay for a book costing $24.00?

Solution: $24 \times \frac{10}{100} = 2.40$
$24.00 - 2.40 = 21.60

Example: The local power company advertised that 8% of your power bill could be saved by installing a timer on the water heater. If Mark's electric bill was $165 last month, how much could he expect to save a month by installing the timer?

Solution: $165 \times \frac{8}{100} = 13.2$
$13.20

ARITHMETIC WORD PROBLEMS

Example: Find the smallest positive multiple of 4 which leaves a remainder of 2 when divided by 3 and a remainder of 4 when divided by 7.

    (A) 32   (C) 64

    (B) 45   (D) 44

Solution: Since this will be a multiple-choice question, elimination of the choices is a much easier way to proceed than to reconstruct the problem.

(1)   Begin with the first condition that the number is a multiple of 4.

Are all the choices multiples of 4?

32 = 4 × 8
45   not a multiple of 4   *Eliminate choice (B).
64 = 4 × 16
44 = 4 × 11

(2)   The second condition states that when divided by 3, there is a remainder of 2. Check the remaining choices.

32 ÷ 3 = 10 R2
64 ÷ 3 = 21 R1   *Eliminate choice (C).
44 ÷ 3 = 14 R2

(3)   The last condition states that when divided by 7, there is a remainder of 4. Check the remaining choices.

32 ÷ 7 = 4 R4
44 ÷ 7 = 6 R2   *Eliminate choice (D).

(4)   This leaves choice (A) as the correct response.

Example: How many whole numbers leave a remainder of 3 when divided into 42, and a remainder of 1 when divided into 27?

Solution: (1)   Examine the first condition.

If a number divided into 42 leaves a remainder of 3, then 42 − 3 or 39 must divide by these whole numbers without any remainder.

What are the factors of 39? Only 3 and 13

(2)   Examine the second condition using the information from step 1.

27 ÷ 3 = 9 R0
27 ÷ 13 = 2 R1

(3)   Therefore, 13 is the only whole number which satisfies both of the given conditions.

DRILL: WORD PROBLEMS

DIRECTIONS: Select the best answer.

---

1. A brand name tissue costs $1.19 for a box of 175 tissues. A generic brand of comparable quality costs $0.89 for the same amount. How much money is saved if five boxes of the generic brand tissue are purchased instead of the brand name tissue?

    (A) $0.30   (C) $0.56

    (B) $1.50   (D) $2.80

2. The school computer lab is purchasing some new software for the next school year. There is enough money to purchase five "Math Frills" at $49.95 each and three "Science Chills" at $59.95. What will be the total cost for this software?

    (A) $249.75   (C) $408.12

    (B) $179.85   (D) $429.60

3. Of a 45 member school track team, $\frac{1}{9}$ of the members were hurdlers and $\frac{1}{15}$ were shot putters. How many members were either hurdlers or shot putters?

    (A) 5   (C) 8

    (B) 3   (D) 24

4. An art student wants to show a water color painting at a festival later this month. To prepare the painting, she finds the following costs are involved: mounting is $12.00, framing is $85.00, and the glass is $16.00. Fortunately the frame shop has a special offer if you do it yourself for $89.95. How much will the art student save by preparing the painting herself?

    (A) $23.05   (C) $89.95

    (B) $85.00   (D) $113.00

5. Kyle got a job with the local phone company delivering phone books for a two-week period during the summer break. He made $4.50 an hour and earned time-and-a-half if he worked more than 40 hours a week. The first week he worked 48 hours, and the second week he worked 35 hours. How much did Kyle earn working this job?

(A) $11.25   (C) $373.50

(B) $157.50   (D) $391.50

6.   At an office supply store, customers are given a discount if they pay in cash. If a customer is given a discount of $9.66 on a total order of $276, what is the percent of discount?

(A)   2%   (C)   4.5%

(B)   3.5%   (D)   9.66%

7.   The school computer lab has just purchased some new software for the next school year. The bill came to $429.60. For orders over $250 a five percent discount is given. What will be the final bill for this software?

(A) $249.75   (C) $408.12

(B) $179.85   (D) $429.60

8.   Find the smallest positive multiple of 6 which leaves a remainder of 2 when divided by 4 or 5.

(A)   28   (C)   42

(B)   30   (D)   54

9.   How many whole numbers leave a remainder of 2 when divided into 36 and a remainder of 5 when divided into 20?

(A)   0   (C)   2

(B)   1   (D)   3

ARITHMETIC SKILLS

ANSWER KEY

DRILL: RATIONAL NUMBERS

1. **(B)**   3. **(A)**   5. **(B)**   7. **(D)**
2. **(A)**   4. **(D)**   6. **(B)**   8. **(B)**

DRILL: DECIMALS

1. **(A)**   3. **(C)**   5. **(B)**   7. **(D)**
2. **(C)**   4. **(A)**   6. **(A)**   8. **(A)**

DRILL: PERCENT

1. **(B)**   3. **(B)**   5. **(D)**
2. **(C)**   4. **(B)**   6. **(B)**

DRILL: EXPONENTS AND BASE-TEN NUMERATION

1. **(D)**   3. **(C)**   5. **(B)**   7. **(C)**
2. **(A)**   4. **(D)**   6. **(C)**   8. **(A)**

DRILL: CONVERTING DECIMALS, PERCENTS, AND FRACTIONS

1. **(B)**   3. **(B)**   5. **(A)**
2. **(D)**   4. **(A)**

DRILL: ORDER RELATION

1.	**(B)**	3.	**(C)**	5.	**(A)**	7.	**(C)**
2.	**(B)**	4.	**(C)**	6.	**(B)**		

DRILL: ESTIMATION

1. **(C)**
2. **(C)**

DRILL: NUMBER RELATIONSHIPS

1.	**(D)**	3.	**(D)**
2.	**(B)**		

DRILL: WORD PROBLEMS

1.	**(B)**	4.	**(A)**	6.	**(B)**	7.	**(C)**
2.	**(D)**	5.	**(D)**	7.	**(C)**	9.	**(A)**
3.	**(C)**						

ARITHMETIC SKILLS
DETAILED EXPLANATIONS OF ANSWERS

DRILL: RATIONAL NUMBERS

1. **(B)**   Before adding or subtracting fractions, you must have a common denominator. Convert both fractions to twelfths by multiplying the thirds by four and the fourths by three. Add the fractions and the whole numbers.

$$\frac{2}{3} = \frac{8}{12}$$
$$+1\frac{1}{4} = 1\frac{3}{12}$$
$$\overline{1\frac{11}{12}}$$

2. **(A)**   To subtract a mixed number from a whole number, convert the whole number to a mixed number. Convert 7 to $6\frac{9}{9}$. Subtract the fractions and then the whole numbers.

$$7 = 6\frac{9}{9}$$
$$-3\frac{5}{9} = -3\frac{5}{9}$$
$$\overline{3\frac{4}{9}}$$

3. **(A)**   Subtracting a positive number is equivalent to adding a negative number. When adding two negative numbers, if the signs of both terms are alike, keep the signs the same and add the numbers. Add the fractions first and then the whole numbers. Carry the negative sign to the solution.

$$-8\frac{1}{8} = -8\frac{3}{24}$$
$$-2\frac{2}{3} = -2\frac{16}{24}$$
$$\overline{-10\frac{19}{24}}$$

4.   **(D)**   If two signs are directly next to each other, multiply the two signs into one sign. In this case, a negative times a negative equals a positive. Adding a positive number to a negative number is equivalent to subtracting the positive term from the negative one.

Convert the whole number into a mixed number, and subtract the lesser term from the greater one. Since the greater term is negative, the solution is also negative.

$$-5 - \left(-2\frac{1}{6}\right) = -5 + 2\frac{1}{6}$$

$$
\begin{aligned}
-5 &= -4\frac{6}{6} \\
2\frac{1}{6} &= +2\frac{1}{6} \\
\hline
& -2\frac{5}{6}
\end{aligned}
$$

5.   **(B)**   When multiplying two terms, unlike signs are always negative, and like signs are always positive. The solution here will be positive. Since no terms can be reduced or canceled, multiply the numerators and then multiply the denominators.

$$-\frac{2}{3} \times \left(-\frac{4}{5}\right) = \frac{8}{15}$$

6.   **(B)**   In order to multiply, change $5\frac{1}{3}$, which is a mixed number, to an improper fraction. Then cancel any numerators with any denominators. Now you can multiply the numerators and denominators.

$$5\frac{1}{3} \times \frac{3}{8} =$$

$$\frac{\cancel{16}^{2}}{\cancel{3}_{1}} \times \frac{\cancel{3}^{1}}{\cancel{8}_{1}} = 2$$

7.   **(D)**   In order to divide fractions, change any mixed numbers to improper fractions. When dividing fractions, you must: (1) take the reciprocal (or reverse) of the term after the division sign and (2) change the division sign to a multiplication sign. Then follow your rules for the multiplication of fractions. (Remember: a negative times a negative is a positive.) Cancel when possible and multiply across.

$$-5\frac{1}{4} \div \left(-\frac{7}{10}\right) =$$

$$-\frac{21}{4} \times \left(-\frac{10}{7}\right) =$$

$$-\frac{21^3}{4_2} \times \left(-\frac{10^5}{7_1}\right) = \frac{15}{2} = 7\frac{1}{2}$$

8.   **(B)**   To divide mixed numbers, convert them to improper fractions. When dividing fractions you must: (1) take the reciprocal (or reverse) of the term after the division sign and (2) change the division sign to a multiplication sign. Multiply across. Since one of the two terms is negative, the solution will also be negative. Convert your solution to a mixed number.

$$-7 \div 2\frac{1}{4} =$$

$$-\frac{7}{1} \div \frac{9}{4} =$$

$$-\frac{7}{1} \times \frac{4}{9} = -\frac{28}{9} = -3\frac{1}{9}$$

DRILL: DECIMALS

1.   **(A)**   When adding or subtracting decimals, the decimal points must line up directly underneath each other. Since the signs are different here, subtract the term with the smallest absolute value from the term with the largest absolute value. Since the larger term is positive, the answer will be positive.

$$\begin{array}{c}-3.28 \\ +7.151 \\ \hline\end{array} = \begin{array}{c}+7.151 \\ -3.28 \\ \hline +3.871\end{array}$$

2.   **(C)**   Follow the rules for adding decimals. Since the signs are the same, keep the sign and add the numbers.

$$\begin{array}{r}-12.9215 \\ -\ \ 0.383 \\ \hline -13.3045\end{array}$$

3. **(C)** Subtracting a negative number is equivalent to adding a positive one. Your solution will be positive. Align the columns on either side of the decimal point and add as usual.

$$\frac{\begin{array}{r} + \quad 4.123 \\ - (-11.9) \end{array}}{} = \frac{\begin{array}{r} + \ 4.123 \\ +11.9 \end{array}}{+16.023}$$

4. **(A)** Careful! If a number has no decimal point, it is always understood to be at the extreme right of the whole number. For example, 4 = 4.0; 19 = 19.0. Since the signs are different, subtract the number with the lesser absolute value from the number with the greater absolute value. Since the greater term is negative, the answer will be negative too.

$$\frac{\begin{array}{r} +1.949 \\ -4 \end{array}}{} = \frac{\begin{array}{r} -4.000 \\ + \ 1.949 \end{array}}{- \ 2.051}$$

5. **(B)** When multiplying decimals, the decimal points do *not* have to be aligned. Multiply the normal way, and when you're finished, count the number of decimal places in each factor and add them together. (2 on top and 1 on the bottom; 2 + 1 = 3.) In the answer, count 3 places from the right, and put in your decimal point. Remember, in multiplication, unlike signs produce a negative solution.

$$\frac{\begin{array}{r} 1.03 \\ \times - 2.6 \end{array}}{\begin{array}{r} 618 \\ 2060 \end{array}}$$
$$\frac{}{-2.678}$$

           1.03   (2 decimal places)

    × – 2.6   (1 decimal place)

       618

   2060

–2.678   (3 decimal places)

6. **(A)** When multiplying decimals, the decimal points do not have to be aligned. Multiply as usual. Count the number of decimal places in each factor. Now count that same number of places from the right in the product, in this case, four. Place your decimal point after the fourth digit.

    5.32

  × .04

  .2128

7. **(D)** When dividing decimals, move the decimal in the divisor to the right to get rid of it. Move the decimal in the dividend the same number of places that you moved it in the divisor. Put the decimal point directly above in your answer (quotient) and then divide normally. As with multiplication, unlike terms produce a negative answer.

$$.3\overline{)-25.2} =$$
$$\underline{-84}$$
$$3\overline{)-252}$$

8. **(A)** When dividing decimals, eliminate the decimal point in the divisor by moving it to the right. Move the decimal in the dividend the same number of places to the right. Place the decimal point in your answer (quotient) directly above the one in the dividend. Divide as usual. As with multiplication, unlike terms produce a negative answer.

$$-6.5\overline{)14.95} =$$
$$\underline{-2.3}$$
$$-65\overline{)149.5}$$

DRILL: PERCENT

1. **(B)** Convert a percent to a decimal by placing it over 100. The word "of" is replaced with a multiplication sign. Since the question calls for an increase, add your answer to the original 12.

$$150\% \text{ of } 12 =$$
$$\frac{^3\cancel{150}}{\cancel{100}_{2_1}} \times \frac{\cancel{12}^6}{1} = 18$$
$$18 + 12 = 30$$

2. **(C)** To find 5% of 300, convert the percent to a decimal by putting it over 100. Replace "of" with a multiplication symbol and multiply. Since the question asks for a decrease, subtract your answer from the original number.

$$5\% \text{ of } 300 =$$
$$\frac{5}{\cancel{100}_1} \times \frac{\cancel{300}^3}{1} = 15$$
$$300 - 15 = 285$$

3. **(B)** To find 3% of 80, convert the percent to a decimal by putting it over 100. Replace the word "of" with a multiplication symbol, and multiply as usual. Convert your answer, which is an improper fraction, into a decimal.

$$3\% \text{ of } 80 =$$

$$\frac{3}{\cancel{100}_5} \times \frac{\cancel{80}^4}{1} =$$

$$\frac{12}{5} = 2\frac{2}{5} \text{ or } 2.4$$

4. **(B)** To find 125% of 400, convert the decimal to a percent by putting it over 100. Replace the word "of" with a multiplication symbol and multiply as usual.

$$125\% \text{ of } 400 =$$

$$\frac{125}{\underset{1}{\cancel{100}}} \times \frac{\cancel{400}^4}{1} = 500$$

5. **(D)** Since we don't know the number, set up an equation like the one below. Convert 20% to a fraction by placing it over 100 and simplifying. Divide both sides of the equation by $\frac{1}{5}$, which is the same as multiplying by $\frac{5}{1}$. The solution is 700.

$$140 = 20\% \text{ of ?}$$

$$20\% = \frac{20}{100} = \frac{1}{5}$$

$$\frac{5}{1} \times 140 = 700$$

6. **(B)** Since the percent is missing, set up an equation like the one above. Divide both sides of the equation by 25, which is the same as multiplying by $\frac{1}{25}$. Convert the answer to a percent.

$$35 = ? \text{ of } 25$$

$$\frac{35}{25} = 1.4$$

$$1.4 = 140\%$$

DRILL: EXPONENTS AND BASE-TEN NUMERATION

1. **(D)** An exponent is just repeated multiplication. The exponent tells you how many times the number to the left of it is being multiplied. The 8 is multiplied twice and the 5 is multiplied three times. Simply write out the multiplication.

$$(8^2)\,(5^3) = (8)\,(8)\,(5)\,(5)\,(5)$$

2. **(A)** An exponent is just repeated multiplication. The exponent tells you how many times the number to the left of it is being multiplied. Simply expand the exponent.

$$\frac{5^3}{7^2} = \frac{(5)\,(5)\,(5)}{(7)\,(7)}$$

3. **(C)** An exponent is just repeated multiplication. The exponent tells you how many times the number to the left of it is being multiplied. Simply expand the exponents.

$$2^3 - 6^3 = (2)\,(2)\,(2) - (6)\,(6)\,(6)$$

4. **(D)** An exponent is just repeated multiplication. The exponent tells you how many times the number to the left of it is being multiplied. Simply expand the exponents.

$$9^2 + 3^4 = (9)\,(9) + (3)\,(3)\,(3)\,(3)$$

5. **(B)** Following the rule for exponents, the exponent 3 tells us that 4^5 is being multiplied 3 times.

$$(4^5)^3 = (4^5)\,(4^5)\,(4^5)$$

6. **(C)** The first place to the left of the decimal point is 10^0. The first place to the right of the decimal point is $\frac{1}{10}$; the second place to the right of the decimal point is $\frac{1}{100}$; the third place to the right of the decimal point is $\frac{1}{1,000}$; etc., or, $\frac{1}{10}^1$; $\frac{1}{10}^2$; $\frac{1}{10}^3$; $\frac{1}{10}^4$ (notice that the exponent tells you the number of zeros after the "1"). Choice (C) says: $3 \times 10^0 = 3 \times 1$ (anything to the zero exponent is 1); $2 \times \frac{1}{10}^2 = 2 \times \frac{1}{100} = \frac{2}{100} = .02$; $5 \times \frac{1}{10}^4 = 5 \times \frac{1}{10,000} = \frac{5}{10,000} = .0005$; or, $3.02 + .0005 = 3.0205$.

7. **(C)** The first place to the left of the decimal point is 10^0; so we have $5 \times 10^0 = 5 \times 1 = 5$; anything to the zero exponent is 1.

8. **(A)**

$$
\begin{aligned}
(5 \times 10^4) &= 5 \times 10,000 &+\ (7 \times 10) &+\ (3 \times \tfrac{1}{10}^2) \\
&= 50,000 &+\ 70 &+\ 3 \times \tfrac{1}{100} \\
&= 50,000 &+\ 70 &+\ \tfrac{3}{100} \\
&= 50,070.03
\end{aligned}
$$

DRILL: CONVERTING DECIMALS, PERCENTS, AND FRACTIONS

1.   **(B)**   To change any number to a percent, multiply by 100 and add a percent sign. $^{13}/_{20} \times 100 = 65\%$.

2.   **(D)**   To get rid of a percent sign, put the percent over 100. $84\% = ^{84}/_{100} = ^{21}/_{25}$.

3.   **(B)**   Ignore the whole number 4 at first. Change $^{3}/_{5}$ to a decimal by dividing the numerator by the denominator. $5\overline{)3.0} = .6$. Now, put the 4 in front of it to get 4.6.

4.   **(A)**   To change anything to a percent, multiply by 100 and add a percent sign. $3.61 \times 100 = 361\%$.

5.   **(A)**   The first place to the right of the decimal point is the "tenths"; the second place to the right of the decimal point is the "hundredths"; the third place to the right of the decimal point is the "thousandths"; so, .003 is read "3 thousandths" or $^{3}/_{1,000}$.

DRILL: ORDER RELATION

1.   **(B)**   Any negative number is smaller than any positive number.

2.   **(B)**   It is only necessary to compare $^{5}/_{7}$ with $^{3}/_{4}$, since the 4 is equal in both fractions. Convert both to the lowest common multiple, in this case 28.

$$^{5}/_{7} = ^{20}/_{28}$$
$$^{3}/_{4} = ^{21}/_{28}$$
$$^{20}/_{28} < ^{21}/_{28}$$

3.   **(C)**   In order to compare the two terms, find the smallest common denominator, in this case 72.

$$-^{3}/_{8} = -^{27}/_{72}$$
$$-^{4}/_{9} = -^{32}/_{72}$$

Whichever number is more to the right on the number line, is the larger number; whichever number is more to the left on the number line, is the smaller number.

4. **(C)** Expand the repeating decimals.

$$7.\overline{3} = 7.3333...$$
$$7.\overline{32} = 7.32323232...$$

$7.\overline{3}$ is larger.

5. **(A)** To compare these terms, convert the fraction to a decimal by dividing the numerator by the denominator.

$$^{13}/_{52} = .25$$

The terms are equal.

6. **(B)** An easy method of comparison is to square *both* columns.

$$\sqrt{48}^{\,2} = 48$$
$$7.1^2 = 50.41$$

7. **(C)** An easy method of comparison is to square *both* columns.

$$\sqrt{120}^{\,2} = 120$$
$$10.9^2 = 118.81$$

DRILL: ESTIMATION

1. **(C)** Joni bought approximately 4 gallons of milk, rounded up from 3.5. She was charged approximately $3.00 per book, rounded down from $3.35. 4 gallons times $3.00 is approximately $12.00.

2. **(C)** The average of 3 and 5 is 4.

DRILL: NUMBER RELATIONSHIPS

1. **(D)** Notice that the first number in each pair is larger than the second, indicating either subtraction or division. Since the difference between the two terms from pair to pair is not the same, the operation must be division. Find the divisor that will result in the second term. In this case it is 4, since:

$$4 \div 4 = 1$$
$$10 \div 4 = 2.5$$

$$9 \div 4 = \frac{9}{4}$$
$$1.2 \div 4 = 0.3$$

So,

$$\frac{1}{5} \div 4 =$$
$$\frac{1}{5} \times 4 = \frac{1}{20}.$$

2.   **(B)**   Notice that the first number in each pair is smaller than the second, indicating either addition or multiplication. Since the difference between the terms in each pair is the same number, the relationship is addition. In this case, the number is 2, since:

$$5 + 2 = 7$$
$$0.2 + 2 = 2.2$$
$$-1\frac{1}{3} + 2 = 1\frac{1}{3}$$
$$10 + 2 = 12$$

So,

$$-2 + 2 = 0.$$

3.   **(D)**   Notice that the first number in each pair is smaller than the second, indicating either addition or multiplication. Since the difference between the terms in each pair is not the same, the relationship must be multiplication. In this case, the first term is squared to get the second, since:

$$7^2 = 49$$
$$0.2^2 = 0.04$$
$$\frac{1}{3}^2 = \frac{1}{9}$$
$$-8^2 = 64$$

So,

$$-2^2 = 4.$$

DRILL: WORD PROBLEMS

1.   **(B)**   The more expensive box costs $1.19, and the less expensive box costs $0.89. This saves $0.30 since:

$$\$1.19 - \$0.89 = \$0.30.$$

Five boxes of inexpensive tissues would save $0.30 on each box, or:

$$\$0.30 \times 5 = \$1.50.$$

2.   **(D)**   First determine the amount spent on Math Frills.

$$\$49.95 \times 5 = \$249.75$$

Then determine the amount spent on Science Chills.

$$\$59.95 \times 3 = \$179.85$$

Now, add the two.

$$\$249.75 + \$179.85 = \$429.60$$

3.   **(C)**   To determine how many students were hurdlers, set up the following equation:

$$\tfrac{1}{9} \text{ of } 45 \ =$$
$$\tfrac{1}{9} \times 45 \ =$$
$$\tfrac{45}{9} \ = \ 5$$

Use a similar equation for the shot putters.

$$\tfrac{1}{15} \text{ of } 45 \ =$$
$$\tfrac{1}{15} \times 45 \ =$$
$$\tfrac{45}{15} \ = \ 3$$

To find the number of students who are hurdlers *or* shot putters, add the two products.

$$3 + 5 \ = \ 8$$

4.   **(A)**   First determine the cost of professional framing.

$$\$12.00 + \$85.00 + \$16.00 = \$113.00$$

To find how much the art student would save, subtract the cost of framing the painting herself.

$$\$113.00 - \$89.95 = \$23.05$$

5.   **(D)**   During the first week, Kyle worked 40 hours regular time, and during the second week, he worked 35 hours regular time. Compute his regular wages.

$$40 \times \$4.50 \ = \ \$180.00 \qquad \text{during the first week}$$
$$35 \times \$4.50 \ = \ \$157.50 \qquad \text{during the second week}$$

Find his salary for time-and-a-half.

$$\$4.50 + \tfrac{1}{2}\,(\$4.50) \ =$$
$$\$4.50 + \$2.25 \ = \ \$6.75$$

Now compute overtime wages.

$$8 \times \$6.75 = \$54.00$$

To determine his final earnings, add all of the wages together.

$$\$180.00 + \$54.00 + \$157.50 = \$391.50$$

6. **(B)** To determine what percent of $276.00 is $9.66, use the following equation:

$$?\% \times \$276 = \$9.66$$

Now divide both sides by $276.

$$?\% = {}^{\$9.66}\!/_{\$276}$$

$$?\% = 0.035$$

Convert the answer to a percent by multiplying by 100, or moving the decimal point two places to the right.

$$0.035 \times 100 = 3.5\%.$$

7. **(C)** To find the amount of money discounted, find 5% of $429.60.

$$5\% \times \$429.60$$

Convert 5% to a decimal by multiplying by 100 or moving the decimal point two places to the left.

$$.05 \times \$429.60 = \$21.48$$

Determine the final bill by subtracting the discount from the subtotal.

$$\$429.60 - \$21.48 = \$408.12$$

8. **(C)** Work from the answer choices to find the best answer here. (C), 42, is the only number which is divisible by 6 and leaves a remainder of 2 when divided by 4 or 5.

9. **(A)** Since the question stem uses the word "and," the answer must satisfy both conditions. 17 is the only number that leaves a remainder of 2 when divided into 36; however, 17 will not leave a remainder of 5 when divided into 20. Therefore, the answer is 0.

MEASUREMENT AND GEOMETRY SKILLS

MEASUREMENT

ROUNDING MEASUREMENTS

Given will be either

- a measure which will have to be rounded to a specified place value or

- a measuring tool from which you will have to read the measure of the pictured item and then round to the specified place value.

In either case, proceed as follows:

(1) Read the measure from the measuring tool if the measure is not given.

(2) Identify the place value to which the final measure is to be rounded.

(3) Examine the digit to the right of the place identified in step 2. If this digit is 5 or more, round up.

Example: Round 5,492 feet to the nearest hundred feet.

Solution: 5,<u>4</u>92   (2) Identify the place value.

5,500   (3) Round up since the digit to the right of the designated place value is > 5.

Example: Round 2 feet 5 inches to the nearest foot.

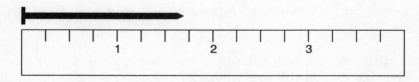

Solution: There are 12 inches in a foot. Since 5 of 12 inches is less than half, do not round up.

Answer: 2 feet

Example: Round the measurement of the nail to the nearest $\frac{1}{4}$ unit.

Solution: The nail measures between $1\frac{1}{2}$ and $1\frac{3}{4}$ units; however, it is closer to $1\frac{3}{4}$.

UNITS OF MEASUREMENT

A diagram or description of a geometric object will be provided. It will be necessary to identify the appropriate unit of measure for the given.

The measures will fall into one of three categories:

- Linear measures are one dimensional like what one could measure with a ruler. Examples would include perimeters, widths, lengths, and heights. Some appropriate units for linear measures include kilometers, meters, decimeters, centimeters, millimeters, miles, yards, feet, and inches.

- Area measures are two dimensional or squared. Any linear measure squared would be an example of an area measure, for example: square meters, square inches, etc.

- Volume measures are three dimensional or cubed. Standard volume units include liters, gallons, pints, or any of the linear measures cubed, such as cubic centimeters, etc.

Example: Which of the following measures would *not* be appropriate to use when discussing the amount of paint necessary to paint a house?

    (A) Liters   (C) Cubic centimeters

    (B) Gallons   (D) Square yards

Solution: The amount of paint is a volume; hence, liters, gallons, and cubic centimeters would all be appropriate units. Square yards is an area measure, and not appropriate for the context of this question. Therefore, (D) is the correct choice.

Example: Which of the following measures would be appropriate to use when discussing the amount of material needed to cover a photo album?

    (A) Cubic inches   (C) Square feet

    (B) Meters   (D) Degrees

Solution: The amount of material to cover a photo album is an area. The only area measure listed above is square feet, so (C) is the correct choice.

Example: Which of the following measures could be used to measure the height of a water tower?

    (A) Liters   (C) Meters

    (B) Gallons   (D) Square feet

Solution: The height of a water tower is a linear measure, and the only linear measure listed is meters. Therefore, (C) is the correct choice.

DRILL: MEASUREMENT

DIRECTIONS: Select the best answer.

---

1. Round 38,203 meters to the nearest ten thousands.

    (A) 40,000 m   (C) 38,000 m

    (B) 30,000 m   (D) 39,000 m

2. Round 25 pounds 7 ounces to the nearest pound.

    (A) 20 lbs   (C) 26 lbs

    (B) 25 lbs   (D) 30 lbs

3. Round 3 weeks 4 days to the nearest week.

    (A) 3 weeks   (C) $3\frac{4}{7}$ weeks

    (B) 3.4 weeks   (D) 4 weeks

4. Round 310 hours 35 minutes to the nearest hour.

    (A) 300 hours   (C) 311 hours

    (B) 310 hours   (D) 320 hours

5. Which of the following measures would be appropriate to use to measure the distance traveled by a wind-up toy train?

    (A) Decimeters   (C) Degrees

    (B) Cubic inches   (D) Square yards

6. Which of the following measures would be appropriate to use to measure the amount of jelly beans necessary to fill a rectangular box?

    (A) Square feet   (C) Cubic centimeters

    (B) Meters   (D) Degrees

7. Which of the following would be appropriate to measure the amount of water needed to fill a child's wading pool?

    (A) Degrees   (C) Cubic centimeters

    (B) Meters   (D) Square yards

DISTANCE, AREA, AND VOLUME

DISTANCE

A geometric figure may be pictured. The figure pictured or described could be a polygon or a circle.

To calculate the perimeter of a polygon:

(1) Draw the figure if it is not presented and carefully label the pieces with the information provided.

(2) Make sure that all the measures are in the same units. Only metric-to-metric or English-to-English conversions will be necessary; no English-to-metric or vice versa will be required.

(3) If the measure(s) of any sides are not given, fill in the missing value from the information presented.

If a side of a right triangle is missing, it may be necessary to use the Pythagorean Theorem:

$$c^2 = a^2 + b^2$$

where c is the length of the hypotenuse and a and b are the lengths of the legs.

(4) Add the measures of all the sides.

Example: What is the distance around this polygon in meters?

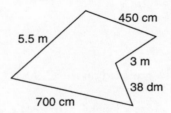

Solution: 450 cm = 4.5 m
700 cm = 7 m
38 dm = 3.8 m

5.5 + 4.5 + 3 + 3.8 + 7 = 23.8 m

Example: What is the distance around this right triangle?

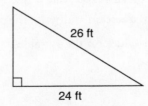

Solution: $26^2 = 24^2 + b^2$ (3) Find the missing side
                $676 = 576 + b^2$ using the Pythagorean
                $100 = b^2$ Theorem.
                  $10 = b$

            $10 + 24 + 26 = 60$ ft   (4) Add.

- The radius of a circle is a line from the center of the circle to any point on the circle.

- The diameter of a circle is a line from one side of the circle to the other passing through the center of the circle.

To calculate the circumference of a circle:

(1) Identify the radius of the circular region described. If the diameter is given, divide this value by 2 for the value of the radius.

(2) Use the formula $C = 2\pi r$ to calculate the distance around the circular region.

    It may not be necessary to substitute a value for pi; however, if it is necessary, use the value given in the problem.

Example: What is the distance around a circular spa that has a diameter of 6 meters?

Solution: diameter = 6 m   (1) Identify the radius.
                radius = $\frac{6}{2}$ = 3 m

            $C = 2\pi r$ (2) Calculate.
               $= 2\pi(3)$
               $= 6\pi$ m

AREA

Area formulas will not be provided on the CLAST, so become familiar with the following formulas:

Area of a rectangle: A = base × height   or A = length × height
           square: A = base × height   or $A = \text{side}^2$
        triangle: $A = \frac{1}{2}$ × base × height
         circle: $A = \pi r^2$, where r is the radius

The surface area of a rectangular solid is the sum of the areas of all the faces: $S = 2lw + 2lh + 2wh$, where l = length, w = width, and h = height.

Units for area or surface area will always be square units. On multiple-choice items, if the units are not squared, the choice can be eliminated.

To calculate the area of a given shape, follow these steps:

(1) Identify the shape in question and write the area formula.

(2) Substitute the given values for the variables.

(3) Calculate the area.

Example: What is the area of a rectangle whose base is 12 cm and whose height is 3 cm?

Solution: Rectangle: $A = \text{base} \times \text{height}$ (1) Identify formula.

$A = 12 \times 3$ (2) Substitute.

$A = 36 \text{ cm}^2$ (3) Calculate.

Example: What is the area of a square whose side measures 11 feet?

Solution: Square: $A = \text{side}^2$ (1) Identify formula.

$A = 11^2$ (2) Substitute.

$A = 121 \text{ ft}^2$ (3) Calculate.

Example: What is the area of a triangle whose base is 10 millimeters and whose height is 3 millimeters?

Solution: Triangle: $A = \frac{1}{2} \times \text{base} \times \text{height}$ (1) Identify formula.

$A = \frac{1}{2} \times 10 \times 3$ (2) Substitute.

$A = 15 \text{ mm}^2$ (3) Calculate.

Example: What is the area of a circular region whose diameter is 10 miles?

Solution: Circle: $A = \pi r^2$ (1) Identify formula.

Diameter $= 10$

Radius $= \frac{10}{2} = 5$

$A = \pi \times 5^2$ (2) Substitute.

$A = 25\pi \text{ mi}^2$ (3) Calculate.

Example: What is the surface area of a rectangular solid whose width is 5 inches, length is 3 inches, and height is 7 inches?

Solution: Rectangular Solid: $S = 2lw + 2lh + 2wh$ (1) Identify formula.

$S = (2 \times 3 \times 5) + (2 \times 3 \times 7) + (2 \times 5 \times 7)$ (2) Substitute.

$S = 30 + 42 + 70$ (3) Calculate.

$S = 142 \text{ in}^2$

VOLUME

Volume formulas will not be provided on the CLAST, so become familiar with the following formulas:

Volume of a rectangular solid: $V = \text{length} \times \text{width} \times \text{height}$

right circular cylinder: $V = \pi r^2 \times \text{height}$

circular cone: $V = \frac{1}{3} \pi r^2 \times \text{height}$

sphere: $V = \frac{4}{3} \pi r^3$

To assist in remembering the above formulas, remember that the volume measures are the area of the base times the height. In the case where the shape comes to a point, take $\frac{1}{3}$ of the full volume.

Units for volume will always be cubic units. On multiple-choice items, if the units are not cubed, the choice can be eliminated.

To calculate the volume of a three-dimensional object:

(1) Identify the object in question and write the volume formula.

(2) Substitute the given values for the variables.

(3) Calculate the volume.

Example: What is the volume of a rectangular solid whose length is 6 m, whose width is 4 m, and whose height is 1.5 m?

Solution: Rectangular Solid: $V = l \times w \times h$ (1) Identify formula.
$$V = 6 \times 4 \times 1.5 \quad \text{(2) Substitute.}$$
$$V = 36 \text{ m}^3 \quad \text{(3) Calculate.}$$

Example: What is the volume of a circular cone whose radius is 3 yards and whose height is 2 feet?

Solution: Circular Cone: $V = \frac{1}{3}\pi r^2 \times h$ (1) Identify formula.
$$3 \text{ yds} = 9 \text{ ft}$$
$$V = \frac{1}{3}\pi(9)^2 \times 2 \quad \text{(2) Substitute.}$$
$$V = \frac{1}{3} \times 81\pi \times 2 \quad \text{(3) Calculate.}$$
$$V = 27\pi \times 2$$
$$V = 54\pi \text{ ft}^3$$

Example: What is the volume of a sphere whose diameter is 4 meters?

Solution: Sphere: $V = \frac{4}{3}\pi r^3$ (1) Identify formula.
radius = $\frac{4}{2} = 2$
$$V = \frac{4}{3}\pi (2)^3 \quad \text{(2) Substitute.}$$
$$V = \frac{4}{3}\pi (8) \quad \text{(3) Calculate.}$$
$$V = \frac{32}{3}\pi \text{ m}^3$$

Example: Find the volume of a right circular cylinder whose radius is 10 decimeters and whose height is 4 centimeters.

Solution: Right Circular Cylinder:
$$V = \pi r^2 \times h \quad \text{(1) Identify formula.}$$
10 decimeters = 100 centimeters
$$V = \pi(100)^2 \times 4 \quad \text{(2) Substitute.}$$
$$V = 10,000\pi \times 4 \quad \text{(3) Calculate.}$$
$$V = 40,000\pi \text{ cm}^3$$

DRILL: DISTANCE, AREA, AND VOLUME

DIRECTIONS: Select the best answer.

---

1.   What is the distance around a square which measures 5 inches a side?

    (A)   10 in   (C)   25 in²

    (B)   20 in   (D)   25 in

2.   What is the distance around a polygon whose sides measure 10 feet, 36 inches, 1 yard, and 5 feet?

    (A)   21 ft   (C)   19 ft

    (B)   52 ft   (D)   20 ft

3.   What is the distance around a right triangle whose legs measure 9 centimeters and 12 centimeters?

    (A)   15 cm   (C)   36 cm

    (B)   21 cm   (D)   225 cm

4.   What is the distance around a circular blade with a 4 inch radius?

    (A) 2π in   (C) 8π in

    (B) 4π in   (D) 16π in

5.   What is the area of a triangle whose base is 8 meters and whose height is 3 meters?

    (A)   11 m   (C)   22 m²

    (B)   12 m²   (D)   24 m²

6.   What is the surface area of a rectangular solid whose length is 10 yards, whose width is 12 yards, and whose height is 2 yards?

    (A)   24 yds   (C)   240 yds²

    (B)   164 yds²   (D)   328 yds²

7.   What is the area of a circular region whose radius is 20 feet?

    (A) 40π ft²   (C) 400π ft²

    (B) 100π ft²   (D) 400π ft

8.   What is the area of a rectangle whose base is $^{10}\!/_3$ centimeters and whose height is 6 centimeters?

(A)   20 cm²   (C) $^{56}\!/_3$ cm²

(B) $^{28}\!/_3$ cm²   (D)   20 cm

9.   What is the volume of a rectangular solid whose length is 9 cm, whose width is 5 cm, and whose height is 12 cm?

(A)   540 cm³   (C)   540 cm²

(B)   26 cm³   (D)   57 cm³

10.   What is the volume of a circular cone whose diameter is 4 miles and whose height is 3 miles?

(A)   48π mi³   (C)   16π mi³

(B)   12π mi³   (D)   4π mi³

11.   Find the volume of a right circular cylinder whose radius is 5 feet and whose height is 3 feet.

(A)   30π ft³   (C)   75π ft²

(B)   75π ft³   (D)   25π ft³

12.   Find the volume of a sphere whose radius is 6 decimeters.

(A)   216π dm³   (C)   216π dm²

(B)   288π dm³   (D)   48π dm³

ANGLES AND LINES

ANGLES

Before beginning examples of the types of problems which could arise in this skill area, familiarize yourself with these vocabulary terms and geometric relationships.

- **Vertical angles** are formed when two lines intersect. These angles are equal.

- **Adjacent angles** are two angles with a common vertex and a common side, but no common interior points.

- A **right angle** is an angle whose measure is 90°.

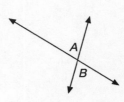

- An **acute angle** is an angle whose measure is between 0° and 90°.

- An **obtuse angle** is an angle whose measure is between 90° and 180°.

- **Complementary angles** are two angles, the sum of the measures of which equals 90°.

- **Supplementary angles** are two angles, the sum of the measures of which equals 180°.

PERPENDICULAR LINES

Two lines are said to be perpendicular if they intersect and form right angles. The symbol for perpendicular is ⊥.

Example: We are given straight lines $\overleftrightarrow{AB}$
and $\overleftrightarrow{CD}$ intersecting at point P.
$PR \perp AB$ and the measure of
$\angle APD$ is 170°. Find the
measures of $\angle 1$, $\angle 2$, $\angle 3$, and $\angle 4$.

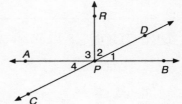

Solution: This problem will involve several of the properties of supplementary and vertical angles, as well as perpendicular lines.

m $\angle APD$ + m $\angle 1$ = 180°	$\angle APD$ and $\angle 1$ are supplementary angles.
170° + m $\angle 1$ = 180°	Given $m \angle APD$ = 170°.
m $\angle 1$ = 10°	Subtract to find the measure of $\angle 1$.
m $\angle 4$ = 10°	$\angle 1$ and $\angle 4$ are vertical angles.
m $\angle 3$ = 90°	$PR \perp AB$.
m $\angle APD$ = m $\angle 3$ + m $\angle 2$	Adjacent angles
170° = 90° + m $\angle 2$	Substitute.
80° = m $\angle 2$	Subtract to find the measure of $\angle 2$.

PARALLEL LINES

Two lines are called parallel if, and only if, they are in the same plane (coplanar) and do not intersect. The symbol for parallel is ||.

If two parallel lines are cut by a transversal, then:

The alternate interior angles are equal.

$$m \angle A = m \angle B$$

The corresponding angles are equal.

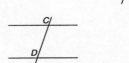

$$m \angle C = m \angle D$$

The same side interior angles are supplementary.

m ∠E = m ∠F = 180°

The alternate exterior angles are equal.

m ∠G = m ∠H

DRILL: ANGLES AND LINES

DIRECTIONS: Select the best answer.

---

1. Find *a*.

    (A)   38°

    (B)   68°

    (C)   78°

    (D)   112°

2. Find *z.*

    (A)   29°

    (B)   54°

    (C)   61°

    (D)   88°

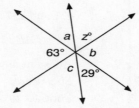

3. $\overleftrightarrow{BA} \perp \overleftrightarrow{BC}$ and m ∠DBC = 53°.
    Find m ∠ABD.

    (A)   27°

    (B)   33°

    (C)   37°

    (D)   53°

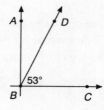

4. If $\overleftrightarrow{m} \perp \overleftrightarrow{p}$, which of the following statements is true?

    (A)   m $\angle 1$ = m $\angle 2$

    (B)   m $\angle 4$ = m $\angle 5$

    (C)   m $\angle 4$ + m $\angle 5$ > m $\angle 1$ + m $\angle 2$

    (D)   m $\angle 3$ > m $\angle 2$

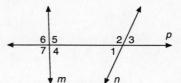

5. In the figure, $\overleftrightarrow{p} \perp \overleftrightarrow{t}$ and $\overleftrightarrow{q} \perp \overleftrightarrow{t}$. Which of the following statements is false?

    (A)   m $\angle 1$ = m $\angle 4$

    (B)   m $\angle 2$ = m $\angle 3$

    (C)   m $\angle 5$ + m $\angle 6$ = 180°

    (D)   m $\angle 2$ > m $\angle 5$

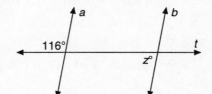

6. If $\overleftrightarrow{a} \parallel \overleftrightarrow{b}$, find z.

    (A)   26°

    (B)   32°

    (C)   64°

    (D)   116°

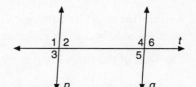

7. If $\overleftrightarrow{m} \parallel \overleftrightarrow{n}$, and $\overrightarrow{p}$ is not perpendicular to $\overleftrightarrow{m}$ or $\overleftrightarrow{n}$, which of the following statements is false?

    (A)   m $\angle 2$ = m $\angle 5$

    (B)   m $\angle 4$ + m $\angle 5$ = 180°

    (C)   m $\angle 3$ = m $\angle 6$

    (D)   m $\angle 1$ = m $\angle 7$

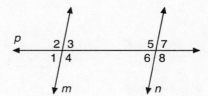

8. If $\overleftrightarrow{r} \parallel \overleftrightarrow{s}$, find m $\angle 2$.

    (A)   17°

    (B)   27°

    (C)   43°

    (D)   73°

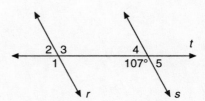

TRIANGLES

A closed three-sided geometric figure is called a triangle. The points of the intersection of the sides of a triangle are called the vertices of the triangle.

- A triangle with no equal sides is called a **scalene triangle**.

- A triangle having at least two equal sides is called an **isosceles triangle**. The third side is called the base of the triangle.

- An **equilateral triangle** is a triangle having three equal sides and three equal angles. Each angle measures 60°.

- An **interior angle** of a triangle is an angle formed by two sides and includes the third side within its collection of points.

- The sum of the three interior angles of any triangle is 180°.

- An **exterior angle** of a triangle is an angle formed outside a triangle by one side of the triangle and the extension of an adjacent side.

- To determine an unknown measure of a side of a triangle, use the Pythagorean Theorem:

$$c^2 = a^2 + b^2$$

  where c is the hypotenuse of a right triangle and a and b are the legs of the right triangle.

- Similar triangles are such that corresponding angles are equal and corresponding sides are proportional in measure.

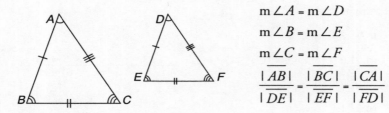

$$m \angle A = m \angle D$$
$$m \angle B = m \angle E$$
$$m \angle C = m \angle F$$
$$\frac{|\overline{AB}|}{|\overline{DE}|} = \frac{|\overline{BC}|}{|\overline{EF}|} = \frac{|\overline{CA}|}{|\overline{FD}|}$$

- The sides opposite congruent angles in a triangle are congruent.

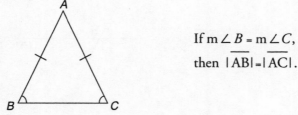

If $m \angle B = m \angle C$,
then $|\overline{AB}| = |\overline{AC}|$.

Example: What type of triangle is $\triangle ABC$?

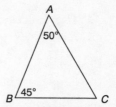

Solution: $\text{m} \angle A + \text{m} \angle B + \text{m} \angle C = 180°$

$50° + 45° + \text{m} \angle C = 180°$

$95° + \text{m} \angle C = 180°$

$\text{m} \angle C = 85°$

$\angle C$ is an acute angle, therefore, $\triangle ABC$ is an acute triangle.

Example: What is the length of the missing side?

Solution: The missing side of this right triangle appears longer than the other two, indicating that it is the hypotenuse. Use the Pythagorean Theorem:

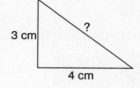

$$a^2 + b^2 = c^2$$

$$3^2 + 4^2 = c^2$$

$$9 + 16 = c^2$$

$$25 = c^2$$

$$\sqrt{25} = c$$

$$5 = c$$

Therefore, the missing side measures 5 cm.

DRILL: TRIANGLES

DIRECTIONS: Select the best answer.

1.   In $\triangle PQR$, $\angle Q$ is a right angle. Find $\text{m} \angle R$.

(A)   27°

(B)   54°

(C)   67°

(D)   157°

2. *MNO* is isosceles. If the vertex angle, ∠*M*, has a measure of 96°, find the measure of ∠*N*.

    (A) 21°

    (B) 42°

    (C) 64°

    (D) 84°

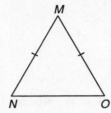

3. Find m ∠1.

    (A) 40°

    (B) 66°

    (C) 74°

    (D) 140°

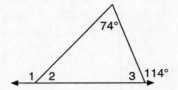

4. Δ*ABC* is a right triangle with a right angle at *B*. Δ*BDC* is a right triangle with right angle at *D*. If m ∠*C* = 36°, find m ∠*A*.

    (A) 18°

    (B) 36°

    (C) 54°

    (D) 72°

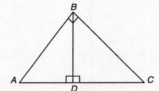

5. The two triangles shown are similar. Find m ∠1.

    (A) 48°

    (B) 53°

    (C) 74°

    (D) 127°

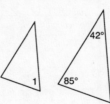

6. The two triangles shown are similar. Find *a* and *b*.

    (A) 5 and 10

    (B) 4 and 8

    (C) 4⅔ and 7⅓

    (D) 5⅓ and 8

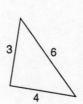
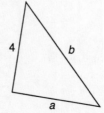

7. Find *b*.

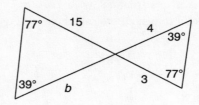

(A) 9

(B) 15

(C) 20

(D) 45

OTHER PLANE FIGURES

In addition to triangles, any of the following types of figures may appear on the CLAST:

- A **quadrilateral** is a polygon with four sides. (Figure 1)

- A **parallelogram** is a quadrilateral whose opposite sides are parallel. (Figure 2)

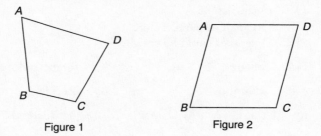

Figure 1   Figure 2

- A **rectangle** is a parallelogram with right angles. The diagonals of a rectangle are equal. (Figure 3)

- A **rhombus** is a parallelogram with two adjacent sides equal. All sides of a rhombus are equal. The diagonals of a rhombus are perpendicular to each other. The diagonals of a rhombus bisect the angles of the rhombus. (Figure 4)

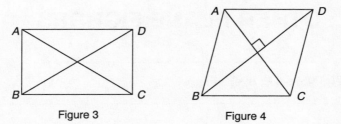

Figure 3   Figure 4

- A **square** is a rhombus with a right angle. A square is an equilateral quadrilateral. A square has all the properties of parallelograms and rectangles. (Figure 5)

- A **trapezoid** is a quadrilateral with two and only two sides parallel. The parallel sides of a trapezoid are called bases. (Figure 6)

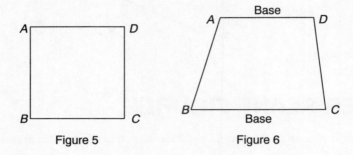

Figure 5   Figure 6

Example: Select the geometric figure that possesses all of the following characteristics:

I.   Quadrilateral
II.   One pair of parallel sides
III. Diagonals could be equal

(A) Square   (C) Trapezoid

(B) Rhombus   (D) Rectangle

Solution: Criterion I.   All shapes listed are quadrilaterals.

Criterion II.   The square, rhombus, and rectangle all have two pairs of parallel sides.

Only the trapezoid has one pair of parallel sides.

We do not need to check Criterion III since we have already eliminated all the choices except choice (C), Trapezoid.

DRILL: OTHER PLANE FIGURES

DIRECTIONS: Select the best answer.

1.   Which of the following is not a polygon with four sides?

(A) Square   (C) Trapezoid

(B) Quadrilateral   (D) Triangle

2.   Which of the following does not have four equal sides?

(A)   Square

(B)   Rectangle

(C)   Rhombus with no right angles

(D)   Rhombus with a right angle

3.   Select the geometric figure that possesses all of the following characteristics:

I.   Quadrilateral
II.   At least one pair of parallel sides
III.   Diagonals are always perpendicular to each other

(A)   Triangle   (C)   Trapezoid

(B)   Rhombus   (D)   Parallelogram

4.   Select the geometric figure that could possess all of the following characteristics:

I.   Triangle
II.   Has an angle of 10° and another angle of 20°

(A)   Rhombus   (C)   Isosceles triangle

(B)   Scalene triangle   (D)   Acute triangle

GEOMETRIC FORMULAS

Two to four diagrams will be pictured with specific characteristics of each figure labeled depicting a specific measurement. This measure may represent area, volume, surface area, angle measurement, perimeter, or circumference. It will be necessary to make a generalization from the given information and apply the generalization to a similar figure.

To cover all possibilities would be impossible, so listed below are some problem-solving hints applicable to this situation:

(1)   Construct a simple table organizing the data.

(2)   Look for a pattern.

(3)   Apply the pattern to the similar figure to find the missing data.

Example: Study the given figures and calculate the area of the shaded region of a square whose sides measure 6 units.

Side measure:	2	3	4
Square area:	4	9	16
Shaded area:	1π	$9\pi/4$	4π

Solution:

Side measure	Square area	Shaded area
2	4	1π
3	9	$9\pi/4$
4	16	4π
6		

The pattern in going from the side measure to the square area is to square the side measure. Therefore, for a square of side 6, the area would be 36.

The pattern in going from the square area to the shaded area is multiply by π and divide by 4. Therefore, the shaded area for a square of side 6 would be $36 \times \pi / 4$ or 9π.

Example: Study the given figures and calculate the missing angle measure and the missing arc measure.

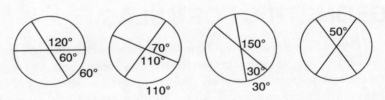

Solution:

Given angle	Adjacent angle	Arc
120°	60°	60°
70°	110°	110°
150°	30°	30°
50°		

The given angle and the adjacent angle are supplementary since they together form a straight angle. To calculate the adjacent angle subtract the given angle from 180°.

The arc measure is equal to the measure of the adjacent angle. Therefore, the missing adjacent measure is 130° and the missing arc measure is 130°.

In addition to this type of problem, you will also be asked to examine a diagram of a two- or three-dimensional figure and identify the correct formula for calculating a specified measure.

- A two-dimensional figure could consist of any combination of three and four sided simple shapes as well as circles and semicircles.

- Three-dimensional figures may include rectangular solids, right circular cylinders, and right cylinder cones.

The measure in question may be length, perimeter, area, surface area, or volume. To determine the correct formula, follow the given steps.

(1)   Think of the figure given in its component parts.

(2)   Write the appropriate formula(s) for the calculation of the specified measure in terms of the given variables.

(3)   Add the component formulas together.

(4)   Simplify or rearrange the formula to match one of the choices.

Example: What is the formula for the surface area of the given prism?

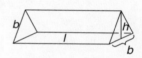

Solution: The prism consists of the
(1)
following component parts:
   2 triangles
   3 rectangles

Component parts.

Area of 1 triangle: $A_T = \frac{1}{2}b \times h$ (2) Formulas.
Area of 2 triangles: $A_T = 2(\frac{1}{2}b \times h)$

Area of 1 rectangle: $A_R = l \times b$
Area of 3 rectangles: $A_R = 3(l \times b)$

$SA = 2(\frac{1}{2}b \times h) + 3(1 \times b)$ (3) Add the formulas.

$SA = b \times h + 3(l \times b)$ (4) Simplify.

Example: Again using the above prism, what is the linear sum of all the edges?

Solution: Perimeter of 1 triangle: $P_T = 3b$ (2) Formulas.
Perimeter of 2 triangles: $P_T = 2(3b)$

In addition to the perimeter of the two triangles is the length of the three edges, each measuring l: $3l$.

$P = 2(3b) + 3l$ (3) Add.

$P = 6b + 3l$ (4) Simplify.

DRILL: GEOMETRIC FORMULAS

> **DIRECTIONS:** Select the best answer.

1. Study the given figures and calculate the surface area of a cylinder with a radius of 5 and a height of 5.

    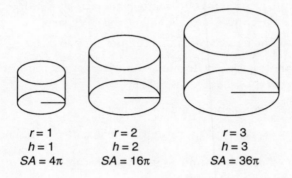

    $r = 1$
    $h = 1$
    $SA = 4\pi$

    $r = 2$
    $h = 2$
    $SA = 16\pi$

    $r = 3$
    $h = 3$
    $SA = 36\pi$

    (A) 40π

    (B) 64π

    (C) 100π

    (D) 125π

2. Study the given figures and calculate the missing median.

    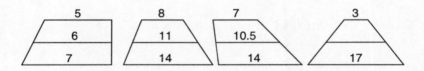

    (A) 6

    (B) 10

    (C) 20

    (D) 51

3. Calculate the area of the nonshaded region within the square.

    (A) $s^2 - \pi s^2$

    (B) $\dfrac{\pi s^2}{4 - s^2}$

    (C) $s^2 - \dfrac{\pi s^2}{4}$

    (D) $\dfrac{\pi s^2}{4}$

    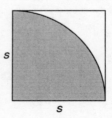

4. What is the area of the shaded region? The figure is a square within a circle with the radius $\sqrt{2}$.

(A) $4 - 2\pi$

(B) $\pi - \frac{1}{2}$.

(C) $2\pi - 3$

(D) $2\pi - 4$

GEOMETRY WORD PROBLEMS

As with the previous word problems in the arithmetic section, these problems will be taken from the same host of contexts. Again, since the area of coverage is so vast and problem types are almost unlimited, the following problem-solving tips may help:

(1) Read the problem carefully to understand what is being asked.

(2) Identify the relevant information and eliminate that which is irrelevant. Also, check for unit measure consistency.

(3) Solve the problem using an appropriate formula for perimeter, area, or volume.

(4) Reread the problem to be sure you have answered the question being asked and that your answer is reasonable.

Example: Calculate the volume of the pictured iceskating rink if the ice is 4 inches thick.

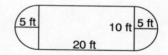

Solution: The dimensions of the rink are given in feet and the thickness of the ice is in inches. Convert 4 inches to feet: $\frac{4}{12}$ or $\frac{1}{3}$ foot.

The area of the rink is made up of a rectangular region and two semicircles which together make a complete circle with a radius of 5 feet.

Area of rectangle: $A_R = 20 \times 10 = 200$ sq ft
Area of circle: $A_C = \pi \times (5)^2 = 25\pi$ sq ft

Total area: $A = 200 + 25\pi$ sq ft

Volume: $V = (200 + 25\pi) \times (\frac{1}{3})$ cu ft

Example: What will be the cost of painting a 12 foot by 14 foot room that is 8 feet high if a can of paint which costs $14.50 a can covers 200 square feet?

Solution: Find the dimensions of the walls:
2 walls are 12×8
2 walls are 14×8

Total surface area of the walls:
$$S = 2(12 \times 8) + 2(14 \times 8)$$
$$S = 192 + 224$$
$$S = 416 \text{ sq ft}$$

If one can of paint covers 200 square feet, it will be necessary to purchase $^{416}/_{200}$ or 2.08 cans of paint. Since this is not done, we must buy 3 cans of paint at $14.50 a can or $3 \times \$14.50 = \$43.50$.

You will also need to solve word problems using the Pythagorean Theorem, which states:

$$c^2 = a^2 + b^2$$

where c is the hypotenuse of a right triangle and a and b are the legs of the right triangle.

Example: A farmer must drive from his barn directly north 3 miles then directly east 4 miles to get to a field. The farmer plans to put in a path through the woods to make a direct path from the barn to the field. If it costs $200 per mile to clear the path, what would be the cost of making the path?

Solution:

$c^2 = a^2 + b^2$	Pythagorean Theorem
$c^2 = 3^2 + 4^2$	Substitute.
$c^2 = 9 + 16$	
$c^2 = 25$	
$c = 5$	The path would be 5 miles.

At $200 per mile, the path would cost 200×5 or $1,000.

Example: The Mann family wishes to purchase a framed mural for the den. The entrance to the room measures 4 feet by 7 feet 6 inches. One dimension must be under what measure to fit through the entrance?

Solution: To fit through the entrance, one dimension would have to be less than the diagonal of the entrance.

7 feet 6 inches = 7.5 feet	Convert to uniform units.
$c^2 = a^2 + b^2$	Pythagorean Theorem
$c^2 = 4^2 + 7.5^2$	Substitute.
$c^2 = 16 + 56.25$	
$c^2 = 72.25$	
$c = 8.5$	At least one dimension must be 8.5 feet or less.

DRILL: GEOMETRY WORD PROBLEMS

DIRECTIONS: Select the best answer.

1. $\triangle PQR$ is a scalene triangle. The measure of $\angle P$ is 8 more than twice the measure of $\angle R$. The measure of $\angle Q$ is two less than three times the measure of $\angle R$. Determine the measure of $\angle Q$.

    (A) 29

    (B) 53

    (C) 60

    (D) 85

    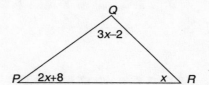

2. A bottle of medicine containing 2 kg is to be poured into smaller containers that hold 8 grams each. How many of these smaller containers can be filled from the 2 kg bottle?

    (A) 0.5   (C) 50

    (B) 5   (D) 250

3. $\angle A$ and $\angle B$ are supplementary. The measure of $\angle A$ is 5 more than four times the measure of $\angle A$. Find the measure of $\angle B$.

    (A) 35   (C) 140

    (B) 125   (D) 145

4. $\triangle RUS$ is isosceles with base $\overline{SU}$. Each leg is 3 less than 5 times the length of the base. If the perimeter of the triangle is 60 cm, find the length of a leg.

    (A) 6   (C) 27

    (B) 12   (D) 30

MEASUREMENT AND GEOMETRY SKILLS

ANSWER KEY

DRILL: MEASUREMENT

1.	**(A)**	3.	**(D)**	5.	**(A)**	7.	**(C)**
2.	**(B)**	4.	**(C)**	6.	**(C)**		

DRILL: DISTANCE, AREA, AND VOLUME

1.	**(B)**	4.	**(C)**	7.	**(C)**	10.	**(D)**
2.	**(A)**	5.	**(B)**	8.	**(A)**	11.	**(B)**
3.	**(C)**	6.	**(D)**	9.	**(A)**	12.	**(B)**

DRILL: ANGLES AND LINES

1.	**(B)**	3.	**(C)**	5.	**(D)**	7.	**(B)**
2.	**(D)**	4.	**(B)**	6.	**(C)**	8.	**(D)**

DRILL: TRIANGLES

1.	**(C)**	3.	**(D)**	5.	**(B)**	7.	**(C)**
2.	**(B)**	4.	**(C)**	6.	**(D)**		

DRILL: OTHER PLANE FIGURES

1.	**(D)**	3.	**(B)**
2.	**(B)**	4.	**(B)**

DRILL: GEOMETRIC FORMULAS

1. **(C)**   3.   **(C)**
2. **(B)**   4.   **(D)**

DRILL: GEOMETRY WORD PROBLEMS

1. **(D)**   3.   **(D)**
2. **(D)**   4.   **(C)**

MEASUREMENT AND GEOMETRY SKILLS
DETAILED EXPLANATIONS OF ANSWERS

DRILL: MEASUREMENT

1.   **(A)**   To round to the nearest ten thousand, look in the thousands column. If that number is less than 5, round down. If it is greater than 5, round up. Since 8 is greater than 5, round up. Place zeros in all of the columns to the right of the ten thousands column.

2.   **(B)**   Since 7 ounces is less than $\frac{1}{2}$ of a pound, round to 25 lbs.

3.   **(D)**   Since four days is greater than $\frac{1}{2}$ of a week, round to 4 weeks.

4.   **(C)**   Since 45 minutes is more than $\frac{1}{2}$ of an hour, round to 311 hours.

5.   **(A)**   The path of a train is linear, or one-dimensional. Decimeters measure one-dimensional units, or distance in a straight line. All the other answer choices measure area or volume.

6.   **(C)**   The space inside of a box is the same as the volume. Cubic centimeters measure volume. All of the other answer choices do not measure three dimensions.

7.   **(C)**   The volume of a child's wading pool could only be measured by cubic centimeters, since it is a three-dimensional measure.

DRILL: DISTANCE, AREA, AND VOLUME

1.   **(B)**   Multiply 5 inches a side times 4 sides. The distance is 20 inches.

2.   **(A)**   First convert all of the measurements to the same units.

36 inches = 3 feet

1 yard = 3 feet

Now add the units.

3 feet + 3 feet + 10 feet + 5 feet = 21 ft.

3. **(C)** Since this is a right triangle, use the Pythagorean Theorem to determine the missing length of the hypotenuse.

$$a^2 + b^2 = c^2$$
$$9^2 + 12^2 = c^2$$
$$81 + 144 = c^2$$
$$225 = c^2$$
$$15 = c$$

Now add the length of the legs and the hypotenuse to determine the distance.

$$9 + 12 + 15 = 36 \text{ cm}$$

4. **(C)** Use the formula Circumference = $2\pi r$. Since the radius is 4 inches,

$$C = 2\pi(4)$$
$$C = 8\pi \text{ in}$$

5. **(B)** Use the formula Area = $\frac{1}{2}$ base × height.

$$A = \frac{1}{2}(8 \times 3)$$
$$A = \frac{1}{2}(24) = 12 \text{ m}^2$$

6. **(D)** To find the surface area of a rect-angular solid, it helps to visualize the solid. As you can see in the diagram, there are three sets of matching planes: the top and bottom, two sides, and two ends. First find the area of one of each of these planes.

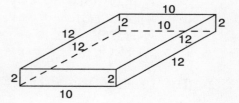

$$10 \times 12 = 120 \qquad \text{area of top}$$
$$10 \times 2 = 20 \qquad \text{area of one side}$$
$$12 \times 2 = 24 \qquad \text{area of one end}$$

Now multiply each plane by two.

$$120 \times 2 = 240 \qquad \text{area of top and bottom}$$
$$20 \times 2 = 40 \qquad \text{area of two sides}$$
$$24 \times 2 = 48 \qquad \text{area of two ends}$$

Add these areas to find the surface area of the entire solid.

$$240 + 40 + 48 = 328 \text{ yds}^2$$

7. **(C)** Use the formula Area = πr^2.

$$A = \pi\, 20^2$$
$$A = 400\pi \text{ ft}^2$$

8. **(A)** Use the formula Area = base × height.

$$A = {}^{10}\!/_3 \times 6$$
$$A = {}^{60}\!/_3$$
$$A = 20 \text{ cm}^2$$

9. **(A)** To find the volume of a rectangular solid, use the formula $V = l \times w \times h$.
$$V = 9 \times 5 \times 12$$
$$V = 540 \text{ cm}^3$$

10. **(D)** Use the formula Volume = $\frac{1}{3}\pi r^2 h$.

$$V = \tfrac{1}{3}\pi \,({}^4\!/_2)^2\,(3)$$
$$V = \tfrac{1}{3}\pi \,(2^2 \times 3)$$
$$V = \tfrac{1}{3}\pi \,(4 \times 3)$$
$$V = \tfrac{1}{3}\pi \,(12)$$
$$V = 4\pi \text{ mi}^3$$

11. **(B)** Use the formula Volume = $\pi r^2 h$.

$$V = \pi \,(5)^2\,(3)$$
$$V = \pi \,(25)\,(3)$$
$$V = \pi \,(75)$$
$$V = 75\pi \text{ ft}^3$$

12. **(B)** Use the formula Volume = $\frac{4}{3}\pi r^3$.

$$V = {}^4\!/_3 \,\pi 6^3$$
$$V = {}^4\!/_3 \pi 216$$
$$V = {}^4\!/_3 \pi 216$$
$$V = 288\pi \text{ dm}^3$$

DRILL: ANGLES AND LINES

1. **(B)** $\angle a$ is supplementary to the angle measuring 112°. Therefore, subtract 112 from 180 to determine the measure of $\angle a$, which is 68°.

2. **(D)** Vertical angles are equal, so the measure of $\angle z$ would be equivalent to the measure of $\angle c$. Find the measure of $\angle c$ with the following equation:

$$29° + 63° + \angle c = 180°$$
$$92° + \angle c = 180°$$
$$\angle c = 88°$$

Therefore, $\angle z$ also measures 88°.

3.   **(C)**   Since $\overleftrightarrow{BA} \perp \overleftrightarrow{BC}$, $\angle ABC$ is a right angle. $\angle ABD$ is complementary to $\angle DBC$. Therefore, to find the measure of $\angle ABD$, use the following equation:

$$90° - 53° = 37°.$$

4.   **(B)**   Since $\overleftrightarrow{m} \perp \overleftrightarrow{p}$, all the angles are right angles. We are not told if $\overleftrightarrow{n} \perp \overleftrightarrow{p}$, so we cannot determine anything about angles 1, 2, or 3. Therefore, choice (B) is the only choice which can be determined from the information given, since we know that $\angle 4$ and $\angle 5$ are both right angles.

5.   **(D)**   Since both $\overleftrightarrow{p}$ and $\overleftrightarrow{q}$ are perpendicular to $\overleftrightarrow{t}$, all of the angles shown are right angles. This means that they are all equal. Therefore, $\angle 2$ cannot be greater than $\angle 5$.

6.   **(C)**   If $\overleftrightarrow{a} \parallel \overleftrightarrow{b}$, then $\angle z$ is supplementary to the angle measuring 116°. Determine the measure using the following formula:

$$180° - 116° = 64°.$$

7.   **(C)**   Angles 3 and 6 are called interior angles, and since $\overleftrightarrow{m} \parallel \overleftrightarrow{n}$, the angles are supplementary, and cannot be equal.

8.   **(D)**   Line r is parallel to line s. $\angle 1$ and the angle measuring 107° are corresponding angles, so they must be equal. $\angle 2$ is supplementary with both of these angles, so its measure can be found using the following formula:

$$180° - 107° = \angle 2$$
$$73° = \angle 2$$

DRILL: TRIANGLES

1.   **(C)**   The sum of the angles of a triangle is always 180°. The sum of angles P and Q is:

$$90° + 23° = 113°.$$

Find the measure of R with the following equation:

$$180° - 113° = 67°.$$

2.   **(B)**   The base angles of an isosceles triangle are equal, meaning $\angle M$ and $\angle Q$ are equal. Therefore, to find their measure, first subtract the measure of $\angle N$ from 180°.

$$180° - 96° = 84°$$

Since $\angle M$ and $\angle N$ are equal, divide the degree measure by 2.

$$84° \div 2 = 42°$$

3.   **(D)**   Angle 3 is the supplement of 114°, so it measures:

$$180° - 114° = 66°.$$

Angles 2, 3, and 74° are all in the triangle, so their sum is 180°. Find the measure of ∠2.

$$180° - (66° + 74°) = 40°.$$

Since ∠2 and ∠1 are supplementary,

$$180° - 40° = 140°.$$

4.   **(C)**   Remember that the sum of the interior angles of a triangle is always 180°. Since we know that ∠*B* is a right angle, it is 90°. The measure of ∠*C* is given as 36°. Use the following formula to find the measure of ∠*A*:

$$36° + 90° + ∠A = 180°$$
$$126° + ∠A = 180°$$
$$∠A = 54°$$

5.   **(B)**   Remember that the sum of the interior angles of a triangle is always 180°. Therefore, the missing angle in the larger triangle measures 53°, since:

$$42° + 85° + X° = 180°$$
$$127° + X° = 180°$$
$$X = 53°$$

Since the triangles are similar, the corresponding angles must be equal. Therefore, ∠1 = 53°.

6.   **(D)**   Since the triangles are similar, the corresponding sides are in proportion. To solve for *a*, set up a proportion.

$\frac{3}{4} = \frac{4}{a}$	Cross multiply.
$3a = 16$	Divide.
$a = \frac{16}{3}$	Simplify.
$a = 5\frac{1}{3}$	

To solve for *b*, set up a proportion.

$\frac{3}{6} = \frac{4}{b}$	Cross multiply.
$3b = 24$	Divide.
$b = 8$	

7.   **(C)**   Since the angles are equal, the triangles are similar. Set up a proportion using the corresponding sides of similar triangles.

$\frac{b}{4} = \frac{15}{3}$	Cross multiply.
$3b = 60$	Divide.
$b = 20$	

DRILL: OTHER PLANE FIGURES

1.   **(D)**   A triangle is defined as a polygon with three sides.

2.   **(B)**   A square and a rhombus are defined as equilateral quadrilaterals; a rectangle does not have four equal sides.

3.   **(B)**   A rhombus is a quadrilateral, has at least one pair of parallel sides, and its diagonals are always perpendicular to each other.

4.   **(B)**   A scalene triangle could possess a $10°$ and $20°$ angle. It would be impossible for the three other choices.

DRILL: GEOMETRIC FORMULAS

1.   **(C)**   The answer is 100π, since $SA = 2\pi r^2 + 2\pi rh$.

2.   **(B)**   The median is equal to the average of the two bases, so:

$$m = \frac{(b+b)}{2}$$
$$m = \frac{(3+17)}{2}$$
$$m = 10$$

3.   **(C)**   The shaded section is $\frac{1}{4}$ of a circle with the radius s. The area of this section is $\frac{\pi s^2}{4}$; the nonshaded area is $\frac{s^2 - \pi s^2}{4}$.

4.   **(D)**   The radius of the circle is $\sqrt{2}$. The area of the circle is πr^2, so:

$$A = \pi\left(\sqrt{2}\right)^2$$
$$A = 2\pi$$

The area of the square is $2^2 = 4$, so the shaded area is the area of the whole circle minus the area of the square, or:

$$A = 2\pi - 4.$$

DRILL: GEOMETRY WORD PROBLEMS

1.   **(D)**   Draw a sketch of the triangle and label the angles. Two of the angles are compared to $\angle R$, so let x = the measure of $\angle R$. Then

$$\angle P = 2x + 8 \text{ and } \angle Q = 3x - 2.$$

The sum of the measures of the angles of a triangle is 180°, so add the measures of all three angles and this will equal 180°.

$$
\begin{aligned}
x + (2x + 8) + (3x - 2) &= 180 \\
6x + 6 &= 180 \\
6x &= 174 \\
x &= 29
\end{aligned}
$$

The measure of $\angle R$ is 29° and the measure of $\angle Q$ is 3(29) − 2 or 85°.

Check: $29 + [2(29) + 8] + [3(29) - 2] = 180$
$$
\begin{aligned}
29 + 66 + 85 &= 180 \\
180 &= 180
\end{aligned}
$$

2.   **(D)**   Since 1 kg = 1,000 g, then 2 kg of medicine = 2,000 g of medicine. Since each small container will hold 8 g, divide 2,000 g by 8 g.

$2,000 \div 8 = 250$ small containers.

3.   **(D)**   Let A = the measure of $\angle A$ and let B = the measure of $\angle B$. Since the two angles are supplementary, one equation is

$$A + B = 180.$$

Since B is five more than four times the measure of $\angle A$, either subtract five from the measure of $\angle B$ or add five to four times the measure of $\angle A$. The equation becomes

$$B = 4A + 5.$$

Now substitute the value of B into the first equation to get

$$A + (4A + 5) = 180.$$

Solve the equation for A.

$$
\begin{aligned}
5A + 5 &= 180 \\
5A &= 175 \\
A &= 35
\end{aligned}
$$

Then $B = 4(35) + 5 = 145$.

Check: $35 + 145 = 180$ $145 = 4(35) + 5$
                $180 = 180$ $145 = 145$

4.   **(C)**   Draw an isosceles triangle and label each side. Let the length of the base be *x*. Then each leg is five times the base less 3, or $5x - 3$.

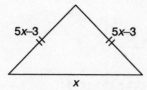

The perimeter is the sum of the sides, so the equation becomes

$$x + (5x - 3) + (5x - 3) = 60.$$

Solve for *x*.

$$11x - 6 = 60$$
$$11x = 66$$
$$x = 6$$

and $5(6) - 3 = 27$

The length of each leg is 27.

Check: $6 + 27 + 27 = 60$
$$60 = 60$$

ALGEBRA SKILLS

REAL NUMBERS

ADDITION AND SUBTRACTION

Most of the numbers used in algebra belong to a set called the real numbers or reals. The set of real numbers is composed of two subsets of numbers; the rational numbers, which were discussed in the Arithmetic Skills section, and the irrational numbers.

The irrational numbers are numeric values which when expressed in decimal form do not repeat or terminate. Some examples of irrational numbers include π, $\sqrt{5}$, $-\sqrt{7}$.

The number line is a graphical representation of the set of real numbers. There is a one-to-one correspondence between each real number and each point on the number line.

To add or subtract real numbers, follow the given steps:

(1) If it is a subtraction problem, convert the problem to an addition problem by changing the subtraction sign to an addition sign and changing the sign of the term following the subtraction symbol.

(2) Before one can combine radical terms, the radicands (the number under the radical signs) must be the same. This is accomplished through simplification.

(3) Combine like terms using the addition rules presented in the Arithmetic Skills section.

Example: $6\sqrt{2} + 2\sqrt{2} = (6+2)\sqrt{2} = 8\sqrt{2}$

Example: $\sqrt{27} - 5\sqrt{3} = \sqrt{9 \times 3} + (-5\sqrt{3}) = 3\sqrt{3} + (-5\sqrt{3}) = -2\sqrt{3}$

Example:
$$7\sqrt{3} + 3\sqrt{48} + 5 = 7\sqrt{3} + 3\sqrt{16 \times 3} + 5 = 7\sqrt{3} + 3 \times 4\sqrt{3} + 5$$
$$= 7\sqrt{3} + 12\sqrt{3} + 5 = 19\sqrt{3} + 5$$

Example: $9\pi + 4 - 2\pi = 7\pi + 4$

MULTIPLICATION AND DIVISION

To multiply two radicals, utilize the law that states, $\sqrt{a} \times \sqrt{b} = \sqrt{ab}$, by proceeding as follows:

(1) If there are whole number coefficients multiplied by the radicals, simply multiply the whole numbers as usual.

(2) Multiply the numbers under the radicals and place this product under a radical sign.

(3) Simplify if possible.

Example: $\sqrt{12} \times \sqrt{5} = \sqrt{60} = \sqrt{4 \times 15} = 2\sqrt{15}$

Example: $3\sqrt{2} \times 4\sqrt{8} = 12\sqrt{16} = 12 \times 4 = 48$

Example: $2\sqrt{10} \times 6\sqrt{5} = 12\sqrt{50} = 12\sqrt{25 \times 2} = 12 \times 5\sqrt{2} = 60\sqrt{2}$

Division of radicals is actually just a process of rationalizing the denominator and then simplifying the resulting expression.

To accomplish this:

(1) Multiply the given expression by 1. This will be demonstrated in the examples.

(2) Simplify the resulting fraction.

Example: $\dfrac{\sqrt{10}}{\sqrt{3}}$

$\dfrac{\sqrt{10}}{\sqrt{3}} \times \dfrac{\sqrt{3}}{\sqrt{3}}$

$\dfrac{\sqrt{30}}{\sqrt{9}} = \dfrac{\sqrt{30}}{3}$

Multiply by 1. In this problem 1 is of the form $\sqrt{3}/\sqrt{3}$ since the denominator of the original fraction is $\sqrt{3}$.

Multiply the numerators and multiply the denominators. Simplify.

Example: $\dfrac{\sqrt{8}}{2\sqrt{5}}$

$\dfrac{\sqrt{8}}{2\sqrt{5}} \times \dfrac{\sqrt{5}}{\sqrt{5}}$

$\dfrac{\sqrt{40}}{2\sqrt{25}} = \dfrac{\sqrt{4 \times 10}}{2 \times 5} = \dfrac{2\sqrt{10}}{10} = \dfrac{\sqrt{10}}{5}$

Multiply by 1. In this problem 1 is of the form $\sqrt{5}/\sqrt{5}$ since the denominator of the original fraction contains $\sqrt{5}$.

Multiply the numerators and multiply the denominators. Simplify.

DRILL: REAL NUMBERS

DIRECTIONS: Select the best answer.

1. $3\sqrt{32} + 2\sqrt{2} =$

    (A) $5\sqrt{2}$ (C) $5\sqrt{34}$

    (B) $14\sqrt{2}$ (D) $\sqrt{43}$

2. $6\sqrt{5} + 2\sqrt{45} =$

    (A) $12\sqrt{5}$ (C) $40\sqrt{2}$

    (B) $8\sqrt{50}$ (D) $12\sqrt{50}$

3. $\sqrt{5} + 6\sqrt{5} - 3\sqrt{5} =$

    (A) $3\sqrt{5}$ (C) $3\sqrt{15}$

    (B) $4\sqrt{5}$ (D) $7\sqrt{15}$

4. $4\pi - 5\pi - 4 =$

    (A) $9\pi - 4$ (C) -5π

    (B) $\pi - 4$ (D) $-\pi - 4$

5. $10\sqrt{2} - 3\sqrt{8} =$

    (A) $6\sqrt{6}$ (C) $7\sqrt{6}$

    (B) $-2\sqrt{2}$ (D) $4\sqrt{2}$

6. $4\sqrt{3} - 2\sqrt{12} =$

    (A) $-2\sqrt{9}$ (C) 0

    (B) $-6\sqrt{15}$ (D) $6\sqrt{15}$

7. $\sqrt{3} \times \sqrt{12} =$

   (A)   3

   (B) $\sqrt{15}$

   (C) $\sqrt{36}$

   (D)   6

8. $\sqrt{7} \times \sqrt{7} =$

   (A)   7

   (B)   49

   (C) $\sqrt{14}$

   (D) $2\sqrt{7}$

9. $3\sqrt{5} \times 2\sqrt{5} =$

   (A) $5\sqrt{5}$

   (B)   25

   (C)   30

   (D) $5\sqrt{25}$

10. $\dfrac{\sqrt{10}}{\sqrt{2}} =$

   (A) $\sqrt{8}$

   (B) $2\sqrt{2}$

   (C) $\sqrt{5}$

   (D) $2\sqrt{5}$

11. $\dfrac{\sqrt{30}}{\sqrt{15}} =$

   (A) $\sqrt{2}$

   (B) $\sqrt{45}$

   (C) $3\sqrt{5}$

   (D) $\sqrt{15}$

12. $\dfrac{\sqrt{48}}{\sqrt{8}} =$

   (A) $4\sqrt{3}$

   (B) $3\sqrt{2}$

   (C) $\sqrt{6}$

   (D)   6

13. $\dfrac{3\sqrt{12}}{\sqrt{3}} =$

   (A) $3\sqrt{15}$ (C)   9

   (B)   6   (D)   12

ORDER OF OPERATIONS

Before solving multiple operation problems, review the rules for the order of operations. Perform operations in this order:

   (1)   operations within grouping symbols (parentheses, brackets, braces, absolute value, etc.) according to the order which follows.

   (2)   operations involving exponents. This includes radicals.

   (3)   multiplication and division from left to right.

   (4)   addition and subtraction from left to right.

Example: $(4 + 8 \times 2) \div (5 - 1) =$

   Solution: $(4 + 16) \div 4$ (1) Eliminate parentheses.
   $= 20 \div 4$
   $= 5$ (3) Divide.

Example: $3^2 + 4 \times 2 - 6 \div 3 =$

   Solution: $9 + 4 \times 2 - 6 \div 3$ (2) Exponents.
   $= 9 + 8 - 6 \div 3$ (3) Multiply.
   $= 9 + 8 - 2$ Divide.
   $= 17 - 2$ (4) Add.
   $= 15$ Subtract.

Example: $\dfrac{7(2a + 3b)}{9 - 2} - 2(4a - 3b) =$

   Solution: $\dfrac{14a + 21b}{7} - 8a + 6b$ (1) Distribute and simplify the denominator.

   $= 2a + 3b - 8a + 6b$ (2) Divide by 7.

   $= -6a + 9b$ (3) Combine like terms.

DRILL: ORDER OF OPERATIONS

DIRECTIONS: Select the best answer.

1. $96 \div 3 \div 4 \div 2 =$

    (A)   64

    (B)   16

    (C)   8

    (D)   4

2. $18 + 3 \times 4 \div 3 =$

    (A)   3

    (B)   5

    (C)   10

    (D)   22

3. $(-3) \times 5 - 20 \div 4 =$

    (A)   −75

    (B)   −20

    (C)   −10

    (D) $-8\frac{3}{4}$

4. $32 \div 2^3 + 4 - 15 \div 3 =$

    (A) $-\frac{7}{3}$

    (B)   7

    (C)   3

    (D)   23

5. $\frac{1}{4} - 3(\frac{1}{2} - \frac{3}{4} + \frac{1}{2})^2 =$

    (A) $\frac{1}{16}$

    (B) $-\frac{1}{2}$

    (C) $\frac{5}{2}$

    (D) $4\frac{1}{8}$

6. $8a - \dfrac{14b}{7} + 4a \times 5 =$

    (A) $12a - 10b$

    (B) $28a - 2b$

    (C) $6ab + 20a$

    (D) $24a - 10b$

SCIENTIFIC NOTATION

To effectively perform operations with very large and/or very small numbers, it is easier to perform the operations with the numbers in scientific notation form. To perform these operations, proceed as follows:

(1) Convert all numbers to scientific notation. Scientific notation dictates that the leading digit be between 1 and 9 inclusive with the remainder of the digits after the decimal point. This value will then be multiplied by an appropriate power of 10. To find this power, count the number of decimal places the decimal point is being moved. If the original number is less than 1, the exponent will be negative. If the original number is greater than 1, the exponent will be positive.

(2) Multiply or divide as the problem will indicate.

- To multiply:
  multiply the decimal numbers and add the exponents on the power of ten. Use this sum as the new power of 10.

- To divide:
  divide the decimal numbers and subtract the exponent on the power of ten in the denominator from the exponent on the power of ten in the numerator. Use this difference as the new power of 10 in the numerator.

Example: $0.000873 \div 291{,}000{,}000 =$

Solution: $8.73 \times 10^{-4} \div 2.91 \times 10^{8}$ (1) Scientific notation.
$= (8.73 \div 2.91) \times (10^{-4} \div 10^{8})$ (2) Subtract exponents.
$= 3.00 \times 10^{-12}$

Example: $(6.2 \times 10^{8}) \times (3.11 \times 10^{-5}) =$

Solution: $(6.2 \times 3.11) \times (10^{8} \times 10^{-5})$
$= 19.282 \times 10^{3}$
$= 19{,}282$ (2) Multiply 19.282 by 1,000.

DRILL: SCIENTIFIC NOTATION

DIRECTIONS: Select the best answer.

---

1. $28{,}500{,}000 \times 0.000000021 =$

(A) 5.985×10^{-1} (C) 5.985×10^{-2}

(B) 5.985×10^{-2} (D) 5.985

2. $0.00023 \times 8{,}000{,}000 =$

(A) 1.84×10^{2} (C) 1.84×10^{4}

(B) 1.84×10^{3} (D) 1.84

3.   73,000,000 × 20,000 =

    (A) 1.46×10^{10} (C) 1.46×10^{12}

    (B) 1.46×10^{11} (D) 1.46^{12}

4.   98,800,000 ÷ 0.000004 =

    (A) 2.47×10^{13} (C) 2.47×10^{11}

    (B) 2.47×10^{12} (D) 2.47^{12}

5. $(3.51 \times 10^{-7}) \div (1.17 \times 10^{-12}) =$

    (A)   300   (C)   30,000

    (B)   3,000   (D)   300,000

LINEAR EQUATIONS AND INEQUALITIES

LINEAR EQUATIONS

An equation is defined as a statement that two separate expressions are equal. Think of these equivalent expressions as sitting on a balance scale, and whatever we do to one side of the equation, we must do to the other in order to keep the scale balanced. Thus, if we add a term to one side, we must add the same term to the other side and the same holds with the other operations.

Therefore, to solve a linear equation:

(1)   Eliminate any grouping symbols.

(2)   Combine like terms on each side of the equation.

(3)   Group like terms across the equation sign by adding or subtracting.

(4)   Divide both sides by the coefficient on the variable.

(5)   Optional: Check the solution by replacing the variable in the given equation with the value of the variable. If both sides equal when simplified, the solution is correct.

Example: If $3x - 8 = 7x + 8$, then

Solution:

$$
\begin{array}{rl}
3x - 8 &= 7x + 8 \\
-7x &\quad -7x \\
\hline
-4x - 8 &= 8 \\
+8 &\quad +8 \\
\hline
-4x &= 16 \\
\overline{-4} & \overline{ -4} \\
\end{array}
$$

(3) Subtract $7x$.

(3) Add 8.
(4) Divide by -4.

$$x = -4$$

Example: If $3x - 5(2 - x) = 4$, then

Solution:

$$
\begin{aligned}
3x - 10 + 5x &= 4 \\
8x - 10 &= 4 \\
+10 \phantom{{}-10} &+10 \\
\hline
\frac{8x}{8} &= \frac{14}{8} \\
x = \frac{14}{8} &= \frac{7}{4}
\end{aligned}
$$

(1) Eliminate parentheses.
(2) Combine like terms.
(3) Add 10.
(4) Divide by 8.

LINEAR INEQUALITIES

An inequality is a statement where the value of one quantity or expression is unequal to another. The symbolism used is as follows:

> greater than
≥ greater than or equal to
< less than
≤ less than or equal to

To solve linear inequalities, one follows the same steps as when solving linear equations with one additional constraint.

When multiplying or dividing by a negative number the direction of the inequality must be changed.

Why?   If $2 < 3$, then

$$2 \times (-4) \; ? \; 3 \times (-4)$$
$$-8 > -12$$

(1) Multiply both sides by –4.
(2) The direction of the inequality changes.

Example: If $2x + 5 > 9$, then

Solution:

$$
\begin{aligned}
2x + 5 &> 9 \\
-5 &-5 \\
\hline
2x &> 4 \\
x &> 2
\end{aligned}
$$

(1) Subtract 5.
(2) Divide by 2.

Example: If $4x + 3 < 6x + 8$, then

Solution:

$$
\begin{aligned}
4x + 3 &< 6x + 8 \\
-6x &\phantom{<}-6x \\
\hline
-2x + 3 &< 8 \\
-3 &\phantom{<}-3 \\
\hline
-2x &< 5 \\
x &> -\frac{5}{2}
\end{aligned}
$$

(1) Subtract 6x.

(2) Subtract 3.
(3) Divide by –2.
(4) Change the direction of the inequality.

DRILL: LINEAR EQUATIONS AND INEQUALITIES

> **DIRECTIONS:** Select the best answer.

1. If $7z + 1 - z = 2z - 7$, then
   - (A) $z = -2$.
   - (B) $z = 0$.
   - (C) $z = 1$.
   - (D) $z = 2$.

2. If $4(3x + 2) - 11 = 3(3x - 2)$, then
   - (A) $x = -3$.
   - (B) $x = -1$.
   - (C) $x = 2$.
   - (D) $x = 3$.

3. If $4(2c - 3) = 8$, then
   - (A) $c = 1\frac{1}{8}$.
   - (B) $c = -\frac{1}{2}$.
   - (C) $c = 12$.
   - (D) $c = \frac{5}{2}$.

4. If $3x - 4(x + 1) = 0$, then
   - (A) $x = -4$.
   - (B) $x = \frac{4}{7}$.
   - (C) $x = 4$.
   - (D) $x = 1$.

5. If $-3p - 1 \geq 16$, then
   - (A) $p \geq -5$.
   - (B) $p \geq -\frac{17}{3}$.
   - (C) $p \leq -\frac{17}{3}$.
   - (D) $p \leq -5$.

6. If $9x - 5(2x + 3) > 0$, then
   - (A) $x < -15$.
   - (B) $x > -15$.
   - (C) $x < 15$.
   - (D) $x > 15$.

7. If $4 - 2a \leq 9 - a$, then
   - (A) $a \leq -5$.
   - (B) $a \geq -5$.
   - (C) $a \leq 5$.
   - (D) $a \geq 5$.

8. If $5(x - 3) > 14$, then

(A) $x > {}^{29}\!/_5$.

(B) $x > {}^{17}\!/_5$.

(C) $x < {}^{17}\!/_5$.

(D) $x < -\frac{1}{5}$.

ALGEBRAIC FORMULAS

A formula will be given with specific values for some of the variables. In order to compute the result, follow the given steps:

(1) Substitute the given values into the appropriate variables.

(2) Simplify to find the result.

Example: The formula for finding the interest (I) on a loan is $I = P \times R \times T$. How much interest will Jerry pay on his loan of $400 ($P$) for 60 ($T$) days at 6% ($R$) per year?

Solution:
$$\begin{aligned} I &= P \times R \times T \\ &= 400 \times 0.06 \times {}^{60}\!/_{365} \\ &= 3.94 \\ & \$3.94 \end{aligned}$$

Example: Given $T = (3S - 4R)^2$, if $S = 400$ and $R = 200$, find T.

Solution:
$$\begin{aligned} T &= (3S - 4R)^2 \\ T &= (3 \times 400 - 4 \times 200)^2 \\ T &= (1{,}200 - 800)^2 \\ T &= (400)^2 \\ T &= 160{,}000 \end{aligned}$$

DRILL: ALGEBRAIC FORMULAS

DIRECTIONS: Select the best answer.

1. The formula for finding the interest (I) on a loan is $I = P \times R \times T$. How much interest will Mr. Smith receive on $300 if the rate is 3% for three years?

(A) $9

(B) $27

(C) $270

(D) $2,700

2.   Given $y = (2x - 3)^3$, if $x = 1$, find y.

   (A)   −1   (C)   1

   (B)   0   (D)   3

3.   The formula for calculating a T score is given by $T = 50 + 10\dfrac{X - \overline{X}}{\sigma}$. Samantha's score, or X, was 80 on a recent exam and she wishes to calculate her T score. The mean $\left(\overline{X}\right)$ was 75 and the standard deviation $\left(\sigma\right)$ was 5. Find her T score.

   (A)   40   (C)   60

   (B)   50   (D)   70

4.   The formula for calculating the distance (D) traveled is $D = R \times T$. If Melissa drove for 3 hours (T) at a rate of 45 mph (R), how far did she travel?

   (A)   135 miles   (C)   135 hours

   (B)   48 miles   (D)   48 hours

5.   Given $R = H - L + 1$, if $H = 100$ and $L = 35$, find R.

   (A)   76   (C)   65

   (B)   66   (D)   −64

FUNCTIONS

Given will be a function, $f(x)$, and a value to substitute for x.

To find the value of the function, replace the variable x with the given value and simplify using the order of operations rules.

Example: Given $f(x) = 5x^2 - 2x + 3$, find $f(-1)$.

   Solution: $f(-1)$ = $5(-1)^2 - 2(-1) + 3$

   = $5(1) + 2 + 3$

   = $5 + 2 + 3$

   = 10

Example: Given $f(x) = 4 - x^2 + x^3$, find $f(\tfrac{1}{2})$.

   Solution: $f(\tfrac{1}{2})$ = $4 - (\tfrac{1}{2})^2 + (\tfrac{1}{2})^3$

   = $4 - \tfrac{1}{4} + \tfrac{1}{8}$

   = $\tfrac{32}{8} - \tfrac{2}{8} + \tfrac{1}{8}$

   = $\tfrac{31}{8}$

DRILL: FUNCTIONS

DIRECTIONS: Select the best answer.

---

1. Given $f(x) = x^2 + 5x - 3$, find $f(-2)$.

   (A) −17
   (B) −9
   (C) 3
   (D) 11

2. Given $f(x) = 3 - x^3$, find $f(-1)$.

   (A) 0
   (B) 2
   (C) 4
   (D) 6

3. Given $f(x) = x^3 - 5x^2 + 2x - 8$, find $f(3)$.

   (A) −200
   (B) −118
   (C) −23
   (D) −20

4. Given $f(x) = 5 + 2x - x^2$, find $f(4)$.

   (A) −3
   (B) 5
   (C) 12
   (D) 29

5. Given $f(x) = 7x^4 - 12x^2 + x - 5$, find $f(-2)$.

   (A) 80
   (B) 72.5
   (C) 55
   (D) 57

QUADRATIC EXPRESSIONS AND EQUATIONS

FACTORING QUADRATIC EXPRESSIONS

The general quadratic expression is of the form $ax^2 + bx + c$.
To assist in factoring, remember the following rules:

(1) Write two sets of parentheses, using the following chart to determine the signs in the parentheses.

$\underline{a}$	$\underline{b}$	$\underline{c}$	signs within the parentheses
+	+	+	(+) (+)
+	−	+	(−) (−)
+	+	−	(+) (−) or (−) (+)
+	−	−	(+) (−) or (−) (+)

(2) List the factors of the *a* term and write these in the first position of each set of parentheses.

(3) List the factors of the *c* term and write these in the second position of each set of parentheses.

(4) Multiply the first and last terms of alternate parentheses. Add these terms together and compare this value with the *b* term. If they match, the quadratic has been factored correctly. If they do not match, try other combinations of the factors until you find one which gives you the *b* value.

Example: What are the linear factors of $x^2 - 6x + 8$?

Solution: (−) (−) (1) Identify the signs.

Factors of 1: 1 and 1 (2) Factors of the *a* term.
$(x-)(x-)$

Factors of 8: 8 and 1 (3) Factors of the *c* term.
           4 and 2
$(x- 8)(x- 1)$

$-x - 8x = -9x$ (4) Check.

Is $-9x = -6x$? NO!

$(x- 4)(x- 2)$ Try again.

$-2x - 4x = -6x$ Check.

Is $-6x = -6x$? YES!!!

Therefore, $(x- 4)(x- 2)$ are the correct factors.

Example: What are the linear factors of $2x^2 + 5x - 3$?

Solution: (+) (−) (1) Identify the signs.

Factors of 2: 2 and 1 (2) Factors of the *a* term.
$(2x+)(x-)$

Factors of 3: 3 and 1 (3) Factors of the *c* term.
$(2x + 3)(x- 1)$

$-2x + 3x = x$ (4) Check.
Is $5x = x$? NO!

$(2x + 1)(x- 3)$ Try again.

$-6x + x = -5x$

Is $-5x = 5x$? NO!   (When the absolute values are the same, just change the signs within the parentheses.)

$(2x - 1) (x + 3)$ Try again.

$6x - x = 5x$ Check.

Is $5x = 5x$? YES!!!

Therefore, $(2x - 1) (x + 3)$ are the correct factors.

FINDING THE ROOTS OF A QUADRATIC EQUATION

A second degree equation in x of the type $ax^2 + bx + c = 0$, where $a = 0$, and a, b, and c are real numbers, is called a quadratic equation.

When finding the roots or solutions of a quadratic equation, you are simply finding the values which satisfy a given quadratic equation.

A quadratic equation has a maximum of two roots. These roots are the points at which the graph of the quadratic equation crosses the x-axis. The roots of all quadratic equations can be extracted by using the quadratic formula; however, some quadratics can also be solved by factoring.

To find the roots of a quadratic equation that factors, follow the given steps:

(1)   Write the given quadratic equation in standard form: $ax^2 + bx + c = 0$.

(2)   Factor the quadratic as you did in the prior skill area.

(3)   Set each factor equal to zero because if $a \times b = 0$ then either $a = 0$ or $b = 0$.

(4)   Solve each resulting linear equation.

Example: Find the correct solutions to $6x^2 - x - 2 = 0$.

    Solution: $(\quad + \quad) (\quad - \quad) = 0$

                Factors of 6:   6 and 1
                                  3 and 2

                Factors of 2:   2 and 1

                $(2x + 1) (3x - 2) = 0$

                $2x + 1 = 0$ or $3x - 2 = 0$
                $2x = -1$ $3x = 2$
                $x = -\frac{1}{2}$ $x = \frac{2}{3}$

If a quadratic does not factor or if you simply prefer to use the quadratic formula to solve quadratic equations, proceed as follows:

(1)   Write the quadratic equation in standard form: $ax^2 + bx + c = 0$.

(2)   Identify the values for a, b, and c for the specific problem.

(3)   Substitute the values for a, b, and c into the quadratic formula.

$$x = \frac{-b \pm \sqrt{b^2 - 4ac}}{2a}$$

(4)   Simplify using the order of operations rules.

Example: Find the correct solutions to $x^2 = 12x - 8$.

Solution: $x^2 - 12x + 8 = 0$ (1) Write in standard form.

$a = 1, b = -12, c = 8$ (2) Identify a, b, and c.

$$x = \frac{12 \pm \sqrt{(-12)^2 - 4(1)(8)}}{2(1)}$$ (3) Substitute.

$$= \frac{12 \pm \sqrt{144 - 32}}{2}$$ (4) Simplify.

$$= \frac{12 \pm \sqrt{112}}{2}$$

$$= \frac{12 \pm 4\sqrt{7}}{2}$$

$$= 6 \pm 2\sqrt{7}$$

DRILL: QUADRATIC EXPRESSIONS AND EQUATIONS

DIRECTIONS: Select the best answer.

---

1. Which is a linear factor of $x^2 - 2x - 8$?

     (A) $(x + 4)$ (C) $(x - 2)$

     (B) $(x - 4)$ (D) $(x + 1)$

2. Which is a linear factor of $x^2 + x - 6$?

     (A) $(x + 2)$ (C) $(x - 6)$

     (B) $(x - 3)$ (D) $(x - 2)$

3. Which is a linear factor of $6x^2 - 5x - 6$?

     (A) $(6x - 1)$ (C) $(2x + 3)$

     (B) $(3x - 2)$ (D) $(3x + 2)$

4. Find the correct solutions to $12x^2 + 5x = 3$.

   (A) $\frac{1}{3}$ and $-\frac{1}{4}$ (C) $\frac{1}{3}$ and -4

   (B) 4 and $\frac{1}{6}$ (D) $-\frac{3}{4}$ and $\frac{1}{3}$

5. Find the correct solution(s) to $x^2 - 3x + 1 = 0$.

   (A) $\dfrac{3 \pm \sqrt{5}}{2}$ (C) $\frac{1}{3}$ and 1

   (B) $\dfrac{-3 \pm \sqrt{5}}{2}$ (D) $\dfrac{3 \pm \sqrt{13}}{2}$

6. Find the correct solution to $3x^2 - 2x = 4x + 2$.

   (A) $\dfrac{-3 \pm \sqrt{15}}{3}$ (C) $\dfrac{3 \pm \sqrt{3}}{3}$

   (B) $\dfrac{3 \pm \sqrt{15}}{3}$ (D) $3 \pm \sqrt{15}$

7. Find the correct solutions to $12x^2 + 5x = 2$.

   (A) $-\frac{1}{4}$ and $\frac{2}{3}$ (C) $\frac{1}{6}$ and $-\frac{1}{2}$

   (B) $\frac{1}{4}$ and $-\frac{2}{3}$ (D) $\frac{1}{3}$ and $-\frac{3}{4}$

SYSTEMS OF LINEAR EQUATIONS

A linear equation is of the form $ax + by = c$. If graphed, this would be a straight line with every point on the line a solution to the equation.

When solving a 2×2 system of linear equations, three outcomes are possible.

A. The two lines could intersect in exactly one point with this point, an ordered pair (x, y), being the common solution.

B. The two lines could be parallel and not intersect, hence having no shared point in common or no solution.

C. The two lines could be actually the same line, and hence result in an infinite number of common solutions.

There are numerous methods for solving a 2 × 2 system of linear equations. The Elimination Method will be presented here. To use this method, follow the given steps:

(1) Write both equations in standard form: $ax + by = c$.

(2) If necessary, multiply the equation(s) by a number(s) that will make the coefficients of one unknown additive inverses.

(3) Add the two equations together. One of three cases will result:

  A. One variable will cancel, leaving one equation with one unknown. If this is the case, there is one solution, an ordered pair. Solve the resulting equation for the unknown. Substitute the value into one of the original equations to find the other unknown.

  B. Both variables will cancel leaving a true numeric statement. If this is the case, the two lines are one in the same and the solution will look like $\{(x, y) \mid ax + by = c\}$ where the linear equation is either of the original equations.

  C. Both variables will cancel leaving a false numeric statement. If this is the case, the lines do not intersect and there is no solution.

Example: Choose the correct solution set for the system of linear equations.

$$6x + 9y = 6$$
$$2x + 3y = 7$$

Solution: Multiply the second equation by −3 so that the coefficients on x are additive inverses: $-3(2x + 3y = 7)$.

$$
\begin{array}{rcr}
6x + 9y &=& 6 \\
+\ -6x - 9y &=& -21 \\
\hline
0 &=& -15
\end{array}
$$

Both variables cancelled and the resulting numeric statement is false. The two original equations happen to be parallel and do not intersect. This means that there is no common solution, so the solution for the system is the empty set.

DRILL: SYSTEMS OF LINEAR EQUATIONS

> **DIRECTIONS:** Select the best answer.

1. Choose the correct solution set for the system of linear equations.
   $$x + 2y = 8$$
   $$3x + 4y = 20$$

   (A) $\{(4, 2)\}$

   (B) $\{(8, 0)\}$

   (C) $\{(x, y) \mid x + 2y = 8\}$

   (D) The empty set

2. Choose the correct solution set for the system of linear equations.
   $$4x + 2y = -1$$
   $$5x - 3y = 7$$

   (A) $\{(2, 1)\}$

   (B) $\{(\frac{1}{2}, -\frac{3}{2})\}$

   (C) $\{(x, y) \mid 4x + 2y = -1\}$

   (D) The empty set

3. Choose the correct solution set for the system of linear equations.
   $$3x + 4y = -2$$
   $$6x + 8y = 4$$

   (A) $\{(2, -2)\}$

   (B) $\{(2, -1)\}$

   (C) $\{(x, y) \mid 3x + 4y = -2\}$

   (D) The empty set

4. Choose the correct solution set for the system of linear equations.
   $$2x + y = -10$$
   $$6x + 3y = -30$$

   (A) $\{(0, -10)\}$

   (B) $\{(-5, 0)\}$

   (C) $\{(x, y) \mid 2x + y = -10\}$

   (D) The empty set

5. Choose the correct solution for the system of linear equations.
   $$x + 8y = 25$$
   $$x + 4y = 15$$

   (A) $\{(4, 8)\}$

   (B) $\{(5, \frac{5}{2})\}$

   (C) $\{(\frac{5}{2}, -\frac{5}{4})\}$

   (D) $\{(5, -\frac{5}{2})\}$

PROPERTIES OF OPERATIONS

The properties of real numbers to be applied in this skill area include:

Real Number Properties

Property	Addition	Multiplication
Commutative Property	$a + b = b + a$	$a \times b = b \times a$
Associative Property	$(a + b) + c = a + (b + c)$	$(a \times b) \times c = a \times (b \times c)$
Identity Property	$a + 0 = a$	$a \times 1 = a$
Inverse Property	$a + (-a) = 0$	$a \times \frac{1}{a} = 1$
Distributive Property of Multiplication over Addition		$a(b + c) = a \times b + a \times c$

To narrow in on the property being illustrated in each question, proceed as follows:

(1) Look for the use of the commutative property. The order of two terms will be switched. This is usually easy to spot and requires no additional work.

(2) If the commutative property does not apply, look for the associative property. There must be at least three terms. The order of the terms will remain the same, but the grouping will change. This is also rather easy to spot and requires no additional work.

(3) If steps 1 and 2 fail to identify a choice, look for a 0 added to a term and not present in a choice or for a 1 multiplied by a term and not present in a choice or vice versa.

(4) The last visual check is to see if the negative of a term is added to itself resulting in a 0 or if a term is multiplied by its multiplicative inverse resulting in a 1.

(5) If the first four visual checks fail to identify a correct choice, the property being illustrated must be the distributive property. In this case, multiply the term outside the parentheses by each term inside the parentheses and see if that result is an option.

Example: Choose the expression equivalent to $7 + 3r$.

(A) $3 + 7r$ (C) $3r - 7$

(B) $3r + 7$ (D) $10r$

Solution: Is the order switched on one choice? This could be $3r + 7$ or $7 + r \times 3$. Yes, choice (B).

Example: Choose the expression equivalent to $5(r + 2s)$.

(A) $(5 + r)2s$ (C) $10rs$

(B) $5r + 2s$ (D) $5r + 10s$

Solution: Is the order switched on one choice? This could be $5(2s + r)$ or $(r + 2s)5$. No.

Regrouping does not apply since the first operation is multiplication and the second operation is addition. The operations must be the same for the associative property.

Are we adding a 0 or multiplying by 1? No.

Are we multiplying into the parentheses by the term 5? This would look like: $5r + 10s$. Yes, choice (D).

Example: Choose the expression equivalent to $9[(x + 3)(x - 3)]$.

(A) $9x^2 - 9$ (C) $9[x^2 - 3]$

(B) $[9(x + 3)](x - 3)$ (D) $9[x^2 - 6]$

Solution: Is the order switched on one choice? No.

Is the grouping switched on one choice? Yes, choice (B).

If the problem is as follows, apply the questions to each choice until you find one that does not meet the requirements.

Example: Choose the statement that is *not* true for all real numbers.

(A) $-x + x = 0$

(B) $3 \times (-\frac{1}{3}) = 1$

(C) $3 + r = r + 3$

(D) $[(a + b)(b + c)](c + d) = (a + b)[(b + c)(c + d)]$

Solution: Choice (A) represents the inverse property.
Choice (B) is not a represented property. $3 \times (-\frac{1}{3}) = -1$.
Choice (C) represents the commutative property.
Choice (D) represents the associative property.

Choice (B) is the correct response.

DRILL: PROPERTIES OF OPERATIONS

DIRECTIONS: Select the best answer.

---

1.   Choose the expression equivalent to $3x + (-3x)$.

   (A)   1   (C) $-9x$

   (B)   0   (D) $-9x^2$

2.   Choose the expression equivalent to $3 \times 4(a + 2)$.

   (A) $7(a + 2)$ (C) $3 \times 4(a + 2) + 1$

   (B) $(4 + 3)2a$ (D) $4 \times 3(a + 2)$

3.   Choose the expression equivalent to $(2x + 3y) + 4z$.

   (A) $2x + (3y + 4z)$ (C) $2x + 7yz$

   (B) $5xy + 4z$ (D) $9xyz$

4.   Choose the statement which is *not* true for all real numbers.

   (A) $(x + 1)(x - 1) = (x - 1)(x + 1)$

   (B) $n \times 1 = n + 1$

   (C) $4(r + 2s) = 4(2s + r)$

   (D) $6(r + 3) = 6r + 18$

ABSOLUTE VALUE

   The absolute value of a number is represented by two vertical lines around the number, and is defined to be the distance of the point representing the number on a number line from the zero point. Since distance is a nonnegative value, the absolute value of any number is nonnegative.

   Some examples: $|5| = 5$

   $|-8| = 8$

To determine whether a given number is a solution to an equation/inequality:

   (1)   Substitute the given value into each equation/inequality given.

   (2)   Simplify to see if the value satisfies the equation/inequality.

Example: For each of the statements below, determine whether $x = 3$ is a solution.

I. $|x - 5| = 2$
II. $x^2 + 3x - 4 = 4$
III. $2x - 5 > 7x + 2$

Solution: I.
$$|3 - 5| = 2$$
$$|-2| = 2$$
Is $2 = 2$ Yes.

II.
$$3^2 + 3(3) - 4 = 4$$
$$9 + 9 - 4 = 4$$
Is $14 = 4$ No.

III.
$$2(3) - 5 > 7(3) + 2$$
$$6 - 5 > 21 + 2$$
Is $1 > 23$ No.

Therefore, I is the only correct response.

Example: For each of the statements below, determine whether $x = \frac{3}{4}$ is a solution.

I. $|3 + x| < 4$
II. $(x + 3)(4x - 3) = 0$
III. $8x + 2 = 8$

Solution: I.
$$|3 + \tfrac{3}{4}| < 4$$
$$|2\tfrac{1}{4}| < 4$$
Is $2\tfrac{1}{4} < 4$ Yes.

II.
$$(\tfrac{3}{4} + 3)(4(\tfrac{3}{4}) - 3) = 0$$
$$(3\tfrac{3}{4})(0) = 0$$
Is $0 = 0$ Yes.

III.
$$8(\tfrac{3}{4}) + 2 = 8$$
$$6 + 2 = 8$$
Is $8 = 8$ Yes.

Therefore, I, II, and III are all correct responses.

DRILL: ABSOLUTE VALUE

<u>DIRECTIONS:</u> Select the best answer.

1.   For each of the statements below, determine whether $x = -5$ is a solution.

I. $x + 3 < 5x - 4$
II. $x^2 + 4x - 5 = 0$
III. $|x + 5| \leq 0$

(A)   II only   (C)   I and III only

(B)   I and II only   (D)   II and III only

2.   For each of the statements below, determine whether $x = \frac{1}{3}$ is a solution.

I. $9x^2 - 1 < 0$
II. $12x - 5 = 1$
III. $|3x - 5| \geq 0$

(A)   I only   (C)   I and III only

(B)   III only   (D)   II and III only

3.   For each of the statements below, determine whether $x = -4$ is a solution.

I. $|2x - 1| = 5 - x$
II. $x^2 - 6 = 10$
III. $(x - 9)^2 \geq 0$

(A)   II only   (C)   I and II only

(B)   III only   (D)   I, II, and III

PROPORTIONALITY AND VARIATION

This skill area will deal with proportionality and two types of variation, direct and inverse.

Direct variation implies that as the value of the independent variable increases, the value of the dependent variable increases. Likewise, as the value of the independent variable decreases, the value of the dependent variable decreases. Direct variation is usually represented as $y = kx$, where k is the constant of proportionality; however, it is usually easier to set up direct variation problems as a proportion with the numerators having the same units and the denominators having the same units.

Inverse variation implies that as the value of an independent variable increases, the value of the dependent variable decreases and vice versa. Inverse variation is usually represented as $y = \frac{k}{x}$, where k is the constant of proportionality. Again, inverse variation problems can be set up as a proportion with same unit fractions making up the proportion with one of the fractions inverted.

When dealing with direct or inverse variation problems, follow the given steps:

(1)   Identify the type of variation applicable to the problem.

(2)   Substitute the given values and variable into the correct proportion.

(3)   Examine the options to select an equivalent expression.

Example: Martha can make 20 cheesecakes during her 8 hour shift at the bakery. Let *C* represent the number of cheesecakes Martha can bake in 9 hours. Select the correct statement of the given condition.

(A) $\frac{8}{20} = \frac{9}{C}$ (C) $\frac{20}{8} = \frac{9}{C}$

(B) $\frac{8}{20} = \frac{C}{9}$ (D) $\frac{20}{9} = \frac{C}{8}$

Solution: This is a direct variation because with more time, more cheesecakes can be made.

$$\frac{20}{8} = \frac{C}{9}$$

This proportion does not exactly match with any of the choices, but choice (A) is equivalent to $\frac{20}{8} = \frac{C}{9}$.

Example: Sam is driving to Tallahassee next week on business. Last time she made the trip in 6 hours driving at 55 mph. Let *H* represent the number of hours to Tallahassee traveling at 65 mph. Select the correct statement of the given condition.

(A) $\frac{6}{55} = \frac{H}{65}$ (C) $\frac{6}{H} = \frac{55}{65}$

(B) $\frac{H}{6} = \frac{65}{55}$ (D) $\frac{6}{65} = \frac{H}{55}$

Solution: This is an inverse variation because as one's speed increases, the time to get there decreases.

$$\frac{6}{H} = \frac{65}{55}$$

This proportion does not exactly match with any of the choices, but choice (D) is equivalent to $\frac{6}{H} = \frac{65}{55}$.

Note: If you are having a difficult time seeing that these proportions are equivalent, cross multiply the answer and each of the choices to compare.

Answer:	$\frac{6}{H} = \frac{65}{55}$	===>	$6 \times 55 = 65 \times H$
Choice (A):	$\frac{6}{55} = \frac{H}{65}$	===>	$6 \times 65 = 55 \times H$
Choice (B):	$\frac{H}{6} = \frac{65}{55}$	===>	$H \times 55 = 6 \times 65$
Choice (C):	$\frac{6}{H} = \frac{55}{65}$	===>	$6 \times 65 = H \times 55$
Choice (D):	$\frac{6}{65} = \frac{H}{55}$	===>	$6 \times 55 = 65 \times H$

This additional step may make it easier to compare but it does require more time; however, better to spend a little additional time and get a correct answer.

DRILL: PROPORTIONALITY AND VARIATION

DIRECTIONS: Select the best answer.

---

1. The interest earned on two savings accounts is the same. One account contained $1,000 at 5% interest while the other account contained $1,200 at an unknown interest I. Select the correct statement of the given condition.

    (A) $5/_I = 1{,}000/_{1{,}200}$

    (B) $5/_I = 1{,}200/_{1{,}000}$

    (C) $5/_{1{,}000} = I/_{1{,}200}$

    (D) $5/_{1{,}000} = 1{,}200/_I$

2. It takes two workers five days to reshingle a roof. It is the rainy season and the job needs to be completed quickly. Let W represent the number of workers needed to do the job in three days. Select the correct statement of the given condition.

    (A) $2/_5 = W/_3$

    (B) $2/_5 = 3/_W$

    (C) $7/_W = 8/_2$

    (D) $2/_W = 3/_5$

3. If R is directly proportional to S, and $R = 17$ when $S = 3$. Select the correct statement of the given condition if $R = 5$.

    (A) $17/_3 = 5/_S$

    (B) $17/_5 = S/_3$

    (C) $17/_3 = S/_5$

    (D) $5/_{17} = 3/_S$

4. If P is inversely proportional to L, and $P = 200$ when $L = 0.25$. Select the correct statement of the given condition if $L = 0.34$.

    (A) $200/_{0.25} = P/_{0.34}$

    (B) $200/_{0.25} = 0.34/_P$

    (C) $200/_P = 0.34/_{0.25}$

    (D) $200/_P = 0.25/_{0.34}$

REGIONS OF THE COORDINATE PLANE

The Cartesian or rectangular coordinate plane consists of a pair of perpendicular lines called coordinate axes. The horizontal axis is the *x*-axis and the vertical axis is the *y*-axis. The point of intersection of these two axes is called the origin; it is the zero point of both axes. Furthermore, points to the right of the origin on the *x*-axis or above the origin on the *y*-axis represent positive real numbers. Points to the left of the origin on the *x*-axis or below the origin on the *y*-axis represent negative real numbers.

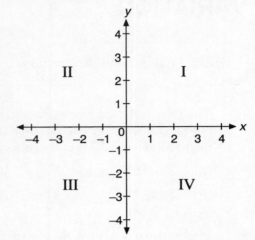

The four regions cut off by the coordinate axes are, in counterclockwise direction from the top right, called the first, second, third, and fourth quadrants, respectively. Each point on the coordinate plane is identified by the ordered pair (x, y). The *x*-coordinate is the first number and the *y*-coordinate is the second number.

To identify regions in the coordinate plane, follow the given steps:

(1) Examine the shaded region. If the region is in only one quadrant, use the information below to eliminate choices which do not describe the quadrant which contains the shaded region.

The first quadrant contains all points with two positive coordinates (+, +), or $x > 0$ and $y > 0$.

Points in quadrant II have a negative *x*-coordinate and a positive *y*-coordinate (−, +), or $x < 0$ and $y > 0$.

Both coordinates are negative in the third quadrant (−, −), or $x < 0$ and $y < 0$.

And points in quadrant IV have a positive *x*-coordinate and a negative *y*-coordinate (+, −), or $x > 0$ and $y < 0$.

(2) Use the information below to further eliminate choices.

A dotted vertical line will be of the form $x > a$ or $x < a$, and a solid vertical line will be of the form $x = a$, $x \geq a$, or $x \leq a$, where a is a real number.

A dotted horizontal line will be of the form $y > b$ or $y < b$, and a solid horizontal line will be of the form $y = b$, $y \geq b$, or $y \leq b$, where b is a real number.

An oblique line, a line with both *x* and *y* variables, will be dotted if the inequality is > or <, and solid if =, ≥, or ≤.

(3) If you are not down to one choice remaining yet, pick a point on each pictured line and substitute it into the remaining equations. If the point does not satisfy the equation, eliminate the choice.

(4) If there is still more than one choice remaining, pick a point in the shaded region to further eliminate a choice.

Example: Identify the conditions which correspond to the shaded region of the plane.

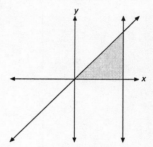

(A) $x \geq y$ and $y \geq 0$ and $x \leq 4$

(B) $x \geq y$ and $y \leq 0$ and $x \geq 4$

(C) $x \leq y$ and $y \leq 0$ and $x \leq 4$

(D) $x \leq y$ and $y \geq 0$ and $x \geq 4$

Solution: The shaded region is in quadrant I. Therefore, $x > 0$ and $y > 0$. Eliminate choices (B) and (C).

The vertical line is $x = 4$.

Since the area to the left of that line is shaded, the inequality must be $x \leq 4$. Eliminate choice (D).

Choice (A) is the correct response.

Example: Identify the conditions which correspond to the shaded region of the plane.

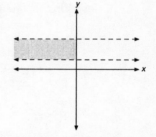

(A) $x < 0$ and $y > 1$ and $y > 3$

(B) $y < 0$ and $x > 1$ and $x > 3$

(C) $y < 0$ and $y \geq 1$ and $x \leq 3$

(D) $x < 0$ and $y > 1$ and $y < 3$

Solution: The shaded region is in quadrant II. Therefore, $x < 0$ and $y > 0$. Eliminate choices (B) and (C).

The difference between the two choices which remain are: one has $y > 3$ and the other has $y < 3$. Since the area shaded is below the line $y = 3$, the correct choice would have $y < 3$. Eliminate choice (A).

Choice (D) is the correct response.

Example: Which shaded region identifies the portion of the plane which corresponds to the conditions $2x + y \geq 5$ and $x - y > 1$?

(A)

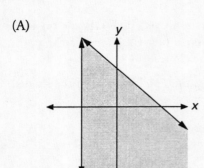

(C)

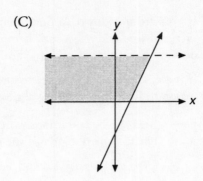

(B)

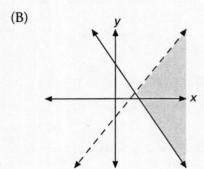

(D)

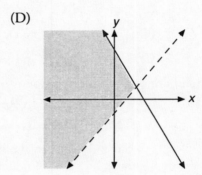

Solution: The given lines are oblique (not horizontal or vertical). Hence, we can eliminate choices (A) and (C).

Since the lines on choices (B) and (D) are the same, check a point in the shaded region of one of the graphs. Choose (0, 0). Substitute (0, 0) into the first inequality.

$$2x + y \geq 5$$

$$2(0) + 0 \geq 5$$

Is $0 \geq 5$?   No.

Since (0, 0) does not satisfy the inequality, it is not a solution, and we can eliminate choice (D) because (0, 0) is part of the solution pictured on the graph.

Choice (B) is the correct response.

DRILL: REGIONS OF THE COORDINATE PLANE

> **DIRECTIONS:** Select the best answer.

1. Identify the conditions which correspond to the shaded region of the plane.

   (A) $y > x$ and $y > -x$

   (B) $y = x$ and $x < 0$

   (C) $y < x$ and $y > -x$

   (D) $y > x$ and $y < -x$

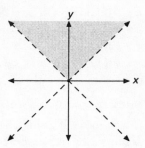

2. Identify the conditions which correspond to the shaded region of the plane.

   (A) $y < 0$ and $x > -2$

   (B) $y < 0$ or $x < -2$

   (C) $x < 0$ or $y < -2$

   (D) $x < 0$ and $y < -2$

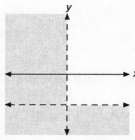

3. Which shaded region identifies the portion of the plane which corresponds to the conditions $x > 0$ and $y < 3$?

   (A)

   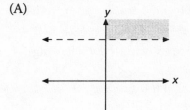

   (C)

   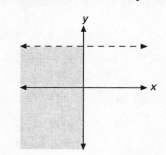

   (B)

   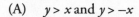

   (D)

   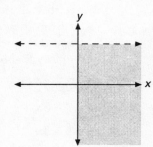

SELECTING EQUIVALENT EQUATIONS AND INEQUALITIES

In this skill area, an equation or inequality will be given. You will be asked to recognize a single step transformation of the original equation or inequality. The algebraic properties used to justify the transformation are as follows:

A. $a = b$ if and only if $a + c = b + c$;
B. $a = b$ if and only if $ac = bc$, $c = 0$;
C. $a > b$ if and only if $a + c > b + c$;
D. $a > b$ if and only if $ac > bc$ and $c > 0$;
E. $a > b$ if and only if $ac < bc$ and $c < 0$; and
F. if $a > b$ and $b > c$, then $a > c$.

To identify the transformed equation or inequality, proceed as follows:

(1) Check to see if a single term has been added or subtracted from both sides as illustrated in properties A and C above.

(2) Check to see if a single term has been multiplied by or divided into both sides as illustrated in properties B, D, and E above.

(3) Check to see if two inequalities have been combined into a single inequality as illustrated in property F above.

Example: Choose the equality which is equivalent to the following:
$$8x - 3 = 2x + 1$$

(A) $10x - 3 = 1$ (C) $4x - 3 = x + 1$

(B) $6x - 3 = 1$ (D) $8x + 1 = 2x - 3$

Solution: The first logical step in solving this equation would be to begin by combining like terms across the equal sign. If we subtract $2x$ from both sides, we arrive at choice (B).

Example: Choose the inequality which is equivalent to the following:
$$-5x < 55$$

(A) $x < -11$ (C) $x < 11$

(B) $x > -11$ (D) $x > 11$

Solution: In examining the choices before deciding on a plan to pursue, we see that all the x coefficients are 1. This would most likely result from dividing the inequality by -5. In so doing, $^{55}/_{-5}$ is -11 and the direction of the inequality must change as shown in property E above. Therefore, the correct choice is (B).

Example: If $x < 0$, then $x^2 > 4x - 3x^2$ is equivalent to which of the following?

(A) $x > 4 - 3x$ (C) $x > x - 3$

(B) $x < 4 - 3x$ (D) $x < x - 3$

Solution: Since $x \neq 0$, the inequality can be divided by x; however, since we are dividing by a negative term, the direction of the inequality must change. This process results in choice (B).

DRILL: SELECTING EQUIVALENT EQUATIONS AND INEQUALITIES

<u>**DIRECTIONS:**</u> Select the best answer.

1. If $x > 0$, then $8x < 3x - x^2$ is equivalent to which of the following?

   (A) $8 < 3 - x$ (C) $8 < x - 2$

   (B) $8 > 3 - x$ (D) $8 > x - 2$

2. Choose the equality which is equivalent to $4x + 3 = 5x - 6$.

   (A) $9x + 3 = -6$ (C) $-x + 3 = -6$

   (B) $4x = 5x - 3$ (D) $-x - 6 = 3$

3. Choose the inequality which is equivalent to $4 < -4x < 12$.

   (A) $1 < x < 3$ (C) $-1 < x < -3$

   (B) $-1 > x > -3$ (D) $8 > x > 16$

WORD PROBLEMS INVOLVING VARIABLES

Problems in this skill area, as with other prior word or story problems, will be taken from a host of contexts. The following steps in problem solving should simplify the process:

(1) Read the problem carefully to understand what is being asked.

(2) Identify the relevant information and eliminate that which is irrelevant. Also, check for unit measure consistency.

(3) Solve the problem.

(4) Reread the problem to be sure you have answered the question being asked and that your answer is reasonable.

Example: If a plane travels five hours from New York to California at a speed of 600 mph, how many miles does the plane travel? The formula for rate problems is Distance = Rate × Time.

Solution:
$$D = R \times T$$
$$= 600 \times 5$$
$$= 3,000$$

Answer: 3,000 miles

Example: Interest = Principal × Rate × Time is the formula used to calculate simple interest. How long would it take Jerry to earn $72 in interest on a principal of $400 at 6%.

Solution:

$I = P \times R \times T$	Given formula.
$72 = 400 \times 0.06 \times T$	Substitute the givens.
$72 = 24 \times T$	Solve for T.
$3 = T$	

Answer: 3 years

Example: Four college friends started a business of remodeling and selling old automobiles during the summer. They paid $600 to rent an empty barn for the summer. They obtained the cars from a dealer for $250 each, and it takes an average of $410 in materials to remodel each car. How many automobiles must be sold at $1,440 each to obtain a gross profit of $7,000? Some formulas to consider are:

Profit = Revenue – Cost
Profit = Selling Price – Expenses
Gross Profit = Total Revenues – Total Cost
Gross Profit = Revenue – [Variable Cost + Fixed Cost]

Solution:
Let a = number of cars   Revenue = $1,440a$
Variable Cost = $(250 + 410)a$ Fixed Cost = $600
The desired gross profit is $7,000.
$$7,000 = 1,440a - [660a + 600]$$
$$7,000 = 1,440a - 660a - 600$$
$$7,600 = 780a$$
$$9.74 = a$$

Answer: 10 cars

DRILL: WORD PROBLEMS INVOLVING VARIABLES

<u>DIRECTIONS:</u> Select the best answer.

1.   Two towns are 420 miles apart. A car leaves the first town traveling toward the second town at 55 mph. At the same time, a second car leaves the other town and heads toward the first town at 65 mph. How long will it take for the two cars to meet?

(A)   2 hr   (C)   3.5 hr

(B)   3 hr   (D)   4 hr

2.   One bank pays 6.5% a year simple interest on a savings account while a credit union pays 7.2% a year. If you had $1,500 to invest for three years, how much more would you earn by putting the money in the credit union?

(A) $10.50   (C) $97.50

(B) $31.50   (D) $108

3.   An item costs a storeowner $50. She marked it up 40% and advertised it at that price. How much profit did she make if she later sold it at 15% off the advertised price?

(A) $7.50   (C) $10.50

(B) $9.50   (D) $39.50

STRUCTURE AND LOGIC OF ALGEBRA

The highlighting of key words in a skill area such as this is common practice. However, key words can take on different meanings relative to the context of the problem, so proceed carefully when relying on such. For this reason, key words will not be presented here. The best advice is to read the problems carefully and practice what has been presented in the way of problem solving tips.

Example: Two consecutive odd integers sum to 36. Which equation should be used to find the numbers if one of the numbers is represented by n?

(A) $(2n - 1) + (2n + 1) = 36$

(B) $n + (n + 1) = 36$

(C) $(2n-1)(2n+1) = 36$

(D) $n(n+1) = 36$

Solution: We are looking for the sum of two numbers. Sum means to add. Therefore, we can eliminate choices (C) and (D).

Consecutive odd means the integers are two apart; therefore, we can also eliminate (B).

Therefore, the correct response is (A).

Two consecutive odd integers could be interpreted as n and $n + 2$; however, this does not guarantee n is odd. A better representation of an odd integer is $2n - 1$ or $2n + 1$. Doubling an integer is always even and adding 1 to an even integer is always odd.

Example: The tens digit of a two-digit number is twice the units digit. If the number itself is equal to 17 more than the tens digit squared, which equation should be used to find the digits if the units digit is represented by u?

Solution: Units digit: u
Tens digit: $2u$
Number: $10(2u) + u$

The number equals 17 more than the tens digit squared. Translation: $10(2u) + u = 17 + (2u)^2$

DRILL: STRUCTURE AND LOGIC OF ALGEBRA

DIRECTIONS: Select the best answer.

---

1.   The sum of two numbers is 41. One number is one less than twice the other. Which equation should be used to find the numbers if one of the numbers is represented by n?

(A) $n(2n-1) = 41$ (C) $n(1-2n) = 41$

(B) $n + (2n-1) = 41$ (D) $n + (1-2n) = 41$

2.   The difference between two integers is 12. The sum of the two integers is 2. Which equation should be used to find the numbers if the greater of the integers is represented by n?

(A) $n + (n + 12) = 2$ (C) $n - (n - 12) = 2$

(B) $n - (2 - n) = 12$ (D) $n + (2 - n) = 12$

3.   A two-digit integer is equal to five more than six times the sum of the digits. If T represents the tens digit and U represents the units digit, which equation mathematically represents the conditions of the problem?

(A) $T + U = 6(T + U) + 5$ (C) $10T + U = 6(T + U) - 5$

(B) $10T + U = 6(T \times U) + 5$ (D) $10T + U = 6(T + U) + 5$

ALGEBRA SKILLS

ANSWER KEY

DRILL: REAL NUMBERS

1.	**(B)**	5.	**(D)**	8.	**(A)**	11.	**(A)**
2.	**(A)**	6.	**(C)**	9.	**(C)**	12.	**(C)**
3.	**(B)**	7.	**(D)**	10.	**(C)**	13.	**(B)**
4.	**(D)**						

DRILL: ORDER OF OPERATIONS

1.	**(D)**	3.	**(B)**	5.	**(A)**
2.	**(D)**	4.	**(C)**	6.	**(B)**

DRILL: SCIENTIFIC NOTATION

1.	**(A)**	3.	**(C)**	5.	**(D)**
2.	**(B)**	4.	**(A)**		

DRILL: LINEAR EQUATIONS AND INEQUALITIES

1.	**(A)**	3.	**(D)**	5.	**(C)**	7.	**(B)**
2.	**(B)**	4.	**(A)**	6.	**(A)**	8.	**(A)**

DRILL: ALGEBRAIC FORMULAS

1.	**(B)**	3.	**(C)**	5.	**(B)**
2.	**(A)**	4.	**(A)**		

DRILL: FUNCTIONS

1. **(B)**   3. **(D)**   5. **(D)**
2. **(C)**   4. **(A)**

DRILL: QUADRATIC EXPRESSIONS AND EQUATIONS

1. **(B)**   3. **(D)**   5. **(A)**   7. **(B)**
2. **(D)**   4. **(D)**   6. **(B)**

DRILL: SYSTEMS OF LINEAR EQUATIONS

1. **(A)**   3. **(D)**   5. **(B)**
2. **(B)**   4. **(D)**

DRILL: PROPERTIES OF OPERATIONS

1. **(B)**   3. **(A)**
2. **(D)**   4. **(B)**

DRILL: ABSOLUTE VALUE

1. **(D)**   3. **(D)**
2. **(B)**

DRILL: PROPORTIONALITY AND VARIATION

1. **(B)**   3. **(A)**
2. **(D)**   4. **(C)**

DRILL: REGIONS OF THE COORDINATE PLANE

1. **(A)**   3. **(D)**
2. **(C)**

DRILL: SELECTING EQUIVALENT EQUATIONS AND INEQUALITIES

1. **(A)**   3.   **(B)**
2. **(C)**

DRILL: WORD PROBLEMS INVOLVING VARIABLES

1. **(C)**   3.   **(B)**
2. **(B)**

DRILL: STRUCTURE AND LOGIC OF ALGEBRA

1. **(B)**   3.   **(D)**
2. **(B)**

ALGEBRA SKILLS
DETAILED EXPLANATIONS OF ANSWERS

DRILL: REAL NUMBERS

1. **(B)** Simplify $\sqrt{32}$ into two multiples, one being a perfect square and the other equivalent to the second term.

$$3\sqrt{32} + 2\sqrt{2} = 3\sqrt{16 \times 2} + 2\sqrt{2}$$
$$= 3 \times 4\sqrt{2} + 2\sqrt{2}$$
$$= 12\sqrt{2} + 2\sqrt{2}$$
$$= 14\sqrt{2}$$

2. **(A)** Simplify $\sqrt{45}$ into two parts so that one part is a perfect square.

$$6\sqrt{5} + 2\sqrt{45} = 6\sqrt{5} + 2\sqrt{9 \times 5}$$
$$= 6\sqrt{5} + 2 \times 3\sqrt{5}$$
$$= 6\sqrt{5} + 6\sqrt{5}$$
$$= 12\sqrt{5}$$

3. **(B)** When the numbers under the square root sign are the same you can just combine the coefficients.

$$1\sqrt{5} + 6\sqrt{5} - 3\sqrt{5} = 4\sqrt{5}$$

4. **(D)** Combine like terms.
$$4\pi - 5\pi = -\pi = -\pi - 4$$

5. **(D)** Simplify $\sqrt{8}$ into two parts so that one part is a perfect square.

$$10\sqrt{2} - 3\sqrt{8} = 10\sqrt{2} - 3\sqrt{4 \times 2}$$
$$= 10\sqrt{2} - 3 \times 2\sqrt{2}$$
$$= 10\sqrt{2} - 6\sqrt{2}$$
$$= 4\sqrt{2}$$

6. **(C)** Simplify $\sqrt{12}$ into two parts so that one part is a perfect square.

$$4\sqrt{3} - 2\sqrt{12} = 4\sqrt{3} - 2\sqrt{4 \times 3}$$
$$= 4\sqrt{3} - 2 \times 2\sqrt{3}$$
$$= 4\sqrt{3} - 4\sqrt{3}$$
$$= 0$$

7. **(D)** Multiply the numbers under the radical signs.

$$\sqrt{3} \times \sqrt{12} = \sqrt{36}$$

Simplify by extracting the square root of the product.

$$\sqrt{36} = 6$$

8. **(A)** The square roots being multiplied are identical, so the product is simply the absolute value of the term beneath the radical sign.

$$\sqrt{7} \times \sqrt{7} = \sqrt{49}$$

Take the square root of the product.

$$\sqrt{49} = 7$$

9. **(C)** Multiply like terms together.

$$3\sqrt{5} \times 2\sqrt{5} =$$
$$3 \times 2 = 6$$
$$\sqrt{5} \times \sqrt{5} = \sqrt{25}, \text{ or } 5$$

Now multiply the products:

$$\left(6\right)\left(\sqrt{25}\right) \text{ or } 6\left(5\right)$$

to get the result

$$6\sqrt{25} \text{ or } 30.$$

10. **(C)** Combine the terms under the radical sign, keeping the operation intact.

$$\frac{\sqrt{10}}{\sqrt{2}} = \sqrt{\frac{10}{2}}$$
$$= \sqrt{5}$$

11. **(A)**   Both the numerator and denominator are square roots. Therefore, they may be combined under the radical sign.

$$\frac{\sqrt{30}}{\sqrt{15}} = \sqrt{\frac{30}{15}}$$
$$= \sqrt{2}$$

12. **(C)**   Both the numerator and denominator are square roots. Therefore, they may be combined under the radical sign.

$$\frac{\sqrt{48}}{\sqrt{8}} = \sqrt{\frac{48}{8}}$$
$$= \sqrt{6}$$

13. **(B)**   Place the portions of the equation that are under square root signs under one sign.

$$\frac{3\sqrt{12}}{\sqrt{3}} = 3\sqrt{\frac{12}{3}} = 3\sqrt{4}$$

Take the square root.

$$3\sqrt{4} = 3 \times 2 = 6$$

DRILL: ORDER OF OPERATIONS

1. **(D)**   This problem only involves division so just work from left to right as the numbers appear.

$$96 \div 3 \div 4 \div 2 = 32 \div 4 \div 2$$
$$= 8 \div 2$$
$$= 4$$

2. **(D)**   Remember to do multiplication first.

$$18 + 3 \times 4 \div 3 =$$
$$18 + 12 \div 3$$

Division is the next order of operation.

$$18 + 12 \div 3 =$$
$$18 + 4$$

Addition is the last operation.

$$18 + 4 = 22$$

3. **(B)** Multiplication is the first operation.

$$(-3) \times 5 - 20 \div 4 =$$
$$-15 - 20 \div 4$$

Division is next.

$$-15 - 20 \div 4 =$$
$$-15 - 5$$

Finally, we add the two negatives.

$$-15 - 5 = -20$$

4. **(C)** Do the exponents portion first.

$$32 \div 2^3 + 4 - 15 \div 3 =$$
$$32 \div 8 + 4 - 15 \div 3$$

The next operation is division.

$$32 \div 8 + 4 - 15 \div 3 =$$
$$4 + 4 - 5$$

Do the addition.

$$4 + 4 - 5 =$$
$$8 - 5$$

Subtraction is last.

$$8 - 5 = 3$$

5. **(A)** The first thing to do in this problem is to tackle the parentheses.

$$\tfrac{1}{4} - 3(\tfrac{1}{2} - \tfrac{3}{4} + \tfrac{1}{2})^2 = \tfrac{1}{4} - 3(1 - \tfrac{3}{4})^2$$
$$= \tfrac{1}{4} - 3(\tfrac{1}{4})^2$$

Square the number in the parentheses.

$$\tfrac{1}{4} - 3(\tfrac{1}{16})$$

The parentheses are still there, so we should multiply.

$$\tfrac{1}{4} - \tfrac{3}{16}$$

Find a common denominator.

$$\tfrac{4}{16} - \tfrac{3}{16}$$

Subtract.

$$\tfrac{1}{16}$$

6. **(B)**   Multiply first.

$$8a - \frac{14b}{7} + 4a \times 5 =$$

$$8a - \frac{14b}{7} + 20a$$

Do the division next.

$$8a - \frac{14b}{7} + 20a =$$

$$8a - 2b + 20a$$

Combine like terms.

$$8a - 2b + 20a =$$
$$28a - 2b$$

DRILL: SCIENTIFIC NOTATION

1. **(A)**   Multiply the two numbers together.

$$28,500,000 \times .000000021 = .598500000$$

When moving the decimal point to the right to make the scientific notation correct, the exponent is negative. Because you are moving the decimal point one place, the correct notation is 5.985×10^{-1}.

2. **(B)**   Multiply

$$.00023 \times 8,000,000 = 1,840$$

In this case, the decimal point is being moved to the left. The exponent will therefore be positive. The point is being moved three places, so the correct notation is 1.84×10^3.

3. **(C)**   Do the multiplication.

$$73,000,000 \times 20,000 = 1,460,000,000,000$$

To put into scientific notation, we are moving the decimal point to the left 12 places, so the exponent will be positive.

$$1.46 \times 10^{12}$$

4. **(A)**   Do the division first.

$$98,800,000 \div .000004$$

Remember, you must move the decimal point in the divisor.

$$.000004 \overline{)98,800,000.000000}$$

The answer is 24,700,000,000,000. To put this into proper scientific notation, the decimal point is moved 13 places to the left. The exponent will be positive.

$$2.47 \times 10^{13}$$

5. **(D)** When dividing with terms in scientific notation form, divide the portion in the dividend by its corresponding portion in the divisor.

$$(3.51 \times 10^{-7}) \div (1.17 \times 10^{-12})$$
$$3.51 \div 1.17 \text{ and } 10^{-7} \div 10^{-11}$$
$$3.51 \div 1.17 = 3$$

When dividing with exponents with the same base, subtract the exponent in the divisor from the exponent in the dividend.

$$10^{-7} \div 10^{-12} = 10^{-7-(-12)} = 10^{-7+12} = 10^{5}$$

Multiply both portions and get

$$3 \times 10^{5} = 3 \times 100,000 = 300,000.$$

DRILL: LINEAR EQUATIONS AND INEQUALITIES

1. **(A)** Combine like terms on both sides of the equation first.

$$7z + 1 - z = 2z - 7$$
$$6z + 1 = 2z - 7$$

Next, bring the terms with variables to one side of the equation.

$$6z - 2z + 1 = -7$$
$$4z + 1 = -7$$

Bring all other terms to the other side of the equation.

$$4z = -7 - 1$$
$$4z = -8$$

Divide by 4 to obtain the value of the variable.

$$\frac{4z}{4} = -\frac{8}{4}$$
$$z = -2$$

2.   **(B)**   Multiply on both sides of the equation to remove the parentheses.

$$4(3x + 2) - 11 = 3(3x - 2)$$
$$12x + 8 - 11 = 9x - 6$$

Combine like terms.

$$12x - 3 = 9x - 6$$

Bring the variables to one side of the equation.

$$12x - 9x - 3 = -6$$

Combine like terms.

$$3x - 3 = -6$$

All other quantities should be moved to the other side of the equation.

$$3x = -6 + 3$$
$$3x = -3$$

Divide by 3 to get the value of the variable.

$$\frac{3x}{3} = \frac{-3}{3}$$
$$x = -1$$

3.   **(D)**   Multiply to remove the parentheses.

$$4(2c - 3) = 8$$
$$8c - 12 = 8$$

Set up the equation so that the variable is on one side and all other terms are on the other side of the equation.

$$8c = 8 + 12$$
$$8c = 20$$

Divide by 8 to get the value of the variable.

$$\frac{8c}{8} = \frac{20}{8}$$
$$c = \frac{20}{8} = \frac{5}{2} \text{ or } 2\frac{1}{2}$$

4.   **(A)**   Multiply to remove the parentheses first.

$$3x - 4(x + 1) = 0$$
$$3x - 4x - 4 = 0$$

Combine like terms.

$$-x - 4 = 0$$

Move the variable to one side (preferably so that it is a positive amount) and all other terms to the other.

$$-x - 4 = 0$$
$$-4 = x$$

5. **(C)** Treat the inequality sign as though it is an equals sign and work on both sides of it.

$$-3p - 1 \geq 16$$
$$-3p - 1 = 16$$

Move terms so that the variable is on one side of the equation, and all other terms are on the other side.

$$-3p - 1 = 16$$
$$-3p = 16 + 1$$
$$-3p = 17$$

Divide both sides by -3 to get the value of the variable.

$$\frac{-3p}{-3} = \frac{17}{-3}$$
$$p = -\frac{17}{3} \text{ or } p = -5\frac{2}{3}$$

Replace the equals sign with the inequality sign.

$$p \geq -\frac{17}{3}$$

Remember, however, that you divided both sides by a negative number. This means the inequality sign must be reversed.

$$p \geq -\frac{17}{3} \text{ becomes } p \leq -\frac{17}{3}$$

6. **(A)** Multiply to remove the parentheses.

$$9x - 5(2x + 3) > 0$$
$$9x - 10x - 15 > 0$$

Combine like terms.

$$-x - 15 > 0$$

Treat the inequality as though it is an equals sign.

$$-x - 15 = 0$$

Move terms to find the value of the variable.

$$-x - 15 = 0$$
$$-x = 15$$

Replace the equals sign with the inequality sign.

$$-x > 15$$

The variable should be positive so divide both sides by −1 and remember to reverse the sign.

$$x < -15$$

7. **(B)** Treat the inequality as though it is an equals sign.

$$4 - 2a \leq 9 - a$$
$$4 - 2a = 9 - a$$

Move the variable to one side of the equation and all other terms to the other side.

$$4 - 2a = 9 - a$$
$$4 - a = 9$$
$$-a = 5$$

Replace the equals sign with the inequality sign.

$$-a \leq 5$$

The variable should be positive, so divide both sides by −1 and remember to reverse the sign.

$$\frac{-a}{-1} \leq \frac{5}{-1}$$
$$a \geq -5$$

8. **(A)** Multiply to remove the parentheses.

$$5(x - 3) > 14$$
$$5x - 15 > 14$$

Treat the inequality like an equals sign.

$$5x - 15 > 14$$
$$5x - 15 = 14$$

Move terms to get the variable alone on one side.

$$5x - 15 = 14$$
$$5x = 29$$

Divide by 5.

$$\frac{5x}{5} = \frac{29}{5}$$

$$x = \frac{29}{5}$$

Replace the equals sign with the inequality sign.

$$x > \frac{29}{5}$$

DRILL: ALGEBRAIC FORMULAS

1.   **(B)**   The formula is Interest = Principle × Rate × Time. Fill in the numbers according to the problem.

$I = \$300 \times 3\% \times 3$ years

Convert 3% to a decimal.

$3\% = .03$
$I = 300 \times .03 \times 3$

Multiply.

$I = 27$

Mr. Smith's interest is $27.

2.   **(A)**   We are given the value of x, so just plug it into the equation to get the value of y.

$y = (2x - 3)^3$
$y = ((2 \times 1) - 3)^3$
$y = (2 - 3)^3$

Do the work in the parentheses first.

$y = (-1)^3$

Cube -1 and you get

$y = -1$.

3.   **(C)**   Although this problem may seem difficult if you have never done T-scores, you are given the formula and all of the values. Just plug the numbers into their corresponding places in the formula and work it out.

$$T = 50 + 10\left(\frac{X - \overline{X}}{\sigma}\right)$$

$$T = 50 + 10\left(\frac{80 - 75}{5}\right)$$

$$T = 50 + 10\left(\frac{5}{5}\right)$$

$$T = 50 + 10(1)$$

$$T = 50 + 10$$

$$T = 60$$

4. **(A)** The distance formula is $D = R \times T$. Plug in the numbers provided in the problem.

$$D = 45 \text{ mph} \times 3 \text{ hrs.}$$

Because the rate and time are in the same measurements (hours), just multiply.

$$D = 135 \text{ miles}$$

5. **(B)** Plug the numbers into the formula.

$$R = H - L + 1$$
$$R = 100 - 35 + 1$$
$$R = 65 + 1$$
$$R = 66$$

DRILL: FUNCTIONS

1. **(B)** For all occurrences of x, substitute (-2).

$$f(x) = x^2 + 5x - 3$$
$$f(x) = (-2)^2 + 5(-2) - 3$$
$$f(x) = 4 + -10 - 3$$
$$f(x) = -6 - 3$$
$$f(x) = -9$$

2. **(C)** Substitute -1 for the variable x in the problem.

$$f(x) = 3 - x^3$$
$$f(x) = 3 - (-1)^3$$
$$f(x) = 3 - (-1)$$
$$f(x) = 3 + 1$$
$$f(x) = 4$$

3.   **(D)**   The number 3 should be substituted for x every time it occurs in the problem.

$$f(x) = x^3 + 5x^2 + 2x - 8$$
$$f(x) = (3)^3 - 5(3)^2 + 2(3) - 8$$
$$f(x) = 27 - 5(9) + 6 - 8$$
$$f(x) = 27 - 45 + 6 - 8$$
$$f(x) = -20$$

4.   **(A)**   For all occurrences of x, substitute 4.

$$f(x) = 5 + 2x - x^2$$
$$f(x) = 5 + 2(4) - (4)^2$$
$$f(x) = 5 + 8 - 16$$
$$f(x) = -3$$

5.   **(D)**   Put in -2 for all occurrences of x.

$$f(x) = 7x^4 - 12x^2 + x - 5$$
$$f(x) = 7(-2)^4 - 12(-2)^2 + (-2) - 5$$
$$f(x) = 7(16) - 12(4) - 2 - 5$$
$$f(x) = 112 - 48 - 2 - 5$$
$$f(x) = 64 - 2 - 5$$
$$f(x) = 57$$

DRILL: QUADRATIC EXPRESSIONS AND EQUATIONS

1.   **(B)**   In a quadratic expression, if the terms are written in descending order, if the last sign is a minus, the two factors will have different signs. Find the factors of 8.

$$8 = 1 \times 8 \text{ or}$$
$$8 = 4 \times 2$$

Because the first term is a square, we can set up the factors as such:

$$(x \quad)(x \quad)$$

We know that the two factors will have different signs.

$$(x - \quad)(x + \quad)$$

Looking at the factors of 8, 2, and 4 seem to be the most logical choice to use. The middle sign is negative, so the larger of the two numbers should be negative.

$$(x - 4)(x + 2)$$

Use the FOIL method to check your work.

$$(x-4)(x+2) = x^2 - 4x + 2x - 8$$
$$= x^2 - 2x - 8$$

2. **(D)**   Again the last sign is negative, so the two factors will have different signs. The factors of 6 are 1, 2, 3, and 6. 2 and 3 seem to be the logical selection.

$$(x- \quad)(x+ \quad)$$

The middle sign is positive, so the larger factor will have the plus sign.

$$(x-2)(x+3)$$

Check your work.

$$(x-4)(x+2) = x^2 - 4x + 2x - 8$$
$$= x^2 - 2x - 8$$

3. **(D)**   The last sign is a minus, so the factors will have different signs. The factors of 6 are 1, 2, 3, and 6. For both instances of 6, try 2 and 3.

$$(3x+ \quad)(2x- \quad)$$

The larger factor should get the negative sign because the middle term is negative.

$$(3x+2)(2x-3)$$

Check these two factors and compare it to the original equation.

$$(3x+2)(2x-3) = 6x^2 + 4x - 9x - 6$$
$$= 6x^2 - 5x - 6$$

4. **(D)**   First, move all of the terms to one side of the equal sign so that the equation equals zero.

$$12x^2 + 5x = 3$$
$$12x^2 + 5x - 3 = 0$$

Next, do the factoring. The last term is negative, and they are in descending order. Therefore, the signs will be different for the two factors. The two factors of 3 are 1 and 3. The factors of 12 are 1, 2, 3, 4, 6, and 12. This may take some trial and error, but remember, the larger factor will have the positive sign because the middle term is positive.

$$(4x+3)(3x-1)$$

Set each factor equal to zero and solve for both answers.

$$4x + 3 = 0$$
$$3x - 1 = 0$$

Get the variables on one side of the equation.

$$4x = -3$$
$$3x = 1$$

Divide.

$$\frac{4x}{4} = \frac{-3}{4} \qquad \frac{3x}{4} = \frac{1}{3}$$

$$x = \frac{-3}{4} \qquad x = \frac{1}{3}$$

5.　**(A)**　This quadratic equation is not factorable. Therefore, use the quadratic formula for completing the square.

$$x = \frac{-b \pm \sqrt{b^2 - 4ac}}{2a}$$

where a is the coefficient of x^2 and b is the coefficient of x and c is the constant term. Plug in the values.

$$x = \frac{-(-3) \pm \sqrt{(-3)^2 - 4(1 \times 1)}}{2(1)}$$

$$x = \frac{3 \pm \sqrt{9 - 4}}{2}$$

$$x = \frac{3 \pm \sqrt{5}}{2}$$

6.　**(B)**　Set the equation equal to zero.

$$3x^2 - 2x = 4x + 2$$
$$3x^2 - 2x - 4x - 2 = 0$$
$$3x^2 - 6x - 2 = 0$$

Use the quadratic formula.

$$a = 3, \ b = -6, \ c = -2$$

$$x = \frac{-b \pm \sqrt{b^2 - 4ac}}{2a}$$

$$x = \frac{-(-6) \pm \sqrt{(-6)^2 - 4(3 \times -2)}}{2(3)}$$

$$x = \frac{6 \pm \sqrt{36 - 4(-6)}}{6}$$

$$x = \frac{6 \pm \sqrt{36 + 24}}{6}$$

$$x = \frac{6 \pm \sqrt{60}}{6}$$

Factor 60 so that one of the factors is a perfect square.

$$x = \frac{6 \pm \sqrt{4 \times 15}}{6}$$

$$x = \frac{6 \pm 2\sqrt{15}}{6}$$

Divide by 2.

$$x = \frac{3 \pm \sqrt{15}}{3}$$

7. **(B)** Move terms to get the equation equal to zero.

$$12x^2 + 5x = 2$$
$$12x^2 + 5x - 2 = 0$$

Use the quadratic formula.

$$a = 12, \ b = 5, \ c = -2$$

$$x = \frac{-b \pm \sqrt{b^2 - 4ac}}{2a}$$

$$x = \frac{-5 \pm \sqrt{5^2 - 4(12 \times -2)}}{2(12)}$$

$$x = \frac{-5 \pm \sqrt{25 - 4(-24)}}{24}$$

$$x = \frac{-5 \pm \sqrt{25 + 96}}{24}$$

$$x = \frac{-5 \pm \sqrt{121}}{24}$$

$$x = \frac{-5 \pm 11}{24}$$

Set each factor equal to zero.

$$\frac{-5 + 11}{24} = 0 \qquad \frac{-5 - 11}{24} = 0$$

$$\frac{6}{24} = 0 \qquad \frac{-16}{24} = 0$$

Simplify.

$$\frac{1}{4} = x \qquad -\frac{2}{3} = x$$

DRILL: SYSTEMS OF LINEAR EQUATIONS

1.   **(A)**   Try to get the coefficients of one of the variables to be the same by using a common denominator. The signs should be the opposite of each other. Multiply the first equation by (–3) and the second equation by (1). Add the two equations together.

$$
\begin{array}{r}
-3(x + 2y = 8) \\
-1(3x + 4y = 20) \\
\hline
-3x - 6y = -24 \\
3x + 4y = 20 \\
\hline
-2y = -4 \\
y = 2
\end{array}
$$

Now take this value of *y* and put it into either of the original equations, and solve for *x*.

$$
\begin{array}{rcl}
x + 2y & = & 8 \\
x + 2(2) & = & 8 \\
x + 4 & = & 8 \\
x & = & 4
\end{array}
$$

So the solution is $x = 4$ and $y = 2$, or (4, 2).

2.   **(B)**   Multiply the first equation by 3 and the second equation by 2. Then add them together.

$$
\begin{array}{r}
3(4x + 2y = -1) \\
2(5x - 3y = \;\; 7) \\
\hline
12x + 6y = -3 \\
10x - 6y = 14 \\
\hline
22x = 11 \\
x = \tfrac{1}{2}
\end{array}
$$

Take this value of *x* and put it into either original equations, and solve for *y*.

$$
\begin{array}{rcl}
4x + 2y & = & -1 \\
4(\tfrac{1}{2}) + 2y & = & -1 \\
2 + 2y & = & -1 \\
2y & = & -3 \\
y & = & -\tfrac{3}{2}
\end{array}
$$

The answers are $x = \tfrac{1}{2}$ and $y = -\tfrac{3}{2}$ or $(\tfrac{1}{2}, -\tfrac{3}{2})$

3.   **(D)**   If we multiply the first equation by (–2) *both* the x and y terms will drop out, telling us that there is no solution, or it is an empty set.

$$-2(3x + 4y = -2)$$
$$6x + 8y = 4$$
$$\overline{-6x - 8y = 4}$$
$$6x + 8y = 4$$

4.   **(D)**   Multiply the first equation by (–3). If you then add the equations together, the x and y *both* drop out. The solution is an empty set.

$$-3(2x + y = -10)$$
$$6x + 3y = -30$$
$$\overline{-6x - 3y = 30}$$
$$6x + 3y = -30$$

5.   **(B)**   Multiply the first equation by (–1). Then add the two equations together.

$$-1(x + 8y = 25)$$
$$x + 4y = 15$$
$$\overline{-x - 8y = -25}$$
$$x + 4y = 15$$
$$\overline{-4y = -10}$$
$$y = \tfrac{5}{2}$$

Put this value of y into either of the original equations and solve for x.

$$x + 8y = 25$$
$$x + 8(\tfrac{5}{2}) = 25$$
$$x + 20 = 25$$
$$x = 5$$

$x = 5$ and $y = \tfrac{5}{2}$ or $(5, \tfrac{5}{2})$

DRILL: PROPERTIES OF OPERATIONS

1.   **(B)**   If two signs are next to each other, multiply them together to create one sign. Two positives and two negatives multiplied together will yield a positive. A positive and a negative multiplied together will yield a negative.

$$3x + (-3x) = 3x - 3x$$
$$= 0$$

2.   **(D)**   The order of multiplication does not matter

$$a \times b = b \times a$$

Therefore,

$$3 \times 4(a + 2) = 4 \times 3(a + 2)$$

3. **(A)** By the associative property of addition, we can say

$$(2x + 3y) + 4z = 2x + (3y + 4z).$$

4. **(B)** Remember that addition and multiplication are not commutative. We are asked which statement is *not* true.

$$n \times 1 \neq n + 1$$

DRILL: ABSOLUTE VALUE

1. **(D)** Plug in –5 for x in the first statement.

$$\begin{aligned} x + 3 &< 5x - 4 \\ -5 + 3 &< 5(-5) - 4 \\ -2 &< -25 - 4 \\ -2 &< -29 \end{aligned}$$

This is false, so we know I is not a solution and (B) and (C) are incorrect. Plug in –5 for x in the second statement.

$$\begin{aligned} x^2 + 4x - 5 &= 0 \\ (-5)^2 + 4(-5) - 5 &= 0 \\ 25 + (-20) - 5 &= 0 \\ 25 - 25 &= 0 \end{aligned}$$

This is a true statement. (A) and (D) are potential answers. Plug –5 into the last statement.

$$\begin{aligned} |x + 5| &\leq 0 \\ |-5 + 5| &\leq 0 \\ |0| &\leq 0 \end{aligned}$$

This is a true statement, so statements II and III are correct. (D) is the answer.

2. **(B)** Plug in $\frac{1}{3}$ for x in the first statement.

$$\begin{aligned} 9x^2 - 1 &< 0 \\ 9(\tfrac{1}{3})^2 - 1 &< 0 \\ 9(\tfrac{1}{9}) - 1 &< 0 \\ 1 - 1 &< 0 \end{aligned}$$

Subtract.

$$0 < 0$$

This is a false statement. I cannot be correct. Therefore (A) and (C) are incorrect. Plug $\frac{1}{3}$ in for x in the second statement.

$$12x - 5 = 1$$
$$12(\tfrac{1}{3}) - 5 = 1$$
$$4 - 5 = 1$$
$$-1 = 1$$

This is also incorrect. Statement II is false, so (D) cannot be the answer. This leaves (B) as the only possible choice. Test out III just to be sure.

$$|\,3x - 5\,| \geq 0$$
$$|\,3(\tfrac{1}{3}) - 5\,| \geq 0$$
$$|\,1 - 4\,| \geq 0$$
$$|-3\,| \geq 0$$
$$3 \geq 0$$

This is true, so (B) is correct.

3.   **(D)**   Substitute -4 for x in the first statement.

$$|\,2x - 1\,| = 5 - x$$
$$|\,2(-4) - 1\,| = 5 - (-4)$$
$$|-8 - 1\,| = 5 + 4$$
$$|-9\,| = 9$$
$$9 = 9$$

This statement is true. Therefore, (A) and (B) cannot be possible answers. Plug -4 in for x in statement II.

$$x^2 - 6 = 10$$
$$(-4)^2 - 6 = 10$$
$$16 - 6 = 10$$
$$10 = 10$$

This statement is also true. Choices (C) and (D) are still possible answers. Plug -4 in for x in the last statement.

$$(x - 9)^2 \geq 0$$
$$(-4 - 9)^2 \geq 0$$
$$(-13)^2 \geq 0$$
$$169 \geq 0$$

This statement is true also. All three statements are correct making (D) the correct answer.

DRILL: PROPORTIONALITY AND VARIATION

1. **(B)** Set up a proportion with the given information.

$$\frac{\text{Interest of first account}}{\text{Interest of second account}} = \frac{\$1,200}{\$1,000}$$

$$\frac{5\%}{I} = \frac{1,200}{1,000}$$

2. **(D)** Set up a proportion.

workers $\rightarrow$ days

$$\frac{2}{W} = \frac{3}{5}$$

3. **(A)** Follow the given proportion: $R/_S$

$$\frac{17}{3} = \frac{5}{S}$$

4. **(C)** Remember that P is inversely proportional to L.

$$\frac{200}{P} = \frac{.34}{.25}$$

You must end up with $200(.25) = P(.34)$.

DRILL: REGIONS OF THE COORDINATE PLANE

1. **(A)** Figure A is the graph of $y > x$; Figure B is the graph of $y > -x$; and Figure C is their intersection or solution.

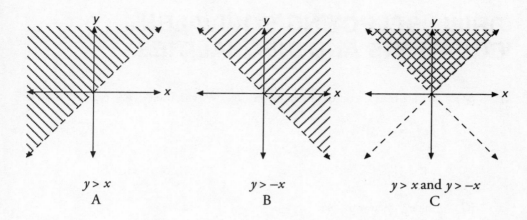

$y > x$
A

$y > -x$
B

$y > x$ and $y > -x$
C

2. **(C)** Figure A is $x < 0$; Figure B is $y < -2$; and Figure C is $x < 0$ or $y < -2$.

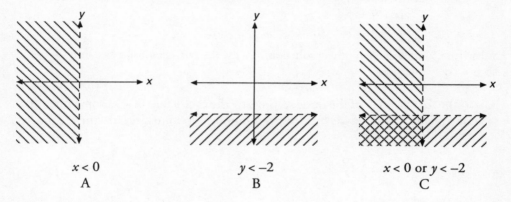

$x < 0$
A

$y < -2$
B

$x < 0$ or $y < -2$
C

3. **(D)** Figure A is $x > 0$; Figure B is $y < 3$; and Figure D is $x > 0$ and $y < 3$.

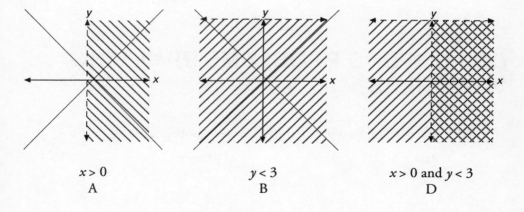

$x > 0$
A

$y < 3$
B

$x > 0$ and $y < 3$
D

DRILL: SELECTING EQUIVALENT EQUATIONS AND INEQUALITIES

1.   **(A)**   We are told $x > 0$, so it must be positive. We can then divide each term by x.

$$\frac{8x}{x} < \frac{3x}{x} - \frac{x^2}{x}$$
$$8 < 3 - x$$

2.   **(C)**   Solve for the variable.

$$4x + 3 = 5x - 6$$
$$4x + 3 + 6 = 5x$$
$$4x + 9 = 5x$$
$$9 = x$$

Substitute 9 for x in each of the solutions. (C) is the correct choice because $-9 + 3 = -6$ is a true statement.

3.   **(B)**   Divide each of the three sections by the coefficient of -4. Remember that in an inequality, if you divide by a negative number, you must reverse the inequality sign.

$$\frac{4}{-4} < \frac{-4x}{-4} < \frac{12}{-4}$$
$$-1 < x < -3$$

Reverse the signs.

$$-1 > x > -3$$

DRILL: WORD PROBLEMS INVOLVING VARIABLES

1.   **(C)**   Use the formula of rate $\times$ time = distance for both cars.

Rate	$\times$	Time	=	Distance
55		T		$55T$
65		T		$65T$
				420

The two vehicles must travel 420 miles between the two of them.

$$55T + 65T = 420$$
$$120T = 420$$
$$T = 3.5$$

It will take 3.5 hours before the cars meet.

2.   **(B)**   First, find the difference between the two percentages.

$$7.2\% - 6.5\% = .7\%$$

Convert the percent to a fraction.

$$.7\% = \frac{7}{1,000}$$

Multiply this number with the amount invested.

$$\frac{7}{1,000} \times \$1,500 = \frac{21}{2} = 10.5$$

The difference is $10.50 for one year. We must determine the difference for three years.

$$3 \times \$10.50 = \$31.50$$

3.   **(B)**   First find the markup price.

$$\$50 \times 40\%$$
$$50 \times .4 = \$20$$

Add this to the original price.

$$\$50 + \$20 = \$70$$

Now, take 15% of this sum.

$$\$70 \times 15\%$$
$$70 \times .15 = \$10.50$$

Add this product to the original price.

$$\$50 + \$10.50 = \$60.50$$

Subtract this sum from the price of the item after the markup to determine the profit.

$$\$70.00 - \$60.50 = \$9.50$$

DRILL: STRUCTURE AND LOGIC OF ALGEBRA

1.   **(B)**   If n represents one of the numbers, then the other number must be $2n - 1$. Add the two numbers together to get 41.

$$n + 2n - 1 = 41.$$

Be sure to put in parentheses to signify the subtraction must be done first.

$$n + (2n - 1) = 41$$

2.   **(B)**   If n represents one of the numbers, then the other number must be $2 - n$. Their difference is 12, so this indicates subtraction.

$$n - 2 - n = 12$$

Again, add parentheses to indicate priority.

$$n - (2 - n) = 12$$

3.   **(D)**   Any two-digit number may be represented by $10T + U$, where T is the tens digit and U is the units digit. Their sum can be represented by $T + U$. Therefore:

$$10T + U = 6(T + U) + 5.$$

STATISTICS SKILLS, INCLUDING PROBABILITY

GRAPHS

The information requested from reading the graph and performing a calculation or two will be limited to obtaining:

A.   sums and differences of frequencies;

B.   a percent of the whole; and

C.   a frequency from a percent.

Example: Examine the bar graph below.

Number of bushels (to the nearest 5 bushels) of wheat
and corn produced by farm RQS from 1975–1985

Wheat: ▤   Corn: ▥

Question 1: In which year was the least number of bushels of wheat produced?

Solution: The number of bushels of wheat produced is represented by the vertical columns, as indicated in the legend below the graph.

By inspection of the graph, we find that the shortest bar representing wheat production is the one for 1976.

Thus, the least number of bushels of wheat was produced in 1976.

Question 2: How many more bushels of corn were produced in 1981 than in 1975?

Solution: The number of bushels of corn produced is represented by the dotted vertical columns, as indicated by the legend under the graph.

By reading the height of the vertical column for corn for the year 1981, we see that approximately 110 bushels were produced. The reading for 1975 is approximately 80 bushels. This is a difference of 110 – 80 or 30.

Thus, there were 30 more bushels of corn produced in 1981 than in 1975.

Question 3: What was the total number of bushels of wheat produced from 1983 to 1985?

Solution: The readings for wheat production in 1983, 1984, and 1985 are approximately 250, 240, and 245, respectively.

Since the question asks for the total number of bushels, add the three values: 250 + 240 + 245 = 735.

Thus, there was a total of 735 bushels of wheat produced from 1983 to 1985.

Example: Examine the line graph below.

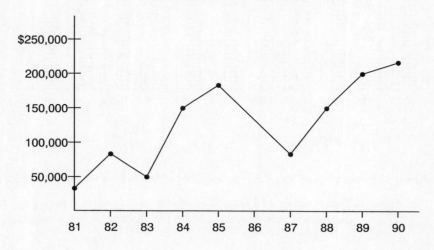

Amount of Scholarship Money Awarded to Graduating Seniors
West High — 1981–1990

Question 1: Between what two years did scholarship money increase the most?

Solution: With a visual inspection, one can see that the greatest increase occurred between the years of 1983 and 1984.

Question 2: In what year(s) did scholarship money actually decrease from the year before?

Solution: A decrease would be indicated by a data point for a particular year below the data point for the previous year. Through visual inspection, we see that scholarship money decreased in 1983, again in 1986, and again in 1987.

Example: Examine the pie chart below.

Sample Family Budget

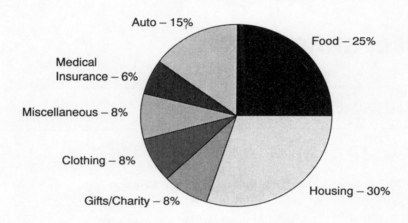

Question 1: Using the budget shown, a family with an income of $2,000 a month would plan to spend what amount on food?

Solution: We see from the chart that the budget allocates 25% of the monthly income to food.

Thus, we need to calculate 25% of $2,000.

$2,000 \times {}^{25}\!/_{100} = 2,000 \times {}^{1}\!/_{4} = 500$

Answer: $500

Question 2: A family with a monthly income of $1,200 spends $72 on clothing. What percent of their monthly income are they actually spending on clothing?

Solution: To calculate the percentage, we will set up a proportion as covered in a previous skill area.

$$^{72}/_{1,200} = {}^{P}/_{100}$$
$$72 \times 100 = 1,200 \times P \qquad \text{Cross multiply.}$$
$$7,200 = 1,200 \times P \qquad \text{Simplify.}$$
$$6 = P$$

Answer: 6%

Question 3: Using the budget shown, a family with an income of $2,000 a month would plan to spend what amount on medical insurance or auto?

Solution: The combined percentage allocated to medical insurance and auto is 6% + 15% or 21%.

Thus, we need to calculate 21% of $2,000.
$2,000 \times {}^{21}/_{100} = 20 \times 21 = 420$

Answer: $420

DRILL: GRAPHS

DIRECTIONS: Select the best answer.

Questions 1–3 refer to the following bar graph.

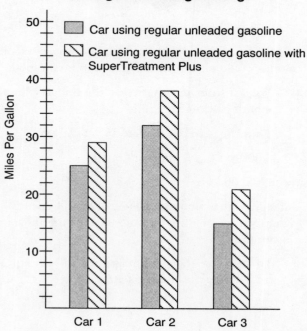

Changes in Average Mileage

1. By how much did the mileage increase for Car 2 when the new product was used?

    (A)   5 mpg   (C)   7 mpg

    (B)   6 mpg   (D)   10 mpg

2. Which car's mileage increased the most in this test?

    (A)   Car 2   (C)   Cars 1 and 2

    (B)   Car 3   (D)   Cars 2 and 3

3. According to the bar graph, if your car averages 25 mpg, what mileage might you expect with the new product?

    (A)   21 mpg   (C)   31 mpg

    (B)   29 mpg   (D)   35 mpg

MEAN, MEDIAN, AND MODE

The mean, median, and mode are all three measures of central tendency. They describe the "middle" or "center" of the data.

MEAN

The mean is the arithmetic average. It is the sum of the data points divided by the number of items in the sample.

Example: Find the mean salary for four company employees who make $5/hr., $8/hr., $12/hr., and $15/hr.

   Solution: The mean salary is the average.

   $5 + 8 + 12 + 15 = 40$ Sum the salaries.

   $^{40}/_4 = \$10/hr$ Divide by the number of items.

Example: Find the mean length of five fish with lengths of 7.5 in, 7.75 in, 8.5 in, 8.5 in, and 8.25 in.

   Solution: The mean length is the average length.

   $7.5 + 7.75 + 8.5 + 8.5 + 8.25 = 40.5$ Sum the lengths.

   $^{40.5}/_5 = 8.1$ in   Divide by the number of items.

MEDIAN

The median is the middle value in a set of items which is arranged in ascending or descending order.

To find the median,

(1)   arrange the items in ascending or descending order and

(2)   count in from each end the same number of items until one or two items remain.

If one item remains, that value is the median.

If two items remain, average the two values to find the median.

Example: Find the median of the following set of numbers:

5, 2, 8, 9, 3

Solution: Arrange in ascending order: 2 3 5 8 9
Count in toward the center: 2̶ 3̶ 5 8̶ 9̶
One item remains, 5, and that is the median.

Example: Find the median of the following set of numbers:

9, 5, 11, 10, 2, 3

Solution: Arrange in ascending order: 2 3 5 9 10 11
Count in toward the center: 2̶ 3̶ 5 9 1̶0̶ 1̶1̶
Two items remain, 5 and 9.
Average the two values: $(5 + 9)/2 = 7$
Thus, 7 is the median.

MODE

The mode is the most frequently occurring value in the set of items. It is possible that a set of items could have no mode or have a number of modes. A set with two modes is said to be bimodal.

Example: Find the mode of the following set of numbers:

4, 5, 8, 3, 8, 2

Solution: Since 8 occurs twice while the other values occur only once, 8 is the mode.

Example: For the given data, find the mean, median, and mode.
500, 600, 800, 800, 900, 900, 900, 900, 900, 1000, 1100

Solution: To find the mean:
500 + 600 + 800 + 800 + 900 + 900 + 900 + 900 + 900 + 1,000 + 1,100 = 9,300

$9300/11 = 845.45$

To find the median:
The items are already in ascending order, so count toward the middle. We arrive at one item, 900.

To find the mode:
See which item appears most frequently. That would be 900 which appears five times.

COMPARING THE MEAN, MEDIAN, AND MODE IN A VARIETY OF DISTRIBUTIONS

Mean, median, and mode were discussed earlier in terms of how to calculate each; however, in this skill area, you will be asked to make comparisons about the relative values of each without being able to calculate the exact values.

In order to make these comparisons, proceed as follows:

(1) If a bar graph is not provided, sketch one from the information given in the problem.

The graph will either be skewed to the left, skewed to the right, or approximately normal.

A graph skewed to the left will look like Figure I and the order of the three terms will be mean < median < mode (alphabetical order).

A graph skewed to the right will look like Figure II and the order of the three terms will be mode < median < mean (reverse alphabetical order).

A graph that is approximately normal will look like Figure III and the mean = median = mode.

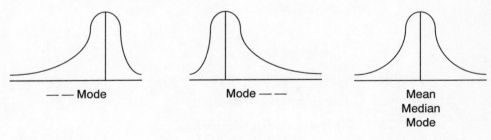

— — Mode	Mode — —	Mean Median Mode
Figure I	Figure II	Figure III

(2) Write the word mode under the highest column of the bar graph, because the mode is the most frequent. If the graph is skewed right or left the positioning of the mode established the order for the remaining two terms according to the information provided above. If the graph is approximately symmetrical, the value of all three terms are approximately equivalent.

Example: On a trip to the Everglades, students tested the pH of the water at different areas. Most of the pH tests were at 6. A few read 7, and one read 8. Select the statement that is true about the distribution of the pH test results.

(A)   The mode and the mean are the same.

(B)   The mode is less than the mean.

(C)   The mode is greater than the median.

(D)   The median is less than the mode.

Solution: Sketch a bar graph.
The graph is skewed to the right.
The mode is furthest left.
Thus, mode < median < mean.

Choices (A), (C), and (D) do not coincide with what has been established in terms of relative order. (B) is the only choice which does follow from our conclusions. Thus, (B) is the correct response.

Example: The graph below represents the mean grade point average of students by classification. Select the statement that is true about the students' GPAs.

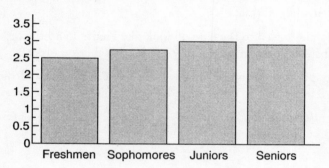

(A)   The mode and median are equal.

(B)   The mode is less than the median.

(C)   The mean is greater than the mode.

(D)   The mean is less than the median.

Solution: The graph is skewed to the left.
Thus, mean < median < mode.

Choices (A), (B), and (C) do not coincide with what has been established in terms of relative order. (D) is the only choice which does follow from our conclusions. Thus, (D) is the correct response.

DRILL: MEAN, MEDIAN, AND MODE

> **DIRECTIONS:** Select the best answer.

1. What is the mean of the data in the following sample?
    12, 15, 18, 24, 31

    (A)   18   (C)   20

    (B)   19.3   (D)   25

2. What is the median of the data in the following sample?
    19, 15, 21, 27, 12

    (A)   19   (C)   21

    (B)   15   (D)   27

3. What is the mode of the data in the following sample?
    16, 14, 12, 16, 30, 28

    (A)   6   (C)   16

    (B)   14   (D) $19.\overline{3}$

4. Mrs. Brandish cans tomatoes. She finds that most often she gets 10 tomatoes in each jar. Sometimes she can squeeze 11 in and once she managed to get 12 in one jar. Select the statement that is true about the number of tomatoes in each jar.

    (A)   The mode equals the mean.

    (B)   The mean is less than the mode.

    (C)   The median is greater than the mean.

    (D)   The mode is less than the median.

THE FUNDAMENTAL COUNTING PRINCIPLE

The fundamental counting principle deals with identifying the number of outcomes of a given experiment and can be broken down into the following three areas.

THE COUNTING RULE

If one experiment can be performed in *m* ways, and a second experiment can be performed in *n* ways, then there are *m* × *n* distinct ways both experiments can be performed in this specified order. The counting principle can be applied to more than two experiments.

Example: A new line of children's clothing is color-coordinated. Niki's mother bought her five tops, three shorts, and two pairs of shoes for the summer. How many different outfits can Niki choose from?·

Solution: How many choices are there for a top?   5
How many choices are there for shorts?   3
How many choices are there for shoes?   2

Apply the counting principle: 5 × 3 × 2 or 30.

Thus, Niki has 30 different outfits.

PERMUTATIONS

A permutation is an arrangement of specific objects where order is of particular importance. To determine the number of possible permutations, the following formula can be used:

$$n^P r = \frac{n!}{(n-r)!}$$

(where *n* is the number of objects in the given set, *r* is the number of objects being ordered, and ! is the notation used for factorial)

or, more simply, use the counting rule described above.

Example: Ten children in Ms. Berea's fifth grade class competed in the school's science fair. First, second, and third place trophies will go to the top three projects. In how many ways can the trophies be awarded?

Solution: Order is of definite importance here.

How many children have a chance at the first place trophy? 10
How many children have a chance at the second place trophy? 9
How many children have a chance at the third place trophy? 8

Apply the counting principle: 10 × 9 × 8 = 720.

Thus, there are 720 ways these 10 children could finish first, second, or third.

COMBINATIONS

A combination is an arrangement of specific objects where order is NOT of particular importance. To determine the number of possible combinations, use the following formula:

$$n^C r = \frac{n!}{r!(n-r)!}$$

(where *n* is the number of objects in the given set, *r* is the number of objects being chosen, and ! is the notation used for factorial)

$3! = 3 \times 2 \times 1$

$12! = 12 \times 11 \times 10 \times ... \times 3 \times 2 \times 1$

$n! = n \times (n-1) \times (n-2) \times ... \times 3 \times 2 \times 1$

Example: Simon has 10 compact discs and his player holds three discs at a time. How many combinations of three discs are possible?

Solution:
$$10^C 3 = \frac{10!}{3!(10-3)!}$$
$$= \frac{10!}{3! \times 7!}$$
$$= \frac{10 \times 9 \times 8 \times \cancel{7} \times \cancel{6} \times \cancel{5} \times \cancel{4} \times \cancel{3} \times \cancel{2} \times \cancel{1}}{(3 \times 2 \times 1) \times (\cancel{7} \times \cancel{6} \times \cancel{5} \times \cancel{4} \times \cancel{3} \times \cancel{2} \times \cancel{1})}$$
$$= \frac{720}{6}$$
$$= 120$$

Thus, there are 120 combinations of discs taken three at a time.

DRILL: THE FUNDAMENTAL COUNTING PRINCIPLE

DIRECTIONS: Select the best answer.

1. A local developer has five different floor plans, and each plan has two different elevations. How many different homes are available?

    (A) 5   (C) 10

    (B) 7   (D) 25

2. A radio station is running a contest. They have eight phone lines, all of which light up instantly when the word "PYRAMID" is broadcast. The first caller will win $1,000, the second caller will win $250, and the third caller will win $25. In how many different ways can the callers be selected to win the prizes?

    (A) 21   (C) 336

    (B) 56   (D) 40,320

3. From six sections of college algebra and four sections of calculus, a researcher will choose two college algebra sections and two calculus sections to be the subjects of a research study. How many different groupings can be selected?

(A) 6

(C) 90

(B) 24

(D) 360

SELECTING AN UNBIASED SAMPLE

If a subset of a population is chosen such that every member had an equal and likely chance of being selected, then we would say that this subset is an unbiased or random sample.

To choose the most appropriate procedure for selecting a random sample,

(1) first make sure that the sample is coming from the target population, and

(2) second make sure that each member of the target population has an equal and likely chance of being selected.

Example: Two homeowners in a 250 home development are interested in starting an association. They decide to conduct a survey to find out if the other homeowners are interested. Which procedure would be the most appropriate for obtaining a statistically unbiased sample?

(A) Poll the homes directly adjacent to their own homes.

(B) Poll shoppers at the local supermarket on Saturday morning.

(C) Poll a random sample of homeowners within the development.

(D) Poll the parents of the children at the local playground.

Solution: Are there any choices which do not sample the target population? Yes, choices (B) and (D), so eliminate these.

Are there choices which do not allow for every member to have an equal and likely chance of being selected? Yes, choice (A), so eliminate this one.

Choice (C) remains and the sample is taken from the target population and every member has an equal and likely chance of being selected.

Example: A local health agency wishes to conduct a survey of the type and amount of health insurance carried on elementary school children. Which procedure would be the most appropriate for obtaining a statistically unbiased sample?

(A) Randomly select an elementary school in the district and send a questionnaire to the parents of every third grader.

(B)   Survey the elementary school closest to the health agency and send a questionnaire home with every child whose last name begins with the letter A.

(C)   Survey a random sample of homeowners in the area.

(D)   Randomly select an elementary school in the district and then survey the parents of a random sample of children attending that school.

Solution: Are there any choices which do not sample the target population? Yes, choice (C). Eliminate it.

Are there choices which do not allow for every member to have an equal and likely chance of being selected? Yes, choices (A) and (B), so eliminate these.

Choice (D) remains and the sample is taken from the target population and every member has an equal and likely chance of being selected.

DRILL: SELECTING AN UNBIASED SAMPLE

DIRECTIONS: Select the best answer.

---

1.   A college librarian wants to determine if students are being fully served by the current library hours. She decides to conduct a survey. Which procedure would be the most appropriate for obtaining a statistically unbiased sample?

(A)   Get a list of students enrolled at the college from the registrar and select a random sample.

(B)   Place a questionnaire at the check-out desk.

(C)   Survey the first 50 students entering the library Tuesday morning.

(D)   Survey students at the student union building.

2.   The Student Council at a local high school wants to raise money for a field day in the spring. They have five possible fundraisers and decide to conduct a survey to see which would be most supported by the student body. Which procedure would be the most appropriate for obtaining a statistically unbiased sample?

(A) Survey the advanced English classes from each grade level.

(B) Survey a random sample of students from a list of all registered students.

(C) Survey the first 100 students entering the cafeteria for lunch.

(D) Survey all seniors.

PROBABILITY

Before discussing the actual calculation of a probability, examine the following probability facts.

(1) Probabilities are values ranging from 0 to 1 inclusive: $0 \leq P(E) \leq 1$. Probabilities cannot be negative or greater than 1.

   a. A probability of 0 means that the event cannot or did not occur.

   b. A probability of 1 means that the event must occur or always occurred.

(2) The sum of the probabilities of all possible events in any given experiment is 1.

(3) The notation used for the probability of an event E not happening is: $P(E')$, where E' is read E compliment.

(4) Combining facts (2) and (3), we then see that: $P(E) + P(E') = 1$. That is the probability of an event happening or its compliment happening is 1. This formula may also be applied in the following form: $1 - P(E) = P(E')$, depending on the context of the problem.

Example: Past records indicate that 25% of the students drop college algebra. What is the probability that a student does not drop college algebra?

   Solution: 25% means $^{25}/_{100}$ or $^1/_4$ of the students drop algebra.

   Those who do drop algebra and those who do not drop it constitute the entire universal set.

   Apply the formula: $1 - P(E) = P(E')$.
   $1 - ^1/_4 = ^3/_4$

   Thus, $^3/_4$ or .75 is the probability that a student does not drop college algebra.

The mathematical formula associated with the probability of a simple event is: $P(E) = ^m/_n$, where m is the number of favorable outcomes relative to event E, and n is the total number of possible outcomes.

Example: Given that Jeffrey gets two hits out of three times at bat at every T-ball game, what is the probability that Jeffrey will get a hit his next time up to bat?

Solution: The number of favorable outcomes, i.e., the number of hits, is two. The number of possible outcomes is three. Thus, the probability of a hit is $\frac{2}{3}$.

The mathematical formula which allows us to find the probability of obtaining either event A or event B is:

$$P(A \text{ or } B) = P(A) + P(B) - P(A \text{ and } B).$$

Note: If events A and B are mutually exclusive, $P(A \text{ and } B) = 0$, then the formula above simplifies to $P(A \text{ or } B) = P(A) + P(B)$.

Example: On a field trip, the teachers counted the orders for a snack and sent the information in with a few people. The orders were for 94 colas and 56 fries. If there were 133 orders, what was the probability of an order for a cola and fries?

Solution: Before using the formula presented above, we must determine $P(\text{cola})$, $P(\text{fries})$, and $P(\text{cola or fries})$.

$P(\text{cola}) = \frac{94}{133}$
$P(\text{fries}) = \frac{56}{133}$
$P(\text{cola or fries}) = \frac{133}{133}$

$$P(A \text{ or } B) = P(A) + P(B) - P(A \text{ and } B)$$
$$\tfrac{133}{133} = \tfrac{94}{133} + \tfrac{56}{133} - P(\text{cola and fries})$$
$$\tfrac{133}{133} = \tfrac{150}{133} - P(\text{cola and fries})$$
$$P(\text{cola and fries}) = \tfrac{150}{133} - \tfrac{133}{133}$$

$$P(\text{cola and fries}) = \tfrac{17}{133}$$

From the conditional probability formula: $P(A \mid B) = \dfrac{P(A \text{ and } B)}{P(B)}$,

we can derive the multiplication rule: $P(A \text{ and } B) = P(A \mid B) \times P(B)$. It is not necessary to fully understand what conditional probability is as long as you are able to apply the counting rules discussed earlier.

Example: If Kyle has eight pairs of socks, four white, two black, one blue, and one red, what is the probability that he randomly chooses two pairs of white socks to wear on consecutive days?

Solution: What is the probability of selecting one pair of white socks? $\frac{4}{8}$

Given that Kyle already chose a pair of white socks, what is the probability that he chooses another pair of white socks? $\frac{3}{7}$ Why?

How many pairs of white socks are left to choose? 3
How many total pairs of socks are left? 7

Thus, the probability of drawing two pairs of white socks is: $\frac{4}{8} \times \frac{3}{7}$ or $\frac{3}{14}$.

If the occurrence of event *A* in no way effects the occurrence or nonoccurrence of event *B*, then events *A* and *B* are said to be independent.

If events *A* and *B* are independent, then $P(A \text{ and } B) = P(A) \times P(B)$.

Example: The probability that a child born is male is 0.5. What is the probability that the next three children born at Memorial Hospital to unrelated parents are all boys?

Solution: The birth of three children to unrelated parents would be considered independent events.

$$P(3 \text{ males}) = (0.5)(0.5)(0.5)$$
$$= 0.125$$

Thus, the probability of three males is 0.125 which is 12.5%.

PROBABILITY WORD PROBLEMS

As with all prior real-world problems, the context of the problems is vast. A table or graph will provide the necessary information to calculate a single outcome, multiple outcome, or conditional probability or an expected value.

Example: The students at a local college voted for a new student body president. The following table is a breakdown of the vote for the student who won the election.

	Freshman	Sophomore	Junior	Senior
Male	9%	17%	10%	9%
Female	16%	13%	15%	11%

Question 1: If a student who voted for the winner is selected at random, what is the probability that that person is a sophomore and a male?

Solution: By locating the correct cell in the table, we see that 17% of votes were from sophomore males. This gives a probability of 0.17.

Question 2: What is the probability of a randomly selected student not being a senior?

Solution: Locate the senior cells.
9% males + 11% females = 20% seniors

Nonseniors: 100% − 20% = 80%

Thus, the probability of not being a senior is 0.80.

Question 3: Knowing that a selected person is a junior, what is the probability that the person is a female?

Solution: This is a conditional probability problem.

To solve such a problem, we need to identify how many are in the given category, in this case juniors.

Locate the junior cells.

10% males + 15% females = 25% juniors

The numerical value associated with the given, the person is a junior, is the denominator for the fraction.

Of the juniors, identify the percent that are females: 15%. This is the numerator.

Thus, the probability that the person is female given that the person is a junior is $^{15}/_{25}$ or 0.60.

Question 4: If in this election there were 500 votes for the winner, how many females cast votes for the winner?

Solution: Total number of females: 16% + 13% + 15% + 11% = 55%

55% of 500 is $^{55}/_{100} \times 500 = 275$

Thus, 275 females cast votes for the winner.

DRILL: PROBABILITY

<u>DIRECTIONS:</u> Select the best answer.

1. A note card manufacturer discovered that the packaging machine was sometimes inserting nine cards into a box which was to contain eight cards. The company opened 10 boxes and discovered that three contained the additional card. What is the probability that a randomly selected box would have nine cards?

   (A) $^{1}/_{10}$ (C) $^{8}/_{10}$

   (B) $^{3}/_{10}$ (D) $^{9}/_{10}$

2. Refer back to problem 1. If 30% of the boxes contain nine cards, what is the probability of selecting two boxes with nine cards from a shipping crate containing 100 boxes?

   (A) $^{29}/_{330}$ (C) $^{1}/_{15}$

   (B) $^{9}/_{100}$ (D) $^{9}/_{50}$

3. If the probability that a student is selected to be a National Merit Scholar is 0.02 and that the student is a female is 0.40, what is the probability that a female is selected to be a National Merit Scholar?

   (A) 0.42   (C) 0.38

   (B) 0.008   (D) 0.20

> **DIRECTIONS:** Questions 4–6 refer to the following information.

Mr. Bennett's 6th grade mathematics class is collecting data on eye color and gender. They organize the data they collected into the following table.

	Brown	Blue	Green
Male	22%	18%	10%
Female	18%	20%	12%

4. If a student is chosen at random, what is the probability that the student is a female with brown eyes?

    (A) 0.18   (C) 0.45

    (B) 0.40   (D) 0.50

5. What is the probability of a randomly selected student not having green eyes?

    (A) 0.22   (C) 0.88

    (B) 0.78   (D) 0.90

6. Given that the student selected has blue eyes, what is the probability that the student is a male?

    (A) 0.18   (C) 0.47

    (B) 0.20   (D) 0.53

PREDICTIONS FROM STATISTICAL DATA

In this skill area, a table, histogram, broken line graph, scatter diagram, or line graph will be given. From this information, you will be asked to infer relationships and/or make predictions. More precisely, the types of questions which may be asked include:

A. commenting on the relationship between two variables;

    A most critical concept to remember is that just because two variables appear to be related, there is no justification in presuming that one variable *causes* the other.

B. commenting on the trend of a single variable;

C. interpolating; and

D. extrapolating.

Example: Tuition and average textbook price are given in the following table. Which statement best describes the relationship between tuition and average textbook price?

Year	Tuition	Average Textbook Price
1985	$3,000	$32.50
1986	$3,200	$31.75
1987	$3,800	$39.62
1988	$3,800	$41.94
1989	$4,500	$40.79
1990	$4,700	$45.21
1991	$5,000	$44.97
1992	$5,700	$49.52
1993	$6,100	$53.10

(A) An increase in the tuition caused an increase in textbook price.

(B) An increase in textbook price caused an increase in tuition.

(C) There appears to be a positive association between tuition and textbook price.

(D) There appears to be a negative association between tuition and textbook price.

Solution: Be cautious of cause-and-effect relationships. Unless there is a direct link between two variables, the relationship can be coincidental. Eliminate choices (A) and (B).

Examine the tuition column and the textbook price column. Both columns are effectively increasing over time. If two variables change in the same direction, both increase or both decrease, we say this is a positive relationship. If one increases while the other decreases, we say this is a negative relationship. Thus, we can eliminate (D) and realize that (C) is the correct choice.

Example: Consider the following line graph. Which of the following best describes the trend in pledge money?

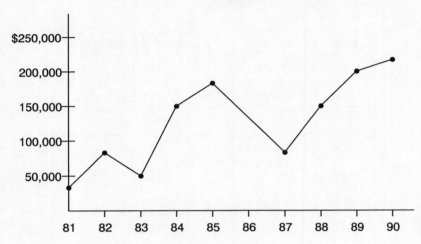

Amount of Money Pledged to Public Television during Telethons
1981-1990

(A) Pledge money has fluctuated but has in general increased over time.

(B) There is no trend in pledge money for any time.

(C) Pledge money actually decreased from 1987 to 1990.

(D) There was more pledge money available in the early 1980s than in the latter part of the decade.

Solution: Visually, we can see that pledge money has in general increased over time. Thus, we can eliminate (B).

Choice (C) is incorrect because pledge money increased from 1987 to 1990.

Choice (D) is incorrect because there was more money in the later 1980s than in the earlier 1980s.

This leaves choice (A). Even though pledge money has not consistently increased, it has in general over time.

Example: Using the same line graph from the previous example, between what two years was the increase in pledge money the most significant?

(A) 1981 – 1982   (C) 1985 – 1986

(B) 1983 – 1984   (D) 1987 – 1988

Solution: To determine the greatest increase, we must compare the differences between each two-year period.

1981 – 1982	80,000 – 40,000 = 40,000
1983 – 1984	150,000 – 50,000 = 100,000
1985 – 1986	120,000 – 175,000 = –55,000
1987 – 1988	150,000 – 70,000 = 80,000

We can see that the greatest increase came between 1983 – 1984, and this is choice (B).

DRILL: PREDICTIONS FROM STATISTICAL DATA

DIRECTIONS: Select the best answer.

1. Family income and food cost are given in the following table. Which statement best describes the relationship between family income and food cost?

Year	Family Income	Food Cost as a Percent of Income
1985	$23,000	25%
1986	$25,200	23%
1987	$28,800	20%
1988	$30,800	19%
1989	$34,500	17%
1990	$34,700	17%
1991	$35,000	16%
1992	$35,700	16%
1993	$38,100	15%

(A) As a family's income increases, they spend less money on food.

(B) An increase in income causes a decrease in the percent of that income spent on food.

(C) There appears to be a positive association between a family's income and the percent spent on food.

(D) There appears to be a negative association between a family's income and the percent spent on food.

2.   Refer to the table in problem 1 above. Which of the following best describes the percent of income spent on food beyond 1993?

(A)   Provided the family continues in the same trend, the percent of income spent on food will continue to decrease slightly.

(B)   The percent spent on food will never drop below 15%.

(C)   It is not possible to predict what will happen beyond 1993 because the trends represented here are unstable.

(D)   Since 15% is such a small percent to pay for food, one would expect the percent to begin increasing independent of income.

3.   Refer to the following scatter diagram showing students' scores on the math and science sections of a test. If a student scored 550 on the math section, what would you estimate the science score to be?

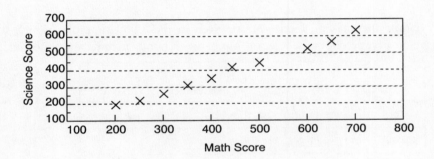

(A)   Around 200   (C)   Around 480

(B)   Around 340   (D)   Impossible to predict

4.   Using the same scatter diagram in problem 3, if a student scored 600 on the math section, what would you expect that same student to score on the verbal section?

(A)   Around 400   (C)   Around 700

(B)   Around 550   (D)   Impossible to predict

INTERPRETING DATA FREQUENCY AND CUMULATIVE FREQUENCY TABLES

In this skill area, a frequency table or cumulative frequency table will be given. The questions in the following example represent the types of questions which may be asked.

Example: The following table represents the distribution of the homes in a given area by the total square footage of the home.

Square Footage	Proportion of Homes
1,000 – 1,200	0.02
1,200 – 1,400	0.08
1,400 – 1,600	0.15
1,600 – 1,800	0.18
1,800 – 2,000	0.22
2,000 – 2,200	0.25
2,200 – 2,400	0.10

Question 1: What is the mode of the distribution?

Solution: The mode is the most frequent.

Thus, the mode would be homes in the 2,000 – 2,200 square foot range because 25% of the homes fall within this range, more than any other frequency.

Question 2: What is the median of the distribution?

Solution: The median is the middle term. We will need to find the point at which half of the homes are above and half of the homes are below. To do this begin adding the decimal values until you reach .50 or just above.

$$0.02 + 0.08 = 0.10$$
$$+ 0.15 = 0.25$$
$$+ 0.18 = 0.43$$
$$+ 0.22 = 0.65$$

Since the value which put us over the 0.50 mark was 0.22, which represented the 1,800 – 2,000 square foot homes, this range is the median. In a case such as this, it is sometimes customary to use the midpoint of the range, 1,900 square feet, as the median.

Question 3: What is the mean of the distribution?

Solution: The mean is the arithmetic average.

To find the mean of this distribution, we must find the class mark, the middle value of each range, and multiply that value by the respective proportion.

$$1,100 \times 0.02 = \quad 22$$
$$1,300 \times 0.08 = \quad 104$$
$$1,500 \times 0.15 = \quad 225$$
$$1,700 \times 0.18 = \quad 306$$
$$1,900 \times 0.22 = \quad 418$$
$$2,100 \times 0.25 = \quad 525$$
$$2,300 \times 0.10 = \quad \underline{230}$$
$$1,830$$

Thus, the mean is 1,830 square feet.

Question 4: What portion of the homes have more than 2,000 square feet?

Solution: Homes with more than 2,000 square feet would be the 2,000 – 2,200 with a proportion of 0.25 and 2,200 – 2,400 with a proportion of 0.10.

This means the 0.25 + 0.10 or 0.35 or 35% of the homes have more than 2,000 square feet.

Question 5: What portion of the homes have between 1,200 and 1,800 square feet?

Solution: Homes in this range are:

1,200 – 1,400	0.08
1,400 – 1,600	0.15
1,600 – 1,800	0.18
	0.41

Thus, 0.41 or 41% of the homes have between 1,200 and 1,800 square feet.

DRILL: INTERPRETING DATA FREQUENCY AND CUMULATIVE FREQUENCY TABLES

DIRECTIONS: Questions 1–5 refer to the following information.

The following table represents the number of presidents by age at the time of inauguration.

Age	Frequency
40 – 44	2
45 – 49	5
50 – 54	12
55 – 59	11
60 – 64	7
65 – 69	3

1.   What is the mean of the distribution?

(A)   52   (C)   57

(B)   55   (D)   67

2.   What is the median of the distribution?

(A)   52   (C)   57

(B)   55   (D)   67

3.   What is the mode of the distribution?

(A)   52   (C)   57

(B)   55   (D)   67

4.   What portion of the presidents was under 55 years of age when inaugurated?

(A)   0.175   (C)   0.525

(B)   0.475   (D)   0.75

5.   What portion of the presidents was in their fifties when inaugurated?

(A)   0.12   (C)   0.425

(B)   0.23   (D)   0.575

STATISTICAL SKILLS, INCLUDING PROBABILITY

ANSWER KEY

DRILL: GRAPHS

1. **(B)**   3. **(B)**
2. **(D)**

DRILL: MEAN, MEDIAN, AND MODE

1. **(C)**   3. **(C)**
2. **(A)**   4. **(D)**

DRILL: THE FUNDAMENTAL COUNTING PRINCIPLE

1. **(C)**   3. **(C)**
2. **(C)**

DRILL: SELECTING AN UNBIASED SAMPLE

1. **(A)**
2. **(B)**

DRILL: PROBABILITY

1.	**(B)**	3.	**(B)**	5.	**(B)**
2.	**(A)**	4.	**(A)**	6.	**(C)**

DRILL: PREDICTIONS FROM STATISTICAL DATA

1.	**(D)**	3.	**(C)**
2.	**(A)**	4.	**(D)**

DRILL: INTERPRETING DATA FREQUENCY AND CUMULATIVE FREQUENCY TABLES

1.	**(B)**	3.	**(A)**	5.	**(D)**
2.	**(C)**	4.	**(B)**		

STATISTICAL SKILLS, INCLUDING PROBABILITY
DETAILED EXPLANATIONS OF ANSWERS

DRILL: GRAPHS

1. **(B)**   Each line on the graph represents two gallons. You will notice a difference of two lines between the two types of gas for Car 2 on the miles per gallon axis.

$$3 \times 2 = 6 \text{ mi.}$$

2. **(D)**   Both Cars 2 and 3 increased three lines on the miles per gallon axis when treated with Super Treatment Plus. Therefore, they increased by the same mileage.

3. **(B)**   Car 1 has the closest nontreatment average to 25 miles per gallon. After it was treated, the car's average increased to 29 miles per gallon.

DRILL: MEAN, MEDIAN, AND MODE

1. **(C)**   To find the mean, add all of the numbers and divide by the amount of terms.

$$12 + 15 + 18 + 24 + 31 = 100$$

There are 5 terms, so:

$$100 \div 5 = 20$$

2. **(A)**   To find the median, put the numbers in order from smallest to largest. The median will be the middle number. Because there is an odd number of items (5), the median will be the number with the same amount of terms on either side of it.

$$12, 15, 19, 21, 27$$

The answer is 19.

3. **(C)**   The mode is the number that occurs most frequently. Notice that 16 appears in the list twice. This is more than any other number.

4.   **(D)**   Mrs. Brandish can fit 10, 11, or 12 tomatoes in a jar. The median is 11. Since the most frequent amount is given, we know the mode is 10. Since 10 is less than 11, the mode is less than the median.

DRILL: THE FUNDAMENTAL COUNTING PRINCIPLE

1.   **(C)**   The numbers given in this problem are independent of one another. Just multiply them to determine the possible number of homes.

$$2 \times 5 = 10$$

2.   **(C)**   The first caller has eight chances of winning because all eight lines are available. The second caller has only seven chances because the one line is occupied by the first caller. The third caller only has six chances because two lines are being occupied by the other callers. Multiply these quantities together to find the number of ways.

$$8 \times 7 \times 6 = 336$$

3.   **(C)**   The researcher will choose two sections in each subject. For algebra, he will have six options for the first test choice and five options for the second test choice, or:

$$\frac{6 \times 5}{1 \times 2} \quad \frac{\text{number of options}}{\text{times he will be choosing}}$$

$$= \frac{30}{2}$$

$$= 15$$

For calculus, he will have four options for his first choice and three options for his second choice, or:

$$\frac{4 \times 3}{1 \times 2} \quad \frac{\text{number of options}}{\text{times he will be choosing}}$$

$$= \frac{12}{2}$$

$$= 6$$

Of the amount of options determined above, the researcher may organize the study in $6 \times 15 = 90$ ways.

DRILL: SELECTING AN UNBIASED SAMPLE

1.   **(A)**   A list of students enrolled at the college would be most appropriate since it is the only sample independent of time, location, and library hours.

2.   **(B)**   A random sample of students would be most appropriate since it is the only sample independent of time, age, or ability.

DRILL: PROBABILITY

1.   **(B)**   Probability $= \dfrac{\text{Favorable ways}}{\text{Total number of samples/ways checked}}$

Since 10 boxes were checked, and three boxes were found containing extra cards, then the probability is $\frac{3}{10}$ that a randomly selected box would have nine cards.

2.   **(A)**   In problem 1, you determined the probability of a randomly selected box with nine cards is $\frac{3}{10}$. This ratio can be converted to $\frac{30}{100}$, or 30 boxes out of a sample of 100.

Each choice from a box is independent of the last; you have an equal chance of choosing a box with eight or nine cards in it, regardless of the last box chosen. Only one factor changes with each choice: the amount of boxes in the crate. This amount decreases with each choice, as does the amount of nine-card boxes.

To determine the probability of finding two nine-card boxes, work backwards from the three box probability. The first time you choose, there are 30 nine-card boxes per crate. After that box is chosen, there are only 29 nine-card boxes left in a crate of 99 boxes.

To find the probability of selecting two boxes with nine cards, multiply the two independent probabilities.

$$\frac{30}{100} \times \frac{29}{99} = \frac{87}{990}$$
$$= \frac{29}{330}$$

3.   **(B)**   These two probabilities are independent of each other, so multiply them together.

$$(.02)\,(.40) = .0080 \text{ or } .008$$

4.   **(A)**   The chart lists the probability for a female having green eyes as 18%.

5.   **(B)**   Add the percentages of males and females with green eyes.

$$10\% + 12\% = 22\%$$

Students not having green eyes would be the whole class, or 100%, minus 22% of students with green eyes, or:

$$100\% - 22\% = 78\%$$

6.   **(C)**   In the entire class, 18% of males have blue eyes and 20% of females have blue eyes, meaning 38% of the class has blue eyes. The probability that a blue-eyed person would be male is 18% of the 38% of all blue-eyed people.

$$^{18}\!/_{38} = {}^{9}\!/_{19}$$

To convert to a decimal, divide 9 by 19.

$$^{9}\!/_{19} = .47$$

To convert to a percent, multiply by 100.

$$.47 \times 100 = 47\%$$

DRILL: PREDICTIONS FROM STATISTICAL DATA

1.   **(D)**   The chart indicates that the family spends a smaller percentage on food as their income increases. Do not confuse this with a smaller amount of money; the amount may remain constant.

2.   **(A)**   The trend on the chart demonstrates a slight decrease in the percentage of income spent on food as the income increases.

3.   **(C)**   If you trace an imaginary line through the graph, you can estimate the science score to fall around 480.

4.   **(D)**   Since the verbal section was not listed in the scatter diagram, it would be impossible to predict the outcome.

DRILL: INTERPRETING DATA FREQUENCY AND CUMULATIVE FREQUENCY TABLES

1.   **(B)**   To find the mean, take the "middle" number in each age group and multiply by the number in the frequency column.

Middle Number	×	Frequency		
42	×	2	=	84
47	×	5	=	235
52	×	12	=	624
57	×	11	=	627
62	×	7	=	434
67	×	3	=	201
		40		2,205 (total) divided by the total in the frequency column: $^{2205}/_{40} = 55\%$

2.   **(C)**   There are 40 scores; the middle one is $20\frac{1}{2}$, which is between 55–59, or 57.

3.   **(A)**   The most frequent is 12, which is age 50–54, or 52.

4.   **(B)**   If you look at the chart, the number of presidents that were under 55 years of age was 12 + 5 + 2 = 19; there are 19 out of a total of 40. Therefore, $^{19}/_{40} = .475$.

5.   **(D)**   Looking at the chart, the number of presidents that were in their fifties when inaugurated is 12 + 11 = 23 out of a total of 40; therefore, $^{23}/_{40} = .575$.

LOGICAL REASONING

VENN DIAGRAMS

A set is any collection of well-defined objects called elements.

Venn diagrams can be used to represent sets. These diagrams consist of circle(s) enclosed within a rectangular region which help to visualize the relationship between members or objects of a set. The rectangular region is called the Universal set, *U*, and the individual circles represent the various sets in question.

A Venn diagram will be given along with four statements depicting set relations whose truth must be evaluated relative to the given diagram.

When evaluating the truth of a statement, begin by placing an "X" in each region of the first set mentioned. Decide if each "X" placed is included in the second set mentioned. If this is true for all "X's" placed, then the statement is probably true.

Example: Sets *A*, *B*, *C*, and *U* are related as shown in the diagram. Which of the following statements is true assuming none of the regions is empty?

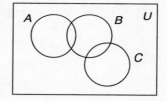

(A) Any element which is a member of set *B* is also a member of sets *A* and *C*.

(B) Any element which is a member of set *A* is also a member of set *C*.

(C) Any element which is a member of set *U* is also a member of set *B*.

(D) No element is a member of all three sets *A*, *B*, and *C*.

Solution: Statement (A): Mark an "X" in each of the three regions which make up set B. Are all three "X's" also members of both sets *A* and *C*? No. Eliminate choice (A).

Statement (B): Mark an "X" in each of the two regions which make up set *A*. Are both "X's" also members of set *C*? No. Eliminate choice (B).

Statement (C): Mark an "X" in all six regions of the diagram. Are all six "X's" also members of set *B*? No. Eliminate choice (C).

Statement (D): Different question! Can you place one "X" anywhere in the diagram such that it belongs to sets *A*, *B*, and *C* at the same time? No. Choice (D) is the correct response, because there is no element which is a member of all three sets.

Example: Sets *A*, *B*, *C*, and *U* are related as shown in the diagram. Which of the following statements is true assuming none of the regions is empty?

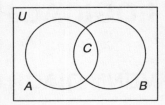

(A) Any element which is a member of set *C* is also a member of sets *A* and *B*.

(B) Any element which is a member of set *A* is also a member of set *C*.

(C) Any element which is a member of set *U* is also a member of set *B*.

(D) None of the above statements is true.

Solution: Statement (A): Mark an "X" in set *C*. Is the X also a member of both sets *A* and *B*? Yes. Choice (A) is the correct response.

Statement (B): Mark an "X" in each of the two regions which make up set *A*. Are the two "X's" also members of set *C*? No. Eliminate choice (B).

Statement (C): Mark an "X" in all four regions of the diagram. Are all four "X's" also members of set *B*? No. Eliminate choice (C).

Statement (D): Choice (A) was true. Eliminate choice (D).

DRILL: VENN DIAGRAMS

DIRECTIONS: Select the best answer.

---

1. Sets *A*, *B*, *C*, and *U* are related as shown in the diagram. Which of the following statements is true assuming none of the regions is empty?

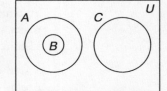

(A) Any element which is a member of set *A* is also a member of set *B*.

(B) Any element which is a member of set *A* is also a member of set *C*.

(C) Any element which is a member of set *B* is also a member of set *A*.

(D) None of the above statements is true.

2.　Sets *A*, *B*, *C*, and *U* are related as shown in the diagram. Which of the following statements is true assuming none of the regions is empty?

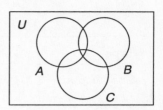

(A) Any element which is a member of sets *B* and *C* is also a member of set *A*.

(B) Any element which is a member of set *A* is also a member of set *C*.

(C) Any element which is a member of set *B* is also a member of set *U*.

(D) No element is a member of all three sets *A*, *B*, and *C*.

LOGICAL STATEMENTS

IDENTIFYING STATEMENTS EQUIVALENT TO THE NEGATIONS OF SIMPLE AND COMPOUND STATEMENTS

A statement is a sentence which can be judged to be true or false.

If a statement conveys a single idea, it is said to be a simple statement. Example: The tomato is green. It is customary to use the symbols *p*, *q*, or *r* to represent a simple statement.

The negation of a statement is read as "not." To negate the statement "The tomato is green," one would say "The tomato is not green." To negate the statement "The tomato is not green," one would say "The tomato is green." A double negation is the same as the original statement.

Quantified terms begin with such words as "all," "none," or "some." To negate a quantified term, change the wording as follows:

　　　　All are <===> Some are not
　　None are <===> Some are

Example:　Select the statement that is the negation of the statement "All dinosaurs are extinct."

(A) No dinosaurs are extinct.

(B) Some dinosaurs are extinct.

(C) Some dinosaurs are not extinct.

(D) Some extinct animals are not dinosaurs.

Solution:　The given statement is of the form: All are. We see above that All are ===> Some are not. Choice (C) follows this transformation; therefore, (C) is the correct choice.

If a statement conveys more than one idea, it is said to be a compound statement. Compound statements of concern in this skill area include:

Compound Statements

Type	Format	Example
Conjunctions	*p* **and** *q*	The book has 500 pages **and** that cat has four legs.
Disjunctions	*p* **or** *q*	Kevin will go to the beach **or** Kevin will go shopping.
Conditionals	**If** *p*, **then** *q*	If I have $2, **then** I will buy you a giant cookie.

To negate a conjunction (*p* and *q*), the resulting statement becomes **not** *p* **or** **not** *q*.

Example: Select the statement that is the negation of the statement "Joni is 18 years old and Lindsay is 3 years old."

(A) Joni is not 18 years old and Lindsay is 3 years old.

(B) Joni is not 18 years old and Lindsay is not 3 years old.

(C) Joni is not 18 years old or Lindsay is not 3 years old.

(D) If Joni is not 18 years old, then Lindsay is not 3 years old.

Solution: We see above that the negation of (*p* and *q*) is (not *p* or not *q*). Choice (C) states this transition.

To negate a disjunction (*p* or *q*), the resulting statement becomes **not** *p* **and** **not** *q*.

Example: Select the statement that is the negation of the statement "A cat does not say moo or a dog does bark."

(A) A cat does say moo and a dog does not bark.

(B) A cat does say moo or a dog does not bark.

(C) A cat does not say moo and a dog does not bark.

(D) A cat does not say moo or a dog does not bark.

Solution: The negation of a negative statement is a positive statement. Keeping this in mind and applying the form above for the negation of a disjunction, we see that choice (A) is the correct response.

To negate a conditional (If *p*, then *q*), the resulting statement becomes *p* **and** **not** *q*.

Example: Select the statement that is the negation of the statement "If Ryan does not go to bed before 10 p.m., then he will be too tired to play at the park tomorrow."

(A) Ryan does not go to bed before 10 p.m. and he is not too tired to play at the park tomorrow.

(B) Ryan does not go to bed before 10 p.m. or he is not too tired to play at the park tomorrow.

(C) Ryan does go to bed before 10 p.m. and he is too tired to play at the park tomorrow.

(D) If Ryan does go to bed before 10 p.m., then he will not be too tired to play at the park tomorrow.

Solution: We have a form (If p, then q) and the negation is (p and not q) as cited above.

Eliminate choice (B) because it uses the word "or."

Choice (D) can be eliminated because it is still of the "If, then" form.

The correct response must have the same beginning statement as the given. Choice (C) does not.

Therefore, choice (A) is the correct response.

DETERMINING EQUIVALENCE OR NONEQUIVALENCE OF STATEMENTS

As in the previous skill area, a statement will be given and it is to be determined which of the choices is an equivalent statement, that is having the same meaning but stated differently. Again, the statements will be limited to conjunctions, disjunctions, conditionals, and negations.

The symbol $\sim$ is customarily used in place of the word "not." For example $\sim p$ would be read "not p." The same symbol is also used in place of the words, "It is not true that…" For example $\sim(p$ and $q)$ would read "It is not true that p and q."

Following is a list of equivalent statements from the previous skill area: (The symbol $\equiv$ is read "is equivalent to.")

1. $\sim(p$ and $q) \equiv \sim p$ or $\sim q$
2. $\sim(p$ or $q) \equiv \sim p$ and $\sim q$
3. $\sim($If p, then $q) \equiv p$ and $\sim q$
4. $\sim($All are$) \equiv$ Some are not
5. $\sim($Some are not$) \equiv$ All are
6. $\sim($None are$) \equiv$ Some are
7. $\sim($Some are$) \equiv$ None are

To this list, we also want to add:

8.   If p, then $q \equiv \sim p$ or q
9.   If p, then $q \equiv q$ or $\sim p$
10. If p, then $q \equiv$ If $\sim q$, then $\sim p$

Example: Select the statement below that is logically equivalent to "If Mia is ill, then she must stay inside."

  (A) If Mia does not stay inside, then she is not ill.

  (B) If Mia is not ill, then she does not have to stay inside.

  (C) If Mia is ill, then she does not have to stay inside.

  (D) If Mia does stay inside, then she is ill.

Solution: p = Mia is ill.
  q = She must stay inside.

The given form is: If p, then q.

The choices are also of the form: If, then.

Consult the list above, 1 through 10, to see which equivalence statement applies to this structure.

10 is the only selection in which both the given and result are in the "If, then" form.

We are then looking for a statement "If $\sim q$, then $\sim p$."

Choice (A) is of this form, and hence the correct response.

Example: Select the statement below that is logically equivalent to "It is not true that Jenny is a blonde or Katie has freckles."

  (A) Jenny is not a blonde or Katie does not have freckles.

  (B) Jenny is not a blonde and Katie does not have freckles.

  (C) If Jenny is not a blonde, then Katie does not have freckles.

  (D) If Katie does not have freckles, then Jenny is not a blonde.

Solution: p = Jenny is a blonde.
  q = Katie has freckles.

The given form is: $\sim$ (p or q).

This form is number 2 above.

Hence, we are looking for a choice of: $\sim p$ and $\sim q$.

Choice (B) is the only one which is equivalent to the given and hence the correct choice.

Example: Select the statement below that is logically equivalent to "It is not true that some dogs can talk."

  (A) If the animal is a dog, then it cannot talk.

  (B) All dogs can talk.

(C)   Some dogs cannot talk.

(D)   No dogs can talk.

Solution: p = some dogs can talk.

The given form is: ~(Some can).

This form is number 7 above.

Hence, we are looking for a choice of: None are.

Choice (D) is the only one which is equivalent to the given and hence the correct choice.

TRANSFORMING STATEMENTS WITHOUT AFFECTING THEIR MEANING

A pair of statements which are logically equivalent will be given. Generalize the statements into symbolic form and select the appropriate structure from the choices given.

Some possibilities may include:

1.   ~(~p) $\equiv$ p
2.   ~(p and q) $\equiv$ ~p or ~q
3.   ~(p or q) $\equiv$ ~p and ~q
4.   If p, then q $\equiv$ If ~q, then ~p
5.   If p, then q $\equiv$ ~p or q $\equiv$ q or ~p
6.   ~(If p, then q) $\equiv$ p and ~q
7.   ~(All are) $\equiv$ Some are not
8.   ~(Some are not) $\equiv$ All are
9.   ~(None are) $\equiv$ Some are
10.   ~(Some are) $\equiv$ None are

Example: Select the rule of logical equivalence which directly (in one step) transforms statement I into statement II.

I.   It is not true that all girls are not pretty.
II.   Some girls are pretty.

(A)   "Not (not p)" is equivalent to "p."

(B)   "If p, then q" is equivalent to "some are p."

(C)   "Not all are p" is equivalent to "some are not p."

(D)   "All are not p" is equivalent to "some are p."

Solution: The symbolic representation of I is: ~(All are p), where p = all girls are not pretty.

The symbolic representation of II is: Some are not p.

Choice (C) gives this transformation.

Example: Select the rule of logical equivalence which directly (in one step) transforms statement I into statement II.

    I.   If the dryer is too hot, then the clothes will shrink.
    II.   If the clothes did not shrink, then the dryer was not too hot.

(A)   "Not (if p, then q)" is equivalent to "p and not q."

(B)   "If p, then q" is equivalent to "some are p."

(C)   "If p, then q" is equivalent to "not p or q."

(D)   "If p, then q" is equivalent to "If not q, then not p."

Solution: The symbolic representation of I is: If p, then q,
where p = the dryer is too hot and
q = the clothes will shrink.

The symbolic representation of II is: If $\sim q$, then $\sim p$.

Choice (D) gives this transformation.

Example: Select the rule of logical equivalence which directly (in one step) transforms statement I into statement II.

    I.   It is not true that calculators and computers complicate your life.
    II.   Calculators do not complicate your life or computers do not complicate your life.

(A)   "Not (p or q)" is equivalent to "not p and not q."

(B)   "Not (p and q)" is equivalent to "not p or not q."

(C)   "Not (not p)" is equivalent to "p."

(D)   "All p and q are" is equivalent to "no p and q are."

Solution: The symbolic representation of I is: $\sim(p$ and $q)$,
where p = calculators complicate your life and
q = computers complicate your life.

The symbolic representation of II is: $\sim p$ or $\sim q$.

Choice (B) gives this transformation.

DRILL: LOGICAL STATEMENTS

<u>**DIRECTIONS:**</u> Select the best answer.

1. Select the statement that is the negation of the statement "If I am hungry, then I will have a snack."

    (A) If I am not hungry, then I will not have a snack.

    (B) I am not hungry and I will have a snack.

    (C) I am hungry or I will not have a snack.

    (D) I am hungry and I will not have a snack.

2. Select the statement that is the negation of the statement "Sam is not a baseball player and Michael is a soccer player."

    (A) Sam is a baseball player and Michael is not a soccer player.

    (B) Sam is a baseball player or Michael is not a soccer player.

    (C) Sam is not a baseball player and Michael is a soccer player.

    (D) Sam is not a baseball player or Michael is not a soccer player.

3. Select the statement that is the negation of the statement "Jelly beans are sweet or licorice is not tart."

    (A) Jelly beans are not sweet and licorice is tart.

    (B) Jelly beans are not sweet or licorice is tart.

    (C) Jelly beans are not sweet and licorice is not tart.

    (D) Jelly beans are sweet or licorice is tart.

4. Select the statement below that is logically equivalent to "It is not true that if the phone rings, I will answer it."

    (A) The phone rings and I do not answer it.

    (B) The phone does not ring and I answer it.

    (C) If the phone does not ring, then I will not answer it.

    (D) If the phone rings, then I will not answer it.

5. Select the statement below that is logically equivalent to "If the batteries are dead, then the calculator will not work."

    (A)   If the batteries are not dead, then the calculator works.

    (B)   If the calculator works, then the batteries are not dead.

    (C)   The batteries are dead or the calculator works.

    (D)   The batteries are not dead and the calculator works.

6. Select the statement below that is logically equivalent to "It is not true that no swimming pools are round."

    (A)   All swimming pools are round.

    (B)   All swimming pools are not round.

    (C)   Some swimming pools are round.

    (D)   Some swimming pools are not round.

7. Select the rule of logical equivalence which directly (in one step) transforms statement I into statement II.

    I.   It is not true that some bananas are pink.
    II.   No bananas are pink.

    (A)   "Not (some are p)" is equivalent to "None are p."

    (B)   "Not (not p)" is equivalent to "p."

    (C)   "Not (p and q)" is equivalent to "not p or not q."

    (D)   "If p, then q" is equivalent to "not p or q."

8. Select the rule of logical equivalence which directly (in one step) transforms statement I into statement II.

    I.   It is not true that exercise is a waste of time or too bothersome.
    II.   Exercise is not a waste of time and exercise is not too bothersome.

    (A)   "Not (p and q)" is equivalent to "not p or not q."

    (B)   "Not (p or q)" is equivalent to "not p and not q."

    (C)   "Not p" is equivalent to "p."

    (D)   "If p, then q" is equivalent to "not p or q."

9.   Select the rule of logical equivalence which directly (in one step) transforms statement I into statement II.

   I.   It is not true that baby girls cannot wear blue.
   II. Baby girls can wear blue.

   (A)   "Not all p" is equivalent to "some are p."

   (B)   "Not (not p)" is equivalent to "p."

   (C)   "Not p" is equivalent to "p."

   (D)   "If p, then q" is equivalent to "not p or q."

DRAWING LOGICAL CONCLUSIONS FROM DATA

The data presented will be in one of two forms; conditions or a syllogism.
The following is an example of data presented in conditional form.

Example: Read the requirements for extracurricular clubs at Highland University and each club's qualifications. Then identify which of the clubs would be permitted.

In order for the Highland University to sanction a club, the club must have a faculty sponsor and elected officers. The club's members may only consist of currently registered Highland University students.

The Lynx Club has Professor Von Gutten as a faculty sponsor. The club's constitution requires that new officers be elected within the first two weeks of classes each fall and that any registered Highland University student or alumni may join.

The Pyramid Club has Professor Smyth as a faculty sponsor. The club elects new officers each semester and only currently registered students may be active members.

The Ping-Pong Club has Assistant Professor Sprunger as a faculty sponsor. Only currently enrolled students are members, and the officers are appointed depending on their ping-pong ability each semester.

   (A)   The Pyramid Club

   (B)   The Lynx Club and The Pyramid Club

   (C)   The Lynx Club and The Ping-Pong Club

   (D)   None of the clubs meet the qualifications.

Solution: Make a list of the qualifications:
          Faculty sponsor
          Elected officers
          Members must be currently registered students

Compare the description of each club. For each qualification met, mark a check. For each qualification not met, mark an "X." If only checks appear for any club(s), these clubs are permitted.

The Lynx Club:
✓ Faculty sponsor
✓ Elected officers
✗ Members must be currently registered students
The Lynx Club would not be permitted.

The Pyramid Club:
✓ Faculty sponsor
✓ Elected officers
✓ Members must be currently registered students
The Pyramid Club would be permitted.

The Ping-Pong Club:
✓ Faculty sponsor
✗ Elected officers
✓ Members must be currently registered students
The Ping-Pong Club would not be permitted.

Thus, of the three clubs, only the Pyramid Club would be permitted. This means that choice (A) is the correct response.

A syllogism or syllogistic argument consists of a finite set of premises followed by a conclusion. One presumes the premises to be true, and only judges the validity or fallacy of the conclusion. The basis of this decision rests on whether the conclusion follows from the given set of premises.

The validity of a syllogism is perhaps best determined using Euler diagrams. This allows a visual representation of the structure of the set of premises.

If a premise states that "All As are Bs," the representation would resemble Figure 1.

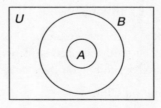

Figure 1

If a premise states that "No As are Bs," the representation would resemble Figure 2.

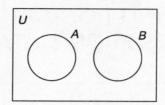

Figure 2

If a premise states that "Some *A*s are *B*s," the representation would resemble Figure 3.

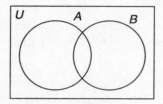

Figure 3

Example: Given that:

I.   No children like spinach.
II.   Tyler is a child.

determine which conclusion can be logically deduced.

(A)   Tyler is not a child.

(B)   Tyler does like spinach.

(C)   Tyler does not like spinach.

(D)   None of the above.

Solution: Draw the appropriate Euler diagram for "No children like spinach."

Place an "X" for Tyler in the children circle.

From the diagram one can see that Tyler is not in the spinach circle; therefore, he does not like spinach.

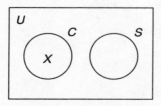

DRILL: DRAWING LOGICAL CONCLUSIONS FROM DATA

> **DIRECTIONS:** Select the best answer.

1. Read the requirements and each applicant's qualifications for participation in the Summer Beach Awareness Program. Then identify which of the applicants are eligible to participate.

    To be eligible for the program, the applicant must be between the ages of eight and 12, have two teacher references, and pass a Red Cross Life Saving Class.

    Bill Greene is nine years old and has references from his second and third grade teachers. He failed to pass the Red Cross Life Saving Class

    Jill Maddison is 13 years old and has references from her middle school art and English teachers. She passed the Red Cross Life Saving Class.

    Mindy Calahan is eight years old and has a reference from her second grade teacher. She passed the Red Cross Life Saving Class.

    (A)   Mindy Calahan

    (B)   Jill Maddison

    (C)   Bill Greene

    (D)   None of these applicants are eligible to participate.

2. Given that:

    I.   Some shrubs flower.
    II.   An Alamanda is a shrub.

    determine which conclusion can be logically deduced.

    (A)   An Alamanda flowers.

    (B)   An Alamanda does not flower.

    (C)   An Alamanda is not a shrub.

    (D)   None of the above.

3. Given that:

    I.   No programmers are skiers.
    II.   All programmers are hikers.

determine which conclusion can be logically deduced.

(A)   All hikers are skiers.   (C)   No hikers are skiers.

(B)   All skiers are hikers.   (D)   None of the above.

VALIDITY OF ARGUMENTS

Four choices will be given, all with true conclusions. One of the conclusions, even though true, will not be justified by the premises. The objective is to identify the one invalid argument.

Example: All of the following arguments have true conclusions, but one of the arguments in not valid. Select the argument that is not valid.

(A)   All tomatoes are edible and all fruits are edible. Therefore, a tomato is a fruit.

(B)   All tomatoes are fruits and all fruits are edible. Therefore, a tomato is edible.

(C)   All tomatoes are red and all tomatoes are fruits. Therefore, some fruits are red.

(D)   All fruits are edible. A pine cone is not edible. Therefore, a pine cone is not a fruit.

Solution: Construct a Euler diagram for choice (A). Tomatoes (T) and fruits (F) are contained within the larger circle edible (E). We can see that the premises do not lead to the conclusion that a tomato is a fruit.

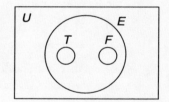

Thus, choice (A) is the correct choice.

Even though it is not necessary to continue, the other Euler diagrams will be constructed.

In choice (B), we have tomatoes (T) contained within the fruits (F) circle which in turn is contained within the edible (E) circle. (T) is contained within (E) and thus a valid argument.

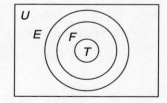

In choice (C), the red (R) circle and the fruit (F) circle must overlap since tomatoes (T) is in both. Thus, the conclusion is valid.

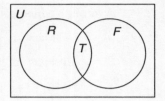

In choice (D) fruits (F) is contained within edible (E). The pine cone (P) is located outside E, and therefore, it is impossible for a pine cone to be a fruit. The conclusion is valid.

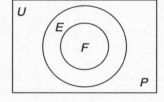

DRILL: VALIDITY OF ARGUMENTS

DIRECTIONS: Select the best answer.

1. All of the following arguments have true conclusions, but one of the arguments in not valid. Select the argument that is not valid.

    (A) All clowns have red noses and all people who cry a lot have red noses. Therefore, clowns cry a lot.

    (B) All circus performers are brave people and lion tamers are circus performers. Therefore, all lion tamers are brave people.

    (C) All acrobats have great balance. All acrobats are circus performers. Therefore, some circus performers have great balance.

    (D) All clowns have red noses. Mr. Samuals does not have a red nose. Therefore, Mr. Samuals is not a clown.

2. All of the following arguments have true conclusions, but one of the arguments in not valid. Select the argument that is not valid.

    (A) All Halloween masks are scary and all scary things cause nightmares. Therefore, Halloween masks cause nightmares.

    (B) All cats have green eyes. Felix is a cat. Therefore, Felix has green eyes.

    (C) All witches wear pointed hats. All witches ride on broom sticks. Therefore, some broomstick riders wear pointed hats.

    (D) All ghosts are scary. Franklin is not a ghost. Therefore, Franklin is not scary.

REASONING PATTERNS

The objective in this skill area is to identify a conclusion from the given premises to form a valid argument.

Expect to find such forms as follows:

Premises:	If p, then q	If p, then q	p or q	If p, then q
	p	$\sim q$	$\sim p$	If q, then r
Conclusion:	q	$\sim p$	q	If p, then r

Example: Select the conclusion that will make the following argument valid.

If you eat a candy apple, then you must brush your teeth.
If you brush your teeth, then you will not get cavities.

(A) If you do not eat a candy apple, then you will not get cavities.

(B) If you eat a candy apple, then you will not get cavities.

(C) If you do not eat a candy apple, then you will get cavities.

(D) If you brush your teeth, then you ate a candy apple.

Solution: p = you eat a candy apple.
q = you brush your teeth.
r = you will not get cavities.

The structure of the given is: If p, then q
                                 If q, then r

From the possibilities listed above, we see that a valid conclusion would be: If p, then r, which is choice (B).

Example: Select the conclusion that will make the following argument valid.

Sam is the pitcher or Joe is not the catcher.
Sam is not the pitcher.

(A) Joe is the catcher.

(B) Joe is not the catcher.

(C) Sam is the pitcher.

(D) If Sam is not the pitcher, then Joe is the catcher.

Solution: p = Sam is the pitcher.
q = Joe is not the catcher.

The structure of the given is: p or q
                                 $\sim p$

From the possibilities listed above, we see that a valid conclusion would be: q, which is choice (B).

DRILL: REASONING PATTERNS

DIRECTIONS: Select the best answer.

---

1.   Select the conclusion that will make the following argument valid.

If the computer is down, then I will not finish my project on time. The computer is down.

(A)   I will finish my project on time.

(B)   I will not finish my project on time.

(C)   If I do not finish my project on time, then the computer was down.

(D)   If I finish my project on time, then the computer was not down.

2.   Select the conclusion that will make the following argument valid.

If the lights are on, then I am home. I am not home.

(A)   If I am home, then the lights are on.

(B)   If I am home, then the lights are not on.

(C)   The lights are on.

(D)   The lights are not on.

DRAWING LOGICAL CONCLUSIONS BASED ON GIVEN FACTS

An argument, in the form of two to four premises, will be given. The objective is to select a logical conclusion from the given argument.

If the premises include the words "if, then," "and," or "or," generalize the statements into symbolic form, write the symbolic conclusion, and identify the appropriate conclusion from the given choices.

Example: Study the given information below. If a logical conclusion is given, select that conclusion. If none of the conclusions given is warranted, select the option expressing this condition.

If you go to the beach, you will get sun burnt. If you go to the museum, you will not get sun burnt. You go to the museum.

(A)   You will get sun burnt.

(B)   You will not get sun burnt.

(C) You will meet a friend at the museum.

(D) None of the above is warranted.

Solution: p = you go to the beach.
q = you will get sun burnt.
r = you go to the museum.
$\sim q$ = you will not get sun burnt.

Sentence 1:   If p, then q
Sentence 2:   If r, then $\sim q$
Sentence 3: r

From sentence 2 and part of 3, we see:

$$\begin{array}{l} \text{If } r, \text{ then } \sim q \\ \underline{\quad r \quad} \\ \hfill \sim q \end{array}$$

From which we can conclude: the correct response is (B).

If the premises include the words "all," "none," or "some," use Euler diagrams to arrive at a logical conclusion.

Example: Study the given information below. If a logical conclusion is given, select that conclusion. If none of the conclusions given is warranted, select the option expressing this condition.

All types of lettuces are vegetables. All types of cabbages are vegetables. All vegetables are edible. A kale is a hardy cabbage.

(A) Kale is a type of lettuce.

(B) Kale is not edible.

(C) Kale is an edible vegetable.

(D) Kale is a nonedible vegetable.

Solution: Construct a Euler diagram.

We have lettuce (L) and cabbage (C) contained within vegetables (V). Vegetables (V) is contained within edible (E). The "X" represents kale.

From the diagram, we can see that kale is not a lettuce but it is a cabbage, a vegetable, and edible.

Thus, the correct response is (C).

DRILL: DRAWING LOGICAL CONCLUSIONS BASED ON GIVEN FACTS

DIRECTIONS: Select the best answer.

---

1. Study the given information below. If a logical conclusion is given, select that conclusion. If none of the conclusions given is warranted, select the option expressing this condition.

    All engineers are successful. All scientists are successful. Robert is a scientist.

    (A) Robert is an engineer.

    (B) Robert is not successful.

    (C) Robert is successful.

    (D) None of the above is warranted.

2. Study the given information below. If a logical conclusion is given, select that conclusion. If none of the conclusions given is warranted, select the option expressing this condition.

    If I buy a new dress, then I will buy a matching belt. I bought a new dress or a new beach towel. I did not buy a new beach towel.

    (A) I bought a new beach towel.

    (B) I did not buy a new dress.

    (C) I bought a matching belt.

    (D) None of the above is warranted.

LOGICAL REASONING

ANSWER KEY

DRILL: VENN DIAGRAMS

1. **(C)**
2. **(C)**

DRILL: LOGICAL STATEMENTS

1.	**(D)**	4.	**(A)**	6.	**(C)**	8.	**(B)**
2.	**(B)**	5.	**(B)**	7.	**(A)**	9.	**(B)**
3.	**(A)**						

DRILL: DRAWING LOGICAL CONCLUSIONS FROM DATA

1. **(D)**   3. **(D)**
2. **(D)**

DRILL: VALIDITY OF ARGUMENTS

1. **(A)**
2. **(D)**

DRILL: REASONING PATTERNS

1. **(B)**
2. **(D)**

DRILL: DRAWING LOGICAL CONCLUSIONS BASED ON GIVEN FACTS

1. **(C)**
2. **(C)**

LOGICAL REASONING
DETAILED EXPLANATIONS OF ANSWERS

DRILL: VENN DIAGRAMS

1.　**(C)**　Since *B* is completely in *A*, any element which is a member of set *B* is also a member of set *A*.

2.　**(C)**　Since set *B* is contained in the universal set (set *U*), any element which is a member of set *B* is also a member of set *U*.

DRILL: LOGICAL STATEMENTS

1.　**(D)**　Let *p* = if I am hungry.
　　　　Let *q* = I will have a snack.
　　　　Then the original statement is: If *p*, then *q*.
　　　　The negation is: ⁓(if *p*, then *q*) = *p* and not *q*.

To negate a conditional: If *p*, then *q*, the result is *p* and not *q*. Therefore, the negation of the original statement is: "I am hungry and I will not have a snack."

2.　**(B)**　Let *p* = Sam is a baseball player.
　　　　Let *q* = Michael is a soccer player.
　　　　Then the original statement is: not *p* and *q*.
　　　　The negation is: ⁓(⁓*p* and *q*) = *p* or ⁓*q*.

The negation of the conjunction "*p* and *q*" is "not *p* or not *q*". Therefore the negation of the original statement is: "Sam is a baseball player or Michael is not a soccer player."

3.　**(A)**　Let *p* = jelly beans are sweet.
　　　　Let *q* = licorice is tart.
　　　　Then the original statement is: *p* or not *q*.
　　　　The negation is: ⁓(*p* or not *q*) = ⁓*p* and *q*.

To negate a disjunction "*p* or *q*," the result is "not *p* and not *q*." Therefore, the negation of the original statement is: "Jelly beans are not sweet and licorice is tart."

4. **(A)**   Let p = if the phone rings.
Let q = I will answer it.
Then the original statement is: $\sim$(If p, then q).
The negation is: p and $\sim q$.

The statement should read "The phone rings and I do not answer it."

5. **(B)**   Let p = the batteries are dead.
Let q = the calculator will work.
The original statement is: If p, then $\sim q$.
The contrapositive (which is the inverse of the converse) always has the same
    truth value as the original statement.
Therefore, the contrapositive is: If q, then $\sim p$.

The statement should read "If the calculator works, then the batteries are not dead."

6. **(C)**   Let p = swimming pools are round.
Let $\sim$(No p) = some are.
The negation of "No or None" is "some."
Therefore, the statement should read: "some swimming pools are round."

7. **(A)**   The negation of "some are pink" is: $\sim$(some are pink) = none are pink.
The negation of "some" is "none."

8. **(B)**   Let p = exercise is a waste of time.
Let q = exercise is too bothersome.
The negation of $\sim$(p or q) = $\sim p$ and $\sim q$.

9. **(B)**   Let p = baby girls can wear blue
Let $\sim(\sim p) = p$
The negation of a negation gives you back the original statement.

DRILL: DRAWING LOGICAL CONCLUSIONS FROM DATA

1. **(D)**   Mindy (A) is not eligible because she has only one reference. Jill (B) is not
eligible because she is older than 12. Bill (C) is not eligible because he did not pass the
class. This leaves (D), none are eligible, as the only choice.

2. **(D)**   Choices (A) and (B) cannot be logically deduced because only *some* shrubs
flower. Choice (C) cannot be logically deduced because it is a contradiction of statement
II "An Alamanda is a shrub." This leaves (D) as the correct answer.

3. **(D)**   Choices (A), (B), and (C) cannot be logically deduced because there is no
information connecting hikers with skiers. Choice (D) is therefore correct.

DRILL: VALIDITY OF ARGUMENTS

1.   **(A)**   There is no correlation between the two groups. You could be in one of the two groups without being in the other.

2.   **(D)**   It is possible for Franklin not to be a ghost and still be scary.

DRILL: REASONING PATTERNS

1.   **(B)**   I will not finish my project on time.

$$\text{If } p, \text{ then } q$$
$$\frac{p}{q}$$

2.   **(D)**   The lights are not on.

$$\text{If } p, \text{ then } q$$
$$\frac{\sim q}{\sim p}$$

DRILL: DRAWING LOGICAL CONCLUSIONS BASED ON GIVEN FACTS

1.   **(C)**   All engineers are successful. All scientists are successful. Robert is a scientist. Robert is successful.

2.   **(C)**   If I buy a new dress, then I will buy a matching belt. I bought a new dress or a new beach towel. I did not buy a new beach towel. I bought a matching belt.

Test 1

This test is also on CD-ROM in our special inter-active CLAST TEST*ware*®. It is highly recommended that you first take this exam on computer. You will then have the additional study features and benefits of timed conditions and instantaneous, accurate scoring. See page 5 for guidance on how to get the most out of our CLAST software.

ESSAY SECTION

ENGLISH LANGUAGE SKILLS SECTION

(You have 80 minutes to complete both the English Language and Reading Skills Sections.)

DIRECTIONS: From the given choices, select the word or phrase that best fits the context of the sentence.

---

1. Janice's friends find her _____ of constantly chewing gum annoying.

    (A) addiction

    (B) hobby

    (C) habit

2. In the late sixties, the _____ manner of the adult actress Goldie Hawn proved to be very appealing to audiences.

    (A) childish

    (B) childlike

    (C) infantile

DIRECTIONS: From the given choices, select the underlined portion which is not needed in the passage and mark its corresponding letter on your answer sheet.

---

3. In order to understand <u>fully</u> a written text, a student might need to reread it
    _A
    <u>again</u>. <u>Some</u> texts are difficult, and comprehension does not come easily the
    _B   _C
    first time around. Experts say<u>, however,</u> that the <u>increased</u> effort will pay off
    _D   _E
    in better understanding of the material.

    (A) fully

    (B) again

    (C) Some

    (D) , however,

    (E) increased

4. It was the <u>consensus of</u> opinion of all the volunteers that they <u>should</u> begin a
    A B
    <u>special</u> project to help the homeless with <u>everyday</u> problems of cleanliness,
    C D
    <u>health</u>, and nutrition.
    E

    (A) consensus of

    (B) should

    (C) special

    (D) everyday

    (E) health

DIRECTIONS: Select the sentence that clearly and effectively states the idea and has no structural errors.

---

5. (A) The shape of a swan, with its broad breast like the stern of a ship tapering to the rear, is superbly adapted to life in the water.

    (B) Superbly adapted to life in the water with its broad breast, the shape of the swan tapers to the rear.

    (C) The shape of the swan is superbly adapted to life in the water with its broad breast like the stern of a ship tapering to the rear.

6. (A) Being made of glass, Rick handled the tabletop carefully.

    (B) Because the tabletop was made of glass, Rick handled it carefully.

    (C) Rick handled the tabletop carefully, being made of glass.

7. (A) Thinking logically, organizing ideas coherently, and clear expression are the major ingredients of good writing.

    (B) To think logically, coherent organization, and clear expression are the major ingredients of good writing.

    (C) Logical thought, coherent organization, and clear expression are the major ingredients of good writing.

8. (A) There are times when one should keep his or her opinions to themselves.

    (B) There are times when people should keep their opinions to themselves.

    (C) There are times when they should keep their opinions to himself or herself.

DIRECTIONS: Select the option that best states the meaning of the underlined sentence.

---

9. I had been interested in my parents' piano for a couple of years when I finally took private lessons. <u>After I learned the piano keyboard, my playing improved a great deal, and I will soon give my first public performance.</u>

(A) After I learned the piano keyboard, my playing improved a great deal, and I will soon give my first public performance.

(B) I will soon give my first public performance because my playing improved a great deal after I learned the piano keyboard.

(C) My playing improved a great deal, and I will soon give my first public performance since I learned the piano keyboard.

(D) After my playing improved when I learned the keyboard, I will soon be giving my first public performance.

10. One of the most popular tourist destinations in the United States is Orlando, Florida. <u>Visitors may come for the theme parks, both Disney and Universal; the spectacular resorts, such as the Swan and the Dolphin; or for the fine local dining which attracts thousands of out-of-towners yearly.</u>

(A) Visitors may come for the theme parks, both Disney and Universal; the spectacular resorts, such as the Swan and the Dolphin; or for the fine local dining which attracts thousands of out-of-towners yearly.

(B) Thousands of out-of-towners yearly are attracted to the theme parks and the spectacular resorts: they come for Disney and Universal, the Swan and the Dolphin, and they come for the fine dining.

(C) Out-of-towners may come because they are attracted by the thousands to the Disney and Universal theme parks as well as the fine dining and spectacular resorts such as the Swan and the Dolphin.

(D) The theme parks, both Disney and Universal, the spectacular resorts, such as the Swan and the Dolphin, and the fine dining may attract thousands of out-of-towners yearly.

DIRECTIONS: Select the sentence that correctly and logically presents the comparison.

---

11. (A) Tanya is motivated as, if not more motivated than, Bob.

(B) Tanya is as motivated as, if not more motivated than, Bob.

(C) Tanya is as motivated, if not more motivated, than Bob.

12. (A) The desire to live longer is as strong as, if not stronger than, any other desire in motivating smokers to give up their habit.

    (B) The desire to live longer is as strong, if not stronger, than any desire in motivating smokers to give up their habit.

    (C) The desire to live longer is strong as, if not stronger than, any other desire in motivating smokers to give up their habit.

13. (A) Mount Everest is higher than any Asian mountain.

    (B) Mount Everest is the highest in Asia.

    (C) Mount Everest is higher than any other Asian mountain.

14. (A) The coach realized that the members of his softball team, who were shorter and slower, just weren't going to stand a chance against their opponents.

    (B) The coach realized that the members of his softball team, who were shorter and slower than the other team's players, just weren't going to stand a chance against their opponents.

    (C) The coach realized that the members of his softball team, who were shortest and slowest, just weren't going to stand a chance against their opponents.

DIRECTIONS: Select the correct response.

---

15. After he had <u>lied</u> in bed all morning, my brother decided he had better start studying for the upcoming test.

    (A) laid

    (B) lay

    (C) lain

    (D) No change is necessary.

16. He finally had to face the textbooks he had <u>laid</u> on his desk two days ago.

    (A) lay

    (B) lain

    (C) lied

    (D) No change is necessary.

DIRECTIONS: The passages that follow contain some errors, which might appear in the underlined part of the test questions. Read each passage and then answer each item by selecting the one that corrects the underlined mistake. Only one underlined mistake will come up in each item. If there is no error, select the "No change is necessary" option.

PASSAGE ONE

A century ago the typical family was an extended one with uncles, aunts, grandparents, parents, and children all under one roof but today's typical family is a nuclear one with parents and perhaps only one child. According to surveys and interviews, many young people today say that they want no children or that they wanted to postpone having a child until their late 30s or even 40s. More women work outside the home, aparantly because they choose to do so rather than because of necessity. Once a couple lives on two salaries, the partners become accustom to a higher income, and having children is put off until much later. If the couple later decide to have a child, they may find that their biological clocks have run down.

Some young people now put off marriage until much later than did their parents' generation. Between 1950 and 1970, the median age for a male to marry for the first time was about 23; by 1987 the median age for them was 26, almost as high as in 1890. Some choosing to stay single. With its increase in mature and financial security, one would think the current trend toward later marriages that include two-income partners would lower the divorce rate. The old saying that "money doesn't buy happiness" must still be true. Today, more than one out of five children live in a one-parent home, children are still the real losers in a divorce.

17. A century ago the typical family was an <u>extended one with</u> uncles, aunts,
      A
   <u>grandparents, parents,</u> and children all under <u>one roof but</u> today's typical
      BC
   family is a nuclear one with parents and perhaps only one child.

   (A) extended one, with

   (B) grandparents parents

   (C) one roof, but

   (D) No change is necessary.

18. According to surveys and interviews, many young people today say that they want no children or that they <u>wanted</u> to postpone having a child until their late 30s or even 40s.

   (A) want

(B) had wanted

(C) were wanting

(D) No change is necessary.

19. More women work outside the home, <u>aparantly</u> because they choose to do so rather than because of necessity.

    (A) appearantly

    (B) apparently

    (C) apearantly

    (D) No change is necessary.

20. Once a couple <u>lives</u> on two salaries, the partners become <u>accustom</u> to a higher
    A   B
    income, and having children <u>is</u> put off until much later.
    C

    (A) live

    (B) accustomed

    (C) are

    (D) No change is necessary.

21. Some young people now put off <u>marriage until</u> much <u>later than</u> did their
    A   B
    <u>parents'</u> generation.
    C

    (A) marriage, until

    (B) later, than

    (C) parent's

    (D) No change is necessary.

22. Between 1950 and 1970, the median age for a male to marry for the first time was

    <u>about 23; by 1987</u> the median age for <u>them</u> was <u>26, almost</u> as high as in 1890.
    A   B   C

    (A) about 23, by 1987

    (B) him

    (C) 26; almost

    (D) No change is necessary.

23. Some <u>choosing</u> to stay single.

    (A) choice

    (B) choose

    (C) chosing

    (D) No change is necessary.

24. With its increase in <u>mature</u> and financial <u>security, one</u> would think the current
    A   B

    trend toward later marriages that include two-income partners <u>would</u> lower
    C

    the divorce rate.

    (A) maturity

    (B) security one

    (C) would have

    (D) No change is necessary.

25. The old saying <u>that "money</u> doesn't buy <u>happiness</u>" must still be true.
    A, B   C

    (A) that "Money

    (B) that, "money

    (C) happiness,"

    (D) No change is necessary.

26. <u>Today</u> <u>more than</u> one out of five children live in a one-parent <u>home, children</u>
    A   B   C

    are still the real losers in a divorce.

    (A) Today's

    (B) more of

    (C) home. Children

    (D) No change is necessary.

PASSAGE TWO

Modern technology have enabled scientists to learn a great deal about the human brain. Using the most modern equipment, researchers have discovered a great deal of information. About how we learn, about how the brain affects the way we feel, about memory, and about the aging of the brain. Contrary to popular opinion intelligence is determined not by the size of the brain but by the number of and the complexity of dendrites in the brain. These dendrites form connections with nerve cells; thus enabling the brain to receive and use information. Researchers estimate that the human brain functions at only a fraction of their potential. Having lost a portion of the brain to injury or illness, some people are able to function quite effective. Acting as a producer of chemicals, the brain produces and secretes substances which affect intelligence, mood, and remembering information. Because brain function deteriorates with age, some people believe that peoples' ability to learn also declines with age. However, older people who engage in intellectual activity or regularly pursue a learning activity, according to recent studies, actually show little or no loss of learning ability. Therefore, to keep the brain functioning well for a lifetime, a person should continue to learn new things and be involved in stimulating activities.

27. Modern <u>technology</u> <u>have</u> enabled scientists <u>to learn</u> a great deal about the
        A   B   C
   human brain.

   (A) tecnology

   (B) has

   (C) in learning

   (D) No change is necessary.

28. Using the most modern <u>equipment,</u> researchers have discovered a great deal
                           A
   of <u>information. About</u> how we learn, about how the brain affects the way we
               B
   <u>feel, about</u> memory, and about the aging of the brain.
   C

   (A) equiptment

   (B) information about

   (C) feel about

   (D) No change is necessary.

29. Contrary to popular <u>opinion</u> <u>intelligence</u> is determined not by the size of the
                     A   B
   <u>brain but</u> by the number of and the complexity of dendrites in the brain.
   C

   (A) opinion, intelligence

   (B) opinion; intelligence

   (C) brain, but

   (D) No change is necessary.

30. These dendrites form connections with nerve <u>cells; thus</u> enabling the brain to
    A, B
    <u>receive</u> and use information.
    C

    (A) cells thus

    (B) cells, thus

    (C) recieve

    (D) No change is necessary.

31. Researchers <u>estimate</u> that the human brain functions <u>at</u> only a fraction of <u>their</u>
    A   B   C
    potential.

    (A) estimating

    (B) by

    (C) its

    (D) No change is necessary.

32. Having <u>lost a</u> portion of the brain to injury or <u>illness, some</u> people are able to
    A   B
    function quite <u>effective</u>.
    C

    (A) lost, a

    (B) illness some

    (C) effectively

    (D) No change is necessary.

33. Acting as a producer of chemicals, the brain produces and secretes substances
    which <u>affect</u> intelligence, mood, and <u>remembering information.</u>
    A,B   C

    (A) effect

    (B) affects

    (C) memory

    (D) No change is necessary.

34. Because brain function deteriorates with <u>age, some</u> people believe that <u>peoples'</u>
    A   B
    ability to learn also <u>declines</u> with age.
    C

    (A) age; some

    (B) people's

(C) declined

(D) No change is necessary.

35. However, older people who engage in intellectual activity or regularly pursue a learning <u>activity, according</u> to recent studies, actually <u>show</u> little or no loss
     A, B   C
     of learning ability.

    (A) activity according

    (B) activity. According

    (C) shows

    (D) No change is necessary.

36. Therefore, to keep the brain functioning <u>well</u> for a <u>lifetime,</u> a person should
     A   B
     continue to learn new <u>things, and</u> be involved in stimulating activities.
     C

    (A) good

    (B) lifetime;

    (C) things and

    (D) No change is necessary.

DIRECTIONS: Select the correct response.

---

37. Our muscles were tired and <u>sore, nevertheless</u> we kept on jogging.

    (A) sore, nevertheless;

    (B) sore; nevertheless,

    (C) sore. Nevertheless;

    (D) No change is necessary.

38. At the meeting were four persons: Mr. Thomas, the owner and general manager; a referee; the coach, a former star player; and the current trainer of the team.

    (A) Mr. Thomas, the owner, and general manager, a referee, the coach, a former star player, and the current trainer of the team.

    (B) Mr. Thomas, the owner and general manager; a referee; the coach; a former star player; and the current trainer of the team.

(C) Mr. Thomas, the owner and general manager, a referee, the coach a former star player and the current trainer of the team.

(D) No change is necessary.

39. Although the police investigated the murder for months they had no suspects.

(A) Although the police investigated the murder for months, they had no suspects.

(B) Although the police investigated the murder for months. They had no suspects.

(C) Although, the police investigated the murder for months, they had no suspects.

(D) No change is necessary.

40. Tours to England feature stops <u>such as: London,</u> Liverpool, and Stratford-on-Avon.

(A) such as, London,

(B) such as the following: London

(C) such as; London

(D) No change is necessary.

READING SKILLS SECTION

DIRECTIONS: Read the following passage and then choose the best response for each question.

Being born female and black were two handicaps Gwendolyn Brooks states that she faced from her birth, in 1917, in Kansas. Brooks was determined to succeed. Despite the lack of encouragement she received from her teachers and others, she was determined to write and found the first publisher for one of her poems when she was eleven.

In 1945 she marketed and sold her first book; national recognition ensued. She applied for and received grants and fellowships from such organizations as the American Academy of Arts and Letters and the Guggenheim Foundation. Later she received the Pulitzer Prize for Poetry; she was the first black woman to receive such an honor.

Brooks was an integrationist in the 1940s and an advocate of black consciousness in the 1960s. Her writing styles show that she is not bound by rules; her works are not devoid of the truth, even about sensitive subjects like the black experience, life in the ghetto, and city life.

Brooks' reaction to fame is atypical. She continues to work—and work hard. She writes, travels, and helps many who are interested in writing. Especially important to her is increasing her knowledge of her black heritage and encouraging other people to do the same. She encourages dedication to the art to would-be writers.

1. The author's primary purpose in writing this passage is to

   (A) describe Gwendolyn Brooks' writing style and her place in American literature in relation to other writers.

   (B) summarize Gwendolyn Brooks' life as an example of dedication and hard work.

   (C) persuade the reader that Gwendolyn Brooks is one of the twentieth century's greatest poets.

   (D) demonstrate that hard work is always rewarded by success.

2. What is the relationship between the sentence beginning on line 15 ("She continues to work—and work hard") and the previous sentence ("Brooks' reaction...")?

   (A) Cause and effect

   (B) Comparison and contrast

(C) Clarification

(D) Addition

3. The passage suggests that Brooks received less credit than she deserved primarily because

    (A) she tried to publish too early in her career.

    (B) she was aided by funds received through grants.

    (C) she was a frequent victim of racial and gender discrimination.

    (D) her work was too complex to be of widespread interest to others.

DIRECTIONS: Read the following dialogue and then answer the question based on its content.

Martin: Eventually, the resources of Earth will be exhausted, the air will be too polluted to breathe, the water to drink, the soil to raise edible crops. If mankind is to survive, then, it must be on another planet. So, we must begin now to develop the means to travel to and live on other planets in large numbers.

George: Nonsense. The crude rockets and habitat equipment we have could never be used to move and support more than very small expeditions to even a very near planet. Nor do we need more, since careful pollution control rules already in force or soon to be enacted will keep acceptable environmental quality for centuries.

4. George misses Martin's point primarily because of

    (A) a different assessment of the quality of present space program equipment.

    (B) a different evaluation of the effects of environmental pollution.

    (C) a different understanding of the time frame involved.

    (D) a different expectation of the effectiveness of anti-pollution legislation.

    (E) a different commitment to human survival.

DIRECTIONS: Read the following passage and then choose the best response for each question.

A cave is a natural opening in the ground extending beyond the zone of light and large enough to permit the entry of man. Occurring in a wide variety of rock types and caused by widely differing geologic processes, caves range in size from single small rooms to interconnecting passages many miles long. The scientific study of caves is called speleology (from the Greek words *spelaion* for cave and *logos* for study). It is a composite science based on geology, hydrology, biology, and archaeology, and thus holds special interest for earth scientists of the U.S. Geological Survey.

Caves have been natural attractions since prehistoric times. Prolific evidence of early man's interest has been discovered in caves scattered throughout the world. Fragments of skeletons of some of the earliest manlike creatures (Austra-lopithecines) have been discovered in cave deposits in South Africa, and the first evidence of primitive Neanderthal man was found in a cave in the Neander Valley of Germany. Cro-Magnon man created his remarkable murals on the walls of caves in southern France and northern Spain where he took refuge more than 10,000 years ago during the chill of the Ice Age.

5. The author's primary purpose in writing this passage is to

   (A) describe the natural forces that cause the formation of caves.

   (B) explain the origin of the term "speleology."

   (C) tell what caves are and that they have interested man from early times.

   (D) show how man's discovery of caves led to the creation of artworks.

6. What is the relationship between the sentence beginning on line 9 ("Prolific evidence...") and the sentence beginning on line 11 ("Fragments of skeletons... ")?

   (A) Generalization and example

   (B) Cause and effect

   (C) Clarification

   (D) Comparison and contrast

7. The passage suggests that

   (A) the opening of a cave must be large enough to admit man.

   (B) not all openings into the earth are classified as caves.

   (C) caves must be a natural opening in the ground.

   (D) caves must extend beyond the zone of light.

> **DIRECTIONS:** Words have been deleted from the following passage. Select the word or phrase that best completes each blank.

Wading through the mud of a political campaign can be a tedious and messy affair. Frequently, issues become buried under a landslide of name-calling and personal attacks, innuendoes, and allegations. The most frequently used fallacy in political campaigns is an attack on the opponent's personality. Attempting to discredit the opponent's views by attacking his or her character is known as the *ad hominem* fallacy, literally, a Latin phrase, "to the man."

Casting aspersions can divert voters from the facts of the case. ____(8)____ if one of the major issues of a campaign year is inflation, voters might hear how a legislator is so rich and has so many tax shelters that he pays less taxes than the average American. The implication, ____(9)____ is that the legislator is dishonest, or, at the very least, uncaring about the concerns of his potential constituents. A politician who has proved to have a conflict of interests in awarding a lucrative government contract to a previous business partner should be challenged when another government contract is going to be awarded. ____(10)____ a past record of dishonesty does not preclude honesty now or in the future. Also, politicians are only human, and it is to be expected that some will have personal problems. Will these problems affect their record of public service? Do we really need to know all the faults of each public figure running for political office?

8. (A) Instead,

   (B) Eventually,

   (C) Meanwhile,

   (D) For example,

9. (A) of course,

   (B) however,

   (C) as a result,

   (D) finally,

10. (A) Therefore,

    (B) In conclusion,

    (C) However,

    (D) Consequently,

> **DIRECTIONS:** Read the following passage and then choose the best response for each question.

The torpedo is a self-propelled underwater weapon having either a high-explosive or a nuclear warhead. Conventional warheads are loaded with up to 1,000 pounds of HBX explosive.

Underwater explosion of the torpedo warhead increases its destructive effect.
5 When a projectile explodes, a part of its force is absorbed by the surrounding air. Upon explosion of the torpedo warhead, the water transfers almost the full force of the explosion to the hull of the target ship.

Fleet-type and Guppy submarines are fitted with 10 tubes, 6 in the bow and 4 in the stem. Spare torpedoes are carried in ready racks near the tubes. On war
10 patrol, a submarine of this type usually puts to sea with a load of 28 torpedoes aboard.

Torpedoes are propelled by gas turbines or electric motors. Turbine types have maximum speeds of 30 to 45 knots, with a maximum effective range of as much as 7$^1/_2$ miles. Electric torpedoes usually have less speed and range than
15 turbine types, but from the submariners' point of view, they have the advantage of leaving no visible wake.

11. The author's primary purpose in writing this passage is to

    (A) explain what a torpedo is and how it works.

    (B) compare the Fleet-type and Guppy submarines.

    (C) warn the reader about the terrible destructive power of torpedoes.

    (D) explain the difference between turbine-powered and electric-powered torpedoes.

12. What is the relationship between the sentence beginning on line 5 ("When a projectile explodes...") and the sentence beginning on line 4 ("Underwater explosion...")?

    (A) Cause and effect

    (B) Comparison and contrast

    (C) Clarification

    (D) Addition

13. The passage suggests that, since the torpedo is "self-propelled,"

    (A) it is also capable of steering itself after it is fired.

    (B) the turbine or electric motor must be part of the torpedo.

(C) it can inflict greater damage on a moving target.

(D) it uses much less energy than an external power source.

DIRECTIONS: Words have been deleted from the following passage. Select the word or phrase that best completes each blank.

Consumers who believe a company is well run and shows promise of doing well in the stock market will invest in that company's stock. If the company shows a profit, the investor will receive a dividend check. Buying United States Savings Bonds is another well-known way of investing money. Some companies offer a dividend reinvestment plan: the profits, instead of being sent to the investor in the form of a check, can be reinvested automatically in the company's stock. To encourage this practice, companies offer several incentives. _____(14)_____, if the dividend is too small to buy a whole share, most companies allow the investor to purchase part of a share until enough dividends accumulate for a whole share. _____(15)_____, some companies offer shareholders a discount off the market price of their stock. A five percent discount is the usual rate. _____(16)_____, about 70 percent of companies charge no fee if the stockholder wishes to purchase more shares for cash.

14. (A) Although

    (B) Eventually

    (C) For example

    (D) In other words

15. (A) In addition

    (B) On the whole

    (C) First

    (D) As a result

16. (A) In contrast

    (B) Finally

    (C) Second

    (D) Later

DIRECTIONS: Read the following passage and then choose the best response for each question.

It seems to me a perfectly natural feeling that the humanities are a luxury, that they do not help to solve economic problems or to create jobs or to build better mousetraps. The only production that they seem to increase is the production of worth. What good are philosophy or history, language or literature to practical men who need practical skills and practical answers to difficult questions?

That sort of point of view makes a lot of sense until you think that without the humanities, we wouldn't have either the Constitution or the Bill of Rights or any recollection of them and how and why this country was made; we would not have a common language; we would not know any other language in which to communicate with other people; and we would scarcely have a body of ideology or information about what we think of ourselves, what we think about life or the world, our place in them, our purpose in them, in other words about religion or law or social life, or about what others besides us think about these matters.

The humanities are about man, about what man has done, and he's done a lot of terrible things but, also, extraordinary and wonderful things, and they're also about what a man could do and, perhaps, what he should and should not do.

Now, it's something to be able to say that we have done that which no other animal could have done, but it is something more to say that some of us have refused to do what the animal in us wanted to do and that we seek to find that which is specifically human wherever it may have been forgotten or denied or crushed.

These are the things that I submit that make a culture, and culture is what the humanities are about. Without the culture, I don't think that you can have a civilized society, let alone a nation. If that is so, then the humanities are not a superfluous set of games that a few scholars play. They are not luxuries. They are essential disciplines, indispensable to our common life in this country and to planning and ordering our activities beyond this country.

17. The author's primary purpose in writing this passage is to

   (A) explain why he or she feels that the humanities are a luxury.

   (B) examine the origins of the Constitution and the Bill of Rights.

   (C) point out that the practical, problem-solving skills are what counts.

   (D) explain and defend the value of the humanities.

18. What is the relationship between the sentence beginning on line 4 ("What good are...") and the sentence beginning on line 7 ("That sort of point of

view...")?

(A) Cause and effect

(B) Comparison and contrast

(C) Clarification

(D) Addition

19. The passage suggests that the actions of man are based upon

(A) access to technology.

(B) animal instincts.

(C) knowledge of himself.

(D) the Bill of Rights.

DIRECTIONS: Read the following statements and then answer the question based on the information provided.

There are students, as well as faculty, who are active in campus politics. All who are active in campus politics are encouraged to join the University Governing Board.

20. If the statements above are true, which of the following must also be true?

(A) All who are encouraged to join the University Governing Board are active in campus politics.

(B) All who are encouraged to join the University Governing Board are faculty or students.

(C) Some who are encouraged to join the University Governing Board are not students or faculty.

(D) Some students are encouraged to join the University Governing Board.

(E) Some students are not encouraged to join the University Governing Board.

DIRECTIONS: Read the following passage and then choose the best response for each question.

I trembled excessively; I could not endure to think of, and far less to allude to, the occurrences of the preceding night. I walked with a quick pace, and we soon

arrived at my college. I then reflected, and the thought made me shiver, that the creature whom I had left in my apartment might still be there, alive and walking
5 about. I dreaded to behold this monster, but I feared still more that Henry should see him. Entreating him, therefore, to remain a few minutes at the bottom of the stairs, I darted up towards my own room. My hand was already on the lock of the door before I recollected myself. I then paused, and a cold shivering came over me. I threw the door forcibly open, as children are accustomed to do when they expect
10 a spectre to stand in waiting for them on the other side; but nothing appeared. I stepped fearfully in; the apartment was empty, and my bedroom was also freed from its hideous guest. I could hardly believe that so great a good fortune could have befallen me, but when I became assured that my enemy had indeed fled, I clapped my hands for joy and ran down to Clerval.

21. The author's primary purpose in writing this passage is to

    (A) persuade us that monsters are only imaginary beings and are not to be feared.

    (B) argue that it is better to share our fears with others than keep them to ourselves.

    (C) convey what happened to the narrator and describe the narrator's state of mind.

    (D) examine the arguments for and against the existence of monsters.

22. What is the relationship between the sentence beginning on line 5 ("I dreaded to behold this monster...") and the sentence beginning on line 6 ("Entreating him...")?

    (A) Cause and effect

    (B) Comparison and contrast

    (C) Clarification

    (D) Addition

23. The passage suggests that the narrator had left his apartment earlier

    (A) in a timorous state.

    (B) in a state of disbelief.

    (C) in a state of panic.

    (D) in a state of resoluteness.

> **DIRECTIONS:** Words have been deleted from the following passage. Select the word or phrase that best completes each blank.

It is important for a teacher to select appropriate reading materials for students in the classroom. Because students vary widely in their ability to read, the first step should be to assess each child's reading level and assign reading material appropriately. Teachers who instruct from materials above the child's reading level are significantly decreasing that child's chance at educational success. The child who reads at a first grade level will have difficulty with a book on the third grade level. Even if the child reading at the second grade level enjoys and even appreciates stories from a sixth grade reader, _____(24)_____ he or she will likely learn few skills and the child's reading will not be facilitated by being far below grade level in the reading text.

Unfortunately, it is a problem which is difficult to correct. _____(25)_____ a teacher may be well aware of the child's specific reading level, finding a book appropriate for their level may pose some difficulties. Textbook publishers sometimes include materials from varied reading levels within the same text. _____(26)_____, two books designated for the same grade level, because of non-standard labeling procedures, may vary widely in reading difficulty.

24. (A) eventually

    (B) for example,

    (C) of course,

    (D) in short

25. (A) In addition,

    (B) As a result,

    (C) In spite of this,

    (D) Even though,

26. (A) Also

    (B) However

    (C) For example

    (D) In conclusion

DIRECTION: Read the following passage and then choose the best response for each question.

The atmosphere is the medium in which air pollutants are emitted and transported from the source to the receptor. Although this sounds simple on the surface, it is perhaps the most complex and least understood facet of air pollution. Many variables influence the character of a given chemical species from the time
5 it leaves the source until it reaches the receptor. A few examples will suffice to illustrate the complexity of the situation.

First, consider emission. Pollutants can be emitted from a point source such as a power plant, a line source such as a highway, or an area source such as a city or large industrial complex. The emission point may be close to the ground (e.g.,
10 the tailpipe of a car) or over a thousand feet in height (e.g., high stacks of a power plant). Thus, elevation alone has a tremendous influence on how rapidly the pollutant will be <u>dispersed</u> and diluted before it reaches a receptor. The relative size of the pollution source is an obvious variable. Time of emission is important because meteorological conditions vary throughout the day. The atmosphere is
15 more stable at night, and less dilution occurs then. During the day, sunlight plays an important part in transforming the chemical species of pollutants.

Second, consider the transport phenomenon. Many attempts have been made to characterize the vertical and horizontal dispersion of pollution from point and line sources. Many mathematical equations and models have been developed. Each
20 has deficiencies because of the variability of sources, source strength, topography, and other factors. From the receptor standpoint, this is the important phase because, if the pollutants are not adequately dispersed and diluted, atmospheric insults will occur.

There are many factors to consider and it should be kept in mind that a nearby
25 source does not necessarily imply that damage will result.

27. On line 12, the word <u>dispersed</u> means

   (A) sent off in various directions.

   (B) poured into a container.

   (C) cleansed.

   (D) deprived of power.

28. The main idea expressed in this passage is that

   (A) the atmosphere is the medium in which air pollutants are emitted and transported.

   (B) scientists have a high degree of accuracy when calculating the pollutant dispersion.

(C) a nearby pollutant source may be an indication that change will result.

(D) there are many alternatives that influence the character of pollutants.

29. The sentence beginning on line 14 ("The atmosphere is more stable at night...") is a statement of

    (A) fact.

    (B) opinion.

30. The author uses the examples of a car's tailpipe and high stacks of a power plant (lines 10-11) to illustrate which point?

    (A) Human beings are doing more to pollute the air than any other creatures.

    (B) Various chemicals react differently with the chemicals in the atmosphere.

    (C) Sunlight plays an important part in transforming certain pollutants.

    (D) Elevation has a tremendous influence on how rapidly the pollutant will be dispersed and diluted.

DIRECTIONS: Read the following statements and then answer the question based upon them.

I love you. Therefore, I am a lover. All the world loves a lover. Therefore, you love me.

31. In terms of its logical structure, the argument above most closely resembles which of the following?

    (A) Adam is a man. Men are homo sapiens. Therefore, Adam is a homo sapien. Homo sapiens are rational. Therefore, Adam is rational.

    (B) Sam got to work on time yesterday, the day before, and for the last 50 working days. Therefore, Sam is dependable. Dependable people get raises. Therefore, Sam will get a raise.

    (C) I like to talk to Pete. Therefore, I am a patient person. Everyone likes to talk to patient people. Therefore, Pete likes to talk to me.

    (D) An orderly universe had to be created by a rational God. The universe is orderly. Therefore, God is rational. A rational God would not allow sin to go unpunished. You sinned. Therefore, you will be punished.

    (E) Lifting weights strengthens the body. You lift weights, therefore you are strong. Strong people are happy. Therefore, you are happy.

DIRECTIONS: Read the following passage and then choose the best response for each question.

We believe that our Earth is about 4.6 billion years old. At present we are forced to look to other bodies in the solar system for hints as to what the early history of the Earth was like. Studies of our Moon, Mercury, Mars, and the large satellites of Jupiter and Saturn have provided <u>ample</u> evidence that all of these
5 objects were bombarded by bodies with a wide variety of sizes shortly after they had formed. This same bombardment must have affected the Earth as well. The lunar record indicates that the rate of impacts decreased to its present low level about 4 billion years ago. On the Earth, subsequent erosion and crustal motions have obliterated the craters that must have formed during this epoch. Since it is generally
10 believed that life on Earth began during this period, the bombardment must have been part of the environment within which this event occurred.

32. On line 4, the word <u>ample</u> means

(A) ambiguous.

(B) sufficient.

(C) scant.

(D) interesting.

33. The main idea expressed in this passage is that

(A) the Earth is an old body having its beginning about 4.6 billion years ago.

(B) during its early history, the Earth was bombarded by bodies.

(C) Mercury, Mars, Jupiter, and Saturn were in place before Earth.

(D) it is because of the Earth's atmosphere that it shows no aftereffects of the bombardment.

34. The statement beginning on line 9 ("Since it is generally believed...") is a statement of

(A) fact.

(B) opinion.

35. The author mentions our Moon, Mercury, and Mars (line 3) to illustrate which point?

(A) Unlike the Earth, these heavenly bodies were heavily bombarded.

(B) The Earth is much older than any of these heavenly bodies.

(C) By studying these heavenly bodies, we find clues to Earth's history.

(D) The rate of impacts on these heavenly bodies was greater than on Earth.

DIRECTIONS: Read the following passage and then choose the best response for each question.

Life in colonial times was harsh, and the refinements of the mother country were ordinarily lacking. The colonists, however, soon began to mold their English culture into the fresh environment of a new land. The influence of religion permeated the entire way of life. In most Southern colonies, the Anglican church
5 was the legally established church. In New England, the Puritans were dominant; and, in Pennsylvania, the Quakers. Especially in the New England colonies, the local or village church was the hub of community life; the authorities strictly enforced the Sabbath and sometimes banished nonbelievers and dissenters.

Unfortunately, the same sort of religious intolerance, bigotry, and superstition
10 associated with the age of the Reformation in Europe also prevailed in some of the colonies, though on a lesser scale. In the last half of the seventeenth century, during <u>sporadic</u> outbreaks of religious fanaticism and hysteria, Massachusetts and Connecticut authorities tried and hanged a few women as "witches." Early in the seventeenth century, some other witchcraft persecution occurred in Virginia,
15 North Carolina, and Rhode Island. As the decades passed, however, religious toleration developed in the colonies.

Because of the strong religious influence in the colonies, especially in New England, religious instruction and Bible reading played an important part in education. In Massachusetts, for example, the law of 1645 required each commu-
20 nity with 50 households to establish an elementary school. Two years later the same colony passed the "Deluder Satan" law which required each town of 100 families to maintain a grammar school for the purpose of providing religious, as well as general, instruction. In the Southern colonies, only a few privately endowed free schools existed. Private tutors instructed the sons of well-to-do planters, who
25 completed their educations in English universities. Young males in poor families throughout the colonies were ordinarily apprenticed for vocational education.

By 1700, two colleges had been founded: Harvard, established by the Massachusetts Legislature in 1636; and William and Mary, in Virginia, which originated in 1693 under a royal charter. Other cultural activities before 1700 were
30 limited. The few literary products of the colonists, mostly historical narratives, journals, sermons, and some poetry, were printed in England. The *Bay Psalm Book* (1640) was the first book printed in the colonies. Artists and composers were few, and their output was of a relatively simple character.

36. On line 12, the word <u>sporadic</u> means

(A) violent. (B) unfortunate.

(C) occasional.   (D) constant.

37. The main idea expressed in this passage is that

    (A) religious toleration was virtually unknown in the American colonies.

    (B) the American colonists brought their English religion and culture with them and gradually developed them in the new land.

    (C) although the colonists managed to found two colleges before 1700, they did not produce any literature of lasting value.

    (D) when the colonists settled in America, they left behind once and for all the culture and religion of their mother country, England.

38. The sentence beginning on line 23 ("In the Southern colonies, only a few privately endowed free schools existed.") is a statement of

    (A) fact.   (B) opinion.

39. The author mentions the *Bay Psalm Book* in line 31 as an example of

    (A) the many fine literary works produced in the colonies.

    (B) the very few books printed in the colonies.

    (C) the kind of religious intolerance practiced in the colonies.

    (D) the superiority of colonial works to English work.

40. The sentence beginning on line 29 ("Other cultural activities before 1700 were limited.") is a statement of

    (A) fact.   (B) opinion.

DIRECTIONS: Select the word or phrase which identifies best the relationship between the sentence parts.

---

41. Although the bill was hotly debated, Congress passed the measure almost unanimously.

    (A) Cause and effect

    (B) Contrast

    (C) Example

    (D) Spatial order

MATHEMATICS SECTION

(You have 90 minutes to complete this section.)

DIRECTIONS: Select the best answer.

---

1. $-3/5 + 4 =$

   (A) $3\,2/5$

   (B) $4\,3/5$

   (C) $-2\,2/5$

   (D) $-3\,3/5$

2. $(-7) \div (-2/3) =$

   (A) $4\,2/3$

   (B) $10\,1/2$

   (C) $7\,2/3$

   (D) $-4\,2/3$

3. $-7.4 - (-3.286) =$

   (A) -4.114

   (B) 10.686

   (C) 4.114

   (D) -3.212

4. $3.75 \times (-0.6) =$

   (A) -0.225

   (B) 2.25

   (C) -2.25

   (D) -22.5

5. If 16 is increased to 28, what is the percent increase?

   (A) 1.75%

   (B) 57%

   (C) 43%

   (D) 75%

6. 60% of what number is 72?

   (A) 43.2

   (B) 83.3

   (C) 132

   (D) 120

7. $(3^2)(5^3) =$

   (A) $(3 \times 2)(5 \times 3)$

   (B) $(3 \times 3)(5 \times 5 \times 5)$

   (C) $(3 \times 5)^{2 \times 3}$

   (D) $(3 + 3)(5 + 5 + 5)$

8. Select the place value associated with the underlined digit.
   63.7<u>0</u>4

   (A) $1/10^1$

   (B) 10^2

   (C) $1/10^0$

   (D) $1/10^2$

9. 625% =

(A) 0.625   (C) 62.5

(B) 6.25   (D) 62,500

10. Choose the symbol to place in the box which makes the following statement true.

$$\frac{2}{13} \quad \square \quad \frac{1}{7}$$

(A) =   (C) <

(B) >   (D) ≤

11. A produce company shipped 55 boxes of oranges from distribution. The lightest box weighed four pounds and the heaviest box weighed 25 pounds. What is a reasonable estimate of the total weight of the shipment?

(A) 200 pounds   (C) 1,372 pounds

(B) 1,100 pounds   (D) 1,500 pounds

12. Determine the missing term in the following sequence.
    −3, −1, 2, 6, 11, __

(A) 17   (C) 15

(B) 16   (D) 33

13. Two families rented camping equipment for a ten-day vacation. The weekly rate for the equipment was $150 and $25 for each additional day. If the costs were shared equally by each family, how much was spent per family on the rental of the equipment?

(A) $87.50   (C) $175.00

(B) $112.50   (D) $225.00

14. On an average, Indiana has 18 sunny days of 30 during the month of November. This past year, the weather service reported that the state received only 22% of what is normal. Indiana had how many sunny days in the month of November?

(A) 4 days   (C) 7 days

(B) 6 days   (D) 13 days

15. Round 484.67 liters to the nearest ten liters.

    (A) 484.7 liters   (C) 485 liters

    (B) 480 liters   (D) 490 liters

16. What is the distance around this pentagon in centimeters?

    (A) 24 cm

    (B) 240 cm

    (C) .24 cm

    (D) 2,400 cm

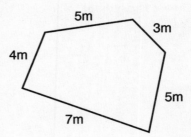

17. What is the area of a circular region whose radius is 5 inches?

    (A) 5π sq. in.   (C) 10π sq. in.

    (B) 25π sq. in.   (D) 100π sq. in.

18. What is the volume of a rectangular solid that is 3 centimeters long, 6 centimeters wide, and 2 centimeters high?

    (A) 30 sq. cm.   (C) 11 cubic cm.

    (B) 36 sq. cm.   (D) 36 cubic cm.

19. Given that lines l_1 and l_2 are parallel, examine the figure and determine which of the following statements is true.

    (A) $m\angle A = m\angle C$

    (B) $m\angle E + m\angle F = 180°$

    (C) $m\angle B = m\angle D$

    (D) $\angle B$ is complementary to $\angle C$.

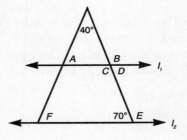

20. What type of triangle is $\triangle ABC$?

    (A) Right triangle

    (B) Equilateral triangle

    (C) Isosceles triangle

    (D) Obtuse triangle

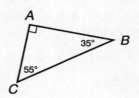

21. Which of the statements is true for the pictured triangle?

    (A) $\dfrac{BD}{DC} = \dfrac{AE}{EC}$

    (B) $\dfrac{DC}{BC} = \dfrac{EC}{AC}$

    (C) $\angle ABC$ is a right angle.

    (D) $m\angle ABC \neq m\angle EDC$

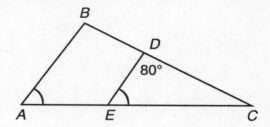

22. Which unit of measure would be appropriate for the amount of gift wrap needed to cover a present?

    (A) Cubic centimeters   (C) Linear feet

    (B) Square centimeters   (D) Liters

23. Study the diagram which contains the individual sides of the rectangular solid shown on the right. Then select the formula for calculating the total surface area (SA) of the rectangular solid.

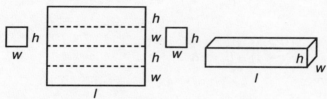

    (A) SA = $l(2 \times w + 2 \times h) + 2(w \times h)$

    (B) SA = $(2 \times l \times w) + (4 \times l \times h)$

    (C) SA = $l \times w \times h$

    (D) SA = $(l \times w) + (l \times h) + (w \times h)$

24. A 10 feet by 15 feet rectangular pool is 6 feet deep. If water costs $0.005 per cubic foot, what is the cost of filling the swimming pool?

    (A) $0.75   (C) $18.00

    (B) $4.50   (D) $45.00

25. $3.4\pi + 2 - 2\pi =$

    (A) 4.4π (C) $1.4\pi + 2$

    (B) 3.4π (D) $3.2\pi + 2$

26. $\sqrt{10} \times \sqrt{5} =$

    (A) $5\sqrt{2}$ (C) $2\sqrt{10}$

    (B) $\sqrt{15}$ (D) $2\sqrt{5}$

27. $1/2 + 5/2 \, (2r)^2 \div 2 =$
    (A) $6r^2$ (C) $0.5 + 5r^2$
    (B) $0.5 + 2.5r^2$ (D) $5.5r^2$

28. $(5.4 \times 10^3) \div (1.8 \times 10^{-2}) =$
    (A) 300,000   (C) 5,220
    (B) 30   (D) .000003

29. If $4(2x - 1) = 5x$, then
    (A) $x = 1/3.$ (C) $x = 4/3.$
    (B) $x = -1/3.$ (D) $x = -4/3.$

30. If $4(x + 5) - 3(2x - 1) \leq 0$, then
    (A) $x \geq 23/2.$ (C) $x \leq 23/2.$
    (B) $x \geq 2.$ (D) $x \geq 17/2.$

31. The formula for finding the distance (d) a moving object covers in a certain amount of time (t) is: $d = 1/2 \, at^2$. What is the distance covered by a falling ball with an acceleration (a) of 32 feet/sec^2 at a time (t) of 3 seconds?
    (A) 192 feet   (C) 1,536 feet
    (B) 21.3 feet   (D) 144 feet

32. Given $f(x) = 3x^2 - 2x + 4$, find $f(-2)$.
    (A) 20   (C) 12
    (B) 44   (D) -4

33. Which is a linear factor of the following expression:
    $2x^2 + x - 3$?
    (A) $x - 3$ (C) $2x + 3$
    (B) $x + 1$ (D) $2x - 3$

34. Solve the following quadratic equation:
    $3x^2 + 6x + 2 = 0$.

    (A) $\dfrac{-3 \pm \sqrt{3}}{3}$

    (B) $-1 \pm \sqrt{2}$

    (C) $\dfrac{-3 \pm \sqrt{5}}{3}$

    (D) $-3 \pm \sqrt{3}$

35. Identify the correct solution set for the given system of linear equations.
    $3x + 7y = -5$
    $2x - y = -9$

    (A) $\{(3, -2)\}$

    (B) $\{(4, 1)\}$

    (C) $\{(-4, 1)\}$

    (D) $\{\ \}$

36. Choose the expression equivalent to the following:
    $4a(3 + 2b)$.

    (A) $3(4a + 2b)$

    (B) $14ab$

    (C) $4a(2b + 3)$

    (D) $20ab$

37. For each statement below, determine if $x = 5$ is a solution.
    I. $4x - 6 = 14 + x$
    II. $(x - 5)(x + 3) = 8$
    III. $x^2 + 6x - 14 \geq 10$

    (A) I and III only.

    (B) I and II only.

    (C) III only.

    (D) None of the above.

38. The Romero family is planning to install a pool. If they borrow \$8,000 at a rate of 7%, the interest is \$560 for the first year. Which is the correct equation to calculate interest I, if the rate is only 5%?

    (A) $\dfrac{560}{I} = \dfrac{5}{7}$

    (B) $\dfrac{I}{8,000} = \dfrac{5}{7}$

    (C) $\dfrac{560}{.05} = \dfrac{I}{.07}$

    (D) $\dfrac{.07}{560} = \dfrac{.05}{I}$

39. Select the correct condition which corresponds to the shaded region in the coordinate plane shown at the right.

    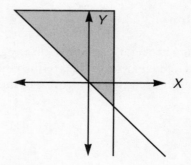

    (A) $x \leq 2$ and $x + y \geq 0$

    (B) $x \geq 0$ and $y \geq 0$

    (C) $y \leq 2$ and $x \geq y$

    (D) $x \leq 2$ and $x \leq y$

40. Select an equivalent inequality to the following:
    $-5r < 20$.

    (A) $r < 4$ (C) $r > 4$

    (B) $r < -4$ (D) $r > -4$

41. A state sales tax on clothing is variable. The first $50 of any item is taxed at two percent. For items over $50, that portion over $50 is taxed at eight percent. What would be the tax on a coat costing $175?

    (A) $11.00   (C) $10.00

    (B) $14.00   (D) $18.00

42. The product of a number decreased by four and the same number increased by 10 is 15 less than the number. Identify the equation which could be used to find the number (n) in question?

    (A) $(n - 4)n + 10 = 15 - n$

    (B) $(n - 4)(n + 10) = n - 15$

    (C) $(-4n)(10n) = n - 15$

    (D) $(n - 4)(n + 10) = 15 - n$

43. The graph below represents the type of footwear worn by students entering the library yesterday afternoon. How many more students were wearing sandals than boots?

    (A) 65

    (B) 25

    (C) 40

    (D) 90

    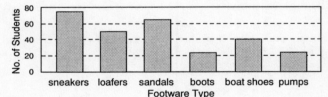

44. Find the median of the following sample data:
    6, 20, 7, 3, 18, 4, 8, 14.

    (A) 7.5   (C) 10

    (B) 8   (D) 80

45. A zoo has eight elephants. On any given day three of the elephants are selected and lined up to give rides to the visitors. How many different arrangements of the three selected elephants are there?

    (A) 21   (C) 336

    (B) 24   (D) 6

46. Of a freshman class, half of the students are enrolled in 15 class hours, most of the remaining freshmen are taking 12 hours with a few students taking 18 hours. Select the statement which is true about this distribution.

    (A) The mode is the same as the mean.

    (B) The median is less than the mean.

    (C) The mean is greater than the mode.

    (D) The mean is less than the median.

47. A toy manufacturer wants to find out which of its demo toys to further develop for sale, based on how well children like the toys. Which of the following procedures would be most appropriate for selecting an unbiased sample?

    (A) Allow the employees at the toy company to take the toys home for their children to play with and report back.

    (B) Take the toys to a preschool, allow the children to play with the toys, and record which are most favored.

    (C) Poll every tenth parent entering a toy store on a given day.

    (D) Arrange for a random sample of children from the distribution area to play with the toys and record which are most favored.

48. Sixty percent of the 5- and 6-year-old children participated in the two sport teams of the city athletic program. Thirty percent of the children played soccer, and 50 percent of the children played T-ball. What is the probability that a randomly selected child played both sports?

    (A) 0.20   (C) 0.25

    (B) 0.80   (D) 1.40

49. Sets *A, B, C,* and *U* are related as shown in the diagram.

    Which of the following statements is true, assuming none of the five regions is empty?

    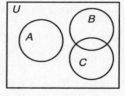

    (A) An element that is a member of set *B* is a member of set *C*.

    (B) An element that is not a member of set *A* is a member of set *B* or set *C*.

    (C) An element that is a member of set *U* is a member of set *A*.

    (D) No element is a member of all three sets *A, B,* and *C*.

50. Select the statement that is the negation of the statement "If it is thundering, then we will not go swimming."

    (A) It is thundering, and we are not going swimming.

    (B) It is thundering, and we will go swimming.

    (C) If it is not thundering, then we will go swimming.

    (D) If we go swimming, then it will not thunder.

51. Select the statement below that is logically equivalent to "If a number is prime, then it is an integer."

    (A) If a number is not prime, then it is not an integer.

    (B) If a number is an integer, then it is prime.

    (C) If a number is prime and an integer, then it is a number.

    (D) If a number is not an integer, then it is not prime.

52. To be eligible for the track team a student must be able to run a mile in less than 10 minutes and throw a medicine ball at least 12 feet. The student must also have a grade point average (GPA) of at least 2.5 and be taking a minimum of three classes.

    The following students wish to try out for the team. Which ones, if any, are eligible?

    Sam is taking 4 classes and has a GPA of 3.2. He runs a mile in 10.3 minutes and throws the medicine ball 14 feet.

    Lee Ann is taking 3 classes and has a GPA of 3.8. She throws the medicine ball 12 feet and runs the mile in 9.9 minutes.

    Ryan is taking 5 classes and has a GPA of 2.6. He throws the medicine ball 12.1 feet and runs the mile in 8.8 minutes.

    (A) Sam and Ryan only

    (B) Lee Ann only

    (C) Lee Ann and Ryan only

    (D) All of the students are eligible.

53. The conclusions to the following arguments are all true. Select the one argument that is not valid.

    (A) All rectangles are parallelograms and all squares are rectangles. Therefore, all squares are parallelograms.

    (B) All dinosaurs are extinct and an archelon was a dinosaur. Therefore, all archelons are extinct.

(C) Some four-legged animals have tails and a horse is a four-legged animal. Therefore, a horse has a tail.

(D) Some parallelograms are trapezoids and all rhombi are parallelograms. Therefore, a rhombus could be a trapezoid.

54. Read the following argument and select the valid conclusion that can be drawn from the given argument.

If I join a health club, then I will exercise at least three times a week. If I exercise at least three times a week, then I will be in shape to go skiing.

(A) If I am in shape to go skiing, then I joined the health club.

(B) If I am not in shape to go skiing, then I did not join the health club.

(C) If I join a health club, then I will be in shape to go skiing.

(D) If I am in shape to go skiing, then I exercised at least three times a week.

55. Which is a logical conclusion that can be drawn from the following?

If you eat well, you will be healthy. If you exercise, you will be healthy. You do not eat well, but you do exercise.

(A) You will be healthy.

(B) You will not be healthy.

(C) You will only be somewhat healthy.

(D) None of these are warranted.

PRACTICE TEST 1

ANSWER KEY

English Language Skills

1 **(C)**	11. **(B)**	21. **(D)**	31. **(C)**
2. **(B)**	12. **(A)**	22. **(B)**	32. **(C)**
3. **(B)**	13. **(C)**	23. **(B)**	33. **(C)**
4. **(A)**	14. **(B)**	24. **(A)**	34. **(B)**
5. **(A)**	15. **(C)**	25. **(D)**	35. **(D)**
6. **(B)**	16. **(D)**	26. **(C)**	36. **(C)**
7. **(C)**	17. **(C)**	27. **(B)**	37. **(B)**
8. **(B)**	18. **(A)**	28. **(B)**	38. **(D)**
9. **(B)**	19. **(B)**	29. **(A)**	39. **(A)**
10. **(A)**	20. **(B)**	30. **(B)**	40. **(B)**

Reading Skills

1. **(B)**	12. **(C)**	23. **(C)**	34. **(B)**
2. **(C)**	13. **(B)**	24. **(B)**	35. **(C)**
3. **(C)**	14. **(C)**	25. **(D)**	36. **(C)**
4. **(C)**	15. **(A)**	26. **(A)**	37. **(B)**
5. **(C)**	16. **(B)**	27. **(A)**	38. **(A)**
6. **(A)**	17. **(D)**	28. **(A)**	39. **(B)**
7. **(B)**	18. **(B)**	29. **(A)**	40. **(A)**
8. **(D)**	19. **(C)**	30. **(D)**	41. **(B)**
9. **(A)**	20. **(D)**	31. **(C)**	
10. **(C)**	21. **(C)**	32. **(B)**	
11. **(A)**	22. **(A)**	33. **(B)**	

Mathematics

1. **(A)**	12. **(A)**	23. **(A)**	34. **(A)**	45. **(C)**
2. **(B)**	13. **(B)**	24. **(B)**	35. **(C)**	46. **(D)**
3. **(A)**	14. **(A)**	25. **(C)**	36. **(C)**	47. **(D)**
4. **(C)**	15. **(B)**	26. **(A)**	37. **(C)**	48. **(A)**
5. **(D)**	16. **(D)**	27. **(C)**	38. **(D)**	49. **(D)**
6. **(D)**	17. **(B)**	28. **(A)**	39. **(A)**	50. **(B)**
7. **(B)**	18. **(D)**	29. **(C)**	40. **(D)**	51. **(D)**
8. **(D)**	19. **(B)**	30. **(A)**	41. **(A)**	52. **(C)**
9. **(B)**	20. **(A)**	31. **(D)**	42. **(B)**	53. **(C)**
10. **(B)**	21. **(B)**	32. **(A)**	43. **(C)**	54. **(C)**
11. **(B)**	22. **(B)**	33. **(C)**	44. **(A)**	55. **(A)**

DETAILED EXPLANATIONS OF ANSWERS

ESSAY SECTION
SAMPLE ESSAYS FOR TOPIC #1

WRITING SAMPLE WITH A SCORE OF 5 OR 6

In today's society, many people continue to believe many common misconceptions about other groups that lead to derogatory stereotypes. Different ethnic and racial groups often believe negative stereotypes about other groups. People of both genders have unfavorable beliefs about the other sex. People of different social classes often have suspicious ideas about those who are not of the same class. But one of the most common misperceptions that leads to a negative stereotype is held by people of all races, genders, and social groups. Like all stereotypes, this one is based on fear and misunderstanding. The stereotype I am talking about is that all handicapped people are retarded and somehow contaminating to healthy people.

People instinctively fear what they do not understand. This is a normal reaction. But the rational thing to do when one is faced with something one does not understand is to educate oneself. But most people do not take the time or the effort to do this, and there are many handicapped people whose lives are made more difficult because of the prejudices of non-handicapped people.

Some of the common misperceptions about handicapped people are: 1) all people who are in wheelchairs are mentally, as well as physically, handicapped; 2) a person who cannot speak clearly cannot think clearly either; 3) all handicapped people have trouble feeding themselves and need help to do everything; 4) all handicapped people are born that way; and 5) all handicapped people feel sorry for themselves and everyone else should feel sorry for them, too. Let's look at each of these beliefs individually, and determine the accuracy or inaccuracy of each.

First, that all people in wheelchairs are mentally, as well as physically, handicapped. This is the most obviously false idea about people with physical challenges. Many people who grow up perfectly healthy suffer spinal injuries that leave them either partially or completely paralyzed and necessitate the use of a wheelchair. A car accident, a sports injury, or even a child's game can cause this kind of spinal damage, which affects a person's ability to control his or her movement, but has no effect on the person's brain. There are several debilitating illnesses that confine sufferers to wheelchairs. These diseases range from muscular dystrophy to cancer to diabetes to disorders of the nervous system, almost all of which leave the person's mental abilities unaffected. One can see this stereotype in action when waiters ignore the person in the wheelchair and ask that person's companion what the handicapped person would like to order. Or when people speak very slowly and loudly to someone in a wheelchair, as if they were talking to a deaf person or a child.

The second misperception, that a person who cannot speak clearly cannot think clearly, is also very pervasive. For example, a child who stutters is more likely to be labelled "slow" or "learning disabled," regardless of that child's actual performance. People who stutter or who cannot speak clearly because of paralysis or diseases that affect motor control, like Parkinson's disease, are treated as if they are deaf, or as if they are retarded. People tend to finish their sentences for them, to suggest words when they cannot say what they want to say, to speak to them loudly and slowly, or to talk to them through other people.

The third misperception, that handicapped people are unable to do things for themselves, leads to people offering to perform even mundane tasks for handicapped people. Handicapped people are capable of controlling their own wheelchairs, dialing telephones, taking notes, opening doors and drawers, and most other everyday tasks. If a handicapped person is unable to do something, he or she will usually ask for help; if he or she does not ask, people should not presume to do these tasks for them. Handicapped people often undergo special therapy to learn to cope with their disabilities, and many have specially trained dogs and monkeys to help them with daily tasks. Many able-bodied people are annoyed when others presume to give them unsolicited help; most handicapped people feel the same way, and they deserve the same respect.

The fourth misunderstanding about handicapped people is that they are born that way. As mentioned earlier, there are many types of diseases and accidents that can disable previously non-handicapped people. The important point that people need to understand is that when a person becomes handicapped, it is only their physical attributes that change. They are still the same person as before the accident or illness, with the same feelings and emotions. They might need more help to accomplish certain tasks, but they have not metamorphosed into some totally different person.

The last misperception, that handicapped people feel sorry for themselves and that other people should feel sorry for them, too, is probably the most damaging. While many people go through a period of self-pity after an accident or illness leaves them impaired, this is a normal part of the acceptance process, and eventually the person will get past the "why me?" feeling and will learn to cope with the disability. Handicapped people consider themselves to just be faced with different challenges; most of them realize that self-pity is a useless waste of time. When other people feel sorry for them, and make it clear that they see the handicapped person as someone to be pitied, it is degrading. It implies that a person's physical capabilities define who that person is, rather than personality and ability.

Even persons who have mental handicaps, whether from a congenital problem like Down's syndrome, or from disease or injury, are not less of a person than someone who is not mentally challenged. A mentally handicapped person may not be able to achieve the same intellectual goals as an unimpaired person, but they still experience needs and desires, emotions, and likes and dislikes. Most people who suffer from mental retardation are kind, gentle people who can provide a lot of joy to their families. They maintain lifelong the innocence and sweetness of very young children. Despite society's perceptions, the love and joy these people offer are just as valuable as any contributions a "normal" person can make.

Common misperceptions about the causes and needs of handicapped people, and the fear of the unknown and the misunderstood, lead to derogatory stereotypes about people who face physical and mental challenges. To many people, a handicapped person is somehow less human, but this idea, and the actions it inspires, are demeaning and false. We need to educate ourselves about this issue, so that these stereotypes, and all stereotypes, can be eradicated and replaced with respect and understanding for those who are different.

FEATURES OF THE WRITING SAMPLE SCORING 5 OR 6

The writer of this essay presents a clear thesis and expands that thesis in a logical manner. The arguments presented in support of the thesis are lucid and detailed. The writer offers a well-organized essay that informs the reader of the points to be examined and then proceeds to discuss each of those points rationally. The conclusion sums up the main argument of the essay and refers back to the central thesis. The writer makes very few mistakes in grammar, usage, and mechanics, and demonstrates a clear understanding of the rules of written English. This understanding allows the writer to communicate very effectively.

WRITING SAMPLE WITH A SCORE OF 3 OR 4

A common misperception that leads to a derogatory stereotype is the idea that women are inferior to men. This idea has been around for thousands of years, and even though women have been trying hard to show men that its not true for the last thirty years, most men still believe it.

This misperception has many different sides to it. Like the idea that women are not as smart as men. Many women are just as smart if not smarter than men. The person with the highest ever recorded IQ is a woman. And even if not all women are smart, not all men are smart, either.

Men use this idea that women are not smart to keep women from doing the things they want to do. Like its really hard for women to get top positions in big companies because the men don't think the women can be tough enough to make the big deals.

Men also think that women have this really strong maternal instinct and so even if they hire a woman they don't want to give her a promotion because they think she's going to get pregnant and then she'll have to take a maternity leave. So unless a woman is too old to get pregnant, she doesn't have the chances for promotion that men do.

Men think that women are too emotional, too. They think that if a woman has to deal with men the way men deal with men, that she'll get all emotional and start crying. Male bosses think that they can't criticize a woman employee or she'll start crying, and that makes men really uncomfortable.

Some women have been able to really succeed even though this stereotype exists. A lot of women run their own businesses and make as much money as a lot of men, but the men don't take this as proof that women are just as good as men. They say that either the woman has a rich husband or father who gave her the business, or that she slept with her boss to get her job or her raise. Or they say that the business she runs isn't a "real" business because its a "women's" business, like a beauty parlor or a boutique. Does that mean that a barber shop isn't a real business because its a "men's" business? Of course not!

Men have other untrue stereotypes about women. Like the idea that all women want to get married and have babies. Lots of women don't want to have a husband because they don't want to have to take care of him. And even if they are married, a lot of women don't like children and don't want to have any. But no one believes these women won't change their minds.

Men also think that women aren't as smart. But if a woman is smart, they don't like her. Our society teaches women that they should try to please men, so if being smart doesn't please men, a lot of women will pretend that they are a lot dumber than they really are just so guys will like them. Girls learn about this by the time they are in high school, which is when girls scores on math tests start to go down. Before high school, girls do just as well as boys, if not better, on standardized achievement tests. But when girls get old enough to want to date, they realize that none of the guys are interested in girls who are "brains" and so they stop trying to do as well at math and science.

Men think women can't do things like mechanics or electronics or things like that, either. That's why a lot of places tell women that they need work on their car when they really don't—the men think that the woman doesn't know any better so she'll pay these guys a lot of money to do unnecessary repairs.

These misperceptions about women need to stop. Men need to grow up and accept the fact that women are just as smart as they are and that women can do just about anything men can do. And if any man says that men are stronger than women, he should try having a baby! If men had to have the babies, women would get a lot more respect!

FEATURES OF THE WRITING SAMPLE SCORING 3 OR 4

This writer begins with a fairly clear thesis, and does focus on the topic. But the arguments presented to support that thesis are not presented in a logical manner and are repeated in different places. Poor usage and mechanics also interfere with the clarity of this essay. The writer makes several mistakes with possessive forms of personal pronouns. The conclusion is a statement of the writer's own opinion, rather than a summary of the arguments already presented. The poor organization of the essay and the lack of knowledge of the standards of written English interfere with the writer's ability to communicate effectively.

WRITING SAMPLE WITH A SCORE OF 1 OR 2

People have lots of misperceptions about people. Like a lot of people think Mexican people are lazy. Or black people steal. Or like Chinese people are all real smart.

These ideas make bad stereotypes. Cause if you think all black people are theifs then you won't trust black people. Or if you think all Mexicans are lazy and don't work good, you won't hire them for a job. Or you might hire a Chinese person cause you think there all smart but that one isn't and can't do the job for you.

There are stereotypes about people who have different religions, too. Like Hindus and Buddhists and Muslems. A lot of people think that all these people are terrorists when really most of them are peaceful.

Another stereotype is that all white people are rich and this makes a lot of people think that its ok to steal from them because they have so much money anyway. Or that they are all prejidised against everyone else, so its ok to treat them bad.

So these perceptions lead to derogatory stereotypes that make people think bad about other people, so that different people don't get along.

FEATURES OF THE WRITING SAMPLE SCORING 1 OR 2

This essay does not address the chosen topic. The writer has not chosen one misperception to write about, but instead has just presented a list of different stereotypes and claimed that these stereotypes are bad. The essay does not reflect any attempt to think critically about the topic; rather the writer repeats common notions about stereotypes without any analysis of those ideas. There is no attempt to present a well-defined argument, and there are no supporting details. Spelling and grammar errors also interfere with the writer's ability to communicate clearly and effectively.

SAMPLE ESSAYS FOR TOPIC #2

WRITING SAMPLE WITH A SCORE OF 5 OR 6

The expectation that our statesmen be superheroes is the most dangerous attitude contributing to the decline of leadership in contemporary America. We expect perfection in all areas—physical (including appearance), intellectual, political, and moral, sustained throughout a leader's life. In addition, potential leaders must meet the criteria of diverse segments of the population, as well as withstand the scrutiny of their political opponents, special interest groups, and the media, all of whom have access to ever-increasing banks of information.

Many Americans share the sentiment that we are "dwarves standing on the shoulders of giants." But if one of these past political giants, George Washington, were a candidate today, the famous incident with the cherry tree would be investigated by the media, complete with a video recreation of the young George chopping away with his axe. Questions would be raised about his commitment to the environment, his support for farm workers, his respect for property owners, and even political acumen. After all, should a president be unable to prevaricate when necessary?

Recently, the draft records of Bill Clinton and Dan Quayle have been major election-year issues. The emphasis has been on the fact that both of these men avoided service in the Viet Nam War, rather than on the reasons for their avoidance. This is a clear example of the manipulation of facts so common to today's political campaigns. Clinton was labelled a "draft dodger" for refusing to register for the draft and for publicly protesting the war, even though he, like many of his generation, protested for moral and ethical reasons. Due to the distortion of Clinton's position, many people believe him to be a coward, not realizing that it takes a great deal of courage and personal integrity to maintain one's personal convictions in the face of public opinion. Quayle also avoided military service during the war, but he did so by securing a commission in the National Guard, through the intercession of his wealthy family. To many Americans, it seems more honorable to avoid military service through enrollment in a non-combatant service and not speak out against the war than to refuse any hypocritical quasi-military post and follow one's convictions. This focus on both men's action during the war highlights another aspect of the unrealistic expectations Americans have for their leaders—that the events of youth serve not as character-building incidents, but as a series of possible pitfalls that can entrap a politician in the past. The implication is that a leader must be born with the wisdom of Solomon, able to foresee the possible political repercussions of his every action from adolescence on. While divorce no longer carries a stigma, married candidates come under intense scrutiny of their private lives, including any potential episodes of adultery. Americans have become so open to accusations of adultery that it has become a fairly common campaign tactic to imply that any late-night work sessions with a male candidate and a woman staffer are evidence of an affair. Unmarried candidates also have their private lives examined, with the rumors of homosexuality hovering right below the surface. As the attacks on Attorney General Janet Reno show, the rumors can, and do, surface even in the "conservative" press.

Modern politics also focus on the politician's physical appearance, although this focus is not as blatant. Physical perfection and charming good looks have become tacit (which would have eliminated Abraham Lincoln). In the recent presidential election, comments about Perot's stature and the size of his ears were heard more than discussions about his fitness for political office. Political imperfection in the form of cancer hindered Paul Tsongas in his candidacy, not so much because of fears that he might not live through a four-year term, but because of an irrational fear of the disease itself. The most basic physical characteristics of gender and race often exclude women and minorities from the highest leadership opportunities.

The electorate should move beyond the focus on such physical criteria and evaluate a potential leader's intellectual acumen, the choices made as a mature adult, and the positions on the issues. Instead, these too are attacked by a plethora of self-promoting special interest groups. A candidate who supports abortion rights or equal housing and job opportunities for gays will be denounced by many church and community leaders. Yet a candidate who declines such support or speaks out against these positions will be derided as spineless or rejected outright by women's rights activists, gay and lesbian organizations, and other groups who claim protection under the Constitution's insurance of equal rights. The result? Candidates who say less what they mean and more what the majority of their listeners want to hear. We have lost that tolerance which accepts a *human* leader, someone who has taken risks, made an occasional mistake, but who has learned, matured, and grown thereby, someone who cannot solve all our problems but will respond effectively to emergencies and will make clear and thoughtful decisions.

This intense scrutiny which characterizes contemporary candidacy is in great part a result of our current fascination with the media, which presents information not for our consideration and judgement, but for our entertainment. The sheer volume of documentation available in every area of a candidate's life, and the relish with which tantalizing details are searched out and revealed, are recent phenomena. In earlier eras, because of stricter media ethics and a stronger respect for privacy, the leadership opportunities of Dwight D. Eisenhower and John F. Kennedy were not compromised by the longstanding mistress of one and the series of affairs of the other.

In the end, expecting perfection in our leaders while at the same time supporting efforts to find and dwell upon imperfections will result in many potential candidates declining nominations, or bowing out early rather than risking personal and familial pressure and embarrassment. We must learn to season emotional reactions with reasoned assessment of the political potential of our leaders, *all* of whom have feet of clay, but some of whom might become giants nonetheless.

FEATURES OF THE WRITING SAMPLE SCORING 5 OR 6

The purpose and thesis of the essay are clear from the opening sentence, and the introductory paragraph suggests several specific areas for consideration. The essay proceeds to expand on these suggestions, and the organization is logical and dynamic. The writer presents contemporary and historical examples to support the arguments made. The writer not only enlarges on specific ways in which political leadership is hampered by public expectations, but also analyzes the factors contributing to the new expectations for candidates. The author also theorizes about the long-term consequences of the current attitude, which demonstrates a sophisticated appraisal of the topic. There are few mechanical or usage errors, and the balanced structure of the essay illustrates the writer's command of written English.

WRITING SAMPLE WITH A SCORE OF 3 OR 4

The attitude which I believe has led to the decline of leadership in contemporary America is that we expect too much of our leaders. We expect them to be knowledgeable about everything, to have personal and professional ethics which never fail, and to have a flawless record of choices and votes.

First, we expect them to know a lot about every area of contemporary life and politics. They must be able to lead on biological issues like abortion and euthanasia, on scientific issues like further space exploration and creating life in test tubes, on health issues like medical insurance and pharmaceutical costs, on family issues such as gay rights and family leaves, and on business-labor issues such as unemployment, welfare, taxation, and environmental controls. And these are just *some* of the areas we expect our potential leaders to confront and to know about. *No one* can master all the knowledge available in our world today, so how can we expect this of any leader? We should certainly expect him to have in-depth training and knowledge in a couple of areas, but we need to trust in his ability to choose a team of assistants who will have depth in the areas he only has slight knowledge about. A teacher I once had used to say, if you don't know it, know where to find out about it.

Second, in addition to our expectations for knowledge, we expect a potential leader to have ethics in his personal as well as his political life. This means we can expect him not to be a criminal, murderer, or thief, but also that he has not treated anybody truly unfairly with intention, and that he has been honest in obeying the laws of his country. These are reasonable expectations. But many people and groups expect much more. They want leaders who have married, but have never had extra-marital affairs, or who have been young and carefree and understand students, but have never smoked marijuana themselves, even decades ago, or who have never disagreed with a U.S. war in avoiding the draft. We expect entirely too much, especially of leaders when they were young, when they may not even have realized they would one day be politicians. Even their families are investigated, although they will not be elected. So the early actions of Bill Clinton's wife and mother were subjects of investigation and publicity.

Third, we expect too much of a candidate's record. People grow and change their mind. Some even change political parties, like former president Ronald Reagan. We should not hold honest growth and change against them, calling it vacillation and spinelessness. We should instead look for reasonable decisions made *at the time,* based on a careful consideration of factual evidence. This should be enough to qualify a candidate. Even occasional mistakes which are admitted and altered can be understood, and shouldn't be reason for discarding a candidate.

Finally, we need to be on guard not to expect too much of our leaders. If we don't diminish our expectations, we won't have people who want to hold public office—especially not *good* people.

FEATURES OF THE WRITING SAMPLE SCORING 3 OR 4

This essay meets the higher order criteria for writing: It has a clear purpose and thesis, defined from the first paragraph, and it presents and fulfills a basic, easy-to-follow organization. While there is occasional lack of integration, often at the end of a paragraph (for instance, the words of a former teacher, or the investigations of Clinton's wife and mother), these are minor flaws rather than major faults in the essay's logic. The essay contains a reasonable number of details and some variety of sentence structure, including a conclusion which summarizes, then goes on to evidence concern for future consequences if the described attitude of excessive expectations fails to change.

The greatest weakness is in the writer's attention to details of language. Key words are repeated with little variation, indicating weak vocabulary. Transition words are too obvious, and the arrangement of concepts is sequential (first, second, third), never allowing the essay to achieve the greater complexity of comparison or contrast, for instance. The writing is wordy in places, and there are several lapses in usage and grammar. The writer also employs masculine pronouns instead of preferable gender-neutral language.

WRITING SAMPLE WITH A SCORE OF 1 OR 2

I can think of several attitudes which make being a leader difficult to say the least. For example getting mad at a leader. Many people decide they want to be furious at anything or anyone and who should they pick but the closest leader-type person like their senator or president. Sometimes these people are political cartoonists (like Doonesbury) who get paid to get mad at politicians and that means if they don't do this they don't eat, so I guess they have the right. But I'm not talking about them, just others.

Getting mad for no reason is a character trait of most type-A persons, and it can be dangerous to your health, so these persons should really stay away from all political rallies and events and probably should not even read the newspapers or turn on the TV unless they are going in for counseling about their tendency to get mad when they come into any kind of contact with any political or moral subject, like whether a political person was a child molester or cheated on his or her mate or taxes, or even dodged the draft.

Draft-dodging is not a problem, though, unless no one else at the time was legally doing it, especially with help from their wealthy families; and in addition this is true of marijuana smoking (also called "pot" as well. I mean if someone just takes one puff, it's illegal and that's whether you inhale or you don't, so it doesn't really matter, so there was really no reason for the so-called press to make such a stink about Clinton when he was running for the office of the presidency of the United States.

Which brings us back to being mad as a not always helpful attitude, but sometimes being necessary because if enough people like you and I get mad at the press which doesn't do its job well (especially some talk shows and some supermarket rag sheets).

Finally, getting mad is an attitude too many people have and it ruins your health and outlook on life as well as your chance to be effective as a politician who listens and cares and helps people, and talks sensitively in today's world.

FEATURES OF THE WRITING SAMPLE SCORING 1 OR 2

This writer has many interesting ideas, but unfortunately they are not sorted and ordered into a good essay. At the beginning the writer indicates that he will address people who "get mad" at politicians. This might have resulted in an effective essay about an attitude (anger against politicians) which has led to a decline of American leadership. But even in the first paragraph the writer wanders away from the focus. This straying from the topic continues throughout.

The writer purports to return to the topic when starting paragraph four, through a logically faulty, superficial transition, but there anger is discussed as a means for its affect on press coverage, not potential leadership. There are many other significant errors in this essay, from sentence fragments and run-on sentences to lack of agreement and other grammatical errors, however, this essay suffers most from unclear focus and the absence of logical organization, coherence, and transitions.

ENGLISH LANGUAGE SKILLS SECTION

1. **(C)**   "Habit" (C) is the best choice because the word refers to an action which a person performs regularly or habitually. "Addiction" (A) has strong connotations which would not be appropriate to describe gum chewing. "Hobby" (B) refers to a more complex activity which a person participates in for personal enrichment.

2. **(B)**   The word "childlike" (B) has positive connotations which would agree with the description "very appealing." Both "childish" (A) and "infantile" (C) have negative connotations referring to behavior which is extremely below a person's age level, and, therefore, unappealing.

3. **(B)**   Choice (B) "again" has the same meaning as "reread," and is therefore unnecessary. Choice (A) "fully" is an important distinction used to describe the level of understanding. Choice (C) "Some" distinguishes the difficult texts which require more effort. Choice (D) "however" signals the author's shift in thought. Finally, choice (E) "increased" is important to the meaning of the passage because it describes the higher level of effort which the author is discussing.

4. **(A)**   Choice (A) "consensus of" can be eliminated because a consensus is the opinion of the group. Choice (B) "should" is important to both the meaning and the structure of the sentence. Choice (C) "special" describes the nature of the project, and choice (D) "everyday" describes the nature of the problems. Finally, choice (E) "health" is important because it refers to one of the categories that the volunteers are dealing with.

5. **(A)**   In choice (A), the modifying phrase "with its broad breast like the stern of a ship tapering to the rear" is correctly placed immediately following the thing being described, "the shape of a swan." Choice (B) is phrased awkwardly, and the pronoun "its" is ambiguous since it could refer to the water. In choice (C), the descriptive phrase is incorrectly placed after "water."

6. **(B)**   Choice (B) shows the correct relationship between the two phrases. Both choices (A) and (C) imply that Rick is made of glass because of incorrect or ambiguous placement of the modifying phrase "being made of glass."

7. **(C)**   Choice (C) expresses the ideas in correct parallel form. Choice (A) shifts from "thinking" and "organizing" to simple noun form. Choice (B) shifts from an infinitive "to think" to noun form.

8. **(B)**   Choice (B) shows agreement between the pronouns "their," "themselves" and the antecedent "people." In choice (A), the singular pronouns "one" and "his or her" do not agree with the plural pronouns "themselves."

9. **(B)**   Choice (B) contains the most effective subordination of ideas. Choices (A) and (C) string the clauses together with "and," making the sentence unnecessarily wordy. Choice (D) incorrectly shifts the verb tense.

10. **(A)**   Choice (A) lists the ideas in the clearest, most logical manner. Choice (B) is confusing because it separates the categories from their examples. Choice (C) implies that the visitors have not yet come. Choice (D) also makes this implication, and the ideas do not flow smoothly.

11. **(B)**   When making a comparison with "as," the word "as" must be stated twice to complete the comparison, even if a phrase with "than" is added. (B) is the only choice that makes a complete comparison; choices (A) and (C) are incomplete, since they both omit an "as."

12. **(A)**   Choice (A) is the only one using the word "as" twice to make a complete comparison. Choices (B) and (C) each omit an "as," making the comparison incomplete.

13. **(C)**   Choice (C) makes the most complete and logical comparison. Choice (A) implies that Mount Everest is not an Asian mountain, and choice (B) is vague about the subjects of comparison.

14. **(B)**   Choice (B) makes the clearest comparison between the players of the two teams. Choice (A) uses the comparative "er" form without clearly stating what the players are being compared to. Choice (C) uses the superlative "est" form (used to compare more than two things) when only two things are being compared, in this case the two sets of players.

15. **(C)**   "Lain" (C) is the correct past participle of the verb "lie" (to recline). "Laid" (A) is the past participle for "lay" (to set down), and "lied" (D) is the past participle for "lie" meaning "to not tell the truth."

16. **(D)**   "Laid" (D) is the correct past participle for the verb "lay" (to set down). Choice (A) is in the incorrect tense. Choice (B) is the past participle for "lie" (to recline), and choice (C) is the past participle for "lie" (to not tell the truth).

17. **(C)**   Choice (C) correctly places a comma before a coordinating conjunction joining two independent clauses. Choice (A) uses a comma incorrectly since commas are not necessary before a subordinating conjunction between two phrases. Choice (B) omits the necessary comma between items in a list, which is, in this case "parents" and "grandparents."

18. **(A)**   The present tense verb "want" (A) is needed to agree with the other verb, "say." Choices (B) and (C) are both in the past tense, and are thus not consistent with the preceding verb.

19. **(B)** Choice (B) is the correct spelling. All other choices are misspelled.

20. **(B)** "Accustomed to" (B) is the correct form of the participle. The verb "live" (A) does not agree with the subject "couple." Finally, the verb "are" (C) does not agree with the singular subject "having children."

21. **(D)** The sentence is correct as written (D). Choice (A) incorrectly places a comma before a preposition. Choice (B) incorrectly uses a comma to divide the phrase "later than," and choice (C) incorrectly places the possessive apostrophe before the "s" following a plural noun ending in "s."

22. **(B)** The singular pronoun "him" (B) is needed to agree with the singular noun "male." Choice (A) is a comma splice: the semicolon is the correct punctuation between two independent clauses. The semicolon in choice (C), however, is incorrect since it does not join two independent clauses.

23. **(B)** The sentence requires the verb "choose" (B) to be a complete sentence. With the noun "choice" (A), the phrase is a fragment. Choice (C) is a gerund, not a verb; it is also misspelled. "Choosing" (D) is spelled correctly, but the phrase still lacks a verb.

24. **(A)** The noun "maturity" (A) is consistent with the noun phrase, "financial security." Choice (B) incorrectly omits the comma between the two phrases. Choice (C) is an incorrect verb form.

25. **(D)** The sentence is correct as written (D). A quote beginning in the middle of a sentence as part of that sentence does not require capitalization, as in choice (A). As part of the sentence, it should not be preceded by a comma, as in choice (B), or followed by a comma, as in choice (C).

26. **(C)** Choice (C) correctly places a period rather than a comma between two independent clauses. Choice (A) contains an unnecessary apostrophe. Choice (B) does not make sense; the writer is saying "more than" a certain amount of children live in a one-parent home, not "more of."

27. **(B)** The verb "has" (B) agrees with the singular noun "technology." In choice (A), "technology" is misspelled. Choice (C) is incorrect because the verb "enabled" must be followed by an infinitive "to learn" rather than a participial phrase such as "in learning."

28. **(B)** Choice (B) corrects a fragment by joining the first clause, which is independent, with the second clause, which is dependent. Choice (A) is misspelled. Choice (C) incorrectly omits the comma. The information is about how the brain affects feeling *and* memory, not how we feel about memory, as the phrase implies without the comma.

29. **(A)**   Choice (A) correctly places a comma after an introductory phrase. A semicolon (B) is incorrect because the phrase "contrary to popular opinion" is not independent. Choice (C) is incorrect because a comma is only used if there is an independent clause on either side of the conjunction.

30. **(B)**   Choice (B) correctly places a comma before additional information which is not a complete sentence. Choice (A) is incorrect because the ideas are run together without a pause. In choice (C), "receive" is misspelled. Finally, choice (D) is incorrect because a semicolon cannot be used unless both phrases are independent.

31. **(C)**   The singular pronoun "its" agrees with the singular noun "brain." Choice (A) incorrectly changes the verb "estimate" to a gerund, making the sentence a fragment. Choice (B) is incorrect because the sentence is discussing the capacity at which the brain functions; "by" would be an incorrect preposition to use in this case.

32. **(C)**   Choice (C) is correct because the word "effectively" is describing a verb and should therefore be in adverbial form. Choice (A) incorrectly places a comma after "lost," implying that it is an introductory phrase. Choice (C) is incorrect because it omits the necessary comma after the complete introductory phrase ending with "illness."

33. **(C)**   "Memory" (C) is consistent with the other items in the series ("intelligence" and "mood"). The sentence requires the verb "affect" rather than the noun "effect" (A). Finally, choice (B) is not correct because the verb "affects" does not agree with the plural subject "substances."

34. **(B)**   Choice (B) correctly places the apostrophe before the "s" following a plural noun. Choice (A) incorrectly places a semicolon after an incomplete introductory phrase. Choice (C) is in the incorrect tense.

35. **(D)**   The sentence is correct as written (D). Choice (A) incorrectly omits the comma preceding incidental information placed between the subject "people" and verb "show." It would also be incorrect to use a period, as in choice (B), since the second phrase would be a fragment. Finally, the verb "shows" (C) does not agree with the subject "people."

36. **(C)**   Choice (C) is correct because no comma is used between a compound verb ("learn" and "be involved"). The phrase "to keep the brain functioning" is correctly modified by "well," not "good," as in choice (A), and choice (B) incorrectly uses a semicolon after an introductory phrase.

37. **(B)**   In sentences joined by a conjunctive adverb such as "nevertheless," the conjunctive adverb must be preceded by a semicolon and followed by a comma, as in choice (B). Choice (A) incorrectly reverses this punctuation. Finally, although it is acceptable to use a period before a conjunctive adverb, it is not correct to follow it with a semicolon, as in choice (C).

38. **(D)**   When items in a series contain commas within themselves, each item must be separated by a semicolon, as in choice (D), the original statement. Choice (A) implies a much larger group and uses an unnecessary comma before "and general manager." Choice (B) uses semicolons incorrectly before every phrase, and choice (C) incorrectly omits the commas before "a former star player" and the final "and."

39. **(A)**   When a dependent clause beginning with a subordinating conjunction is joined to a following independent clause, a comma is placed between the two phrases, as in choice (A). Choice (B) is incorrect because the first phrase is a fragment. It is also incorrect to place a semicolon between a dependent and an independent clause, as in choice (C).

40. **(B)**   Colons are used before a list of items introduced by the phrase "the following" (B). Commas are not used after the phrase "such as," as in choice (A). It is also incorrect to follow "such as" with a semicolon, as in choice (D).

READING SKILLS SECTION

1. **(B)** The passage emphasizes from the first sentence that Gwendolyn Brooks was born with two handicaps: being female and being black. All the details are selected to highlight her determination to succeed in spite of these handicaps. Choice (A) is incorrect: only one sentence (beginning on line 12) mentions her writing style, and the passage does not compare her with any other writers. Choice (C) is incorrect: although obviously admiring Brooks' achievements and determination, the author does not propose that she is one of the twentieth-century's greatest poets. Choice (D) is incorrect: it is true that Brooks is presented as an inspiring example of success through hard work and determination, but the author is not *demonstrating* that hard work is *always* rewarded by success. That generalization would be extremely difficult to demonstrate, and the author does not attempt to do so.

2. **(C)** The sentence "She continues to work—and work hard" is an explanation or *clarification* of what the author means in the previous sentence, "Brooks' reaction to fame is atypical." The second sentence clarifies what the author means by "atypical": whereas most people who achieve fame rest on their laurels, Brooks continues to work hard. None of the other choices correctly describes the relationship between the sentences.

3. **(C)** The passage begins with the statement that Brooks lived with two handicaps: being female and being black. The second sentence refers to "the lack of encouragement" she received from teachers and others, thus suggesting (but not saying directly) that this lack of encouragement was due to her being female and black. Choice (A) is incorrect: she did publish early, but there is no hint that early publication hurt her career. Choice (B) is incorrect: she did receive funds through grants, but that amounts to recognition; it is not a reason for her receiving "less credit than she deserved." Choice (D) is incorrect: nowhere does the passage suggest that her work is too complex to be widely appreciated.

4. **(C)** Martin begins with "eventually" and talks about long-term effects. George talks about present and near future objects and activities, at most accepting solutions that will work for centuries. In short, Martin is taking a very long view and George a relatively short one. They probably do not disagree that much on the quality of the present space program equipment, for Martin urges an ongoing improvement of it and George dismisses it as inadequate for Martin's plans. So, (A) does not apply. Nor need their expectations of the effects of pollution (B) or of anti-pollution legislation (D) be that different. George merely sees that the problem can be staved off for a while, even if not forever, while Martin sees that the problem cannot be staved off forever, even if for a little while. They may even be equally committed to human survival (E): George to getting through the present problems, Martin to the long haul. Only the time frames of their concerns are clearly different.

5. **(C)** The first paragraph explains what caves are, and the second paragraph gives examples of prehistoric man's interest in caves. Choice (A) is incorrect: although the phrase in line 3 "caused by widely differing geologic processes" touches on the causes of caves, the passage does not elaborate on these causes. Choice (B) is incorrect: the origin of the term "speleology" is explained, but that explanation is incidental to the main purpose of explaining what caves are. The origin of "speleology" is in parentheses, indicating that it is not crucial to the passage. Choice (D) is incorrect: lines 14 and 15 mention artworks created by Cro-Magnon man, but this is only one example of man's early interest in caves.

6. **(A)** The sentence beginning "Fragments of skeletons" provides an example of the "Prolific evidence" mentioned in the previous sentence. None of the other choices correctly describes the relationship between the sentences.

7. **(B)** The key word in the question is *suggests*. Anything that is stated explicitly and directly cannot be *suggested*. The only statement that is *not* stated explicitly in the definition of a cave is statement (B): that not all openings into the earth are classified as caves. But the definition does *suggest* this because it defines the cave as a particular kind of opening, that is, one that goes beyond the zone of light and is large enough for a man to enter.

8. **(D)** Choice (D), "For example," correctly identifies the sentence as an illustration of the preceding idea. Choices (B) and (C) both indicate time, while choice (A), "Instead," would only be used to link dissimilar ideas.

9. **(A)** Choice (A), "of course," is the only word which indicates similar ideas. Choice (B), "however," implies a contradictory idea. Choice (C), "as a result," indicates a summing up of ideas, and choice (D), "finally," would be used to indicate time or position.

10. **(C)** Choice (C), "However," is correct because it links the contradictory ideas in the sentence. Both choice (A), "Therefore," and choice (D), "Consequently," indicate cause, purpose or result. Choice (B) is wrong because this sentence is in no way a concluding statement.

11. **(A)** The passage begins by defining the torpedo and goes on to inform the reader about how the torpedo works and the types of submarines that use it. Choice (B) is incorrect: even though the third paragraph mentions the two types of submarines that carry torpedoes, the focus of the passage is torpedoes, not submarines. Choice (C) is incorrect: paragraph two explains why an underwater explosion is more destructive than an explosion in the air, but nowhere does the author *warn* us about torpedoes; the author wishes only to *inform* us about them. Choice (D) is incorrect: the author does explain the difference between turbine-powered and electric-powered torpedoes, but that explanation is only part of his larger purpose, namely to tell us what torpedoes are and how they work.

12. **(C)**   The first sentence of the second paragraph is the topic sentence: it states the main idea that the torpedo's destructive effect is increased by the fact that its explosion takes place under water. The second sentence ("When a projectile explodes....") *clarifies* or explains that statement by describing exactly what happens in an airborne explosion. The third sentence then describes an underwater explosion. None of the other choices correctly describes the relationship between the two sentences.

13. **(B)**   Since the author calls the torpedo "self-propelled," and since the turbine and electric motors are described as the torpedo's means of propulsion, these motors must be part of the torpedo. Choice (A) is incorrect: the fact that the torpedo powers itself implies nothing about how it finds its target. Choice (C) is incorrect: the torpedo being self-propelled tells us nothing about how destructive it is. Choice (D) is incorrect: the author neither says nor implies anything about the comparative efficiency of internal and external power sources.

14. **(C)**   Choice (C) is the correct answer. "For example" identifies this sentence as an illustration of the previous idea. Choice (A), "Although," is inappropriate because it indicates a contrast in ideas. Choice (B), "Eventually," indicates a time shift, and choice (D), "In other words," implies a concluding statement.

15. **(A)**   Choice (A), "In addition," correctly links two similar ideas. Choices (B) and (D) both indicate a conclusion, and choice (C), "First," incorrectly indicates time or position.

16. **(B)**   Choice (B), "Finally," is the best transition because it shows that this idea is the last in a series. Therefore, choice (C), "Second," cannot be correct. Choice (A), "In contrast," implies a contradictory idea, and choice (D), "Later," would only be used to indicate a time shift.

17. **(D)**   Although the passage begins with a paragraph that sounds as though the author is questioning the value of the humanities, the rest of the passage makes it clear that the author is explaining and defending the humanities as "essential disciplines, indispensable to our common life..." (line 27). Statement (A) is therefore incorrect: the first sentence of the passage does include the phrase "the humanities are a luxury," but this first sentence is presenting not the author's view but a contrary view against which the author wishes to argue. Statement (B) is incorrect. Although the Constitution and the Bill of Rights are mentioned as examples of documents we would not have without the humanities, they are not the main topic of the passage. Statement (C) is incorrect because the first paragraph is describing a viewpoint against which the author is arguing.

18. **(B)**   The sentence beginning on line 7 is in contrast to the one beginning on line 4 because it points out why the earlier statement is not true: "That sort of point of view makes a lot of sense *until you think that...*" Choices (A), (C), and (D) are incorrect because they describe relationships that simply do not exist between the two sentences.

19. **(C)**   The passage does not state directly that man's actions are based upon knowledge of himself, but it does imply that, especially in lines 10–17: man's thinking about himself, about what he has done and what he should or should not do, has great impact on his actions. Choice (A) is incorrect because the passage mentions nothing about technology. Choice (B) is incorrect because the author states that "we have done that which no other animal could have done"—that is, mankind does not operate solely on the basis of animal instincts. Choice (D) is incorrect because the Bill of Rights is mentioned as a *product* of man's thinking, not as the basis of man's actions.

20. **(D)**   (A) need not be true. That all who are active in campus politics are encouraged to join does not mean that everyone who is encouraged to join is active in campus politics. Some may not be active, yet be encouraged to join. Choice (B) need not be true. The passage states that all faculty and students who are active in campus politics are encouraged to join. This does not necessarily mean that others, who are not students or faculty, are not encouraged to join. Perhaps administrators or community leaders are also encouraged to join. Choice (C) need not be true. It is possible that only faculty and students are encouraged to join, and no one else. The passage does not specify. Choice (D) must be true. The passage states that there are students active in campus politics, and that all those in that category are encouraged to join. Choice (E) need not be true. It is possible that all students are active in campus politics. Therefore, all students would be encouraged to join.

21. **(C)**   The author is telling a story here, so his or her purpose is to relate what happened (or what the author has imagined) and to tell us about the person to whom it happened. Many of the details in the passage reveal the narrator's state of mind: "I trembled," "I then reflected," "I dreaded," etc. Statement (A) is incorrect because the passage is a story, not an attempt to persuade us that monsters are not to be feared. In fact, the passage tries to evoke fear and suspense. Likewise, statements (B) and (D) are wrong because the passage is not advancing an argument.

22. **(A)**   The relationship between the fourth sentence ("I dreaded to behold this monster...") and the fifth sentence ("Entreating him...") is one of cause and effect. It is *because* the narrator fears that Henry should see the monster that he or she entreats Henry to remain at the bottom of the stairs. Since the relationship is cause and effect, it cannot be comparison and contrast (B), clarification (C), or addition (D).

23. **(C)**   Choice (A) is incorrect. Timorous is defined as shrinking from action due to terror. Choice (B) is incorrect. Disbelief is defined as a "mental rejection of something as untrue." The speaker did not mentally reject the monster or he or she would not have cautiously returned to check on its presence. Choice (D) is incorrect. Resoluteness suggests calmness. Nothing in the passage indicates calmness. Choice (C) is correct. The passage presents context clues of "trembled, cold, shivering, stepped fearfully."

24. **(B)**   Choice (B), "for example," is the correct transition word, because the second phrase is an illustration of the concept being discussed. Choice (A) is incorrect because it indicates a shift in time. Choice (C), "of course," does not fit, since it makes too emphatic a statement. Choice (D) indicates a conclusion.

25. **(D)**   Choice (D), "Even though," is the correct transition. Choice (A), "In addition," is incorrect, because the prior sentence discusses a different idea. Choice (C) is not appropriate, since it refers to the previous sentence. Choice (B), "As a result," is a concluding phrase.

26. **(A)**   Choice (A) is the correct answer because it links two similar ideas. Conversely, choice (B), "However," indicates contrast, and choice (D) does not fit because the sentence is not a conclusion. Choice (C) is incorrect because the sentence is not an example of the previous idea being discussed.

27. **(A)**   The word "dispersed" means scattered or sent off in various directions. None of the other choices are similar in meaning. Choice (B) may fit the word "dispensed" but not "dispersed."

28. **(A)**   This is the introductory concept in the first sentence. Choice (B) is incorrect, as the formulas developed by mathematicians have deficiencies, as pointed out by the author in paragraph three. Choice (C) is incorrect. The author makes a statement to the contrary in the last sentence of the selection. Choice (D) is incorrect. The word "alternative" is misused.

29. **(A)**   It is a statement of fact because it can be verified or disproved by observing the differences in the atmosphere by day and night.

30. **(D)**   In the sentence immediately after the examples of the tailpipe and the stacks of a power plant, the author says, "*Thus*, elevation alone has a tremendous influence on how rapidly the pollutant will be dispersed and diluted..." Those two examples were intended to illustrate this point. Statement (A) is incorrect because the passage does not discuss human beings in relation to other creatures. Statement (B) may be true in itself, but it has nothing to do with the examples of the tailpipe and the smokestacks. Statement (C) occurs in lines 15 and 16, but it, too, is unrelated to the examples cited.

31. **(C)**   The argument is structured to show that certain feelings which one person has for another must be reciprocated. In other words, the feelings in the first person must produce like feelings in the second person. Choice (C) best parallels that type of reasoning. Only one difference occurs between the passage and choice (C). In the passage, the object of the feelings is being addressed. In answering the object of the feeling was being spoken of in the third person. Choices (A), (D), and (E) employ standard syllogistic reasoning. The syllogism is the method used in deductive reasoning. The syllogism takes the form:

  If A = A
  And B = C
  Then A = C
In choice (A) the argument is:
  Adam = Man;
  Man = Rational;
  therefore Adam = Rational.
Choice (D) uses a slightly different formulation:
  If A then B;
  A, so B.
  If B, then C cannot be present without D.
  B with C, therefore D follows.
In the passage,
  A = orderly universe;
  B = rational God;
  C = sin.

32. **(B)**   The word "ample" means sufficient, adequate, or abundant. None of the other choices is close in meaning.

33. **(B)**   Beginning with the third sentence, every sentence in the paragraph relates to the bombardment of the Earth by bodies. Choice (B), therefore, must be correct. Choice (A) is true, but it is only a detail leading up to the main idea. Nothing in the passage supports choice (C). Choice (D) may be inferred from the sentence beginning on line 8 ("On the Earth...") but this statement concerns only one aspect of the bombardment. It does not express the central idea that the Earth was bombarded, as choice (B) does.

34. **(B)**   The words "believed" and "must have" indicate that the statement, even though it is very probably true, expresses a reasonable belief based on the evidence available. It is still, however, an opinion, not a fact.

35. **(C)** The second sentence of the paragraph states that we must look to other bodies in the solar system to learn about Earth's history. The heavenly bodies mentioned in the next sentence all show signs of bombardment, and therefore it is reasonable to assume that the Earth was bombarded, too. Statement (A) is wrong because the author is assuming that the Earth must have been bombarded just like the other bodies. Statements (B) and (D) are unsupported by anything in the paragraph.

36. **(C)** "Sporadic" means occurring occasionally, singly, or in isolated instances. None of the other choices is close in meaning to "occasional."

37. **(B)** Everything in the passage is related to the second sentence of the first paragraph: "The colonists, however, soon began to mold their English culture into the fresh environment of a new land." This is the thesis statement of the whole passage, and choice (B) paraphrases it. Choice (A) contradicts lines 10–13 of the passage. Choice (C), while true according to the passage, pertains only to the last paragraph, not to the whole passage. Choice (D) contradicts the thesis statement of lines 2–3.

38. **(A)** The sentence is a statement of *fact* because it can be verified or disproved by checking the records on the number of privately endowed free schools in the Southern colonies.

39. **(B)** The statement about the *Bay Psalm Book* follows the statement that there were few literary works produced in the colonies, and those were printed in England. Choice (A) contradicts that statement. Choice (C) cannot be right because the paragraph is not about religious intolerance. Choice (D) is wrong because nothing is said about the colonies' works being superior to English works. Choice (B) has to be correct because the second sentence of the paragraph says that cultural activities before 1700 were *limited,* and the statements that follow are examples of that limited activity.

40. **(A)** Out of context, this sentence may appear to be an opinion; however, the historical description in the passage validates the statement.

41. **(B)** The word "Although" indicates that the first part of the sentence will be in contrast to the second part. Here the contrast is between the fact that the bill was hotly debated and the fact that it nevertheless passed almost unanimously.

MATHEMATICS SECTION

1.   **(A)**   is the correct response. When adding rational numbers, first find a common denominator: $-3/5$, $4/1$. The common denominator is 5×1 or 5. Write the rational number expression with this common denominator: $-3/5 + 20/5$. Add: $-3/5 + 20/5 = 17/5$. Rewrite as a mixed number: $3\,2/5$.

Choice (B) is obtained from ignoring the sign of the first rational number and adding. Choices (C) and (D) contain errors commonly experienced when working with signed numbers.

2.   **(B)**   is the correct choice. To divide fractions, multiply by the inverse of the second term. The division problem then becomes a multiplication problem. A negative number multiplied by a negative number is a positive number which eliminates choice (D). When multiplying rational numbers, rewrite the expression as:

$$\frac{-7}{-2/3}$$

Multiply both the numerator and denominator by $-3/2$. This gives a 1 in the denominator and the numerator becomes:

$-7/1 \times -3/2 = 21/2$ or $10\,1/2$.

Choices (A) and (C) are obtained by performing the incorrect operation.

3.   **(A)**   is the correct response. Subtracting a negative number translates into: $-7.4 + 3.286$. When adding a positive and a negative number, subtract the lesser absolute valued number from the greater. The answer has the sign of the value with the greater absolute value.

$$-7.4 - (-3.286) = -7.4 + 3.286 = -4.114$$

Choice (C) has the incorrect sign. (B) is obtained by adding the absolute values of the decimal fractions, and (D) is obtained through errors in place value alignment.

4.   **(C)**   is the correct choice. When multiplying a positive number by a negative number, the answer will be negative. This eliminates choice (B). Multiply: $3.75 \times (-0.6) = -2.250$. Since there are 3 total decimal places in the factors, there will be three decimal places in the product. Choices (A) and (D) have incorrect decimal point placement.

5.   **(D)**   is the correct choice. To calculate a percent increase, find the difference between the greater value and the lesser value. Divide this difference by the lesser value and multiply by 100 to convert to a percent.

$$\frac{28 - 16}{16} \times 100 = \frac{12}{16} \times 100 = .75 \times 100 = 75\%$$

(C) is obtained by dividing by 28 instead of 16. (A) and (B) are the results of the use of incorrect formulas.

6.   **(D)**   is the correct response, and is found by establishing the following equation: (.60) A = 72. Divide by .60 to obtain $^{72}/_{.6}$ = 120. Responses (A), (B), and (C) resulted from incorrect placement of the values into the given equation.

7.   **(B)**   is the correct answer. Exponents indicate the number of times one uses a base as a factor. Therefore, $(3^2)(5^3)$ = (3 × 3)(5 × 5 × 5). (A), (C), and (D) are incorrect because they improperly illustrate the meaning of exponents.

8.   **(D)**   is the correct choice. The underlined value (0) is in the hundredths place. (A) represents the tenths position. (C) represents the units position, and (B) represents the hundreds position.

9.   **(B)**   is the correct response. 625% means 625 out of 100 or $^{625}/_{100}$ or 6.25. (A), (C), and (D) all represent misplacement of the decimal point.

10.   **(B)**   is the correct choice. To determine magnitude, multiply the extremes: 2 × 7 or 14 and then the means: 13 × 1 or 13. Since 14 > 13, $^2/_{13}$ > $^1/_7$. (A), (C) and (D) are simply the other choices available.

11.   **(B)**   is the correct response and follows from the process of elimination. If all the boxes weighed 4 lbs., the total weight would be 55 × 4 or 220 lbs. This eliminates (A). If all the boxes weighed 25 lbs., the total weight would be 55 × 25 or 1,375. This eliminates (D). (C) is also unreasonable because at least one box weighs only 4 lbs. and even if the remaining 24 boxes all weigh 25 lbs., the total would be 1,324 lbs. The only choice remaining is (B).

12.   **(A)**   is the correct response. The sequence is being formed by first adding two, then three, then four, and then five. The next term would be found by adding six. Thus arriving at 17. (B), (C), and (D) are incorrect because they are not obtainable values from following the set pattern.

13.   **(B)**   is the correct choice. A 10-day trip would be the weekly package ($150) plus an additional 3 days ($25 × 3 or $75). The total is $225, but this is shared by the two families, so divide $225 by 2 to get $112.50 per family. (A) is the per family rental for an 8-day trip. (C) is the total rental for an 8-day trip. (D) is the total rental of a 10-day trip.

14.   **(A)**   is the correct response. 22% of the 18 sunny days is 18 × .22 or approximately 4 days. (B) and (C) are choices when 22% of 30 days, which is irrelevant to the problem, is calculated. (D) was calculated by incorrectly applying the principles of the problem.

15. **(B)** is the correct answer. When rounding to the nearest ten, look at the units position, in this case the second 4 in the number. Since 4 does not necessitate rounding up, the number in the tens position remains unchanged, and the rounded number is 480. (A) and (C) are obtained by rounding off to the tenths and units positions, respectively. (D) would be correct if the units digit necessitated rounding up.

16. **(D)** is the correct response. By adding the values of each side of the pentagon, we obtain a value of 24 m. 1 m is equivalent to 100 cm, therefore 24 m is equivalent to 2,400 cm. (A), (B), and (C) are incorrect because of improper decimal point placement when converting to centimeters.

17. **(B)** is the correct response. To calculate the area of a circle, use the formula $A = \pi r^2$. So, $A = \pi \times (5)^2$ or 25π sq. in. (A) is found by not squaring the radius. (B) is the circumference of the circle not the area, and (D) is found by using the diameter instead of the radius in the calculation.

18. **(D)** is the correct response. The volume of a rectangular solid is calculated by $V = l \times w \times h$ or $3 \times 6 \times 2$ or 36 cubic cm. The units of (A) and (B) are incorrect for volume. (C) is found by using the incorrect formula.

19. **(B)** is the correct answer. $\angle F = 70°$ because the sum of the interior angles of a triangle equals 180°. $\angle E$ is 110° since it is supplementary to a 70° angle. Therefore, $70° + 110° = 180°$ or $\angle E + \angle F = 180°$. (A) is incorrect because $\angle A = 70°$ and $\angle C = 110°$, and $\angle A = \angle C$. (C) is incorrect because $\angle D = 70°$ and $\angle B = 110°$, and $\angle B = \angle D$. (D) is incorrect because $\angle B$ and $\angle C$ are vertical angles and therefore are equivalent. The sum of their measures is not 90°.

20. **(A)** is the correct answer. The two given angles sum to 90°. Since the angles of a triangle sum to 180°, this leaves 90° for $\angle A$. Since $\angle A$ is 90°, this makes $\triangle ABC$ a right triangle. There is no angle greater than 90°, so $\triangle ABC$ is not an obtuse triangle. Since the angles of $\triangle ABC$ are all different, the sides all have different measures which eliminates (B) and (C).

21. **(B)** is the correct choice. These triangles are similar, and the sides are in proportion. (A) is an incorrect proportion. (C) is incorrect because $\angle ABC$ measures 80°, not 90°. (D) is incorrect because the two angles referenced are equal.

22. **(B)** is the correct answer because it is the only choice which is appropriate for surface area measures. (A) and (C) are unidimensional measures, and (D) is a measure of volume.

23. **(A)**   is the correct answer. To calculate the surface area, it is necessary to calculate the area of each of the laid out pieces. The larger piece is $l \times (h + w + h + w)$ or $l(2w + 2h)$. The area of the end piece is $w \times h$, and since there are two, the total area of the ends is $2(w \times h)$. The surface area of the rectangular solid is then the sum of the larger piece and the two ends. (B), (C), and (D) all result from the incorrect formula for surface area.

24. **(B)**   is the correct choice. To calculate the cost, find the volume of the pool and multiply that by the cost per cubic foot of water: $10 \times 15 \times 6 \times 0.005$ or $4.50. (A), (C), and (D) all contain errors in the proper use of calculating the volume of the pool or decimal point placement.

25. **(C)**   is the correct answer. To simplify the expression, combine the irrational numbers: $3.4\pi + (-2\pi) = 1.4\pi$. Since 2 is not irrational one cannot combine the 1.4π with the 2. Therefore, the answer is $1.4\pi + 2$. (A) and (B) are obtained through errors with the combination of rational and irrational numbers. (D) resulted from improper alignment of decimal places when subtracting the irrational components.

26. **(A)**   is the correct response. When multiplying radical numbers multiply the terms under the radicands: 10×5 or 50. Fifty is the product of 2 and 25 (a perfect square). The square root of 25 is 5. Hence when simplified, the answer is $5\sqrt{2}$. (B), (C), and (D) are the results of errors made in multiplying the radicals or in simplifying.

27. **(C)**   is the correct choice. Begin this problem by squaring $2r$ to get $4r^2$. Multiply this by $^5/_2$ to obtain $10r^2$. Then divide this by 2 for $5r^2$. One cannot add $^1/_2$ to $5r^2$ since they are not like terms, so the correct response is $^1/_2 + 5r^2$ or $0.5 + 5r^2$. (A), (B), and (D) result from errors with order of operations and/or combining unlike terms.

28. **(A)**   is the correct response. Begin by dividing 5.4 by 1.8 to obtain 3. To divide 10^3 by 10^{-2}, simply subtract the exponents: $3 - (-2)$ or 5 for 10^5. So 3×10^5 is equivalent to $3 \times 100,000$ or $300,000$. (B) and (D) are obtained from incorrect decimal placement, and (C) resulted from an error in operation.

29. **(C)**   is the correct answer. Distribute 4 across $2x - 1$ to get $8x - 4 = 5x$. Subtract $5x$ from both sides to combine like terms and get $3x - 4 = 0$. Add 4 to both sides to get $3x = 4$. Divide by 3 to get $x = ^4/_3$. (A), (B), and (D) all stem from algebraic errors common to simplifying equations.

30. **(A)**   is the correct choice. Begin by distributing to get $4x + 20 - 6x + 3 \le 0$. Combine like terms to get $-2x + 23 \le 0$. Subtract 23 to get $-2x \le -23$. When dividing an inequality by a negative number, in this case -2, one must remember to change the direction of the inequality. The result is $x \ge ^{23}/_2$. (C) does not take into account the directional change, and (B) and (D) result from errors in combining like terms and simplifying.

31. **(D)** is the correct choice. Substitute 32 for (*a*) and 3^2 for (t^2) in the given formula. The result is

$$^1/_2 \times 32 \times 9 \text{ or } 144 \text{ feet}$$

(A), (B), and (C) all result from errors made in appropriately using the given formula.

32. **(A)** is the correct answer. Substitute the given value of –2 for *x* in the equation: $\qquad f(-2) = 3(-2)^2 - 2(-2) + 4.$

Simplify: $\qquad\qquad = 3(4) - (-4) + 4$
$$= 12 + 4 + 4$$
$$= 20$$

(B), (C), and (D) all result from errors in simplifying.

33. **(C)** is the correct response. Since 2 (from $2x^2$) and 3 are prime, the only choices for the factors are $2x$ and *x*, and 3 and 1. The choice $(2x + 3)(x - 1)$ when multiplied out gives the original problem. (A), (B), and (D) are likely candidates, but not actual factors of the given quadratic.

34. **(A)** is the correct response. This quadratic equation does not factor, so it is necessary to use the quadratic formula to find the solutions. The quadratic formula is as follows:

$$x = \frac{-b \pm \sqrt{b^2 - 4ac}}{2a} \text{ with } a = 3, b = 6, \text{ and } c = 2.$$
$$x = -6 \pm \sqrt{36 - 4(3)(2)}$$
$$x = \frac{-6 \pm \sqrt{12}}{2a}$$
$$x = \frac{-6 \pm 2\sqrt{3}}{6}$$
$$x = \frac{-3 \pm \sqrt{3}}{3}$$

(B), (C), and (D) all contain errors in the use of the formula or with simplifying.

35. **(C)** is the correct response. To solve a system of linear equations, use one of two methods.

Method 1 — Substitution

Use: $\qquad\qquad\qquad\qquad\qquad\qquad 2x - y = -9$
Solve for *y*: $\qquad\qquad\qquad\qquad\qquad\qquad y = 2x + 9$
Substitute for *y* in $3x + 7y = -5$: $\quad 3x + 7(2x + 9) = -5$
Solve for *x*: $\qquad\qquad\qquad\qquad 3x + 14x + 63 = -5$
$$17x = -68$$
$$x = -4$$

Substitute $x = -4$ into $2x - y = -9$ to find y:
$$2(-4) - y = -9$$
$$-8 - y = -9$$
$$-y = -1$$
$$y = 1$$

Therefore, $\{(-4,1)\}$ is the correct solution set.

<u>Method 2 — Elimination</u>

Multiply: $(2x - y = -9)7$
$$14x - 7y = -63$$
Add: $\underline{3x + 7y = -5}$
$$17x = -68$$
$$x = -4$$

Substitute $x = -4$ into $2x - y = -9$ to find y:
$$2(-4) - y = -9$$
$$-8 - y = -9$$
$$-y = -1$$
$$y = 1$$

Therefore, $\{(-4,1)\}$ is the correct solution set.

36.   **(C)**   is the correct answer. Since addition is commutative, the terms within the parentheses may be interchanged from $3 + 2b$ to $2b + 3$. (A), (B), and (D) all yield different responses from the original as a result of improper property use.

37.   **(C)**   is the correct answer. Substitute 5 for x in each of the three statements.
   (I) yields: $4(5) - 6 = 14 + 5$
$$20 - 6 = 14 + 5$$
$$14 = 19 \qquad \text{...NO...}$$
   (II) yields: $(5 - 5)(5 + 3) = 8$
$$(0)(8) = 8$$
$$0 = 8 \qquad \text{...NO...}$$
   (III) yields: $5^2 + 6(5) - 14 \geq 10$
$$25 + 30 - 14 \geq 10$$
$$41 \geq 10 \qquad \text{...YES...}$$

38.   **(D)**   is the correct choice. Interest = Principal $\times$ Rate $\times$ Time ($I=PRT$). Since the principal of \$8,000 is constant, the rate and interest will vary. Solving for P gives us $P = {}^I/_{RT}$, and since one year is mentioned, we will assume that T is 1 and the equation simplifies to $P = {}^I/_R$. For the initial condition of \$560 of interest at 7%, we have $8,000 = {}^{560}/_{.07}$. For the second condition we have $8,000 = {}^I/_{.05}$. Equating the two fractional terms gives us ${}^{560}/_{.07}$. (D) is the result of inverting this proportion. (A) and (C) set up inappropriate proportions, and (B) uses an incorrect value.

39. **(A)** is the correct response. The inequality $x \leq 2$ includes all points on and to the left of the vertical line $x = 2$. The inequality $x + y \geq 0$ includes all points on and to the upper right of the line passing through the points $(0, 0)$ and $(1, -1)$. The "and" indicates that both conditions must be met. Therefore the solution set consists of all points in the upper wedge. Choice (B) would be the first quadrant. Choice (C) would be the points on and below the horizontal line $y = 2$ and the points on and below the line through $(1, 1)$ and $(0, 0)$. Choice (D) would be the points on and to the left of the vertical line $x = 2$ and the points on and above the line through the points $(1, 1)$ and $(0, 0)$.

40. **(D)** is the correct answer. To solve this inequality divide both sides by -5. When dividing by a negative number, remember to change the direction of the inequality. $^{-5}r/_{-5} < {}^{20}/_{-5}$ or $r > -4$. (B) does not take into account the directional change, and (A) and (C) contain errors with signed numbers.

41. **(A)** is the correct choice. To compute the sales tax, subtract 50 from 175 to find the amount taxed at 8% and find that tax: $(175 - 50)(.08) = \$10$. Then find 2% of the first \$50: $.02(50) = \$1$. Hence, the total tax for the coat would be \$10 + \$1 or \$11. (B) is the result of all of \$175 being taxed at 8%. (C) is a partial answer from above. (D) is a result of an error in understanding the problem.

42. **(B)** is the correct choice. Translating the words into symbols is as follows: "the product of" means multiply, so multiply the first two given expressions, a number decreased by 4 $(n - 4)$ and the same number increased by 10 $(n + 10) \rightarrow$ $(n - 4)(n + 10)$. "Is" means is equal to and 15 less than the number is $(n - 15)$. The full equation is then: $(n - 4)(n + 10) = n - 15$. (A), (C), and (D) are all misrepresentations of the given statement.

43. **(C)** is the correct response. Approximately 65 students were wearing sandals and approximately 25 students were wearing boots. The difference $(65 - 25)$ is 40. (A) and (B) are the values from the graph for the number of students wearing sandals and boots, respectively. (D) is the sum of the number of students wearing sandals or boots.

44. **(A)** is the correct answer. The median is the middle number of a data set in numerical order. First arrange the set in order: 3, 4, 6, 7, 8, 14, 18, 20. Then locate the middle term. In this case the middle term would fall midway between 7 and 8, so the median is 7.5. (B) is from incorrectly rounding the median. (C) is the mean, and (D) is the sum total of the data set.

45. **(C)** is the correct response. Eight elephants are available to be selected for the first position. Given that the first elephant has been selected, only 7 elephants are left to be selected for the second position. The first and second positions have been selected, leaving 6 for the third position. Thus $8 \times 7 \times 6 = 336$. (A), (B), and (D) are incorrect because they do not illustrate the fundamental counting principle for this example.

46. **(D)** is the correct choice. From the information given, the mode and median would be 15, and the mean would be less than 15. So, the mean is less than the median. (A) is incorrect because the mode is not the same as the mean. (B) is incorrect because the median is greater than the mean. (C) is incorrect because the mean is less than the mode.

47. **(D)** is the correct solution because it is the only unbiased sample. When determining if a sampling is unbiased, ask yourself if everyone in the population has an equal and likely chance of being selected. (A), (B), and (C) do not provide for everyone in the population to have an equal and likely chance of being selected.

48. **(A)** is the correct choice. The formula to use is: p (A or B) = p (A) + p (B) − p (A and B). 0.60 represents p (A or B). 0.30 represents p (A) and 0.50 represents p (B). To find p (A and B) substitute the known values into the equation. 0.60 = 0.30 + 0.50 − X. Solving for X gives 0.20. This is the case since some children played both sports. They were counted twice, so we subtract that quantity out to compensate for the double inclusion. (B), (C), and (D) result from incorrect use of the formula.

49. **(D)** is the correct choice. Since set A does not intersect with set B or set C, there can be no element that would be in all three sets A, B, and C. (A) is incorrect because an element could be in region I which is in set B, but not in set C. (B) is incorrect because an element not in set A could be in region V which is not in set B or set C. (C) is incorrect because the element could be in region I, II, III, or V, all within U, but not in set A.

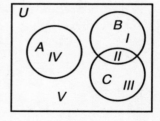

50. **(B)** is the correct choice. In order for a conditional statement to be negated, the premise must be true and the conclusion must be false. Thus, "It is thundering," and "we go swimming," satisfies this condition. (A), (C), and (D) do not satisfy the condition.

51. **(D)** is the correct choice. An equivalent form to the conditional statement (if p then q) is the contrapositive (if not q then not p). Thus, if a number is not an integer, then it is not prime, is the equivalent variation to the given conditional. (A) is the inverse of the conditional and not equivalent. (B) is the converse of the conditional and not equivalent. (C) has no meaning in logic.

52. **(C)** is the correct answer. Sam is ineligible because he requires more than 10 minutes to run the mile. Both Lee Ann and Ryan are eligible as they meet every requirement listed.

53. **(C)** is the correct choice. Even though a horse has a tail, this cannot be logically concluded from the information given. Since some four-legged animals have tails, the horse could be in area I or II of the Venn diagram. There is nothing in the premise which necessitates inclusion in area II.

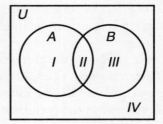

54. **(C)** is the correct answer. From: if p then q
                                    and   if q then r,
we can logically conclude that   if p then r
or in this case: If I join a health club, then I will be in shape to go skiing. (A), (B), and (D) do not follow logically from the above criterion.

55. **(A)** is the correct response. The conjunction "but" is used in place of "and" in the third sentence of the statement which states that you do exercise. The second sentence states that, "If you exercise, you will be healthy." (B) does not follow since you do exercise, and (C) is not valid because we do not know anything about being somewhat healthy.

CLAST

COLLEGE LEVEL ACADEMIC SKILLS TEST

Test 2

This test is also on CD-ROM in our special inter-active CLAST TEST*ware*®. It is highly recommended that you first take this exam on computer. You will then have the additional study features and benefits of timed conditions and instantaneous, accurate scoring. See page 5 for guidance on how to get the most out of our CLAST software.

ESSAY SECTION

DIRECTIONS: The essay portion of this test has a 60-minute time limit. In that time you are to plan, write, and proofread an essay on *one* of the topics listed below. Please read the topics carefully so that you fully understand what you are asked to do.

Topics: 1. A factor in the rising costs of health care.

OR

2. A growing problem with our judicial system.

Reread the topics and select one on which to write your essay. The essay must be on only one of the two topics, and it must address the topic entirely.

In your essay, be sure to introduce the subject, and then do one of the following:

- explain the topic you chose

OR

- assume a position about the topic and support it

Your essay will be judged based on the following criteria:

- Appropriate and effective language
- Proper spelling, grammar, and punctuation
- Well-structured paragraphs and sentences
- Logically developed ideas supported in detail
- Addressing the topic as it has been presented
- Setting up a clear main idea

Take some time to think about what you have to say and how you want to say it before beginning to write. Allow yourself some time toward the end of the section to look over your work and make the necessary corrections.

Handwriting does not affect your score, but it is in your best interest to write legibly so that the evaluators can read and under-stand your essay more easily.

Use the lined pages in the answer sheet at the back of the book to write your essay.

ENGLISH LANGUAGE SKILLS SECTION

(You have 80 minutes to complete both the English Language and Reading Skills sections.)

DIRECTIONS: From the given choices, select the word or phrase that best fits in the context of the sentence.

---

1. There was a feeling of hope and excitement throughout the nation as the new president began his _____ of office.

   (A) reign

   (B) term

   (C) rein

2. I could not see across the street since the fog had begun to _____ the neighborhood.

   (A) wrap

   (B) envelop

   (C) envelope

DIRECTIONS: From the given choices, select the underlined portion which is not needed in the passage and mark its corresponding letter on your answer sheet.

---

3. <u>Today,</u> laser technology is <u>often</u> used in surgery. Because lasers amplify light
      A   B
   to make a <u>powerful</u> beam, doctors can use lasers for <u>delicate</u> operations such
              C   D
   as eye surgery <u>on the eye</u> and removing unhealthy tissue.
                   E

   (A) Today,

   (B) often

   (C) powerful

   (D) delicate

   (E) on the eye

4. Lasers also help shoppers <u>buying groceries</u> check out <u>faster</u> because lasers
   A   B
   "read" the bar codes when groceries <u>that come in boxes</u> are passed over the
                                        C
   beam. In the world of art, photographers create <u>amazing</u> photographs by
                                                    D
   sending a laser beam through everyday objects <u>that we see daily</u>.
                                                 E

   (A) buying groceries

   (B) faster

   (C) that come in boxes

   (D) amazing

   (E) that we see daily

DIRECTIONS: Select the sentence that clearly and effectively states the idea and has no structural errors.

---

5. (A) The instructor told the students to sit down in a loud voice.

   (B) In a loud voice, the instructor told the students to sit down.

   (C) The instructor told the students in a loud voice to sit down.

6. (A) Wearing only pajamas, residents of the burning house were carried out by firemen.

   (B) Residents of the burning house were carried out by firemen wearing only pajamas.

   (C) Firemen carried out residents of the burning house wearing only pajamas.

7. (A) The manager is competent, good natured, and offers help.

   (B) The manager is competent, has a good nature, and offers help.

   (C) The manager is competent, good natured, and helpful.

8. (A) To lick water off the shower curtain, climbing up the side of the house, and sleeping in the kitchen sink are some of my cat's strange habits.

   (B) Licking water off the shower curtain, climbing up the side of the house, and sleeping in the kitchen sink are some of my cat's strange habits.

   (C) Licking water off the shower curtain, climb up the side of the house, and sleeping in the kitchen sink are some of my cat's strange habits.

DIRECTIONS: Select the option that best states the meaning of the underlined sentence.

---

9. When viewing a play in the Elizabethan era, the audiences had to use their imaginations. <u>Since small boys whose voices had not yet changed played the female roles, women were not allowed to perform on the Elizabethan stage.</u>

    (A) Since small boys whose voices had not yet changed played the female roles, women were not allowed to perform on the Elizabethan stage.

    (B) As women were not allowed to perform on the Elizabethan stage, small boys had to play the female roles, although their voices had not yet changed.

    (C) Because women were not allowed to perform on the Elizabethan stage, the female roles were played by small boys whose voices had not yet changed.

    (D) Until small boys whose voices had not yet changed were allowed to play the female roles, women were not permitted to perform on the Elizabethan stage.

10. Advertisers are becoming more interested in consumers between the ages of 55 and 70. <u>In contrast to all other age groups, this age group has more leisure time, more disposable income, and more numbers.</u>

    (A) In contrast to all other age groups, this age group has more leisure time, more disposable income, and more numbers.

    (B) Because this age group is increasing in numbers, they have more leisure time and disposable income.

    (C) Even though this age group has more leisure time and disposable income, their numbers are increasing.

    (D) While this age group does have more leisure time and disposable income, the most important factor to advertisers is their increasing numbers.

DIRECTIONS: Select the sentence that correctly and logically presents the comparison.

---

11. (A) The new methods of teaching reading seem to be much different than the old methods.

    (B) The new methods of teaching reading seem to be very different from the old methods.

    (C) The new methods of teaching reading, seem much more different than the old methods.

12. (A) I found this class to be as challenging as, if not more challenging than, any I have ever taken.

   (B) I found this class to be as challenging, if not more challenging than, any I have ever taken.

   (C) I found this class to be as challenging, if not more challenging, than any I have ever taken.

13. (A) The Volvo is the safest on the market.

   (B) The Volvo is safer than any on the market.

   (C) The Volvo is the safest car on the market.

14. (A) People who once drove to work or school have discovered that cycling is more cheap.

   (B) People who once drove to work or school have discovered that cycling is cheaper.

   (C) People who once drove to work or school have discovered that cycling is cheapest.

DIRECTIONS: Select the correct response.

---

15. I like <u>laying</u> in the sun.

   (A) to lie

   (B) to lay

   (C) having lain

   (D) No change is necessary.

16. He told the delivery man to <u>sit</u> the couch next to the window.

   (A) set

   (B) have set

   (C) setted

   (D) No change is necessary.

DIRECTIONS: The passages that follow contain some errors, which might appear in the underlined part of the test questions. Read each passage and then answer each item by selecting the one that corrects the underlined mistake. Only one underlined mistake will come up in each item. If there is no error, select the "No change is necessary" option.

PASSAGE ONE

Most people are a bit apprehensive about going to the dentist, some people are positively panic-stricken at the thought of a visit to their dentist. The prospect of sitting helplessly in a large mechanical chair while at the mercy of the dentist keeps some people away. These especially fearful people cansel appointments and delay getting checkups. Some frightened people ignore toothaches they would rather put up with pain than go to the dentist. Some of these people suffer from a dental phobia. They have an irrational fear of the dentist.

No one can promise that a visit to the dentist will be painless, however modern technology has made dental treatment much more comfortable. Many people fear the pain of the needle. That delivers the anesthetic. Now some anesthetics can be injected into the gums on a jet of air. The old image of a leering dentist with a huge drill in hand is a common one. Today's dentists; however, use high-speed, water-cooled drills which are fast and virtually painless.

Such sophisticated equipment and techniques does not help to calm all fears; therefore, dentists adopted additional techniques for soothing patients. Some dentists give patients headphones for listening to music during treatment. Others use hypnosis to relax his patients. Getting patients to do relaxing exercises at the beginning of an appointment may also work. Someone who fears dental treatment should tell the dentist of their apprehension. The dentist can then explain the treatment step by step in order to reduce some of the fear.

17. Most people are a bit <u>apprehensive</u> about going to the <u>dentist, some</u> people
                             A   B
     are positively panic-stricken at the thought of a visit to <u>their</u> dentist.
                                                                   C

   (A) aprehensive

   (B) dentist. Some

   (C) his

   (D) No change is necessary.

18. These <u>especially</u> fearful people <u>cansel</u> <u>appointments and</u> delay getting checkups.
      A   B   C

    (A) espesially

    (B) cancel

    (C) appointments, and

    (D) No change is necessary.

19. Some frightened people ignore <u>toothaches they</u> would rather put up with
                                       A

    <u>pain</u> than <u>go to</u> the dentist.
      B   C

    (A) toothaches. They

    (B) pane

    (C) have gone

    (D) No change is necessary.

20. Some of these people suffer from a <u>dental phobia. They</u> have an <u>irrational</u>
                                        A,B   C
    fear of the dentist.

    (A) Dental Phobia

    (B) phobia, they

    (C) irational

    (D) No change is necessary.

21. No one can promise that a visit to the dentist will be <u>painless, however</u>
                                                            A,B
    <u>modern technology</u> has made dental treatment much more comfortable.
         C

    (A) painless; however,

    (B) painless, however;

    (C) Modern Technology

    (D) No change is necessary.

22. Many people fear the pain of the <u>needle. That</u> delivers the <u>anesthetic. Now</u>
                                        A   B
    some anesthetics <u>can</u> be injected into the gums on a jet of air.
                        C

    (A) needle that

    (B) anesthetic, now

    (C) will

    (D) No change is necessary.

23. The old image of a leering dentist with a huge drill in hand is a common one.
    <u>Today's</u> <u>dentists; however,</u> use <u>high-speed, water-</u>cooled drills which are fast
        A   B   C
    and virtually painless.

    (A) Todays'

    (B) dentists, however,

    (C) high-speed water

    (D) No change is necessary.

24. Such sophisticated <u>equipment</u> and techniques <u>does not help</u> to calm all
                          A   B
    <u>fears; therefore</u>, dentists adopted additional techniques for soothing patients.
        C

    (A) equiptment

    (B) do

    (C) fears, therefore

    (D) No change is necessary.

25. Some dentists give patients headphones for listening to music during
    <u>treatment. Others</u> use hypnosis to relax <u>his</u> patients. Getting patients to do
        A   B
    relaxing <u>exercises</u> at the beginning of an appointment may also work.
             C

    (A) treatment others

    (B) their

    (C) exercizes

    (D) No change is necessary.

26. Someone who fears dental treatment should tell the dentist of <u>their apprehension.</u>
                                                                   A,B
    The dentist can then explain the treatment step by <u>step in</u> order to reduce some
                                                        C
    of the fear.

    (A) his or her apprehension

    (B) apprehensions

    (C) step; in

    (D) No change is necessary.

PASSAGE TWO

When they see how little respect and understanding most people have for the animal kingdom, most environmentalists agree with the English Romantic poet William Wordsworth: "Little we see in nature that is ours." That is, the public may not always see the parallels between we humans and the animal kingdom. Anyone with a backyard, however, can observe natural habitate and discern correspondences with human life-styles. There are among the inhabitants a scheme of balancing acts that take place called an ecosystem, Creatures depend upon each other's life-styles for their own existence, that is, the habits of one species enable another species to exist. With respect for the environment. All can survive. Also, nearly all the creatures one could find could teach humans about cooperation. For example most people know that raccoons are fastidious about their food intake, carrying food to a stream to wash it well before eating. Did they also know that raccoons can actually work together to accomplish a task? Two raccoons have been known to work together to help each other reach places neither one could reach on their own. Nature apparently has many lessons for mankind, and she will teach them without a pennies worth of charge.

27. When they see how little respect and understanding most people have for the animal kingdom, most <u>environmentalists</u> agree with the English Romantic
    A
    poet William <u>Wordsworth: "Little</u> we see in nature that is <u>ours."</u>
    B   C

    (A) environmentalists'

    (B) Wordsworth, "Little

    (C) ours".

    (D) No change is necessary.

28. <u>That is,</u> the public may not always see the parallels <u>between</u> <u>we humans</u> and
    A   B   C
    the animal kingdom.

    (A) That is:

    (B) among

    (C) us humans

    (D) No change is necessary.

29. Anyone with a backyard, however, can observe natural <u>habitate</u> and <u>discern</u>
                                                           A   B
    <u>correspondences</u> with human life-styles.
    C

    (A) habitat

    (B) disern

(C) correspondances

(D) No change is necessary.

30. <u>There are among</u> the <u>inhabitants</u> a scheme of balancing acts <u>that take</u> place
       A   B   C
    called an ecosystem.

    (A) there is among

    (B) inhabitant,

    (C) that takes

    (D) No change is necessary.

31. Creatures depend upon each <u>other's</u> life-styles for <u>their</u> own <u>existence, that</u> is,
                               A   B   C
    the habits of one species enable another species to exist.

    (A) others'

    (B) his or her

    (C) existence; that

    (D) No change is necessary.

32. With respect for the <u>environment. All</u> can survive.
                           A,B,C
    (A) environment all

    (B) environment, all

    (C) environment; all

    (D) No change is necessary.

33. For <u>example most</u> people know that raccoons are fastidious about their food
           A
    <u>intake</u>, carrying food to a stream to wash it <u>well</u> before eating.
     B   C
    (A) example, most

    (B) intake:

    (C) good

    (D) No change is necessary.

34. <u>Did</u> they also <u>know that</u> raccoons <u>can</u> actually work together to accomplish a
     A   B   C
    task?

    (A) Don't

    (B) know: that

(C) could

(D) No change is necessary.

35. Two raccoons <u>have been</u> known to work <u>together to</u> help each other reach
                  A   B
    places neither one could reach on <u>their</u> own.
                                          C

    (A) had been

    (B) together, to

    (C) its

    (D) No change is necessary.

36. Nature apparently has many lessons for mankind, and she will teach them
    without a <u>pennies</u> worth of charge.
              A,B,C

    (A) pennies'

    (B) penny's

    (C) pennys

    (D) No change is necessary.

DIRECTIONS: Select the correct response.

---

37. It was true that the boy did not have many of the expensive toys his friends <u>had,
    nevertheless,</u> he was quite happy.

    (A) had. Nevertheless;

    (B) had, nevertheless

    (C) had; nevertheless

    (D) No change is necessary.

38. The radio station invited listeners to choose which of three songs should be
    named the greatest rock-and-roll classic of all time: <u>"Hey, Jude" by the Beatles,
    "Satisfaction" by the Rolling Stones, or "Stairway to Heaven," a Led Zeppelin
    song.</u>

    (A) "Hey Jude;" by the Beatles; "Satisfaction;" by the Rolling Stones; or
    "Stairway to Heaven;" a Led Zeppelin song.

    (B) "Hey Jude," by the Beatles; "Satisfaction," by the Rolling Stones; or
    "Stairway to Heaven," a Led Zeppelin song.

(C) "Hey Jude," by the Beatles, "Satisfaction," by the Rolling Stones, or "Stairway to Heaven," a Led Zeppelin song.

(D) No change is necessary.

39. <u>Because her new shoes feel tight and uncomfortable. Mandy prefers to wear her old sneakers.</u>

(A) Because her new shoes feel tight and uncomfortable, Mandy prefers to wear her old sneakers.

(B) Because her new shoes feel tight and uncomfortable Mandy prefers to wear her old sneakers.

(C) Because her new shoes feel tight and uncomfortable; Mandy prefers to wear her old sneakers.

(D) No change is necessary.

40. The course gave me a great deal of <u>trouble, hundreds</u> of pages of reading, many papers, and essay tests.

(A) trouble. Hundreds

(B) trouble; hundreds

(C) trouble: hundreds

(D) No change is necessary.

READING SKILLS SECTION

DIRECTIONS: Select the word or phrase which identifies best the relationship between the sentence parts.

1. The study of Latin will help you improve your English vocabulary; on the other hand, Spanish will prove more useful in conversation with people.

    (A) Contrast

    (B) Addition

    (C) Spatial order

    (D) Example

DIRECTIONS: Read the following passage and then choose the best response for each question.

Dr. Robert H. Goddard, at one time a physics professor at Clark University, Worcester, Massachusetts, was largely responsible for the sudden interest in rockets back in the 1920s. When Dr. Goddard first started his experiments with rockets, no related technical information was available. He started a new science, industry, and field of engineering. Through his scientific experiments, he pointed the way to the development of rockets as we know them today. The Smithsonian Institute agreed to finance his experiments in 1920. From these experiments he wrote a paper titled "A Method of Reaching Extreme Altitudes," in which he outlined a space rocket of the step (multistage) principle, theoretically capable of reaching the moon.

Goddard discovered that with a properly shaped, smooth, tapered nozzle he could increase the ejection velocity eight times with the same weight of fuel. This would not only drive a rocket eight times faster, but 64 times farther, according to his theory. Early in his experiments he found that solid-fuel rockets would not give him the high power or the duration of power needed for a dependable supersonic motor capable of extreme altitudes. On March 16, 1926, after many trials, Dr. Goddard successfully fired, for the first time in history, a liquid-fuel rocket into the air. It attained an altitude of 184 feet and a speed of 60 mph. This seems small as compared to present-day speeds and heights of missile flights, but instead of trying to achieve speed or altitude at this time, Dr. Goddard was trying to develop a dependable rocket motor.

Dr. Goddard later was the first to fire a rocket that reached a speed faster than the speed of sound. He was first to develop a gyroscopic steering apparatus for rockets. He was the first to use vanes in the jet stream for rocket stabilization

25 during the initial phase of a rocket flight. And he was first to patent the idea of step rockets. After proving on paper and in actual tests that a rocket can travel in a vacuum, he developed the mathematical theory of rocket propulsion and rocket flight, including basic designs for long-range rockets. All of this information was available to our military men before World War II, but evidently its immediate 30 use did not seem applicable. Near the end of World War II we started intense work on rocket-powered guided missiles, using the experiments and developments of Dr. Goddard and the American Rocket Society.

2. The author's primary purpose in writing this passage is to

    (A) explain exactly how a rocket engine operates.

    (B) give the reader a glimpse into the private life of Dr. Robert Goddard.

    (C) summarize Dr. Robert Goddard's contribution to the development of rockets.

    (D) compare Dr. Robert Goddard's achievement with those of other scientists.

3. What is the relationship between the sentence beginning on line 11 ("Goddard discovered...") and the sentence beginning on line 12 ("This would not only drive...")?

    (A) Cause and effect

    (B) Comparison and contrast

    (C) Clarification

    (D) Addition

4. The passage suggests that Goddard's mathematical theory and design

    (A) are applicable to other types of rocket-powered vehicles.

    (B) included basic designs for long-range rockets.

    (C) utilized vanes in jet streams for rocket stabilization.

    (D) tested rocket travel in a vacuum.

DIRECTIONS: Words have been deleted from the following passage. Select the word or phrase that best completes each blank.

A significant development during the Paleolithic period was the emergence of modern man. During this time, one million years ago to 12,000 B.C., man's brain became much larger. There are two suggested reasons for the rapid evolutionary development of man's brain. _____(5)_____ meat eating led to big-game hunting, an activity that necessitated group planning and cooperation; and second, the use of speech facilitated planning and coordination of group activities. Tool making was once thought to be a major factor in the development of a large brain for man, but it is now known that many animals use tools and even make tools.

_____(6)_____ two other factors greatly influenced the emergence of modern man. It seems that about 100,000 years ago, genetic evolution became less important than cultural evolution as man developed the ability to pass on accumulated knowledge. _____(7)_____ food supplies increased significantly after the retreat of the great glaciers about 12,000 years ago. This increase in food supplies may have contributed to the ability of man to increase his own numbers, thus ensuring the survival of his species.

5. (A) Although,

    (B) For this reason,

    (C) Finally,

    (D) First,

6. (A) In conclusion

    (B) Similarly,

    (C) In addition,

    (D) However,

7. (A) Meanwhile,

    (B) Also,

    (C) Nevertheless,

    (D) In spite of this,

DIRECTIONS: Read the following passage and then choose the best response for each question.

A prominent black woman during the Civil War period was Harriet Tubman who was born a slave in 1823. At an early age she was hired out and worked most often as a field hand. She was considered rebellious because of her intolerance of slavery. As a result, she suffered from beatings and whippings by white overseers.
5 In her mid-teens she interfered with an overseer who was beating another slave and was hit in the head with a heavy object. As a result of this injury, she suffered from dizzy spells, blackouts, and seizures for the remainder of her life.

In the late 1840s, Harriet Tubman was determined to escape with her husband and two brothers. Her husband refused to go and her brothers returned to slavery

10 mid-way in their journey. Harriet Tubman continued alone to Delaware and Philadelphia where she worked with white abolitionists. During the next ten years she worked as a "conductor" in the Underground Railroad. She made approximately 19 trips into the South and lead nearly 300 slaves to freedom in the North and Canada. Known as the "Moses of her People," Harriet Tubman traveled, armed

15 and alone, throughout the South. Her enemies placed a $40,000 reward for her capture or death, but she never lost a "passenger" in her many trips.

She was praised and assisted in her efforts by abolitionists in the North, in Canada and in Great Britain. Her exploits were all publicized.

During this period she met John Brown and they became good friends. She

20 helped Brown to plan his noted raid on Harper's Ferry and it was only her own illness that prevented her from joining him.

When the Civil War erupted in 1861, she continued her trips into the South. In 1862 she worked in cooperation with the Union forces which had recently captured the Georgia Sea Islands, serving as a liaison between Federal troops and

25 recently freed blacks and as a volunteer nurse in camp hospitals.

While working in South Carolina, Harriet Tubman served as a spy and a scout for the Union Army. At the request of Federal officers, she organized recently freed blacks into an intelligence service which provided tactical information on Confederate forces to the U.S. forces.

30 In June 1863, Harriet Tubman accompanied Colonel James Montgomery on a raid up the Combahee River in South Carolina. Leading the troops up the river, Harriet Tubman helped them avoid Confederate defenses and participated in the assault which destroyed commissary stores, cotton, and other property valued in the millions and helped over 700 slaves to escape to Union lines.

35 Now known as "General Tubman" by some, Harriet Tubman continued to work with Union forces throughout the war as a cook, nurse, and guide.

Although she worked directly with the Army, she received no pay but she was able, on occasion, to draw rations. At the end of the war, she began a 37-year campaign to receive compensation for her wartime services. Eventually she received

40 a small monthly pension, but it was based on her marriage to a black Union Army veteran who had died a few years after their marriage, not upon her own contributions!

Her postwar activities also included the founding of an old-age home for indigent blacks as well as schools and rest homes for the freed men and their children.

45 Noted and respected by all, she died in 1913, penniless and ignored.

8. The tone of this passage is best described as

(A) angry.

(B) skeptical.

(C) admiring.

(D) detached.

9. In this passage the author expresses bias against

   (A) black people in general.

   (B) the Union Army.

   (C) John Brown.

   (D) Harriet Tubman.

10. The organizational pattern of the second paragraph (lines 8-16) primarily employs

   (A) cause and effect.

   (B) classification.

   (C) chronological order.

   (D) examples.

DIRECTIONS: Read the following dialogue and then answer the question based on its content.

Tiffany: In none of the volleyball games in which I have played did Lisa make a mistake.

Jon: That's not true. Lisa made several mistakes in the game on Tuesday night.

11. Jon's response implies which of the following?

   (A) Tiffany has not played in any games in which Lisa also played.

   (B) Tiffany believes that Lisa is the best player on the team.

   (C) Tiffany has played in every game that Lisa has played in.

   (D) Tiffany played in the game on Tuesday night.

   (E) Tiffany has not watched Lisa's play very closely during the season.

> **DIRECTIONS:** Read the following passage and then choose the best response for each question.

The presence of women in the management ranks of corporations is a reality. We've grown accustomed to seeing this working woman hanging from the subway strap during commuting hours. We may refer disparagingly to her tailored suit and little tie but we no longer visualize her in a housedress with her hair uncombed. The woman who leaves her children to go to work in the morning is no longer a pariah in her community or her family. Her paycheck is more than the pin money; it buys essential family staples and often supports the entire family.

The situation for men has also changed for the better as a result of women's massive entry into the workforce. Men who would once have felt unrelenting pressure to remain with one firm and climb the career ladder are often freed up by a second income to change careers in midlife. They enjoy greater intimacy and involvement with their children.

The benefits for business are also readily apparent. No senior manager in the country would deny that the huge generation of women who entered management seven or eight years ago has functioned superbly, often outperforming men.

Yet the prevailing message from the media on the subject of women and business is one filled with pessimism. We hear about women leaving their employers in the lurch when they go on maternity leave. Or we hear the flip side, that women are overly committed to their careers and neglectful of their families. And in fact, it is true that problems arising from women's new workforce role do exist, side by side with the benefits.

The problems hurt business as well as individuals and their families. Affordable quality childcare, for one example, is still a distant dream. So women are distracted at work, and men who would have felt secure about their children when their wives were home are also anxious and distracted. Distraction also impedes the productivity of some high-achieving women with the birth of their first child and causes some to depart with the birth of their second.

12. The tone of this passage is best described as

   (A) depressed.

   (B) cynical.

   (C) optimistic.

   (D) humorous.

13. In this passage, the author expresses bias against

    (A) the media.

    (B) women in the management ranks.

    (C) husbands who let their wives work.

    (D) men who change careers in midlife.

14. The organizational pattern of the fourth paragraph (lines 18-23) primarily employs

    (A) cause and effect.

    (B) classification.

    (C) chronological order.

    (D) examples.

DIRECTIONS: Words have been deleted from the following passage. Select the word or phrase that best completes each blank.

Consultative teaching models have gained much popularity lately. The Content Mastery program is one such model designed to assist students who have been identified as learning disabled to achieve their maximum potential in normal classroom environments. Learning disabled students are intelligent but need extra skills in order to overcome their disabilities. A learning disabled student who is mainstreamed may have difficulties in a class where the teacher may not have the training necessary to help students with different disabilities. ____(15)____, since class sizes vary, some classes may be too large for the teacher to give individualized instruction necessary for the success of these students. The student who needs extra help can go to the Content Mastery classroom and work on an individualized basis under the guidance of the special programs teacher with the materials available there. Students needing the Content Mastery program exhibit the following character- istics: consistently low grades, poor performance, and gaps in skills.

____(16)____, Content Mastery is not just "a little extra help." It also is not designed to "give" students the answers to worksheets and tests. What Content Mastery does is offer increased stimulus variation in the form of many different strategies. ____(17)____, the Content Mastery materials include taped textbooks, hi-lighted books and worksheets, and supplementary materials (such as laminated charts to practice labeling), as well as small study groups, individual counseling, sessions on test-taking strategies, and other types of problem-solving skills.

15. (A) Also,

    (B) In short,

    (C) In spite of this,

    (D) Therefore,

16. (A) Presently,

    (B) However,

    (C) Conversely,

    (D) For this reason,

17. (A) For example,

    (B) Otherwise,

    (C) In conclusion,

    (D) As a result,

DIRECTIONS: Read the following passage and then choose the best response for each question.

Helping your children enjoy reading is one of the most important things you can do as a parent and well worth the investment of your time and energy. Kids will learn reading skills in school, but often they come to associate reading with work, not pleasure. As a result, they lose their desire to read. And it is that desire—the
5 curiosity and interest—that is the cornerstone to using reading and related skills successfully.

By far the most effective way to encourage your children to love books and reading is to read aloud to them, and the earlier you start, the better. Even a baby of a few months can see pictures, listen to your voice, and turn cardboard pages.
10 Make this time together a special time when you hold your children and share the pleasure of a story without the distractions of TV or telephones. You may be surprised to find that a well-written children's book is often as big a delight to you as it is to the kids.

And don't stop taking the time to read aloud once your children have learned
15 to read for themselves. At this stage, encourage them to read to you some of the time. This shared enjoyment will continue to strengthen your children's interest and appreciation.

Simply having books, magazines, and newspapers around your home will help children to view them as part of daily life. And your example of reading frequently
20 and enjoying it will reinforce that view.

While your children are still very small, it's a good idea to start a home library for them, even if it's just a shelf or two. Be sure to keep some books for little children to handle freely. Consider specially made, extra-durable books for infants, and pick paperbacks and plastic covers for kids who are older but still not quite ready for
25 expensive hardbacks. Allowing little children to touch, smell, and even taste books will help them to develop strong attachments.

How you handle books will eventually influence how your kids treat them. Children imitate, so if they see that you enjoy reading and treat books gently and with respect, it is likely that, in time, they will do the same.

30 When you read aloud together, choose books that you both like. If a book seems dull, put it down and find one that is appealing.

18. The tone of this passage is best described as

   (A) neutral.

   (B) encouraging.

   (C) despondent.

   (D) bitter.

19. In this passage, the author expresses bias against

   (A) adult literature.

   (B) viewing reading as work.

   (C) magazines and newspapers.

   (D) reading aloud.

20. The organizational pattern of the second paragraph (lines 7-13) primarily employs

   (A) comparison.

   (B) definition.

   (C) location order.

   (D) statement and clarification.

DIRECTIONS: Read the following statements and then answer the question based on the information provided.

All basketball players are athletic. Some teenagers are basketball players. Some athletic persons are skaters. No teenagers are skaters.

21. If the statements above are true, which of the following must also be true?

    (A) All skaters are athletic.

    (B) No basketball players are skaters.

    (C) Some teenagers are athletic.

    (D) Some teenagers are skaters.

    (E) All athletic persons are basketball players or skaters.

DIRECTIONS: Read the following passage and then choose the best response for each question.

Child care is much on our minds these days. With quality child care we are developing our young people and, therefore, are developing the future of this community and the future of the nation. Henry Adams, who devoted considerable thought to education, said, "A teacher affects eternity; he can never tell where
5 influence stops." That is the sort of heady stuff inherent in the work of the child development centers we celebrate today. For many years laymen believed that the education of a child begins in first grade. Kindergarten and before were relegated to child's play. Through education of the laity, we are making it known that child's play is "serious business," that play is the work of children through which they
10 develop as human beings, learn to relate to others, find security and develop the self-esteem critical to their maturing as successful and happy adults. By first grade it is too late to begin this serious work. You have been told that students dropping out of high school is a critical problem across the nation and I will tell you that children don't drop out in high school. They drop out in kindergarten and wait ten
15 years to make it official. If you want to improve education, reduce dropouts, produce happy and accomplished citizens, employees, managers, and customers for the future, put your money on preschool and early childhood education. That is where the human being is developed. Count on it.

22. The tone of this passage is best described as

    (A) lighthearted.

    (B) ironic.

    (C) nostalgic.

    (D) concerned.

23. In this passage, the author expresses bias against

    (A) Henry Adams.

    (B) the idea that education begins in first grade.

(C) laymen.

(D) kindergarten teachers.

24. The organizational pattern of this paragraph primarily employs

(A) summary.

(B) statement and clarification.

(C) comparison.

(D) time order.

DIRECTIONS: Read the following passage and then choose the best response for each question.

The biggest enemy of the Civil War soldiers was disease; almost 80 percent of all deaths during the war were the result of sickness. Care for these ill and disabled soldiers was provided by civilians, most of whom were women. Since over 180,000 black men served in the armed forces of the Union army and another 200,000 black
5 men worked in service units, it is clear that large numbers of black women were needed to provide assistance to them.

The most famous of the black women who volunteered to help the troops was Susie King Taylor. Born a slave in 1848 on one of the Georgia Sea Islands, she grew up in Savannah. She learned to read and write in a clandestine school taught by a
10 free black woman.

In her early teens, Susie returned to the Sea Islands and escaped slavery when the Union army occupied the islands in 1862. By now 14, she volunteered to work as a teacher in a school for freedmen on St. Simon's Island. Later that year, she married Edward King and moved to Port Royal Island off the coast of South
15 Carolina.

While on Port Royal, Edward joined the First South Carolina Volunteers, a regiment of black troops being raised by General Hunter, the Union commander. Susie King taught soldiers in her husband's company to read and write as well as helped the men to clean their equipment, and nursed the wounded after battles.

20 In her semi-official position as unit laundress and volunteer nurse, Susie King traveled with her husband's unit, the First South Carolina Volunteers (later the 33d U.S. Colored Troops), throughout the war. In 1863, while at Camp Shaw in Beaufort, South Carolina, she met Clara Barton, the founder of the American Red Cross. She also became acquainted with Colonel Thomas Wentworth Higginson,
25 the commander of the 33d U.S.C.T. and a noted abolitionist.

In February 1866, the 33d U.S.C.T. was disbanded and Susie King moved to Savannah where she opened a night school for adult freedmen. She operated the school through 1868 but upon the death of her husband, she took employment as a house domestic and laundress. In 1874 she moved to Boston with her employers and continued to work as a house servant. In 1879, she married Russell Taylor.

While in Boston, Susie Taylor helped to organize the Boston branch of the Women's Relief Corps, an auxiliary of the Grand Army of the Republic in 1886.

In 1898 her son became ill in Louisiana and she returned to the South to nurse him. Though he needed specialists' care, Jim Crow laws prevented her from taking him back to Boston; he died soon thereafter.

After the war, Colonel Higginson encouraged her to write her wartime memoirs and contributed the foreword to her book. In 1902 Mrs. Taylor published her wartime memoirs and they constitute the only written record of the activities of the black nurses during the Civil War.

25. The tone of this passage is best described as

    (A) ardent.

    (B) arrogant.

    (C) detached.

    (D) indignant.

26. In this passage, the author expresses bias against

    (A) Jim Crow laws.

    (B) army volunteers.

    (C) the American Red Cross.

    (D) Colonel Higginson.

27. The organizational pattern of the third paragraph (lines 11-15) primarily employs

    (A) addition.

    (B) cause and effect.

    (C) generalization and example.

    (D) chronological order.

DIRECTIONS: Words have been deleted from the following passage. Select the word or phrase that best completes each blank.

One of the world's most valuable gems, pearls are valued for their luminous beauty. Pearls are formed when an irritant, like a few grains of sand or a parasite, enters a mollusk. Nacre-forming cells begin to cover the intruder with smooth layers of calcium carbonate until the irritant assumes the same appearance as the inside of the mollusk. Only rarely, and after many years, do the layers of nacre form a pearl.

When a cut pearl is examined under a microscope, concentric layers of nacre are revealed. Tiny crystals of the mineral aragonite, held in place by a cartilage-like substance called conchiolin, reflect light in an iridescent rainbow effect. Jewelers call this iridescence *orient*. Most mollusks do not make iridescent pearls _____(28)_____ their aragonite crystals are too large.

Perfectly round pearls are quite rare in natural occurrence. Most pearls now are cultured. A young oyster receives both a piece of mantle from a donor oyster and a seeding bead of mussel shell. These are tucked into a carefully-made incision in an oyster, which is then lowered into the ocean in a wire cage so it can be cleaned and periodically x-rayed to check on progress. _____(29)_____ the oyster is a living organism, and not a machine in a factory, the oyster may choose to spit out the introduced nucleus, or the resulting pearl may be full of lumps and stains. Minor stains and imperfections, _____(30)_____ may be eliminated by carefully grinding down the surface of the pearl in order to produce a smaller, but more valuable, perfect pearl.

28. (A) although

    (B) because

    (C) provided that

    (D) even though

29. (A) Instead

    (B) Likewise

    (C) Since

    (D) Otherwise

30. (A) therefore,

    (B) meanwhile,

    (C) besides,

    (D) however,

DIRECTIONS: Read the following passage and then choose the best response for each question.

The classroom is not the place to learn decision making, it is not the place to learn interpersonal communication skills, and it is not the place to learn occupational skills, but if we expect a functional population, these things had better be a part of the educational curriculum. In class we prepare passively for action in the future.
5 Most life skills are best learned by direct action and experiencing the consequences. Adolescents need to come face-to-face with reality. Most of the time youth are not allowed to see what life is all about until late in adolescence when we climb over the schoolyard walls, only to find that we don't have the tools to deal with reality. We don't want to be in that world, so we take pills, we take drugs, and sometimes we
10 take our lives. We feel impotent about what to do in the present because we've never done anything in the past. We need the opportunity to make a difference and experience our own mistakes and successes to form our own identity and sense of self-worth. School can be the place which emphasizes participation. We need to advocate that schools allow education to include "action," not merely passive
15 textbook learning. I realize that many of you deal with young people who have already given up on education. The aid you give them is crucial. But, if we ever want to prevent them from becoming long-term clients of the social services, welfare, or justice systems, we must concentrate on the roots of the problems. If we increase the inherent interest of materials taught, if we give the students a sense of discovery,
20 if we teach well, and if what we teach is worth learning, then perhaps people will get more involved in the process of learning than they are right now. That movement has already begun with the work of organizations like Independent Sector, which are trying to shatter the idea that educational curriculum can only refer to that which occurs in a classroom. Let's join that movement.

31. The tone of this passage is best described as

   (A) impassioned.

   (B) malicious.

   (C) incredulous.

   (D) apathetic.

32. In this passage, the author expresses bias against

   (A) adolescents.

   (B) the social services, welfare, and justice systems.

   (C) traditional classroom teaching and learning.

   (D) organizations like Independent Sector.

33. The organizational pattern of the passage primarily employs

    (A) statement and clarification.

    (B) simple listing.

    (C) contrast.

    (D) classification.

DIRECTIONS: Read the following statements and then answer the question based on the information provided.

A teenager claims:

When I am 16, I can be sued, but I also can drive a car.

When I am 18 and have to register for the draft, I can vote.

When I am 21, I have to go to work, but I can drink.

34. Which of the following would be the most plausible conclusions from these claims?

    (A) When I am 65, I have to retire, but I get social security.

    (B) When I am 13 and have to pay adult movie prices, I should be allowed to see adult movies.

    (C) When I am six, I have to go to school, but I should not have to walk to it.

    (D) When I get married, I will need money for a house.

    (E) When I am 35 and have my mid-life crisis, I should make a lot of money.

DIRECTIONS: Select the word or phrase which identifies best the relationship between the sentence parts.

---

35. A longer school year is not the answer to our academic problems; furthermore, such a proposal would never be passed by the legislature.

    (A) Cause and effect

    (B) Addition

    (C) Contrast

    (D) Example

36. The rays of the sun at the horizon pass through a large portion of the atmosphere, which refracts them and makes the sun appear red or orange.

    (A) Cause and effect

    (B) Comparison

    (C) Example

    (D) Spatial order

DIRECTIONS: Read the following passage and then choose the best response for each question.

The high school drop out rate remains high in many southern states. An average of 18 percent of the students who finish sixth grade in Texas, Mississippi, Louisiana, and Alabama do not stay in school long enough to graduate from high school. Maintaining a precise count of the number of dropouts is difficult. Some students may still be listed as enrolled when in fact they have stopped attending school and do not plan to return. A slightly larger percentage of male students drop out of school than females. More students tend to leave school during the eleventh grade. Other times most frequently cited reasons for dropping out include failing grades, suspensions and expulsions, conflict with the school, pregnancy, marriage and economic hardship. Generally, students who are <u>incarcerated</u> are not counted in the total number of dropouts. Some school districts have implemented special programs to encourage teens to stay in school. These retention programs usually include tutoring, counseling and opportunities for part-time employment at the school or in the neighborhood.

37. On line 10, the word <u>incarcerated </u>means

    (A) mentally handicapped.

    (B) incapacitated.

    (C) underage.

    (D) in prison.

38. The main idea expressed in this passage is that

    (A) everyone should graduate from high school.

    (B) more males drop out of school than females.

    (C) there are many reasons why students drop out of school.

    (D) some southern states have large numbers of students who do not graduate from high school.

39. The sentence beginning on line 7 ("More students tend to leave school during the eleventh grade.") is a statement of

    (A) fact.

    (B) opinion.

40. The statement beginning on line 4 ("Some students may still be listed as enrolled...") is used to support which point?

    (A) Maintaining a precise count of the number of dropouts is difficult.

    (B) More male students drop out than females.

    (C) An average of 18 percent of students in the South do not graduate.

    (D) More students tend to leave during the eleventh grade.

DIRECTIONS: Read the following statements and then answer the question based on the information provided.

---

41. Premise: Jill has used her electric can opener thousands of times, and it has never malfunctioned.

    Conclusion: Therefore, it will not give her any problem with the can she is now opening.

    The argument is

    (A) valid.

    (B) invalid.

MATHEMATICS SECTION

(You have 90 minutes to complete this section.)

DIRECTIONS: Select the best answer.

---

1. $-\frac{1}{3} - \frac{1}{4} =$

   (A) $\frac{1}{12}$ (C) $-\frac{7}{12}$

   (B) $-\frac{1}{7}$ (D) $-\frac{2}{7}$

2. $(\frac{2}{5})$ **x** $(-3\frac{1}{2}) =$

   (A) $3\frac{1}{10}$ (C) $\frac{5}{7}$

   (B) -2 (D) $-\frac{7}{5}$

3. $-2.1 + (-7.31) =$

   (A) -5.21 (C) -14.31

   (B) -9.41 (D) 9.41

4. $-0.4 \div 1.6 =$

   (A) -0.025 (C) -0.4

   (B) 4 (D) -0.25

5. What is the result of decreasing 30 by 20% of itself?

   (A) 24   (C) 15

   (B) 6   (D) 10

6. What percent of 300 is 105?

   (A) 2.85%   (C) 28.5%

   (B) 0.35%   (D) 35%

7. $(4^3)^2 =$

   (A) $(4)^9$ (C) $(4)^{3+2}$

   (B) $(12)^2$ (D) $(4^3)(4^3)$

8. Select the numeral equivalent to

   $(7 \times 10^2) + (3 \times 10) + (2 \times \frac{1}{10}) + (6 \times \frac{1}{10^4})$.

   (A) 730.2006   (C) 730.0206

   (B) 73.26   (D) 730.2161

9. $^7/_{20} =$

    (A) 3.5%   (C) 35%

    (B) 0.035   (D) 0.35%

10. Choose the symbol to place in the box which makes the following
    statement true.

    $7.2\overline{6}$ ☐ 7.265

    (A) =   (C) <

    (B) >   (D) ≤

11. Twelve people work at a small print shop. The lowest paid person earns $120
    per week while the highest paid person earns $780 per week. What is a
    reasonable estimate of the average salary per person?

    (A) $110   (C) $570

    (B) $150   (D) $780

12. Look for a linear relationship between the numbers in each ordered-pair.
    Then identify the missing term.
    (0, 0) (7, $^7/_4$) (6, $^3/_2$) (8, 2) (–5, $^{-5}/_4$) (20, __)

    (A) 4   (C) 14

    (B) 5   (D) –4

13. The people on a cruise are forming equal teams to play a game. When the
    people form teams of 2, 3, or 4, there is always one person left. What is the
    smallest number of people wanting to play the game?

    (A) 9   (C) 13

    (B) 12   (D) 25

14. Round the measure of the length of the pictured pencil to the nearest $^1/_4$ cm.

    (A) 10.50 cm

    (B) 10.75 cm

    (C) 11.00 cm

    (D) 11.25 cm

15. What is the distance around
    the right triangle shown?

    (A) 24 miles

    (B) 10 miles

    (C) 100 miles

    (D) 200 miles

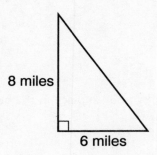

8 miles

6 miles

16. What is the area of a triangular region with a base measure of 6 cm and a height
    of 7 cm?

    (A) 13 sq. cm.   (C) 84 sq. cm.

    (B) 21 sq. cm.   (D) 42 sq. cm.

17. What is the volume of a right circular cylinder that is 10 inches high and has
    a diameter of 8 inches?

    (A) 80π sq. in.   (C) 640π cu. in.

    (B) 160π sq. in.   (D) 160π cu. in.

18. Given that $\overleftrightarrow{AC} \parallel \overleftrightarrow{BD}$ and $\overleftrightarrow{AC} \perp \overleftrightarrow{AB}$,
    examine the figure and determine which
    of the following statements is true.

    (A) $x = y$

    (B) $\angle ACB$ and $\angle DBC$ are complementary angles.

    (C) $\triangle ABC$ is an equilateral triangle.

    (D) $x = z$

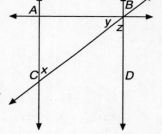

19. Given that $l_1 \parallel l_2$. Which of the
    following pairs are vertical angles?

    (A) 1 and 3

    (B) 1 and 4

    (C) 5 and 7

    (D) 2 and 4

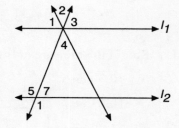

20. Which of the statements is true for the pictured triangles?

    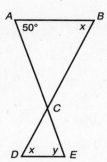

    (A) $x = y$

    (B) $\dfrac{CE}{DE} = \dfrac{CB}{AB}$

    (C) $m\angle ACB = m\angle ECD$

    (D) $z = 50°$

21. Which measure would *not* be appropriate for the total amount of shampoo used yearly by a family of four?

    (A) Gallons   (C) Cubic centimeters

    (B) Square inches   (D) Liters

22. Study the given figures. What is the measure of x?

    (A) 40°

    (B) 60°

    (C) 100°

    (D) 120°

    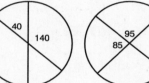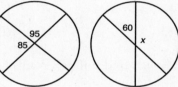

23. The country of Alika is designing a new flag. The original flag will be 6 feet by 8 feet. The design will include red ribbon sewn around the perimeter and across one diagonal. How much ribbon will be needed for the new flag?

    (A) 38 feet   (C) 24 feet

    (B) 58 feet   (D) 28 feet

24. $\sqrt{12} + 4\sqrt{3} =$

    (A) $4\sqrt{15}$ (C) $8\sqrt{3}$

    (B) $6\sqrt{3}$ (D) $5\sqrt{15}$

25. $\dfrac{9}{\sqrt{3}} =$

    (A) 3   (C) $6\sqrt{3}$

    (B) $\sqrt{3}$ (D) $3\sqrt{3}$

26. $\dfrac{6(a + 2b)}{3} - (3a - b) =$

    (A) $-a + 5b$ (C) $a + b/3$

    (B) $-a + b$ (D) $-a + 3b$

27. $0.003 \times 627{,}000 =$

    (A) 1.881×10^4 (C) 2.09

    (B) 188.1 (D) 1.881×10^3

28. If $6a - (a - 3) = 0$, then

    (A) $a = 2.$ (C) $a = 3/5.$

    (B) $a = -1/2.$ (D) $a = -3/5.$

29. If $7 - x > 6 + 2x$, then

    (A) $x < 3.$ (C) $x > 1/3.$

    (B) $x > 13.$ (D) $x < 1/3.$

30. Given E $= mc^2$, find E if $m = 3$ and $c = 4$.

    (A) 36 (C) 49

    (B) 48 (D) 144

31. Given $f(x) = x^3 + 6x - 1$, find $f(3)$.

    (A) 26 (C) 19

    (B) 44 (D) 35

32. Which is a linear factor of the following expression?
    $$10x^2 - x - 2$$

    (A) $2x - 1$ (C) $5x - 2$

    (B) $2x + 1$ (D) $5x - 1$

33. Solve the following quadratic equation.
    $$2x^2 - 1 = 3x$$

    (A) $\dfrac{3 \pm \sqrt{17}}{2}$ (C) $\dfrac{3 \pm \sqrt{17}}{4}$

    (B) $1, 1/2$ (D) $\dfrac{-3 \pm \sqrt{17}}{4}$

34. Identify the correct solution set for the given system of linear equations.
    $$4x - 3y = 8$$
    $$-8x + 6y = 4$$

    (A) $\{(0,12)\}$

    (B) $\{(2, 0)\}$

    (C) $\{\quad\}$

    (D) $\{ (x, y) \mid 4x - 3y = 8; x, y \in R\}$

35. Choose the expression equivalent to the following:
    $(5pq^2)q^3r^3$.

    (A) $25p^2q^2q^3r^3$ (C) $5pq^6r^3$

    (B) $5p(q^2q^3)r^3$ (D) $(5pq)^2q^3r^3$

36. For each statement below, determine if $x = -^1/_2$ is a solution.
    I. $|3x + 2| < 1$
    II. $(2x - 1)(x + 4) = 0$
    III. $4x^2 - 1 = 0$

    (A) I and II only

    (B) I and III only

    (C) III only

    (D) All of the above

37. During a given 24-hour period, 500 cars pass over a bridge. Let n represent the number of cars passing over the bridge during a 6-day period. Select the correct condition for the given information.

    (A) $\dfrac{500}{1} = \dfrac{n}{6}$ (C) $\dfrac{n}{500} = \dfrac{1}{6}$

    (B) $\dfrac{500}{24} = \dfrac{n}{6}$ (D) $\dfrac{n}{500} = \dfrac{6}{24}$

38. Select the shaded region which graphically represents the conditions
$x \geq 0$ and $-3 < y < 3$.

(A)

(B)

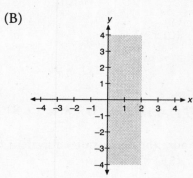

(C)

(D)

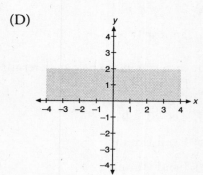

39. Select an equivalent inequality to the following:
$-12 < 4r < 28$.

(A) $-16 < r < 24$ (C) $-3 < r < 7$

(B) $-3 > r < 7$ (D) $3 < r < 7$

40. A circus is traveling from Orlando to Jacksonville. The caravan averages 50 miles per hour for the first 100 miles of the 150 mile trip, but construction slows the pace to 30 miles per hour for the remaining journey. How long will it take for the circus to reach Jacksonville?

(A) 3.67 hours   (C) 2 hours

(B) 1.67 hours   (D) 1 hour

41. Select the appropriate equation for the following narrative: The product of two consecutive odd integers is 195.

(A) $(2n + 1) + (2n + 3) = 195$ (C) $n(n + 3) = 195$

(B) $(2n + 1)(2n + 3) = 195$ (D) $n(n + 1) = 195$

42. The circle graph represents the amount of time a college freshman spends in the given activities during a 24-hour day. What percent of the time is spent studying and eating?

    (A) 8%

    (B) 22%

    (C) 38%

    (D) 46%

eating 2 hr.   sleeping 8 hr.

studying 9 hr.   in class 3 hr.

leisure 2 hr.

43. Find the mean of the following data set:
    11, 4, 2, 7, 15, 2, 5, 8.

    (A) 11   (C) 2

    (B) 6   (D) 6.75

44. Representatives to a student group are being selected to fill vacancies. Two of five freshmen will be selected and three of four sophomores will be selected. In how many different ways can these students be selected?

    (A) 480   (C) 22

    (B) 120   (D) 40

45. If there is a 70% chance that a seed will sprout, what is the probability that a seed will not sprout?

    (A) 0.30

    (B) 0.70

    (C) 1

    (D) Cannot be determined from the information given.

46. The following plot represents an individual's shoe size and height.

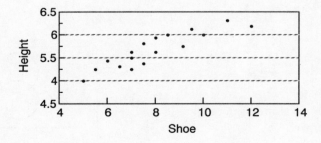

Which of the following best describes the relationship between shoe size and height?

(A) There appears to be no relationship between shoe size and height.

(B) An increase in height causes an increase in shoe size.

(C) There appears to be a negative relationship between shoe size and height.

(D) There appears to be a positive relationship between shoe size and height.

47. The following table depicts the distribution of end of semester grades.

Grades	Percent
A	12
B	26
C	30
D	22
F	10

What percent of the students received a C or higher?

(A) 30%   (C) 68%

(B) 62%   (D) 38%

48. The following information on flavor and topping preference was tabulated at a local yogurt shop.

	Fruit	Candy
Vanilla	25%	35%
Chocolate	5%	10%
Swirl	10%	15%

What is the probability that someone ordered a swirl yogurt?

(A) .15   (C) .05

(B) .10   (D) .25

49. Sets *A, B, C,* and *U* are related as shown in the diagram.

Which of the following statements is true, assuming none of the eight regions is empty?

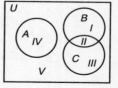

(A) An element that is a member of sets *A* and *B* must be a member of set *C.*

(B) An element that is not a member of set *A* is a member of set *B.*

(C) An element that is a member of sets *A, B,* and *C* is a member of *U*.

(D) None of the above statements is true.

50. Select the statement that is the negation of the statement "The apple is green and it is not ready to eat."

    (A) The apple is not green or it is ready to eat.

    (B) The apple is not green and it is ready to eat.

    (C) If the apple is not green, then it is ready to eat.

    (D) If the apple is ready to eat, then it is green.

51. Given that:

    I. Everything that flies has wings.
    II. Balloons do not have wings.

    Determine a deducible logical conclusion.

    (A) Some balloons fly.

    (B) Balloons have wings.

    (C) Balloons do not fly.

    (D) No logical conclusion can be drawn.

52. The conclusions to the following arguments are all true. Select the one argument that is not valid.

    (A) All cars have four wheels and all station wagons have four wheels. Therefore, a station wagon is a car.

    (B) All whole numbers are integers and all integers are real numbers. Therefore, all whole numbers are real numbers.

    (C) Every trapezoid has four sides and every four-sided figure is called a quadrilateral. Therefore, every trapezoid is a quadrilateral.

    (D) All forks have tines and all tines will pierce meat. Therefore, all forks will pierce meat.

53. Read the following argument and select the valid conclusion which can be drawn from the given argument.

    If the soda bottle is half empty, then it is half full. The soda bottle is not half full.

    (A) The soda bottle is more than half empty.

    (B) The soda bottle is less than half empty.

(C) The soda bottle is not half empty.

(D) The soda bottle is either completely full or empty.

54. Choose the rule of logical equivalence that directly (in one step) transforms statement I into statement II.

  I.   If the printer is unplugged, then it will not work.

  II. The printer is not unplugged or it will not work.

  (A) "If p, then q" is equivalent to "not p or q."

  (B) "If p, then q" is equivalent to "not p or not q."

  (C) "Not (p or q)" is equivalent to "not p or not q."

  (D) "If p, then q" is equivalent to "if not q, then not p."

55. Which is a logical conclusion that can be drawn from the following?

  All astronauts are highly skilled, trained professionals.
  All highly skilled, trained professionals have college degrees.
  Aaron has a college degree.

  (A) Aaron is a highly skilled, trained professional.

  (B) Aaron is an astronaut.

  (C) Aaron is not an astronaut.

  (D) None of these are logical.

PRACTICE TEST 2

ANSWER KEY

English Language Skills

1. **(B)**	11. **(B)**	21. **(A)**	31. **(C)**
2. **(B)**	12. **(A)**	22. **(A)**	32. **(B)**
3. **(E)**	13. **(C)**	23. **(B)**	33. **(A)**
4. **(E)**	14. **(B)**	24. **(B)**	34. **(A)**
5. **(B)**	15. **(A)**	25. **(B)**	35. **(C)**
6. **(A)**	16. **(A)**	26. **(A)**	36. **(B)**
7. **(C)**	17. **(B)**	27. **(D)**	37. **(C)**
8. **(B)**	18. **(B)**	28. **(C)**	38. **(B)**
9. **(C)**	19. **(A)**	29. **(A)**	39. **(A)**
10. **(D)**	20. **(D)**	30. **(A)**	40. **(C)**

Reading Skills

1. **(A)**	12. **(C)**	23. **(B)**	34. **(B)**
2. **(C)**	13. **(A)**	24. **(B)**	35. **(B)**
3. **(A)**	14. **(D)**	25. **(C)**	36. **(A)**
4. **(A)**	15. **(A)**	26. **(A)**	37. **(D)**
5. **(D)**	16. **(B)**	27. **(D)**	38. **(D)**
6. **(C)**	17. **(A)**	28. **(B)**	39. **(A)**
7. **(B)**	18. **(B)**	29. **(C)**	40. **(A)**
8. **(C)**	19. **(B)**	30. **(D)**	41. **(B)**
9. **(B)**	20. **(D)**	31. **(A)**	
10. **(C)**	21. **(C)**	32. **(C)**	
11. **(D)**	22. **(D)**	33. **(A)**	

Mathematics

1. **(C)**	12. **(B)**	23. **(A)**	34. **(C)**	45. **(A)**
2. **(D)**	13. **(C)**	24. **(B)**	35. **(B)**	46. **(D)**
3. **(B)**	14. **(B)**	25. **(D)**	36. **(B)**	47. **(C)**
4. **(D)**	15. **(A)**	26. **(A)**	37. **(A)**	48. **(D)**
5. **(A)**	16. **(B)**	27. **(D)**	38. **(A)**	49. **(C)**
6. **(D)**	17. **(D)**	28. **(D)**	39. **(C)**	50. **(A)**
7. **(D)**	18. **(D)**	29. **(D)**	40. **(A)**	51. **(C)**
8. **(A)**	19. **(D)**	30. **(B)**	41. **(B)**	52. **(A)**
9. **(C)**	20. **(C)**	31. **(B)**	42. **(D)**	53. **(C)**
10. **(B)**	21. **(B)**	32. **(A)**	43. **(D)**	54. **(A)**
11. **(C)**	22. **(D)**	33. **(C)**	44. **(D)**	55. **(D)**

DETAILED EXPLANATIONS OF ANSWERS

ESSAY SECTION
SAMPLE ESSAYS FOR TOPIC #1

WRITING SAMPLE WITH A SCORE OF 5 OR 6

The rising cost of health care in the United States has become more than a national concern — it is now a national crisis. The situation has become so grave that the President made health care costs a major issue in his campaign, and has appointed a task force to investigate ways of providing equitable health care for all Americans. One of the most pressing problems the task force is addressing is health insurance.

The cost of health insurance in this country has skyrocketed in the last two decades. Many middle class Americans cannot afford to insure themselves and their families, despite earning relatively large incomes, and for the working class, health insurance is completely out of reach. The result is that these people literally cannot afford to get sick. An illness means lost work and wages, as well as exorbitant medical bills. Those who can afford to buy health insurance often find that their policy is inadequate for anything beyond rudimentary care. An unexpected surgery can involve thousands of dollars in out-of-pocket expenses, and a chronic disease like cancer or diabetes can eat up a policy's maximum allowable benefits in a matter of weeks or months.

Many employers provide health benefits to their employees as part of their compensation, but while these plans often do not cost the employee to insure himself, adding a spouse and children to the coverage often entails payments of two or three hundred dollars a month. Most employees cannot afford these premiums, and so the worker is covered, but the spouse and children remain uninsured.

Costs of providing this type of group insurance has become so high that many employers, especially smaller companies, are trying to either cut benefits or find some cheaper way of providing coverage, while many prospective employees accept or reject job opportunities on the basis of benefits rather than salary.

Health-maintenance organizations (HMOs) and preferred-provider organizations (PPOs) are two common means that many employers have turned to in their attempts to regulate costs. HMOs and PPOs provide coverage for routine and preventative health care, while keeping costs down by limiting benefits on certain types of care, or by not covering certain expenses at all. Cosmetic surgery, mental health care, and orthodontia, for example, are commonly limited or excluded from coverage. To help control costs, these types of organizations often require second opinions for all surgeries and may limit the number or types of tests that a patient may have. They also often require notification 48 hours in advance before any procedure is performed, and require notification within 24 hours of an emergency for benefits to be paid. To encourage preventative medicine, these organizations often offer very low ($5 to $10) office visit copayments, and provide prescription plans that absorb almost all of the cost of prescriptions.

But these programs have serious limitations. Yearly out-of-pocket deductibles are generally high, and annual maximum benefits can be quite low. This means that for people who are in good overall health, these plans are beneficial, but if a family has an unexpected health emergency, whether it be a serious injury or a debilitating illness, these plans provide little assistance. It is also possible for a person with a rare illness to not be diagnosed because of the limitations on testing imposed by these plans.

The rationale behind these types of health plans is that to keep costs low, preventative treatment is emphasized, and expensive testing and long-term illnesses are often excluded from coverage. But for people who otherwise cannot afford any health care, HMOs and PPOs cover most of the everyday expenses. For those people who cannot afford to join an HMO or a PPO, and who make so little money that they can qualify for government assistance, Medicare and Medicaid can provide coverage, but the income requirements for these forms of aid are so stringent that many Americans fall between the cracks. They make too much money to meet the federal income standards but make far less than they need to be able to buy health insurance.

So what is the answer? That is what the government's task force is trying to determine. Some states are not waiting for the government to come up with a solution. Hawaii has a managed health care program that covers every state resident, and Oregon has recently offered a plan for rationed health care that would cover all of its citizens. But it is the idea of rationed health care that raises the most important ethical questions. Under rationed health care plans, such as Oregon's, all diseases and injuries are ranked by cost of treatment and by frequency of occurrence in the population. Once the ranking has been established, a cut-off number is determined, and all of those illnesses and injuries that have a rank number that is larger than the cut-off number is not covered by the rationed health care plan. Critics say that the state is playing God with this type of plan; by deciding what illnesses or injuries are not treated, the state is also determining who will live and who will die. But supporters say that some illnesses are just too expensive and the chances of survival are so low anyway, that to pay for the treatment is a waste of money that could otherwise save other lives. Some senior citizen advocacy groups argue that this type of rationed health care amounts to a death sentence for the aged, who are often chronically ill.

But the costs of extreme measures to prolong the lives of elderly people is a major contribution to the rocketing costs of health care. Heart surgery alone often costs in the tens or even hundreds of thousands of dollars, and the vast majority of patients who undergo heart surgery are senior citizens. The question that must be answered is, is it fair to spend hundreds of thousands of dollars to give an elderly person five or maybe ten more years of life when that same money could save the lives of critically ill children who have their whole lives ahead of them? There is no easy answer to this moral dilemma, but it is true that the money, effort, and facilities used to prolong the lives of seriously ill senior citizens is money, effort, and facilities that are not used to save children and young adults who have better odds for long-term survival. There are other alternatives than rationed health care, though.

One alternative is to set national limits on how much certain procedures and tests can cost. By standardizing costs and then standardizing how much of the cost is covered by the government health care plan, costs can be managed. Many insurance companies already try to control costs by standardizing how much they will pay for various tests and procedures, but there are no regulations that restricts physicians or medical facilities from charging more than this standard rate. A national health care plan that did regulate fees would prevent some doctors and hospitals from overcharging for services. This type of fee schedule, combined with a sliding scale based on income for the amount of the fee that is covered by the government, could go far to easing this country's health care crisis. Other options are to base national health care on the plans already instituted in other countries. Canada and England are among the other countries that have instituted national health care and managed to control health care costs. A recent study showed that drug costs in Canada were less than half what they are is this country, for the same medications produced by the same companies!

The health care problem in this country has reached crisis proportions. Many people who hold good jobs cannot afford to insure themselves or their families, and the working class and the poor cannot afford to get sick at all. Even those people who can afford health insurance find that the policies they buy do not cover catastrophic illnesses or injuries. Many employers have tried to provide health care coverage for their employees, but escalating costs have made it harder to provide comprehensive coverage. HMOs and PPOs are just two of the alternative forms of health insurance coverage that try to provide managed care at a reasonable cost, but to keep costs low, they have to restrict the health problems they cover and they have to require fairly large deductibles. The federal government does offer Medicare and Medicaid for those people who qualify, but the income requirements for these plans are so tough that many of the working poor who need help the most cannot qualify. Some states have tried to provide statewide care for all their citizens, but these programs are usually based on rationed care, which raises a host of moral and ethical questions that have no easy answer. The only thing that can be said for certain is that health care reform is desperately needed, but the President's task force does not have an easy job ahead of it.

FEATURES OF THE WRITING SAMPLE SCORING 5 OR 6

This essay provides a clear thesis and develops that thesis in a clear and logical manner. The body of the essay expands on various aspects of the thesis, and provides concise and reasonable support. The few usage, structural, and mechanical errors do not interfere with the writer's ability to communicate effectively, and the writer demonstrates a solid understanding of the rules of written English. The essay is well-thought-out and the conclusion relates the various points raised in the essay to the general argument made throughout.

WRITING SAMPLE WITH A SCORE OF 3 OR 4

There are many factors in the rising cost of health care. For instance, unemployment effects health care costs, because unemployed people cannot pay their bills. Another factor is all the new tests available, like ultrasound and CAT scans, that many doctors order just to avoid malpractice suits. But one of the most important factors in the rising cost of health care is the cost of medecine.

The cost of prescription medecations has increased drasticly in the last few years. Some antibiotics cost as much as three or four dollars a pill! Many senior citizens, who are the ones who take the most drugs, spend a large percentage of their fixed income for medecine. Many of them take more kinds of medecine than they really need, too. In fact, a lot of senior citizens who act like their senile are really only like that because they take so many medecines that they interfere with each other.

Some people have serious diseases that have no drugs to treat them. These people cannot get their health back because drug companies say it is too expensive to develop new medecines that might help these people. These people then end up in hospitals because they are too ill to take care of themselves, or else they end up taking a lot of different medecines that don't help very much but are quite expensive. This ends up saving money for the drug companys, but it costs the patient and his family more than they can afford. Many people lose their homes and even their health insurance because of these kinds of illnesses.

There are some drugs that have been developed that would help many people, but they are not available to the public. This is because of government regulations; that say that every drug must be proven safe and effective before it can be marketed. The FDA has such strict procedures for proving a drug is safe. It takes seven to ten years to get a new drug approved! It is very expensive for the drug company because they have to do animal testing and then, test the drug on humans. If the drug is to help a really rare disease, often the drug company won't do all the testing needed to get it approved because it says that it would not be worth it because there won't be enough people using the drug for it to make enough money to reimburse the company for all the testing.

Drug companies say that the cost of developing new drugs is too high already, even for drugs that will be used by a large segment of the population. It can cost millions of dollars to develop one drug! Because these development costs are so high, the government gives drug companies a patent for any new drug. This patent gives the drug company that developed a new drug exclusive rights to make and market the new drug, for several years. This is supposed to let the company recover the cost of developing and testing the new drug before other drug companies can copy it and sell generic versions.

Another factor that makes it so expensive to buy prescription medecines is that many new medecines come from rare plants. Many of these rare plants come from the rainforest and since the rainforests are being destroyed, so are these plants. So a plant that might give us a cure for cancer or diabetes or something gets destroyed before the drug companies can study it and learn how it works and how to make a sinthetic copy of it.

As you can see, the high cost of prescription drugs is one of the factors in the rising cost of health care. There are many reasons why prescription medecines are expensive. But it is also true that many drug companies have returned huge profits to their investors for several years. To cut the cost of drugs, there should be a limit on how much profit a drug company can make. The government should also loosen up the FDA regulations. If a drug has already been approved in Europe or some other country, it shouldn't have to go through all the testing all over again before it can be sold here. There are other ways of controlling the cost of medecines which would lower health care costs for all of us.

FEATURES OF THE WRITING SAMPLE SCORING 3 OR 4

This essay does have a thesis, and the writer does focus on *one* factor in the rising cost of health care. The author does provide some support for the thesis that drug costs are a factor in rising health care costs, but most of this support is anecdotal and superficial. The conclusion raises points not previously mentioned in the body of the essay.

Also, while the writer's intention is apparent, poor usage, sentence structure, and mechanics, as well as spelling problems, interfere with the author's ability to clearly communicate that intent. The author is obviously familiar with some of the issues concerning the costs of prescription medications, but she or he has failed to present these issues in a way that clearly demonstrates their effect on the cost of health care.

WRITING SAMPLE WITH A SCORE OF 1 OR 2

There are lots of factors in the rising cost of health care. There are lots of unemployed people who don't have insurance, so they can't pay their hospital bills.

There are lots of other people who only make minimum wage, so they can't pay their bills, either. Or they can pay the doctor, but they can't buy the medecine he wants them to take, or have the surgury he says they need. Also, lots of doctors make their patients have lots of tests done, and these tests are expensive.

Some of these tests are good. Like the MRI which is sort of like an X-ray, but it shows soft tissue, too. Or ultrasound, which uses sound waves to show if there are any tomurs or anything. Some tests doctors want are not so good, though. Like when they want you to have six or seven different blood tests that all cost $100 each. Or when they make you get both X-rays and a MRI.

So there are a lot of factors to the rising cost of health care. Doctors order too many tests, just so they won't get charged with malpractise. A lot of people can't afford these tests. Some of them can't even afford to go to the doctor at all! This country needs a national health care plan, like Canada or England, to take care of people and lower health care costs.

FEATURES OF THE WRITING SAMPLE SCORING 1 OR 2

This essay lacks structure and a clear thesis statement, and does not address the topic. Instead of focussing on *one* factor in the rising cost of health care, this author mentions several possible factors, without demonstrating *how* any of these factors affect health care costs.

The second paragraph, rather than providing support for the points raised in the introduction, is a rambling list of medical tests that again fails to demonstrate *how* these tests affect health care costs.

The conclusion raises points that were not previously mentioned, and again fails to clearly link these points to the topic of the essay. There is little support for the author's position, and the support provided is illogical and superficial. Poor usage, sentence structure, and spelling errors all interfere with the writer's ability to communicate effectively.

SAMPLE ESSAYS FOR TOPIC #2

WRITING SAMPLE WITH A SCORE OF 5 OR 6

There are many growing problems in our judicial system. Rising crime rates, over-crowded jails, an increase in juvenile crime, and a lack of standard sentencing guidelines are all difficulties that inhibit our country's ability to maintain an effective judicial system. But perhaps the most pressing problem our judicial system faces is the disparity between the treatment of those who have money and those who don't.

Our constitution mandates that those who cannot afford legal representation shall have a court-appointed attorney to defend them. This right is supposed to guarantee that all citizens have access to legal coverage, and the representation provided by a public defender is supposed to be as good as that afforded by a private attorney. Unfortunately, this is usually not the case.

Public defenders work for the state, and like many other state employees who handle a large number of clients, these lawyers are often significantly overworked. A public defender in a large city might represent hundreds of clients every week. Often, case loads are so large that the attorneys only meet their clients a few minutes before going into court. This burden of work has serious consequences for the defendant.

Most importantly, the quality of the defense a public defender can provide his client is necessarily poorer than that of a private attorney. The limited contact with the defendant before going into court means that the public defender has little time to search for precedents that could help the client. It also means that there is little opportunity for the attorney and the client to become acquainted with one another, which makes it difficult for the defendant to trust the attorney. Many of the people forced to rely on public defenders are poorly educated and do not understand the repercussions of intricate legal procedures or the consequences of plea bargaining. If these people do not trust the public defender assigned to their case, they are often uncooperative because they cannot believe that their lawyer really has their best interests at heart. Public defenders are commonly perceived as more concerned with settling the case quickly rather than fairly.

Even if the attorney and his client manage to establish a trusting relationship, time constraints and staff limitations make it difficult for the public defender to thoroughly research the case. Private law firms have large research staffs to search out precedents and to investigate the facts of a case. Public defenders offices often lack these resources, or else the research staff is overwhelmed by the demands of so many attorneys with so many cases. And in these difficult economic times, research staffs are often the first to suffer from budget cuts.

Another factor of this problem is that there is little incentive for public defenders to continue with a case after a client has been convicted. Case loads often dictate that, rather than attempting to establish their client's innocence, public defenders are forced to try to negotiate the most favorable plea bargain. If the client chooses to go to trial and is found guilty, an overworked public defender is less likely to urge the client to appeal the conviction. If the defendant does appeal the conviction, he or she is often forced to deal with a different public defender for the appeal, as the case loads can interfere with the attorney's ability to stay with the case.

This disparity in legal representation has long-term consequences for the poor who find themselves dealing with the legal system. Many people agree to plea guilty in return for a reduced sentence even though that might not be in their best interest. Since these people are often uneducated, they frequently do not understand their legal rights. They do not realize that they have the right to a jury trial, or they might assume that because they are poor, or uneducated, or a minority, that they will not receive a fair trial. With the public defender under pressure to settle as many cases as possible without going to trial, the client is often urged to follow poor legal advice in the interest of expediency.

The problems between the public defender and the defendant are exacerbated by the lack of trust on both sides. Unlike private attorneys, who can choose whom they represent, public defenders must represent everyone assigned to them. They do not have the luxury of selecting only those clients whom they believe to be innocent. Because so many of the clients they represent really are guilty of the crimes they are charged with, it is all to easy for public defenders to become cynical and assume that *all* of their clients are guilty. This presumption of guilt makes it harder for the defendant to place his confidence in the public defender, and it contributes to the antagonistic relationship that is so common between public defenders and their clients.

Those defendants who can afford to hire their own attorney, on the other hand, can provide themselves with an attorney who believes in them and who is committed to making the best defense possible. Because the private attorney and his client have much more time to spend before the client goes into court, the lawyer has more time to prepare an adequate defense and to prepare plans for an appeal in the case of a conviction.

It would be interesting to compare the rates of conviction, appeal, and plea bargaining of people defended by private attorneys to the rates of those defended by public defenders. I believe such a comparison would show that public defenders accept more plea bargains, have a higher conviction rate, and a lower appeal rate. This means that many people are going to jail because they cannot afford to hire a private attorney. This is exactly what the constitutional guarantee of representation is meant to prevent!

The most important growing problem in our judicial system is the difference in legal representation afforded by public defenders and private attorneys. Those people who are forced to accept a public defender do not receive the most competent legal care because their lawyers are overworked and understaffed, and are under pressure to settle as many cases as quickly as possible. Time constraints that dictate that many clients do not even meet their attorneys until minutes before going into court insures that, no matter how well-meaning, public defenders are just not equipped to provide their clients with competent legal advice and representation. Americans are supposed to enjoy equality under the law, but until we invest more money into public defense, that equality will remain out of reach of our poorer citizens.

FEATURES OF THE WRITING SAMPLE SCORING 5 OR 6

This essay provides a clearly defined thesis in the introductory paragraph. The writer then presents logical and convincing supporting arguments throughout the remainder of the essay. The arguments are presented in a rational order and reflect a well-thought-out approach to the topic. The conclusion sums up the major arguments presented in the essay, and cleanly closes the discussion. The writer makes very few grammar, spelling, or usage mistakes, and demonstrates an ability to communicate effectively in written English.

WRITING SAMPLE WITH A SCORE OF 3 OR 4

A growing problem with our judicial system is that too many policemen treat citizens bad.

We all the time see cases in the newspaper about people who get stopped for speeding or something and they end up getting beaten up by the police. Or the police see some kids doing a crime, like trying to steal a car, and they shoot them saying the kids had weapons even when they don't.

The Rodney King case is probably the most famous case of policemen stopping someone and then beating them real badly. But the King case was also one of the most extreme cases, because the cops that stopped King called other police to come and join them, and so a lot of cops ended up beating him.

The cops said that King was a drug addict and resisted arrest and that was why they had to beat him up. But a tape of the beating showed that King didn't try to resist.

Even if he had, how could one guy resist ten people all beating on him with nightsticks?

But even with the videotape, the cops got off on charges that they did the wrong thing. If the tape hadn't been made, probably noone would have believed that King hadn't resisted.

Look at the situation - a lot of white cops said a black man they knew used drugs tried to fight them. A lot of people in this country think that alone is a good enough of a reason to beat someone.

In the second trial, two of the cops were convicted of violating King's rights, but if they hadn't been cops, and if they hadn't been white, they probably would have gone to jail after the first trial.

A lot of young minority kids get killed by cops every year when the cops say that they had to shoot in self-defense. The cops say that the kid made a threatening move or went to grab a gun, but then it turns out that the kid didn't even have a gun!

Of course this don't happen nearly as often if the kids are white, but even so it seems like the cops are trigger happy.

Cops can get out of hand when they do searches too. Even though they have to have a search warrant, they really destroy a place when they search it.

Like if their looking for drugs, they rip open mattresses and other furnature, and they dump everything out of all the drawers.

This isn't fair to the people in the house who don't know anything about the drugs. Sometimes they tear cars apart, too. And they don't always have to have a warrant.

If they pull someone over for bad driving and they smell beer or pot when they talk to the driver, they can claim that they have probable cause to search the car.

And even if they don't find anything, the people who got searched can't do anything about it, because the cops say they were just doing there job.

The biggest growing problem for our judicial system is police who don't respect the citizens.

We're supposed to be innocent until proven guilty but the cops act like we're guilty until we're proven innocent. So a lot of people don't respect the law or the police and commit more crimes.

FEATURES OF THE WRITING SAMPLE SCORING 3 OR 4

This essay does have a clear thesis, and the writer does support that thesis with good examples. However, the structure of the essay is confused—the paragraphs often consist of single sentences, even though the topics of many of these sentences are linked and should form one paragraph.

The writer makes the common error of presenting opinion as fact, without providing adequate support for his or her assertions. Also, errors in grammar, sentence structure, and usage limit the writer's ability to communicate effectively.

WRITING SAMPLE WITH A SCORE OF 1 OR 2

There our lots of problems with our countries judicial system. These problems makes it harder to get criminuls put in jail and makes it easy for them to get out. Because of these problems, we have to many drug dealers and murdurers in our sociatey.

Judges don't give criminuls tuff sentences and they walk away after doing horrible things. Even in jail, they act like they didn't do nothing wrong, and they can get drugs as easy as on the streets.

Teenagers who do crimes don't get sentunced really they get sent to detention or a boy's home and they learn even worse crimes there. Everybody makes excuses for them like they came from a bad home or they didn't have a father. Even if they do get sent to prison they get treated better than a lot of people who never did crimes. People in jail get three meals a day, doctor's, and even TVs. Lots of poor people don't.

Poor people get treated differently than rich people, espesually if their a minority. Rich people can hire fancy laywers and poor people have to have public defenders who don't have any time or staff to really defend people. Some states have started using the death penalty again. Which maybe will stop criminals. Even if it doesn't, at least some of them won't be able to do crimes again.

FEATURES OF THE WRITING SAMPLE SCORING 1 OR 2

This essay has no thesis statement, and it fails to address the chosen topic. The topic asks for a discussion of "a growing problem in our judicial system"; this essay is a rambling list of perceived problems. There is no structure to the essay; material is not presented in any systematic or organized manner. The writer makes no attempt to focus on and explain *one* problem, and no support is presented for any of the statements made. Poor sentence structure, usage, and mechanics interfere with the writer's ability to communicate effectively.

ENGLISH LANGUAGE SKILLS SECTION

1.   **(B)**   "Term" (B) is the correct word to refer to a period of time in a political office. "Reign" (A) refers to a position of royalty, and "rein" (C) is totally out of context, as it refers to holding something back, or something used to restrain something else.

2.   **(B)**   "Envelop" (B) is the best choice to describe how the fog hangs over the neighborhood. "Wrap" (A) is not the best choice because its context is too physical to describe something as ethereal as fog. "Envelope" (C) refers to a letter container.

3.   **(E)**   Choice (E) can be eliminated because it repeats the information just stated. Choice (A) is important for placing the information in the correct time frame. "Often" (B) is important to the meaning of the passage because this technology is not always used. Finally, "powerful" (C) and "delicate" (D) help to distinguish the words they describe.

4.   **(E)**   Choice (E) can be eliminated because it is redundant: ordinary objects are understood to be those we see everyday. Choice (A) helps specify the general term "shoppers." "Faster" (B) explains the major benefit of this particular use of lasers. Choice (C) informs the reader that this technology cannot be used with all groceries. "Amazing" (D), while not essential to the meaning of the passage, emphasizes the interesting nature of this technology.

5.   **(B)**   For clarity, a modifier must be as close as possible to the word or phrase it is describing. Choice (B) correctly places the modifying phrase "In a loud voice" next to the word it is actually describing, the instructor. In choice (A), the phrase appears to be describing the action of the students, and in choice (C) it appears to be describing the students themselves.

6.   **(A)**   Choice (A) is correct because the modifying phrase "wearing only pajamas" is correctly placed directly before what it is describing, "the residents of the burning house." Choice (B) implies that the firemen were wearing pajamas, and choice (C) seems to say the same of the house.

7.   **(C)**   Choice (C) lists the manager's qualities in consistent, parallel form. In choice (A), the phrase "offers help" is not consistent in form with "competent" and "good natured." Although choice (B) is consistent, it is unnecessarily wordy.

8.   **(B)**   Choice (B) consistently lists the cat's habits in "ing" form. Choice (A) shifts from an infinitive "to lick" to the "ing" form. In choice (C), "climb up" is not consistent with the "ing" form and generally does not make sense within the structure of the sentence.

9.   **(C)**   Choice (C) correctly expresses the cause-and-effect relationship between the two ideas: the fact that women were not allowed to perform is the reason for boys

taking female roles. Choice (A) incorrectly implies the opposite relationship, that the boys playing the roles were the reason women were not allowed to perform. Choice (B) implies that boys performed these roles even though their voices had not changed, which is the very reason they were used. Finally, choice (D) implies that women were not allowed to perform until boys played the roles, which does not make sense.

10. **(D)** Choice (D) clearly shows the relationship between the ideas. Choice (A) does not show any relationship between the ideas. The relationships implied in choices (B) and (C) do not make sense.

11. **(B)** Choice (B) is correct because when stating that two things are different, we say that they are "different from" one another. It is incorrect to say they are "different than" each other (A) because "than" implies a comparison of quantity which does not exist. Choice (C) also implies a comparison of quantity: something cannot be more or less different than something else. They are equally different from each other.

12. **(A)** When making a comparison with "as," the word "as" must be stated twice to complete the comparison, even if a phrase with the word "than" is added. Choice (A) is the only one that makes a complete comparison. Choices (B) and (C) are both incomplete since they omit the second "as."

13. **(C)** When comparing more than two things, the superlative form "most" or "est" must be used. Choice (C) uses the correct form. Although choice (A) uses the correct form, it is vague about what is being compared. In choice (B), the comparative form ("more" or "er") used to compare two things, is acceptable, since it is phrased so that one group (the Volvo) is compared to another ("any on the market"); however, it is also too vague about what is being compared.

14. **(B)** When comparing two things (in this case driving and cycling) the comparative form ("more" or "er") is used. Choice (B) uses the correct form. Although choice (A) also uses the comparative form, with adjectives of one syllable ("cheap"), "er" is preferable to "more." Choice (C) incorrectly uses the superlative form.

15. **(A)** "To lie" (A) is the correct infinitive form of the verb "lie" meaning "to recline." "To lay" (B) is incorrect because it means "to set down." Although "having lain" (C) is the correct participial form of "lie," the phrase does not fit the structure of the sentence. Finally, "laying" (D) is the gerund form of "lay," which is incorrect for the same reason as (B).

16. **(A)** "Set" (A), meaning "to place," is the correct word to use based on the context of the sentence. Choice (B) "have set" represents an incorrect shift in tense. "Setted" (C) is not a standard form of the verb "set." Finally, "sit," meaning "to recline," does not fit the context of the sentence.

17. **(B)** Choice (B) corrects the run-on with a period between the two complete sentences. Choice (A) is a misspelling of "apprehensive." The singular pronoun "his," choice (C), does not agree with the plural antecedent "some people."

18. **(B)** "Cancel" (B) corrects the misspelling "cansel." Choice (A) is a misspelling of "especially." Choice (C) incorrectly places a comma between a compound verb; even with a conjunction, a comma is not used unless both phrases contain a subject and verb.

19. **(A)** Choice (A) corrects a run-on by placing a period between the two complete sentences. "Pane" (B) refers to part of a window; the context of the sentence requires the word "pain," meaning "extreme discomfort." Finally, choice (C) incorrectly shifts the verb tense.

20. **(D)** The passage is correct as written (D). Choice (A) incorrectly capitalizes "dental phobia." Choice (B) is a comma splice (a comma used between two independent clauses without a conjunction). Choice (C) is an incorrect spelling of "irrational."

21. **(A)** In choice (A), a semicolon is placed between two independent clauses, correcting the comma splice. Choice (B) is incorrectly punctuated: "however" should be preceded by a semicolon and followed by a comma, not the reverse. Choice (C) incorrectly capitalizes "modern technology," a common noun phrase.

22. **(A)** Choice (A) corrects a fragment by joining the dependent clause "that delivers the anesthetic" to the main clause, "many people fear the pain of the needle." Choice (B) is a comma splice. Choice (C) implies that the procedure described has not yet been used.

23. **(B)** Choice (B) corrects the misuse of the semicolon by adding the comma. A comma always follows the conjunction *however*. Choice (A) misuses the apostrophe. Choice (C) omits a comma between two separate items, causing the reader to run the words "high-speed water" together.

24. **(B)** The verb "do" (B) agrees with the plural subject "equipment" and "techniques." Choice (A) is an incorrect spelling of "equipment," and choice (C) is a comma splice.

25. **(B)** The plural pronoun "their" (B) agrees with the plural antecedent "dentists." Choice (A) is a run-on. Choice (C) is a misspelling of "exercises."

26. **(A)** The singular pronouns "his or her" (A) agree with the singular antecedent "someone." Choice (B) is a plural when a singular is called for, and choice (C) creates a fragment, since a semicolon can only be used between two independent clauses.

27. **(D)**   The passage is correct as written (D). In choice (A), an apostrophe is incorrectly used where possession is implied. In choice (B), a comma is used to introduce an important quotation; in such cases, a colon is the preferred punctuation. Finally, in choice (C), the period is incorrectly placed outside of the quotation marks.

28. **(C)**   When a pronoun directly follows a preposition, such as "between," the pronoun must be in the objective form. In choice (C), the correct form of the pronoun "us" is used. Choice (A) is incorrect because colons are not used to set off a simple introductory phrase such as "that is." "Among" (B) is not a correct preposition to follow "parallels."

29. **(A)**   "Habitat" (A) corrects the misspelling. Choice (B) is a misspelling of "discern." Choice (C) is a misspelling of "correspondences."

30. **(A)**   "There is" (A) agrees with the singular subject "scheme." In choice (B), the "s" is incorrectly omitted after a plural noun. Finally, in choice (C), the verb "takes" does not agree with the plural subject "acts."

31. **(C)**   In choice (C), a semicolon is correctly placed between two independent clauses, correcting a comma splice. In choice (A), the apostrophe is placed incorrectly; "each other" is a singular noun phrase, and the apostrophe must be placed before the "s" in showing possession. "His or her" (B) does not agree with the plural antecedent "creatures."

32. **(B)**   Choice (B) is correct because a comma is generally the standard punctuation between a dependent clause ("with respect for the environment") and an independent clause ("all can survive"). In choice (A), there is no punctuation, so the phrases run together awkwardly. Since one of the phrases is not a complete sentence, it is incorrect to use a semicolon (C) or period (D) between them.

33. **(A)**   Choice (A) is correct because introductory phrases like "for example" are generally followed by a comma. Choice (B) is incorrect because a comma rather than a colon is used between a dependent clause and an independent clause. Choice (C) is incorrect because the adjective "good" is not used to modify a verb ("wash").

34. **(A)**   "Don't" (A) is consistent in tense with the other verbs in the sentence. Choice (B) represents an incorrect use of a colon. Choice (C) implies that the raccoons do not already work together, which is inconsistent with the context of the passage.

35. **(C)**   "Its" (C) agrees with the singular antecedent "neither." Choice (A) implies that the raccoons no longer work together. In choice (B), the comma is superfluous.

36. **(B)**   Choice (B) is the only one containing the correct singular possessive forms. "Pennies'" (A) is an incorrect plural form. Choices (C) and (D) omit the apostrophe needed to indicate possession.

37. **(C)** Conjunctive adverbs like "nevertheless" are generally preceded by a semicolon and followed by a comma. Choice (C) is the only one containing the correct punctuation in the correct order. Although it is acceptable to begin a sentence with a conjunctive adverb, as in choice (A), it would not be correct to follow the conjunctive adverb with a semicolon. Choices (B) and (D) are both comma splices.

38. **(B)** When items in a series contain commas within themselves, each item should be separated by a semicolon. Choice (B) contains this correct punctuation. Choice (A) contains superfluous semicolons. Choice (C) uses commas where semicolons are needed to distinguish the items, and choice (D) omits the necessary commas within the items.

39. **(A)** Choice (A) is correct because a comma generally separates a dependent clause and an independent clause. In choice (B), the lack of any punctuation causes the ideas to run together awkwardly. Because one phrase is a dependent clause, it is incorrect to use a semicolon (C) or a period (D) for punctuation.

40. **(C)** When following a statement with a list or phrase that clarifies the thought or gives examples, a colon is used to introduce the list or phrase, as in choice (C). Choice (A) is a fragment. Choice (B) is incorrect because the list is not a complete sentence. Finally, choice (D) is incorrect because using only a comma implies that "a great deal of trouble" is part of the list when in fact the listed items are examples of the trouble encountered by the student.

READING SKILLS SECTION

1. **(A)** The phrase "on the other hand" signals a *contrast* to what is said in the first part of the sentence. Here the contrast is between the benefit of studying Latin and the benefit of studying Spanish.

2. **(C)** The first sentence establishes the focus of the passage: the importance of Dr. Goddard's work in the development of rockets. The fourth sentence of the first paragraph sums up the content of the passage: "Through his scientific experiments, he pointed the way to the development of rockets as we know them today." Choice (A) is incorrect: the subject of the passage is Dr. Goddard, not the rocket engine. The passage does not go into a technical explanation of how a rocket engine works. Choice (B) is incorrect: nothing is said about Dr. Goddard's private life. Information is limited to his scientific achievements. Choice (D) is incorrect: no other scientists are mentioned.

3. **(A)** The first sentence states Dr. Goddard's discovery concerning the importance of the nozzle design. The second sentence explains the *consequences* or *effects* of the proper design: much greater speed and distance. Therefore, the relationship is one of cause and effect. None of the other choices describes that relationship.

4. **(A)** The sentence beginning on line 26 ("After proving on paper...") mentions Dr. Goddard's mathematical theory and his rocket designs. Since the mathematical theory has to do with the principles of rocket propulsion, it stands to reason that the theory must be applicable to any rocket-powered vehicles, not just the kinds of rockets that Goddard was designing. Choices (B), (C), and (D) are incorrect because they are all stated explicitly in the passage and therefore cannot be "suggested."

5. **(D)** Choice (D) is the clearest transition, since this is the first in a chronological series of events. Choice (C) is obviously incorrect for this reason. Choice (A), "Although," indicates contrasting ideas, and choice (B) implies a causal relationship which does not actually exist.

6. **(C)** Choice (C), "In addition," is correct because the sentence is one in a series of similar ideas. Choice (A), "In conclusion," is wrong because this is not the concluding statement. Choice (B), "Similarly," is a feasible alternative, but not as strong as (C). Choice (D), "however," indicates a contrast.

7. **(B)** Choice (B), "Also," is the best answer. Choice (C), "Nevertheless," and choice (D), "In spite of this," are incorrect because they change the meaning of the sentence. Choice (A), "Meanwhile," imposes a time condition.

8. **(C)** The tone of a piece of writing is the writer's attitude or feeling toward the subject. In this selection, the author expresses *admiration* for Harriet Tubman by characterizing her as a selfless heroine dedicated to the cause of leading slaves to freedom. Any facts about her that might make the reader think less of Harriet Tubman

are not included in the account. At the time of her death she was "noted and respected by all." Choice (A) "angry" is incorrect. Even though the author does seem to feel some anger towards the Union Army for denying Harriet compensation for her services it would be misleading to describe the tone of the whole passage as angry. Choice (B) "skeptical" is incorrect: skeptical means disbelieving, and this author is not at all skeptical about Harriet Tubman's accomplishments and stature as a human being. Choice (D) is incorrect: detached means without any emotion, objective. Again, the author here is emotionally involved because he or she plainly admires Tubman for her dedication, toughness, and compassion.

9.   **(B)**   In the sentence beginning on line 39, the author writes, "Eventually she received a small monthly pension, but it was based on her marriage to a black Union Army veteran, who had died a few years after their marriage, not upon her own contributions!" Here the author expresses dismay that the Army did not reward Tubman for service. The implied criticism of the Army may be considered bias, even if it is justified. Choice (A) is incorrect: there is no hint of bias or predisposition against black people. Choice (C) is incorrect: Harriet Tubman helped John Brown plan his raid on Harper's Ferry, and nothing negative is said or implied concerning Brown. Choice (D) is incorrect because the entire passage recounts Tubman's accomplishments and heroic qualities.

10.   **(C)**   The second paragraph employs chronological order because it begins with Tubman's decision to escape and then recounts in order of time the events that followed that decision. Choice (A) is incorrect: the events are narrated one after the other without any emphasis on cause and effect. Choice (B) is incorrect: nothing is being classified into different kinds. Choice (D) is incorrect: the paragraph does not begin with a general statement and then proceed with examples to support that statement.

11.   **(D)**   Jon's response has two parts. First is the assertion that Tiffany is wrong in saying that Lisa has not made a mistake in any game in which both of them played. Second is the proof of the assertion, that in the game on Tuesday night Lisa made mistakes. For the proof to be valid, Tiffany and Lisa must both have played in the Tuesday night game, (D). If Tiffany has not played in any games with Lisa (A), the fact that Lisa made mistakes on Tuesday night does not prove Jon's assertion. Tiffany may or may not believe that Lisa is the best player on the team, (B). Either way, Tiffany's opinion has nothing to do with the validity of Jon's proof. Jon does not imply that Tiffany has played in every game that Lisa has played in, (C), only that they both played on Tuesday night. There may well have been games in which Tiffany did not play and in which Lisa made mistakes. Tiffany does not say otherwise, so proving otherwise would not weaken her statement. Jon has nothing to say about other games during the season, only the one on Tuesday night, so (E) is not the correct answer.

12. **(C)** The author is generally optimistic about the effects of women's entry into managerial positions. The first three paragraphs enumerate some of the benefits for the women themselves, their husbands, their children, and business. The fourth paragraph criticizes the media for being too negative, and the fifth paragraph points out some real problems—but the overall tone is still optimistic. Because it is optimistic, the tone cannot be described as "depressed" (A) or "cynical" (B). The passage is serious throughout: there is no attempt to be humorous (D).

13. **(A)** The fourth paragraph takes the media to task for its unwarranted pessimism concerning women in the workplace. Choice (B) is incorrect: the author clearly supports women in managerial positions; he or she is not biased against them. Choice (C) is incorrect: the author makes no statement that could be interpreted as biased against husbands who let their wives work. He or she points out the benefits of such an arrangement. Choice (D) is incorrect: the author mentions the possibility of career changes as one of the benefits of women working.

14. **(D)** The paragraph begins with the general statement that the message from the media regarding women in business is "filled with pessimism." The following two sentences provide examples of that pessimistic outlook to support the opening statement. Choice (A) is incorrect: no event is described that was caused by another event. Choice (B) is incorrect: nothing is being classified into various kinds or categories. Choice (C) is incorrect: the order of time is not followed. Rather, we hear about repeated or typical messages from the media.

15. **(A)** Choice (A), "also," correctly links the two similar ideas being discussed. Choice (B), "in short," implies a summing up of ideas. Choice (C) is also incorrect, because it indicates contrast, and choice (D), "therefore," implies a causal relationship.

16. **(B)** Choice (B), "however," is the best transition; it indicates the argument that is the detractor's main objection. Choice (C) is incorrect because it implies a contrast. Choice (A) imposes a time restraint, and choice (D) incorrectly refers to the previous sentence.

17. **(A)** Choice (A) is correct because the sentence gives examples of the kinds of strategies being discussed. Choice (B) indicates a contrast, and choice (C) implies a conclusion. Choice (D) is also incorrect since it indicates a cause, purpose, or result.

18. **(B)** The author of this passage is intent on persuading readers to help their children develop a love for reading. The writer's tone is hopeful and encouraging, emphasizing that teaching a child to read can be very enjoyable and rewarding for both parent and child. (Example: "You may be surprised to find that a well-written children's book is often as big a delight to you as it is to the kids.") Choice (A) is incorrect: the author feels very strongly about the benefits of reading. He or she is not at all neutral. Choice (C) is incorrect: the tone is consistently upbeat and positive, not despondent or depressed. Choice (D) is incorrect: there is no hint of bitterness in the author's voice.

19. **(B)**   The author feels that reading should be enjoyable for adults and children alike, and for children to develop a love for reading, they must experience its joys. The second sentence of the first paragraph most clearly expresses the author's bias against viewing reading as work. Choice (A) is incorrect: the author is especially concerned here with children's literature, but he or she obviously approves of adult reading because if adults do not read, children will not learn to read by imitating adults. Choice (C) is incorrect: the author says that having magazines and newspapers around the home is helpful in itself. Choice (D) is incorrect: the author recommends reading aloud as the "most effective way to encourage your children to love books and reading" (lines 7-8).

20. **(D)**   The topic sentence of the paragraph is the first one, which recommends reading aloud as the best way to nurture a child's love for reading. The following sentences clarify this statement by pointing out how even a baby can enjoy reading, by suggesting that the reading period can be a very special time for the family, and by saying that the parent may well enjoy a children's book as much as the child. Choice (A) is incorrect: two things are not being compared or contrasted. Choice (B) is incorrect: no term is being defined. Choice (C) is incorrect: no physical object or scene is being described.

21. **(C)**   Since all basketball players are athletic, and some teenagers are basketball players, it follows that those teens who are basketball players are athletic. Choice (C) must be true. Choice (A) is not necessarily true. Sentence three says that some athletic persons are skaters, which leaves open the possibility that some nonathletic persons are also skaters. Since all basketball players are athletic, and some athletic persons are skaters, some of the athletic persons who are basketball players may also be skaters. Thus, (B) is not necessarily true. The last sentence of the statement says that no teenagers are skaters. Therefore, choice (D) is wrong. Just because all basketball players are athletic does not mean that all athletic persons are basketball players. Some athletic persons may play baseball. That some athletic persons are skaters does not mean that all are. Again, some may play baseball. Therefore, choice (E) is not necessarily true.

Sometimes it is helpful to use Venn diagrams to answer questions like this one. First, draw a circle to represent athletic persons. Mark it with an A (for athletic). Next, draw a smaller circle within the A circle. Mark it BB for basketball players. We know that A is at least as large as BB, since all BB are A, but we don't know if all A are BB. Next, draw another circle which partially intersects BB and mark it T for teenagers. In the part of T which intersects A only, place a question mark, since we cannot say for sure whether any Ts are A but not BB. Next, draw

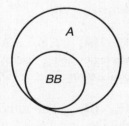

a circle which intersects A and BB. Mark it S for skaters. On the part of S which intersects BB draw a question mark, since it is not clear from the passage if S intersects BB. S and T should not intersect, based on the last sentence of the passage. Your final diagram should be:

Now it is easy, using the diagram, to answer question one. Go through the answer choices one at a time while looking at the diagram. (A) need not be true, since part of S is outside circle A. (B) need not be true, since we don't know if S intersects BB. (C) must be true, since part of T is in BB, which is in A. (D) is obviously false, since T and S do not intersect. (E) is not true, since part of A is in neither S or BB.

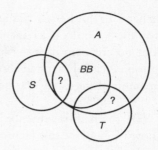

22.   **(D)**   The author is very concerned that more attention be paid to preschool and early childhood education. The writer calls child's play "serious business" (line 9), urging the reader to "put your money on preschool and early childhood education" (line 17). Choice (A) is incorrect: the passage is serious throughout, alerting us to the urgency of the problem. Choice (B) is incorrect: a writer is ironic when he or she says the opposite of what is really meant. Here, the author is straightforward, saying exactly what he or she means. Choice (C) is incorrect: nostalgic means yearning for a past time. Here, the author points out that we know more now about child development than we did in the past.

23.   **(B)**   In lines 6-7, the author says that laymen believed for years that a child's education begins in first grade. It is this idea which the author regards as false and against which he or she argues. Choice (A) is incorrect: the quotation from Henry Adams supports the importance of teachers, a point that the author wishes to stress. Choice (C) is incorrect: although the author says that laymen were wrong to believe that education begins in first grade, he or she does not show bias against them. The writer's desire is to educate laymen. Choice (D) is incorrect: the passage calls attention to the great importance of kindergarten and preschool teachers.

24.   **(B)**   The second sentence of the passage proposes the importance of quality child care for "developing the future of this community and the future of the nation." The remainder of the passage *clarifies* why child care is so important. Therefore, "statement and clarification" best describes the organizational pattern. The passage is not a summary (A) of previous material, it is not comparing (C) two things, and it does not relate events in order of time (D).

25.   **(C)**   The author's tone is best described as detached because the material is present in an objective manner, simply recording the facts of Susie King Taylor's life. Emotional language, which might convey strong feeling on the writer's part, is avoided. Choice (A) is incorrect: ardent means showing strong emotion, fervent. Choice (B) is incorrect: arrogant means haughty or snobbish, and there is no hint of haughtiness here. Choice (D) is incorrect: indignant means feeling offended by an injustice, and the author betrays no such feeling.

26.   **(A)**   In lines 34-35, the author states that Jim Crow laws prevented Susie King Taylor's son from receiving medical specialists' care, and that he subsequently died. Although the author presents these facts dispassionately, the very presentation of the facts calls attention to the terrible consequences of these laws. Choice (B) is incorrect:

Susie King Taylor herself was an army volunteer, and the passage pays tribute to her contribution. Choice (C) is incorrect: the American Red Cross is mentioned in lines 23-24, but no criticism of it is expressed or implied. Choice (D) is incorrect: Colonel Higginson is called "a noted abolitionist" (line 25), and he encouraged Taylor to write her memoir of the Civil War period (lines 36-37).

27. **(D)** The first sentence begins "In her early teens," the second sentence starts "By now 14," and the third sentence begins "Later that year..." The author is recounting events in the order of time (chronological order). None of the other choices, therefore, is appropriate.

28. **(B)** Choice (B), "because," is correct, since it shows a causal relationship. Choices (A) and (D) are both incorrect because they indicate contrast. Choice (C), "provided that," incorrectly implies a condition which does not exist.

29. **(C)** Choice (C), "Since," is the best transition; it indicates the cause of the oyster's behavior. Choice (A), "Instead," and choice (D), "Otherwise," both indicate a contrast. Choice (B), "Likewise," implies the linking of two contrasting ideas.

30. **(D)** Choice (D), "however," is correct because it contrasts two dissimilar ideas. Choice (A), "therefore," would only be used to link similar ideas. Choice (B), "meanwhile," makes no sense because it implies time. Choice (C), "besides," indicates a summing up of ideas.

31. **(A)** Impassioned means filled with strong emotion. Here the author's intense desire to change traditional classroom learning is heard in the repetition of phrases ("The classroom is not the place...it is not the place...and it is not the place..." —lines 1-2; "we take pills, we take drugs, and sometimes we take our lives"—lines 9-10) and in the final exhortation: "Let's join that movement." Choice (B) is incorrect: malicious means intending to hurt— the writer does not seem to want to hurt but to help young people learn to cope in the real world. Choice (C) is incorrect: incredulous means disbelieving. There is nothing that the author is incredulous about. Choice (D) is incorrect: the author's tone is the opposite of apathetic; he or she seems to care very much about educating young people.

32. **(C)** The author feels that traditional classroom learning is too passive and too unrelated to the world after school. The first sentence states the kinds of skills needed in the world and denies that students learn them in the classroom. Choice (A) is incorrect: the author expresses no prejudice or bias against adolescents. Choice (B) is incorrect: the author wants to prevent young people from becoming "long-term clients" of these systems, but that does not mean that he or she is opposed to the systems themselves. Choice (D) is incorrect: the author expressly commends "organizations like Independent Sector" in lines 22-23.

33. **(A)** The opening sentence states the main idea that young people do not learn key skills in the classroom. The rest of the passage clarifies that idea by explaining more fully what the author means. Choices (B), (C), and (D) are incorrect: the passage does not list items of any kind. No contrast is set up between two ideas, people, or things; furthermore, the passage is not classifying items into various categories.

34. **(B)** The pattern set up in the premises is "When I am (age), I have a new obligation but also a new privilege (loosely related to the obligation)." This sets up the claim that each new obligation that comes with age should have a related privilege, the pattern of (B)—seeing R-rated movies to compensate for higher ticket prices. (C) does not demand a new privilege but only that the duty not be doubled with another duty. (A) fits the pattern of the premises exactly but is not marked as a conclusion. If taken as one, it is less plausible than (C) since nothing in the premises supports this further fact—that he will get this particular privilege—only that he ought to get some privilege. (D) does not fit because it is not age related and, again, makes a factual claim. Finally, (E) is about neither an age-triggered duty nor a related privilege.

35. **(B)** The transitional word "furthermore," which begins the second part of the sentence, signals an *additional* point along the same lines as the first point made in the first part of the sentence. Both statements are arguments against a longer school year.

36. **(A)** The first part of the sentence describes the *cause* (the sun's rays passing through a large portion of the atmosphere) of the *effect* described in the second part of the sentence (the rays being refracted and the sun's orange or red appearance).

37. **(D)** *Incarcerated* means "imprisoned." None of the other choices is close in meaning. "Incapacitated" (B) sounds like "incarcerated" but means disabled.

38. **(D)** Although the author of the passage might agree with choice (A), this belief is not expressed in the paragraph. Choices (B) and (C) are both included in the paragraph but neither statement summarizes the content of the whole passage. The correct choice is (D) because it paraphrases the topic of the entire passage which is stated in the first and second sentences.

39. **(A)** The sentence is a statement of *fact* because it can be verified or disproved by checking the statistics of the numbers of students who leave school in various grades.

40. **(A)** The statement beginning on line 4 is explaining why it is difficult to keep an exact count of the number of dropouts. The statement is not directly related to the idea that more male students drop out than females (B), or that an average of 18 percent of students in the South do not graduate (C), or that more students leave school during eleventh grade (D).

41. **(B)** This argument is invalid, since the conclusion does not follow, even if we assume the premise to be true.

MATHEMATICS SECTION

1.   **(C)**   is the correct response. When subtracting rational numbers, find a common denominator: $-1/3$, $1/4$. The common denominator is 3×4 or 12. Write the rational number expression with the common denominator: $-4/12 - 3/12$. Subtract to get $-7/12$. Options (A), (B), and (D) all contain errors in subtracting rational numbers.

2.   **(D)**   is the correct choice. A positive number multiplied by a negative number is a negative number which eliminates options (A) and (C). Convert $-3 1/2$ to an improper fraction: $-7/12$. Rewrite the problem as:

$$2/5 \times -7/2 = -14/10 \text{ or } -7/5.$$

Choice (B) is obtained through errors in operation.

3.   **(B)**   is the correct response. When adding two negative numbers, add the absolute values and assign a negative to the response.

2.1
$\underline{7.31}$
9.41   Answer: -9.41

Option (D) has the incorrect sign. (A) and (C) are obtained through errors in operation.

4.   **(D)**   is the correct option. When dividing a negative number by a positive number, the answer will be negative. This eliminates choice (B). Perform long division:

$$1.6 \overline{\smash{\big)}\ {-0.400}} \quad {-.25}$$

Option (A) has incorrect decimal point placement, and (C) uses improper identification of the product and given factor.

5.   **(A)**   is the correct choice. To calculate the decrease, find 20% of 30: $30 \times .20 = 6$. Subtract that value from the given value: $30 - 6 = 24$. (B) is a partial answer. (C) and (D) are the results of the use of incorrect methods.

6.   **(D)**   is the correct response, and is found by establishing the following equation: $P \times 300 = 105$. Divide by 300 to obtain $105/300 = .35$. To convert to a percent, multiply by 100: $0.35 \times 100 = 35\%$. Responses (A), (B), and (C) resulted from incorrect placement of the values into the given equation.

7.   **(D)**   is the correct choice. Exponents indicate the number of times one uses a base as a factor. Therefore, $(4^3)^2$ means $(4^3)(4^3)$. (A), (B), and (C) are incorrect because they improperly illustrate the meaning of exponents.

8. **(A)** is the correct choice.

$$
\begin{array}{llll}
7 \times 10^2 & \text{means} & 7 \times 100 \text{ or } 700 \\
3 \times 10 & \text{means} & 3 \times 10 \text{ or } 30 \\
2 \times {}^1/_{10} & \text{means} & {}^2/_{10} \text{ or } .2 \\
6 \times {}^1/_{10^4} & \text{means} & {}^6/_{10,000} \text{ or } \underline{.0006} \\
& & 730.2006
\end{array}
$$

(B), (C), and (D) all have errors in place value assignment.

9. **(C)** is the correct response. $^7/_{20} = .35$ which is not an option. However we notice that many of the responses are expressed as a percent. By converting the decimal to a percent (multiplying by 100: $0.35 \times 100 = 35\%$), we find 35%. (A), (B), and (D) all represent misplacement of the decimal point.

10. **(B)** is the correct option. The line over the hundredths position of the numeral on the left means that the number repeats itself and continues on indefinitely to the right: 7.26666... Since the two numbers being compared are equivalent until the thousandths position, we look there to determine magnitude. Since $6 > 5$, 7.26 is the great number. (A), (C), and (D) are simply the other options available.

11. **(C)** is the correct response and follows from the process of elimination. If all the people were paid the lowest salary, the average salary per person would be $120 \times {}^{12}/_{12}$ or $120. This eliminates (A). If all the people were paid the highest salary, the average salary per person would be $780 \times {}^{12}/_{12}$ or $780. This eliminates (D). (B) is also unreasonable because at least one person makes $780 and even if the remaining 11 people all make $120, the average salary would be $780 + 11 \times 120 = \$2,100$ and the average per person would be $^{\$2,100}/_{12}$ or $175. The only option remaining is (C).

12. **(B)** is the correct response. The second term of each ordered pair is $^1/_4$ of the first term. To find the missing term, divide 20 by 4 and the result is 5. (A), (C), and (D) are incorrect because they are not obtainable values from following the set pattern.

13. **(C)** is the correct option. One is looking for a number when divided by 2, 3, or 4, the remainder is always 1. This number is one more than the least common multiple (LCM) of 2, 3, and 4. Write 2, 3, and 4 in prime factor form: 2 is prime, 3 is prime, and $4 = 2 \times 2$. To construct the number in question use the greatest number of prime factors present in any single given number: $2 \times 2 \times 3$ or 12. Since there is always 1 left over, add 1 to 12, so the smallest number of people would be 13. (B) is the LCM. (A) does not have a remainder of 1 when divided by 3, and (D) is not the smallest number of people possible.

14. **(B)** is the correct response. One can see that the pencil is between 10.5 and 11.0. So rounding to the nearest $^1/_4$ cm would be 10.75.

15. **(A)** is the correct choice. Before calculating the distance around the triangle, it is necessary to find the length of the hypotenuse. Since this is a right triangle, any missing side can be calculated using the Pythagorean Theorem: $a^2 + b^2 = c^2$.

We have
$$6^2 + 8^2 = c^2$$
$$36 + 64 = c^2$$
$$100 = c^2 \text{ and } c = 10$$

Therefore, the distance around the triangle is: 6 + 8 + 10 or 24 miles.

16. **(B)** is the correct choice. To calculate the area of a triangle, use the formula $A = \frac{1}{2}b \times h$. So, $A = \frac{1}{2}(6)(7) = 21$ sq. cm. (A), (C), and (D) are obtained from incorrect use of the formula.

17. **(D)** is the correct response. The volume of a right circular cylinder is calculated by $V = \pi r^2 \times h$ or $\pi(4^2) \times 10$ or 160π cubic inches. (A) and (B) have the incorrect units for volume. (C) is the result of using the diameter measure given in the formula instead of the radius value of 4 inches.

18. **(D)** is the correct response. Since lines $\overleftrightarrow{AC}$ and $\overleftrightarrow{BD}$ are parallel and cut by a transversal, $x = z$ because the angles formed are alternate interior angles. (A) and (B) would only be correct if x, y, and $z = 45°$. Since we do not know this, it may not be assumed. (C) is incorrect because an equilateral triangle has three 60° angles.

19. **(D)** is the correct choice. Vertical angles are the nonadjacent or opposite angles formed by the intersection of two lines. The only option of angles which satisfy this condition are 2 and 4. The angles in (A) and (B) are not formed by two lines. The angles in (C) are adjacent.

20. **(C)** is the correct choice. Triangles *ABC* and *EDC* are similar triangles. Therefore, corresponding angles are congruent and corresponding sides are in proportion. The angles formed at point C are corresponding as well as vertical angles and hence equal. (A) is incorrect because even though x could equal y, we are not sure because the angles are not corresponding angles. (D) is incorrect for the same reason, the angles in question are not corresponding angles. (B) is incorrect because the proportion does not include corresponding sides.

21. **(B)** is the correct option. Shampoo would be measured in units of volume. Square inches is the only listed measure which is not a volume measure.

22. **(D)** is the correct choice. Even though the angles are inside a circle, the relationship which exists is that the angles are supplementary because together each pair forms a straight angle. So, 40 + 140 = 180, 85 + 95 = 180, and 60 + ? = 180. The missing value would be 120. (A), (B), and (C) are results from misinterpreting the relationship.

23. **(A)** is the correct choice. To calculate the amount of ribbon needed, we will need to know the measure of the diagonal. To do this use the Pythagorean Theorem: $6^2 + 8^2 = c^2$, where c is the measure of the diagonal and measures 10 feet. So, to go all the way around the flag would require (6 + 8 + 6 + 8) feet of ribbon plus the 10 feet for the diagonal, for a total of 38 feet. (B), (C), and (D) are obtainable from incorrectly calculating the diagonal or the perimeter.

24. **(B)** is the correct choice. Before adding radical expressions, the radicands must equal. Simplify $\sqrt{12}$: $12 = 4 \times 3$, the square root of 4 is 2, so $\sqrt{12} = 2\sqrt{3}$. Then combine $2\sqrt{3}$ and $4\sqrt{3}$ by factoring out the $\sqrt{3}$ which gives us 2 + 4 or $6\sqrt{3}$. (A), (C), and (D) all contain errors in the addition of radical numbers.

25. **(D)** is the correct choice. To simplify the expression, multiply the numerator and denominator by

$$\frac{9}{\sqrt{3}} \times \frac{\sqrt{3}}{\sqrt{3}} = \frac{9\sqrt{3}}{3} = 3\sqrt{3}$$

(A), (B), and (C) all contain errors when simplifying or adding radical numbers.

26. **(A)** is the correct response. To simplify this expression, divide 6 by 3 in the fractional portion to get:

$2(a + 2b) - (3a - b)$ Distribute to remove the parentheses.
$2a + 4b - 3a + b$ Combine like terms.
$-a + 5b$

(B), (C), and (D) are the results of errors made in working with signed numbers or in simplifying.

27. **(D)** is the correct option. $0.003 \times 627{,}000 = 1{,}881$. Converted to scientific notation, 1,881 becomes 1.881×10^3. (A) and (B) result from incorrect place value, and (C) is a result of performing the incorrect operation.

28. **(D)** is the correct response. Begin by distributing to remove the parentheses:

$6a - a + 3 = 0$ Combine like terms.
$5a + 3 = 0$ Subtract 3 from both sides.
$5a = -3$ Divide both sides by 5.
$a = -^3/_5$

(A), (B), and (C) all stem from algebraic errors common to simplifying equations.

29. **(D)** is the correct choice. Begin by combining like terms. Subtract $2x$ from both sides of the inequality.

$7 - 3x > 6$ Subtract 7 from both sides.
$-3x > -1$ Divide both sides by -3.
$x < ^1/_3$ The direction of the inequality sign changes when dividing by a negative.

(A), (B), and (C) all stem from algebraic errors common to simplifying inequalities.

30. **(B)** is the correct option. Substitute the given values into the given formula:

$E = (3)(4^2)$
$\quad = 3 \times 16$
$\quad = 48$

(A), (C), and (D) are the results of improper substitution or errors in the order of operations.

31. **(B)** is the correct choice. Substitute the given value of 3 for x in the equation and simplify.

$$f(3) = 3^3 + 6(3) - 1$$
$$= 27 + 18 - 1$$
$$= 44$$

(A), (C), and (D) all result from errors in simplifying.

32. **(A)** is the correct response. List the factors of 10 (from $10x^2$): 1 and 10 and 2 and 5. Since 2 is prime, the only factors are 2 and 1. The option $(2x - 1)(5x + 2)$ when multiplied out gives the original problem. (B), (C), and (D) are likely candidates, but not actual factors of the given quadratic.

33. **(C)** is the correct response. It is necessary to first write the quadratic in standard form: $2x^2 - 3x - 1$. This quadratic does not factor, so it is necessary to use the quadratic formula to find the solutions. The quadratic formula is as follows:

$$x = \frac{-b \pm \sqrt{b^2 - 4ac}}{2a}$$ with $a = 2$, $b = -3$, and $c = -1$.

$$x = \frac{3 \pm \sqrt{9 - 4(2)(-1)}}{2(2)} = \frac{3 \pm \sqrt{17}}{4}$$

(A), (B), and (D) all contain errors in the use of the formula or with simplifying.

34. **(C)** is the correct response. This system of linear equations is best solved by the elimination method.

Multiply $(4x - 3y = 8)2$
$8x - 6y = 16$
Add $\underline{-8x + 6y = 4}$
$0 = 20$

This statement is never true; hence, there is no solution.

35. **(B)** is the correct choice. Since multiplication is commutative, we can regroup the q's. (A), (C), and (D) all yield different responses from the original as a result of improper property use.

36. **(B)**   is the correct answer. Substitute $-1/2$ for x in each of the three statements.

(I) yields:

$$|3(-1/2) + 2| < 1$$
$$|-3/2 + 2| < 1$$
$$|1/2| < 1$$
$$1/2 < 1 \qquad \text{... YES...}$$

(II) yields:

$$(2(-1/2) - 1)(-1/2 + 4) = 0$$
$$(-2)(31/2) = 0$$
$$-7 = 0 \qquad \text{... NO...}$$

(III) yields:

$$4(-1/2)^2 - 1 = 0$$
$$1 - 1 = 0$$
$$0 = 0 \qquad \text{... YES...}$$

37. **(A)**   is the correct choice. Convert 24 hours into 1 day so that the units will be consistent throughout. The proportion set up from the information given is:

$$\frac{500}{1} = \frac{n}{6}$$

(B) and (D) use inconsistent units of measure. (C) sets up an inappropriate proportion.

38. **(A)**   is the correct response. The inequality $x \geq 0$ identifies the region to the right of the *y-axis*, eliminating choices (C) and (D). The double inequality of $-3 < y < 3$ represents dotted horizontal lines passing through 3 and -3 on the *y*-axis with the area between the lines shaded. Of the two remaining choices, (A) is the only one which satisfies this constraint.

39. **(C)**   is the correct choice. To solve this double inequality divide all terms by 4 the coefficient from the variable r.

$$\frac{-12}{4} < \frac{4r}{4} < \frac{28}{4} \qquad \text{or} \qquad -3 < r < 7$$

(A) uses the improper operation of subtraction, (D) ignores the signed value of -12, and (B) improperly changes the direction of the inequality.

40. **(A)**   is the correct choice. The formula Distance = Rate × Time will be used here. The first portion of the problem provides us with a distance traveled of 100 miles at an average rate of 50 mph. Substituting this information into the formula gives us that it took 2 hours to travel the first leg of the journey: $100 = 50 \times T_1$. $T_1 = 2$ hours. The second leg was 50 miles at a rate of 30 mph. Using the formula again tells us that it took 1.67 hours for this portion: $50 = 30 \times T$. $T_2 = 1.67$ hours. Combining the times tells us that it took $2 + 1.67$ or 3.67 hours to make the journey. (B) and (C) are the partial times for each leg of the journey, and (D) is from errors in using the formula.

41. **(B)** is the correct option. Translating the words into symbols is as follows: "the product of" means multiply (this eliminates (A)). Two consecutive odd integers could be represented by $(2n+1)$ and $(2n+3)$. "Is" is the equals 195. The full equation is then: $(2n+1)(2n+3) = 195$. (C) and (D) are misrepresentations of the given statement.

42. **(D)** is the correct response. Students spend a total of 11 hours out of 24 hours studying and eating. This computes into $^{11}/_{24}$ or .46 or 46%. (A) and (C) are the partial answers from studying and eating separately. (B) is from a misrepresentation of the data.

43. **(D)** is the correct choice. The mean is the average of the numbers. Sum the numbers ($S = 54$) and divide by the number of numbers ($n = 8$) in the set: $^{54}/_8 = 6.75$. (B) is the median. (C) is the mode.

44. **(D)** is the correct response. In how many ways can two of five freshmen be selected:

$$5C_2 \text{ or } \frac{5!}{2!3!} = \frac{5 \times 4 \times 3 \times 2 \times 1}{2 \times 1 \times 3 \times 2 \times 1} = 10$$

Three of four sophomores can be selected in the same manner.

$$4C_3 \text{ or } \frac{4!}{3!1!} = \frac{4 \times 3 \times 2 \times 1}{3 \times 2 \times 1 \times 1} = 4$$

Since the two events are independent, the values are multiplied (10×4 or 40) to determine the number of different ways these students can be selected. (A), (B), and (C) result from the use of inappropriate formulas.

45. **(A)** is the correct choice. We are being asked to find the complement of the given event. Since probabilities sum to 1 and we know that the probability of a seed sprouting is. 70, the only other event that can happen is that it will not sprout. So that probability must be $1 - .70$ or .30.

46. **(D)** is the correct solution. We can see from the figure that as shoe size increases so does height, so there is a positive relationship which rules out (A) and (C). The problem with (B) is that neither variable causes a change in the other variable.

47. **(C)** is the correct option. Sum the percents for the letter grades A, B, and C: $12 + 26 + 30 = 68\%$. (A), (B), and (D) result from misreading the table.

48. **(D)** is the correct choice. From reading the table we can see that swirl yogurt is made up of 10% and 15% for a total of 25% or a probability of .25. (A), (B), and (C) result from misreading the table.

49. **(C)** is the correct choice. If an element is a member of the intersection of all three sets within the universal set, then that member is certainly a member of the universal set. (A) is incorrect because the element in question could still be outside of set *C*. (B) is incorrect because a member not in *A* does not have to be in set *B*.

50. **(A)** is the correct option. In order to negate this statement (*p* and *q*), the logical equivalence is "not *p* or not *q*." This translates into "The apple is not green or it is ready to eat." (B), (C), and (D) are not equivalent negations of the given statement.

51. **(C)** is the correct choice. From the premise we know that things that fly are a subset of things that have wings. Since balloons do not have wings, this set is exterior to the set of things with wings and cannot possibly intersect with the set of things which fly. As a result of this explanation options (A), (B), and (D) can be discarded.

52. **(A)** is the correct choice. From the premise we know that cars and station wagons are both subsets of things with wheels; however, there is nothing which indicates that the set of cars and set of station wagons intersect. So even though the conclusion is valid, it cannot be logically drawn from the premise. The conclusions for options (B), (C), and (D) can all be logically drawn from the premises.

53. **(C)** is the correct option. Given the statement, If *p* then *q* followed by "not *q*," the logical conclusion to draw would be "not *p*" which is "The soda bottle is not half empty." (A), (B), and (D) cannot logically be drawn as a conclusion to the given premises.

54. **(A)** is the correct choice. Let *p* = the printer is unplugged and *q* = it will not work. We see that we begin with the form: If *p* then *q* and transfer to: not *p* or *q*. (B), (C), and (D) do not follow this transformation.

55. **(D)** is the correct response. The set of astronauts is a subset of skilled, highly trained professionals which is in turn a subset of those with college degrees. However, even though Aaron has a college degree, he may or may not be in the set of highly skilled, trained professionals or astronauts.

CLAST

COLLEGE LEVEL ACADEMIC SKILLS TEST

Answer Sheets

CLAST – TEST 1 Essay Section

During the actual exam, you will be given 5 pages of lined paper for your essay. You may ask for more paper if necessary. Uses these pages for the practice test, and use extra paper if you need it.

CLAST – TEST 1

English Language Skills Section

1. Ⓐ Ⓑ Ⓒ Ⓓ Ⓔ
2. Ⓐ Ⓑ Ⓒ Ⓓ Ⓔ
3. Ⓐ Ⓑ Ⓒ Ⓓ Ⓔ
4. Ⓐ Ⓑ Ⓒ Ⓓ Ⓔ
5. Ⓐ Ⓑ Ⓒ Ⓓ Ⓔ
6. Ⓐ Ⓑ Ⓒ Ⓓ Ⓔ
7. Ⓐ Ⓑ Ⓒ Ⓓ Ⓔ
8. Ⓐ Ⓑ Ⓒ Ⓓ Ⓔ
9. Ⓐ Ⓑ Ⓒ Ⓓ Ⓔ
10. Ⓐ Ⓑ Ⓒ Ⓓ Ⓔ
11. Ⓐ Ⓑ Ⓒ Ⓓ Ⓔ
12. Ⓐ Ⓑ Ⓒ Ⓓ Ⓔ
13. Ⓐ Ⓑ Ⓒ Ⓓ Ⓔ
14. Ⓐ Ⓑ Ⓒ Ⓓ Ⓔ
15. Ⓐ Ⓑ Ⓒ Ⓓ Ⓔ
16. Ⓐ Ⓑ Ⓒ Ⓓ Ⓔ
17. Ⓐ Ⓑ Ⓒ Ⓓ Ⓔ
18. Ⓐ Ⓑ Ⓒ Ⓓ Ⓔ
19. Ⓐ Ⓑ Ⓒ Ⓓ Ⓔ
20. Ⓐ Ⓑ Ⓒ Ⓓ Ⓔ
21. Ⓐ Ⓑ Ⓒ Ⓓ Ⓔ
22. Ⓐ Ⓑ Ⓒ Ⓓ Ⓔ
23. Ⓐ Ⓑ Ⓒ Ⓓ Ⓔ
24. Ⓐ Ⓑ Ⓒ Ⓓ Ⓔ
25. Ⓐ Ⓑ Ⓒ Ⓓ Ⓔ
26. Ⓐ Ⓑ Ⓒ Ⓓ Ⓔ
27. Ⓐ Ⓑ Ⓒ Ⓓ Ⓔ
28. Ⓐ Ⓑ Ⓒ Ⓓ Ⓔ
29. Ⓐ Ⓑ Ⓒ Ⓓ Ⓔ
30. Ⓐ Ⓑ Ⓒ Ⓓ Ⓔ
31. Ⓐ Ⓑ Ⓒ Ⓓ Ⓔ
32. Ⓐ Ⓑ Ⓒ Ⓓ Ⓔ
33. Ⓐ Ⓑ Ⓒ Ⓓ Ⓔ
34. Ⓐ Ⓑ Ⓒ Ⓓ Ⓔ
35. Ⓐ Ⓑ Ⓒ Ⓓ Ⓔ
36. Ⓐ Ⓑ Ⓒ Ⓓ Ⓔ
37. Ⓐ Ⓑ Ⓒ Ⓓ Ⓔ
38. Ⓐ Ⓑ Ⓒ Ⓓ Ⓔ
39. Ⓐ Ⓑ Ⓒ Ⓓ Ⓔ
40. Ⓐ Ⓑ Ⓒ Ⓓ Ⓔ

Reading Skills Section

1. Ⓐ Ⓑ Ⓒ Ⓓ Ⓔ
2. Ⓐ Ⓑ Ⓒ Ⓓ Ⓔ
3. Ⓐ Ⓑ Ⓒ Ⓓ Ⓔ
4. Ⓐ Ⓑ Ⓒ Ⓓ Ⓔ
5. Ⓐ Ⓑ Ⓒ Ⓓ Ⓔ
6. Ⓐ Ⓑ Ⓒ Ⓓ Ⓔ
7. Ⓐ Ⓑ Ⓒ Ⓓ Ⓔ
8. Ⓐ Ⓑ Ⓒ Ⓓ Ⓔ
9. Ⓐ Ⓑ Ⓒ Ⓓ Ⓔ
10. Ⓐ Ⓑ Ⓒ Ⓓ Ⓔ
11. Ⓐ Ⓑ Ⓒ Ⓓ Ⓔ
12. Ⓐ Ⓑ Ⓒ Ⓓ Ⓔ
13. Ⓐ Ⓑ Ⓒ Ⓓ Ⓔ
14. Ⓐ Ⓑ Ⓒ Ⓓ Ⓔ
15. Ⓐ Ⓑ Ⓒ Ⓓ Ⓔ
16. Ⓐ Ⓑ Ⓒ Ⓓ Ⓔ
17. Ⓐ Ⓑ Ⓒ Ⓓ Ⓔ
18. Ⓐ Ⓑ Ⓒ Ⓓ Ⓔ
19. Ⓐ Ⓑ Ⓒ Ⓓ Ⓔ
20. Ⓐ Ⓑ Ⓒ Ⓓ Ⓔ
21. Ⓐ Ⓑ Ⓒ Ⓓ Ⓔ
22. Ⓐ Ⓑ Ⓒ Ⓓ Ⓔ
23. Ⓐ Ⓑ Ⓒ Ⓓ Ⓔ
24. Ⓐ Ⓑ Ⓒ Ⓓ Ⓔ
25. Ⓐ Ⓑ Ⓒ Ⓓ Ⓔ
26. Ⓐ Ⓑ Ⓒ Ⓓ Ⓔ
27. Ⓐ Ⓑ Ⓒ Ⓓ Ⓔ
28. Ⓐ Ⓑ Ⓒ Ⓓ Ⓔ
29. Ⓐ Ⓑ Ⓒ Ⓓ Ⓔ
30. Ⓐ Ⓑ Ⓒ Ⓓ Ⓔ
31. Ⓐ Ⓑ Ⓒ Ⓓ Ⓔ
32. Ⓐ Ⓑ Ⓒ Ⓓ Ⓔ
33. Ⓐ Ⓑ Ⓒ Ⓓ Ⓔ
34. Ⓐ Ⓑ Ⓒ Ⓓ Ⓔ
35. Ⓐ Ⓑ Ⓒ Ⓓ Ⓔ
36. Ⓐ Ⓑ Ⓒ Ⓓ Ⓔ
37. Ⓐ Ⓑ Ⓒ Ⓓ Ⓔ
38. Ⓐ Ⓑ Ⓒ Ⓓ Ⓔ
39. Ⓐ Ⓑ Ⓒ Ⓓ Ⓔ
40. Ⓐ Ⓑ Ⓒ Ⓓ Ⓔ
41. Ⓐ Ⓑ Ⓒ Ⓓ Ⓔ

Mathematics Section

1. Ⓐ Ⓑ Ⓒ Ⓓ Ⓔ
2. Ⓐ Ⓑ Ⓒ Ⓓ Ⓔ
3. Ⓐ Ⓑ Ⓒ Ⓓ Ⓔ
4. Ⓐ Ⓑ Ⓒ Ⓓ Ⓔ
5. Ⓐ Ⓑ Ⓒ Ⓓ Ⓔ
6. Ⓐ Ⓑ Ⓒ Ⓓ Ⓔ
7. Ⓐ Ⓑ Ⓒ Ⓓ Ⓔ
8. Ⓐ Ⓑ Ⓒ Ⓓ Ⓔ
9. Ⓐ Ⓑ Ⓒ Ⓓ Ⓔ
10. Ⓐ Ⓑ Ⓒ Ⓓ Ⓔ
11. Ⓐ Ⓑ Ⓒ Ⓓ Ⓔ
12. Ⓐ Ⓑ Ⓒ Ⓓ Ⓔ
13. Ⓐ Ⓑ Ⓒ Ⓓ Ⓔ
14. Ⓐ Ⓑ Ⓒ Ⓓ Ⓔ
15. Ⓐ Ⓑ Ⓒ Ⓓ Ⓔ
16. Ⓐ Ⓑ Ⓒ Ⓓ Ⓔ
17. Ⓐ Ⓑ Ⓒ Ⓓ Ⓔ
18. Ⓐ Ⓑ Ⓒ Ⓓ Ⓔ
19. Ⓐ Ⓑ Ⓒ Ⓓ Ⓔ
20. Ⓐ Ⓑ Ⓒ Ⓓ Ⓔ
21. Ⓐ Ⓑ Ⓒ Ⓓ Ⓔ
22. Ⓐ Ⓑ Ⓒ Ⓓ Ⓔ
23. Ⓐ Ⓑ Ⓒ Ⓓ Ⓔ
24. Ⓐ Ⓑ Ⓒ Ⓓ Ⓔ
25. Ⓐ Ⓑ Ⓒ Ⓓ Ⓔ
26. Ⓐ Ⓑ Ⓒ Ⓓ Ⓔ
27. Ⓐ Ⓑ Ⓒ Ⓓ Ⓔ
28. Ⓐ Ⓑ Ⓒ Ⓓ Ⓔ
29. Ⓐ Ⓑ Ⓒ Ⓓ Ⓔ
30. Ⓐ Ⓑ Ⓒ Ⓓ Ⓔ
31. Ⓐ Ⓑ Ⓒ Ⓓ Ⓔ
32. Ⓐ Ⓑ Ⓒ Ⓓ Ⓔ
33. Ⓐ Ⓑ Ⓒ Ⓓ Ⓔ
34. Ⓐ Ⓑ Ⓒ Ⓓ Ⓔ
35. Ⓐ Ⓑ Ⓒ Ⓓ Ⓔ
36. Ⓐ Ⓑ Ⓒ Ⓓ Ⓔ
37. Ⓐ Ⓑ Ⓒ Ⓓ Ⓔ
38. Ⓐ Ⓑ Ⓒ Ⓓ Ⓔ
39. Ⓐ Ⓑ Ⓒ Ⓓ Ⓔ
40. Ⓐ Ⓑ Ⓒ Ⓓ Ⓔ
41. Ⓐ Ⓑ Ⓒ Ⓓ Ⓔ
42. Ⓐ Ⓑ Ⓒ Ⓓ Ⓔ
43. Ⓐ Ⓑ Ⓒ Ⓓ Ⓔ
44. Ⓐ Ⓑ Ⓒ Ⓓ Ⓔ
45. Ⓐ Ⓑ Ⓒ Ⓓ Ⓔ
46. Ⓐ Ⓑ Ⓒ Ⓓ Ⓔ
47. Ⓐ Ⓑ Ⓒ Ⓓ Ⓔ
48. Ⓐ Ⓑ Ⓒ Ⓓ Ⓔ
49. Ⓐ Ⓑ Ⓒ Ⓓ Ⓔ
50. Ⓐ Ⓑ Ⓒ Ⓓ Ⓔ
51. Ⓐ Ⓑ Ⓒ Ⓓ Ⓔ
52. Ⓐ Ⓑ Ⓒ Ⓓ Ⓔ
53. Ⓐ Ⓑ Ⓒ Ⓓ Ⓔ
54. Ⓐ Ⓑ Ⓒ Ⓓ Ⓔ
55. Ⓐ Ⓑ Ⓒ Ⓓ Ⓔ

CLAST – TEST 2 Essay Section

During the actual exam, you will be given 5 pages of lined paper for your essay. You may ask for more paper if necessary. Uses these pages for the practice test, and use extra paper if you need it.

CLAST – TEST 2

English Language Skills Section

1. Ⓐ Ⓑ Ⓒ Ⓓ Ⓔ
2. Ⓐ Ⓑ Ⓒ Ⓓ Ⓔ
3. Ⓐ Ⓑ Ⓒ Ⓓ Ⓔ
4. Ⓐ Ⓑ Ⓒ Ⓓ Ⓔ
5. Ⓐ Ⓑ Ⓒ Ⓓ Ⓔ
6. Ⓐ Ⓑ Ⓒ Ⓓ Ⓔ
7. Ⓐ Ⓑ Ⓒ Ⓓ Ⓔ
8. Ⓐ Ⓑ Ⓒ Ⓓ Ⓔ
9. Ⓐ Ⓑ Ⓒ Ⓓ Ⓔ
10. Ⓐ Ⓑ Ⓒ Ⓓ Ⓔ
11. Ⓐ Ⓑ Ⓒ Ⓓ Ⓔ
12. Ⓐ Ⓑ Ⓒ Ⓓ Ⓔ
13. Ⓐ Ⓑ Ⓒ Ⓓ Ⓔ
14. Ⓐ Ⓑ Ⓒ Ⓓ Ⓔ
15. Ⓐ Ⓑ Ⓒ Ⓓ Ⓔ
16. Ⓐ Ⓑ Ⓒ Ⓓ Ⓔ
17. Ⓐ Ⓑ Ⓒ Ⓓ Ⓔ
18. Ⓐ Ⓑ Ⓒ Ⓓ Ⓔ
19. Ⓐ Ⓑ Ⓒ Ⓓ Ⓔ
20. Ⓐ Ⓑ Ⓒ Ⓓ Ⓔ
21. Ⓐ Ⓑ Ⓒ Ⓓ Ⓔ
22. Ⓐ Ⓑ Ⓒ Ⓓ Ⓔ
23. Ⓐ Ⓑ Ⓒ Ⓓ Ⓔ
24. Ⓐ Ⓑ Ⓒ Ⓓ Ⓔ
25. Ⓐ Ⓑ Ⓒ Ⓓ Ⓔ
26. Ⓐ Ⓑ Ⓒ Ⓓ Ⓔ
27. Ⓐ Ⓑ Ⓒ Ⓓ Ⓔ
28. Ⓐ Ⓑ Ⓒ Ⓓ Ⓔ
29. Ⓐ Ⓑ Ⓒ Ⓓ Ⓔ
30. Ⓐ Ⓑ Ⓒ Ⓓ Ⓔ
31. Ⓐ Ⓑ Ⓒ Ⓓ Ⓔ
32. Ⓐ Ⓑ Ⓒ Ⓓ Ⓔ
33. Ⓐ Ⓑ Ⓒ Ⓓ Ⓔ
34. Ⓐ Ⓑ Ⓒ Ⓓ Ⓔ
35. Ⓐ Ⓑ Ⓒ Ⓓ Ⓔ
36. Ⓐ Ⓑ Ⓒ Ⓓ Ⓔ
37. Ⓐ Ⓑ Ⓒ Ⓓ Ⓔ
38. Ⓐ Ⓑ Ⓒ Ⓓ Ⓔ
39. Ⓐ Ⓑ Ⓒ Ⓓ Ⓔ
40. Ⓐ Ⓑ Ⓒ Ⓓ Ⓔ

Reading Skills Section

1. Ⓐ Ⓑ Ⓒ Ⓓ Ⓔ
2. Ⓐ Ⓑ Ⓒ Ⓓ Ⓔ
3. Ⓐ Ⓑ Ⓒ Ⓓ Ⓔ

4. Ⓐ Ⓑ Ⓒ Ⓓ Ⓔ
5. Ⓐ Ⓑ Ⓒ Ⓓ Ⓔ
6. Ⓐ Ⓑ Ⓒ Ⓓ Ⓔ
7. Ⓐ Ⓑ Ⓒ Ⓓ Ⓔ
8. Ⓐ Ⓑ Ⓒ Ⓓ Ⓔ
9. Ⓐ Ⓑ Ⓒ Ⓓ Ⓔ
10. Ⓐ Ⓑ Ⓒ Ⓓ Ⓔ
11. Ⓐ Ⓑ Ⓒ Ⓓ Ⓔ
12. Ⓐ Ⓑ Ⓒ Ⓓ Ⓔ
13. Ⓐ Ⓑ Ⓒ Ⓓ Ⓔ
14. Ⓐ Ⓑ Ⓒ Ⓓ Ⓔ
15. Ⓐ Ⓑ Ⓒ Ⓓ Ⓔ
16. Ⓐ Ⓑ Ⓒ Ⓓ Ⓔ
17. Ⓐ Ⓑ Ⓒ Ⓓ Ⓔ
18. Ⓐ Ⓑ Ⓒ Ⓓ Ⓔ
19. Ⓐ Ⓑ Ⓒ Ⓓ Ⓔ
20. Ⓐ Ⓑ Ⓒ Ⓓ Ⓔ
21. Ⓐ Ⓑ Ⓒ Ⓓ Ⓔ
22. Ⓐ Ⓑ Ⓒ Ⓓ Ⓔ
23. Ⓐ Ⓑ Ⓒ Ⓓ Ⓔ
24. Ⓐ Ⓑ Ⓒ Ⓓ Ⓔ
25. Ⓐ Ⓑ Ⓒ Ⓓ Ⓔ
26. Ⓐ Ⓑ Ⓒ Ⓓ Ⓔ
27. Ⓐ Ⓑ Ⓒ Ⓓ Ⓔ
28. Ⓐ Ⓑ Ⓒ Ⓓ Ⓔ
29. Ⓐ Ⓑ Ⓒ Ⓓ Ⓔ
30. Ⓐ Ⓑ Ⓒ Ⓓ Ⓔ
31. Ⓐ Ⓑ Ⓒ Ⓓ Ⓔ
32. Ⓐ Ⓑ Ⓒ Ⓓ Ⓔ
33. Ⓐ Ⓑ Ⓒ Ⓓ Ⓔ
34. Ⓐ Ⓑ Ⓒ Ⓓ Ⓔ
35. Ⓐ Ⓑ Ⓒ Ⓓ Ⓔ
36. Ⓐ Ⓑ Ⓒ Ⓓ Ⓔ
37. Ⓐ Ⓑ Ⓒ Ⓓ Ⓔ
38. Ⓐ Ⓑ Ⓒ Ⓓ Ⓔ
39. Ⓐ Ⓑ Ⓒ Ⓓ Ⓔ
40. Ⓐ Ⓑ Ⓒ Ⓓ Ⓔ
41. Ⓐ Ⓑ Ⓒ Ⓓ Ⓔ

Mathematics Section

1. Ⓐ Ⓑ Ⓒ Ⓓ Ⓔ
2. Ⓐ Ⓑ Ⓒ Ⓓ Ⓔ
3. Ⓐ Ⓑ Ⓒ Ⓓ Ⓔ
4. Ⓐ Ⓑ Ⓒ Ⓓ Ⓔ
5. Ⓐ Ⓑ Ⓒ Ⓓ Ⓔ
6. Ⓐ Ⓑ Ⓒ Ⓓ Ⓔ
7. Ⓐ Ⓑ Ⓒ Ⓓ Ⓔ
8. Ⓐ Ⓑ Ⓒ Ⓓ Ⓔ

9. Ⓐ Ⓑ Ⓒ Ⓓ Ⓔ
10. Ⓐ Ⓑ Ⓒ Ⓓ Ⓔ
11. Ⓐ Ⓑ Ⓒ Ⓓ Ⓔ
12. Ⓐ Ⓑ Ⓒ Ⓓ Ⓔ
13. Ⓐ Ⓑ Ⓒ Ⓓ Ⓔ
14. Ⓐ Ⓑ Ⓒ Ⓓ Ⓔ
15. Ⓐ Ⓑ Ⓒ Ⓓ Ⓔ
16. Ⓐ Ⓑ Ⓒ Ⓓ Ⓔ
17. Ⓐ Ⓑ Ⓒ Ⓓ Ⓔ
18. Ⓐ Ⓑ Ⓒ Ⓓ Ⓔ
19. Ⓐ Ⓑ Ⓒ Ⓓ Ⓔ
20. Ⓐ Ⓑ Ⓒ Ⓓ Ⓔ
21. Ⓐ Ⓑ Ⓒ Ⓓ Ⓔ
22. Ⓐ Ⓑ Ⓒ Ⓓ Ⓔ
23. Ⓐ Ⓑ Ⓒ Ⓓ Ⓔ
24. Ⓐ Ⓑ Ⓒ Ⓓ Ⓔ
25. Ⓐ Ⓑ Ⓒ Ⓓ Ⓔ
26. Ⓐ Ⓑ Ⓒ Ⓓ Ⓔ
27. Ⓐ Ⓑ Ⓒ Ⓓ Ⓔ
28. Ⓐ Ⓑ Ⓒ Ⓓ Ⓔ
29. Ⓐ Ⓑ Ⓒ Ⓓ Ⓔ
30. Ⓐ Ⓑ Ⓒ Ⓓ Ⓔ
31. Ⓐ Ⓑ Ⓒ Ⓓ Ⓔ
32. Ⓐ Ⓑ Ⓒ Ⓓ Ⓔ
33. Ⓐ Ⓑ Ⓒ Ⓓ Ⓔ
34. Ⓐ Ⓑ Ⓒ Ⓓ Ⓔ
35. Ⓐ Ⓑ Ⓒ Ⓓ Ⓔ
36. Ⓐ Ⓑ Ⓒ Ⓓ Ⓔ
37. Ⓐ Ⓑ Ⓒ Ⓓ Ⓔ
38. Ⓐ Ⓑ Ⓒ Ⓓ Ⓔ
39. Ⓐ Ⓑ Ⓒ Ⓓ Ⓔ
40. Ⓐ Ⓑ Ⓒ Ⓓ Ⓔ
41. Ⓐ Ⓑ Ⓒ Ⓓ Ⓔ
42. Ⓐ Ⓑ Ⓒ Ⓓ Ⓔ
43. Ⓐ Ⓑ Ⓒ Ⓓ Ⓔ
44. Ⓐ Ⓑ Ⓒ Ⓓ Ⓔ
45. Ⓐ Ⓑ Ⓒ Ⓓ Ⓔ
46. Ⓐ Ⓑ Ⓒ Ⓓ Ⓔ
47. Ⓐ Ⓑ Ⓒ Ⓓ Ⓔ
48. Ⓐ Ⓑ Ⓒ Ⓓ Ⓔ
49. Ⓐ Ⓑ Ⓒ Ⓓ Ⓔ
50. Ⓐ Ⓑ Ⓒ Ⓓ Ⓔ
51. Ⓐ Ⓑ Ⓒ Ⓓ Ⓔ
52. Ⓐ Ⓑ Ⓒ Ⓓ Ⓔ
53. Ⓐ Ⓑ Ⓒ Ⓓ Ⓔ
54. Ⓐ Ⓑ Ⓒ Ⓓ Ⓔ
55. Ⓐ Ⓑ Ⓒ Ⓓ Ⓔ